Business, Human Rights and Transitional Justice

This book considers the efficacy of transitional justice mechanisms in response to corporate human rights abuses.

Corporations and other business enterprises often operate in countries affected by conflict or repressive regimes. As such, they may become involved in human rights violations and crimes under international law – either as the main perpetrators or as accomplices by aiding and abetting government actors. Transitional justice mechanisms, such as trials, truth commissions, and reparations, have usually focused on abuses by state authorities or by non-state actors directly connected to the state, such as paramilitary groups. Innovative transitional justice mechanisms have, however, now started to address corporate accountability for human rights abuses and crimes under international law and have attempted to provide redress for victims. This book analyzes this development, assessing how transitional justice can provide remedies for corporate human rights abuses and crimes under international law. Canvassing a broad range of literature relating to international criminal law mechanisms, regional human rights systems, domestic courts, truth and reconciliation commissions, and land restitution programmes, this book evaluates the limitations and potential of each mechanism. Acknowledging the limited extent to which transitional justice has been able to effectively tackle the role of corporations in human rights violations and international crimes, this book nevertheless points the way towards greater engagement with corporate accountability as part of transitional justice.

A valuable contribution to the literature on transitional justice and on business and human rights, this book will appeal to scholars, researchers and PhD students in these areas, as well as lawyers and other practitioners working on corporate accountability and transitional justice.

Irene Pietropaoli is a Research Fellow in Business and Human Rights at the British Institute of International and Comparative Law (BIICL) in London.

Part of the
TRANSITIONAL JUSTICE
series

Series editor
Kieran McEvoy, *Queen's University Belfast, UK*

for information about the series and details of previous and forthcoming titles, see
https://www.routledge.com/Transitional-Justice/book-series/TRANJ

A GlassHouse book

Business, Human Rights and Transitional Justice

Irene Pietropaoli

Routledge
Taylor & Francis Group

a GlassHouse book

First published 2020
by Routledge
2 Park Square, Milton Park, Abingdon, Oxon OX14 4RN

and by Routledge
52 Vanderbilt Avenue, New York, NY 10017

a GlassHouse book

Routledge is an imprint of the Taylor & Francis Group, an informa business

British Library Cataloguing-in-Publication Data
A catalogue record for this book is available from the British Library

Library of Congress Cataloging-in-Publication Data
Names: Pietropaoli, Irene, author.
Title: Business, human rights and transitional justice / Irene Pietropaoli.
Description: Abingdon, Oxon ; New York, NY : Routledge, 2020. |
Series: Transitional justice | Based on author's thesis (doctoral - Middlesex
University, 2017) issued under title: Remedy for corporate human
rights abuses in transitional justice contexts. |
Includes bibliographical references and index.
Identifiers: LCCN 2020000640 (print) | LCCN 2020000641 (ebook) |
ISBN 9780367376024 (hardback) | ISBN 9780367809546 (ebook)
Subjects: LCSH: Liability for human rights violations. |
Tort liability of corporations. | Transitional justice.
Classification: LCC K935 .P54 2020 (print) | LCC K935 (ebook) |
DDC 346.03/3–dc23
LC record available at https://lccn.loc.gov/2020000640
LC ebook record available at https://lccn.loc.gov/2020000641

ISBN: 978-0-367-37602-4 (hbk)
ISBN: 978-0-367-80954-6 (ebk)

Typeset in Galliard
by Taylor & Francis Books

Contents

Acknowledgements   vi
Introduction   vii

1 Business and human rights and transitional justice   1

2 Nuremberg and international criminal law   18

3 Regional human rights systems   50

4 Domestic criminal and civil liability   66

5 Truth-seeking processes   143

6 Administrative reparation programmes   187

7 Institutional reform   209

Conclusion   235

Bibliography   251
Index   270

Acknowledgements

This book is largely the product of my doctoral research carried out at the Faculty of Law of Middlesex University. I would like to thank Nadia Bernaz and Joshua Castellino for their expert advice and supervision during that time. I would also like to thank Olga Martin Ortega and Cathal Doyle for useful comments on the thesis.

During the research and writing of this book I was grateful I had the support of my former employer, Business & Human Rights Resource Centre, and current one, the British Institute of International and Comparative Law. Lise Smit, in particular, always encouraged me.

Katherine Laidler did a fantastic job copyediting this book.

Finally, I would like to thank my family for their constant support and my husband, Daniel Aguirre, who inspired many changes to this book over breakfast in the tea shops of Myanmar.

Introduction

Corporations and other business enterprises[1] often operate in countries affected by conflict or repressive regimes, and their involvement in human rights violations and crimes under international law, as the main perpetrator or as accomplices by aiding and abetting government forces, has been well documented.[2] In the words of the former UN Special Representative on business and human rights: 'The most egregious business-related human rights abuses take place in conflict-affected areas and other situations of widespread violence.'[3] A report for the UN Office of the High Commissioner for Human Rights highlights a number of cases where business enterprises were complicit in gross human rights abuses, the majority of which committed in conflict-affected areas.[4]

1 For the purposes of this research, business activities include all activites of business entities, whether they operate transnationally or whether their activities are purely domestic, whether fully privately owned or state-owned, regardless of size, sector, location, ownership and structure. 'Transnational corporations and other business enterprises' is the way the UN refers to this issue: see UN Special Representative to the Secretary-General on human rights and translational corporations and other business enterprises. For short, often this research uses the term 'business enterprises' or 'business' or 'corporations'.

2 For example, UN Office of the High Commissioner for Human Rights (OHCHR), 'Improving accountability and access to remedy for victims of business-related human rights abuse' A/HRC/32/19, 10 May 2016; J Zerk, 'Corporate liability for gross human rights abuses: towards a fairer and more effective system of domestic law remedies', Feb 2014, www.ohchr.org/Documents/Issues/Business/DomesticLawRemedies/StudyDomesticLawRemedies.pdf; International Committee of the Red Cross (ICRC), *Business and International Humanitarian Law: An Introduction in the Rights and Obligations of Business Enterprises under International Humanitarian Law* (ICRC 2006); JP Bohoslavsky and M Rulli, 'Corporate Complicity and Finance as a "Killing Agent": The Relevance of the Chilean Case' (2010) 8 *JICJ* 829; S Tripathi, 'Business in Armed Conflict Zones: How to Avoid Complicity and Comply with International Standards' (2010) 50 *Politorbis* 131.

3 UN Human Rights Council, Report of the Special Representative of the Secretary-General on the issue of human rights and transnational corporations and other business enterprises, John Ruggie, 'Business and human rights in conflict-affected regions: challenges and options towards State responses' (2011) A/HRC/17/32.

4 Zerk (n 2) 17–23.

In transitional justice contexts, the trials, truth commissions and reparations typically included within the set of remedy mechanisms have focused primarily on abuses by state authorities or by non-state actors directly connected to the state, such as paramilitary groups or death squads.[5] Innovative uses of transitional justice mechanisms across the world, however, have started to address, even if still only in a marginal way, corporate accountability for human rights abuses and crimes under international law, and have attempted to provide redress for victims.[6] This book analyzes this development.

While there are a large number of sources on business and human rights, as well as on transitional justice in general, there is little literature that links the two areas. There is only one book, edited by Sabine Michalowski and titled *Corporate Accountability in the Context of Transitional Justice*, that compiles different cases.[7] Scholarship in this area has mostly focused on the analysis of one specific country (mostly South Africa and, more recently, Argentina and Colombia),[8] one specific mechanism (in particular the Nuremberg trial against German industrialists, and the South Africa Truth and Reconciliation Commission),[9] one type of rights violation (e.g. the unlawful corporate exploitation of natural resources) or one specific issue (such as financial complicity).[10] For example, *Cuentas Pendientes* ('outstanding

---

5 UN Office of the High Commissioner of Human Rights (OHCHR), Analytical Study on Human Rights and Transitional Justice, A/HRC/12/18, 2009; P de Greiff, 'Theorizing Transitional Justice' in M Williams, R Nagy, and J Elster (eds), *Transitional Justice* (NYU Press 2012); P Hayner, *Unspeakable Truths: Facing the Challenge of Truth Commissions* (Routledge 2001); G Bass, *Stay the Hand of Vengeance: The Politics of War Crimes Tribunals* (Princeton University Press 2000); N Kritz (ed.), *Transitional Justice: How Emerging Democracies Reckon with Former Regimes* (US Institute of Peace Press 1995).

6 A Clapham, 'Extending International Criminal Law beyond the Individual to Corporations and Armed Opposition Groups' (2008) 6 *JICJ* 899; E Duruigbo, 'Corporate Accountability and Liability for International Human Rights Abuses: Recent Changes and Recurring Challenges' (2008) 6 *Northwestern JIHR* 222; S Beale, 'A Response to the Critics of Corporate Criminal Liability' (2009) 46 *American Crim LR* (2009) 1481; D Stoitchkova, 'Towards Corporate Liability in International Criminal Law' (2010) 38 *Intersentia*; A Batesmith, 'Corporate Criminal Responsibility for War Crimes and Other Violations Of International Humanitarian Law: The Impact of the Business and Human Rights Movement', in C Harvey, J Summers, and N White (eds), *Contemporary Challenges to the Laws of War: Essays in Honour of Professor Peter Rowe* (Cambridge: Cambridge University Press 2014), 285; LA Payne and G Pereira, 'Corporate Complicity in Dictatorships' (Saïd Business School and University of Oxford).

7 S Michalowski (ed.), *Corporate Accountability in the Context of Transitional Justice* (Routledge 2013).

8 NC Sánchez León, *Tierra en transición. Justicia transicional, restitución de tierras y política agrarian en Colombia* (Bogotá: Centro de Estudios de Derecho, Justicia y Sociedad, Dejusticia, 2017).

9 L Bilsky, *The Holocaust, Corporations, and the Law: Unfinished Business* (University of Michigan Press, 2017).

10 For example, G Koska, 'Corporate Accountability in Times of Transition: The Role of Restorative Justice in the South African Truth and Reconciliation Commission' (2016) 4(1) *Restorative Justice* 41.

debts') by Juan Pablo Bohoslavsky, the UN Independent Expert on the effects of foreign debt, covers economic complicity in Argentina.[11] Anita Ramasastry, a member of the UN Working Group on Business and Human Rights, has published on the role of banks in repressive regimes from Nazi's Germany to Marcos's Philippines.[12] Some scholars and activities have argued that transitional justice should engage with the unlawful exploitation of natural resources.[13] Occasionally, transitional justice is mentioned in discussions on corporate complicity.[14] In an area related to human rights, transitional justice concepts have been used to analyze issues of justice raised by climate change regulation.[15]

Some research has been done in relation to restorative justice and corporate accountability, with some authors proposing that a restorative justice approach to business can be effective in regulating and punishing corporate entities.[16] In particular, John Braithwaite has developed theories on 'reintegrative shaming' and on 'responsive regulation', which rely on the moral agency of a corporation in order to activate a response to shame and ultimately to change corporate behaviour.[17] Social scientists have also recognized the business logic behind corporate complicity in dictatorships and armed conflict. Guillermo O'Donnell's theory of the bureaucratic authoritarian state, for example, views businesses as crucial to the particular development strategy that emerged in the 1960s and 1970s in Latin American countries.[18]

This book is the first monograph linking business and human rights and transitional justice in a comprehensive manner. It assesses how remedies for corporate human rights abuses and crimes under international law can be achieved in transitional justice contexts. To do so this book first analyzes how different mechanisms (judicial processes at the international and domestic level, truth-seeking initiatives, reparations programmes and institutional reform) have dealt, or failed to deal, with

11 JP Bohoslavsky and H Verbitsky, *Cuentas Pendientes* (Siglo Ventiuno Editores 2015).
12 A Ramasastry, 'Secrets and Lies? Swiss Banks and International Human Rights' (1998) 31 *Vand J Transnatl L* 325.
13 EE Harwell and P Le Billon, *Natural Connections: Linking Transitional Justice and Development Through a Focus on Natural Resources* (International Center of Transitional Justice 2009).
14 D Gray, 'Devilry, Complicity and Greed: Transitional Justice and Odious Debt' (2007) 70 *L Contemporary Problems* 137; Michalowski and Bohoslavsky, 'Ius Cogens, Transitional Justice and Other Trends in the Debate on Odious Debts: A Response to the World Bank Discussion Paper on Odious Debt' (2009) 48 *Colum J Transnatl L* 59.
15 S Klinsky and J Brankovic, *The Global Climate Regime and Transitional Justice* (Routledge 2018).
16 D Roche, 'Dimensions of Restorative Justice' (2006) 62(2) *J Social Issues* 217, 227; J Goodstein and K Butterfield, 'Extending the Horizon of Business Ethics: Restorative Justice and the Aftermath of Unethical Behaviour' (2010), 20(3) *Business Ethics Quarterly* 453.
17 J Braithwaite, *Crime, Shame, and Reintegration* (CUP 1989), 126–27, *Restorative Justice and Responsive Regulation* (OUP 2002), 30–31; J Braithwaite and B Fisse, *Corporations, Crime, and Accountability* (CUP 1993), 141–45.
18 GA O'Donnell, *Modernization and Bureaucratic-Authoritarianism: Studies in South American Politics* (Institute of International Studies, University of California, 1973).

remedy for victims of corporate human rights abuses. It then examines their outcomes, the results those processes have achieved and the obstacles they have faced. Remedies for corporate human rights abuses include both corporate accountability and reparations for victims. Corporate accountability is a broad concept, not limited to corporate liability (the consequences of the breach of a legal obligation), but referring to responsibilities for the consequences of a conduct.[19] In the context of this book it includes measures to hold corporations and other business enterprises legally liable, or otherwise accountable, for violations of human rights they may have committed,[20] either directly or in complicity with the state.

Despite differences in definitions, transitional justice necessarily implies a particular set of measures to deal with legacies of violations that occurred during armed conflicts or under authoritarian regimes.[21] It deals with the legacy of past atrocities by applying three different branches of international law: international human rights law; international humanitarian law; and international criminal law.[22] These four sub-fields of international law have framed transitional justice. First, by emphasizing the state obligation to investigate and prosecute alleged perpetrators of gross violations of human rights and serious violations of international humanitarian law, and to punish those found guilty.[23] Second, by creating the legitimate expectation to

19 N Bernaz, 'Enhancing Corporate Accountability for Human Rights Violations: Is Extraterritoriality the Magic Potion?' (2013) 117 *J Business Ethics* 494.

20 In this book the phrases 'corporate human rights abuses' and 'corporate human rights violations' are used interchangeably and are intended to mean the same thing: the negative impacts of business on human rights. In international law literature and practice, the term 'human rights violations' is often restricted to the actions of states, while the actions of businesses are usually described as 'human rights abuses' or as 'having an adverse human rights impact'. This practice is based on the argument that international law does not impose direct human rights obligations on corporations and thus they cannot legally commit violations against human rights.

21 P de Greiff, 'Theorizing Transitional Justice' in M Williams, R Nagy, and J Elster (eds), *Transitional Justice* (NYU Press 2012); DN Sharp, 'Economic Violence in the Practice of African Truth Commissions and Beyond' in DN Sharp (ed.), *Justice and Economic Violence in Transition* (Springer 2014), 165–201; C Sandoval, L Filippini and R Vidal, 'Linking Transitional Justice and Corporate Accountability' in Michalowski (n 7), 11.

22 P de Greiff, Report of the Special Rapporteur on the Promotion of Truth, Justice, Reparation and Guarantees of Non-Recurrence, A/HRC/21/46 (9 August 2012).

23 Universal Declaration of Human Rights (UDHR), Art 8; International Covenant on Civil and Political Rights (ICCPR), Art 2, 6; Convention against Torture and Other Cruel, Inhuman, Degrading Treatment or Punishment (CAT), Art 4, 5, 7, 12; International Convention for the Protection of All Persons from Enforced Disappearance (ICPPED), Art 3, 6, 7, 11; International Convention on the Elimination of All Forms of Racial Discrimination (CERD), Art 6; Convention on the Rights of the Child (CRC), Art 39; American Convention on Human Rights, Art 25, 63; African Charter on Human and Peoples' Rights, Art 7; European Convention on Human Rights, Art 5, 13, 41. See also UN Updated Set of principles for the protection and promotion of human rights through action to combat impunity, 2005 E/CN.4/2005/102/Add.1, principles 1, 19. For violations of the ICCPR, the Human Rights Committee has stressed the need for judicial remedies in cases of serious violations of the Covenant: views of the Human Rights Committee under Art 5, para 4, of the Optional Protocol

uncover the truth about past abuses.[24] Third, by establishing, through state practice, the right to reparations for victims of gross violations of human rights and international humanitarian law.[25] Fourth, in reiterating the state obligation to prevent the recurrence of such violations in the future.[26] On the operational level, four processes, based on the above principles, constitute the core of transitional justice: (i) justice processes – criminal prosecution initiatives and civil claims at both the international and national levels – that aim to bring perpetrators of abuses to justice and to punish them for the crimes committed; (ii) truth-seeking initiatives, such as

to the ICCPR (*Bithashwiwa and Mulumba v. Zaire*), UN CCPR, Com. No. 241/1987, 14, CCPR/C/37/D/241/1987 (1989). Regional human rights systems have further codified and interpreted those obligations. For example, Article 1.1 of the American Convention on Human Rights (as interpreted) by the Inter-American Court on Human Rights in the *Velásquez-Rodríguez v. Honduras* (ser. C) No. 1, 91 (1987) and in *Ituango Massacres v. Colombia*, (2006) Series C No. 148; the European Court of Human Rights in the procedural objections as interpreted, for example, in *Timurtas v. Turkey* ECHR 221 App. No. 23531/94 (2000), *Turkey, Aksoy v. Turkey*, 26 Eur. Ct. H.R. 2260 (1996), *Mentes v. Turkey*, 59 Eur. Ct. H.R. 2689 (1997), *Conka v. Belgium* (App. No. 51564/99) (2002). See also N Roht-Arriaza, 'State Responsibility to Investigate and Prosecute Grave Human Rights Violations in International Law' (1990) 78 *Calif L Rev* 451.

24 The right of victims and their families to know the truth in relation to past human rights abuses as such is not explicitly recognized as a substantive right in the UDHR or other human rights treaties with the exception of the Convention on Enforced Disappearances (art 24) and in the Geneva Conventions (art 32). Other UN treaties imply the right to truth. See e.g. International Covenant on Civil and Political Rights, art 2. See also Principles to combat impunity, Principles 2–5; Basic Principles, art 22. The Inter-American Court of Human Rights has traced the contours of the truth as the first step and an essential component of an effective remedy, in the wake of enforced disappearances, starting with the seminal *Velásquez Rodríguez case* (n 110). See also, T Antkowiak, 'Truth as Right and Remedy in International Human Rights Experience' (2002) 23 *Mich J Intl L* 977, 995; Hayner (n 5), 24.

25 UDHR, Art 8; ICCPR, Art 2(3); CERD, Art 6; CAT, Art 6, 13, 14; ICPPED, Art 23; CRC Art 39; Articles on Responsibility of States for Internationally Wrongful Acts elaborated by the International Law Commission, A/RES/56/83, article 31 (1). See also General comment No. 31 of the Human Rights Committee which reaffirms the central importance of the right to reparation, and its integral relationship with the right to an effective remedy, paras 15–16; Basic Principles, art 24. See also D Shelton, 'The United Nations Principles and Guidelines on Reparations: Context and Contents' in KS De Feyter and others (eds), *Out of the Ashes: Reparation for Victims of Gross and Systematic Human Rights Violations* (Intersentia, 2006), 11–33); P de Greiff, 'Truth Telling and the Rule of Law' in TA Borer (ed.), *Telling the Truths: Truth Telling and Peacebuilding in Post-Conflict Societies* (University of Notre Dame Press 2006).

26 ICCPR, Art 2; CAT, Art 2; ICPPED, Art 23. See also Principles to combat impunity, principle 35. See also MB Ndulo and R Duthie, 'The Role of Judicial Reform in Transitional Justice and Development' in ICTJ Research Unit, *Transitional Justice and Development*; B Fernando, 'Institutional Reforms as an Integral Part of a Comprehensive Approach to Transitional Justice' (2014) 8 *Intl J Transitional Justice*, 187; DJ Scheffer, 'The Tool Box, Past and Present, of Justice and Reconciliation for Atrocities' (2001) 95(4) *AJIL* 970.

truth and reconciliation commissions (TRCs), to investigate past violations and establish the facts; (iii) reparation processes, to redress victims for the harm suffered; and (iv) institutional reform processes, to transform the military, police and judiciary to ensure that violations do not happen again.[27] Effective transitional justice programmes use comprehensive approaches that integrate the full range of these judicial and non-judicial processes or a combination of them.[28] Within this framework, this book is divided into seven chapters, each assessing how the different transitional justice mechanisms (judicial processes, truth-seeking initiatives, reparations programmes, institutional reform) have achieved, or failed to achieve, corporate accountability and remedy for victims in transitional justice contexts.

Chapter 1 links the fields of business and human rights and transitional justice. The following three chapters focus on judicial processes, at the international (Chapter 2), regional (Chapter 3) and domestic levels (Chapter 4). Judicial processes are key mechanisms to achieving justice in times of transition, are an instrument for ensuring corporate legal accountability, and are, equally, a key aspect of the right to remedy for victims of corporate human rights abuses. The UN Guiding Principles on business and human rights state that 'effective judicial mechanisms are at the core of ensuring access to remedy'[29] and that 'States should take appropriate steps to ensure the effectiveness of domestic judicial mechanisms when addressing human rights-related claims against business'.[30] Chapters 2, 3 and 4 explore how different judicial remedies at the international, regional and national level have addressed, or failed to address, violations of human rights and crimes under international criminal law committed by corporations during times of conflict or repression, and whether they have achieved reparations for victims. The aim of these chapters is to analyze the normative and practical challenges often resulting in corporate impunity and lack of remedy for victims, and to present options for future development.

Chapter 2 explores both the limitations and the potential of international criminal law in this area, through the assessment of historical and contemporary cases, from Nuremburg to the International Criminal Court. Chapter 3 aims to contribute to the research on transitional justice and corporate accountability by analyzing mechanisms that are rarely associated with the two areas: the regional systems for human rights protection. While these are not transitional justice mechanisms *per se* and cannot directly adjudicate the responsibility of companies, this chapter aims to demonstrate how regional systems, and in particular the Inter-American and African

27 OHCHR, Analytical Study on Human Rights and Transitional Justice (2009) A/ HRC/12/18.
28 UN Security Council Report of the Secretary-General, The Rule of Law and Transitional Justice in Conflict and Post-Conflict Societies (2004) S/2004/616, 8.
29 UN Guiding Principles on Business and Human Rights: Implementing the United Nations 'Protect, Respect and Remedy' Framework, annexed to Report of the Special Representative of the Secretary-General on the issue of Human Rights and Transnational Corporations and Business Enterprises, John Ruggie, A/HRC/17/31 (21 March 2011), principle 26.
30 Ibid.

systems, have indirectly provided, and could further provide, remedies for victims of corporate abuses and shape national reparation programmes in transitional justice contexts. The analysis in Chapter 4 turns to assessing the efforts to achieve corporate legal accountability and reparation at the domestic level, through criminal prosecutions, and civil litigation, which focuses on cases litigated under the United States' Alien Tort Statute over allegations of corporate abuses committed during times of conflict or repressive regimes.

The book then moves to a different mechanism to achieve justice in times of transition: truth-seeking initiatives. The search for the truth about past human rights abuses is the cornerstone of almost every transitional or post-conflict process established across the world. Parallel to the evolution of the right to truth as remedy in international tribunals, TRCs, commissions of inquiry or other truth-seeking bodies have become an increasingly common mechanism for societies seeking to move forward as they emerge from a period conflict or repression.[31] Chapter 5 analyzes how different truth-seeking initiatives (TRCs as well as other investigative bodies, such as UN-mandated fact-finding missions and expert panels) have addressed the responsibility of corporations for human rights violations or international crimes committed during times of conflict or repression, and have recommended reparations from business. This chapter focuses on the South African TRC, but also offers commentary on truth commissions established in other countries (such as Liberia, East Timor, Sierra Leone, Argentina, and Brazil). It examines the outcomes of these findings and assesses whether or not they have achieved corporate accountability and reparations for victims. The aim of this chapter is to present the limitations of truth-seeking bodies in this area, but also to highlight the innovations they have put forward and how these could be expanded further.

After the analysis of reparations ordered or recommend by international and national courts and truth commissions, Chapter VI turns to the assessment of administrative reparation programmes – programmes established by national legislation. This chapter looks at programmes dealing with a particular type of reparation, land restitution, which can include the restitution of land taken for economic reasons during an armed conflict or time of repression. There are a number of reasons for the focus on land restitution: land acquisition is often a driver of conflict; illegal land confiscation, forced evictions and population displacement are common during conflict; land disputes are a key aspect that countries in transition need to address; land is often the most important asset that victims seek back after a transition; corporations are often involved in unlawful land confiscation either directly or in complicity with the state; land rights abuses are some of the most widespread corporate human rights abuses; and innovative reparation programmes have tried to deal with victims' grievance in this area. This chapter focuses on efforts to return land that was seized for economic projects in transitional countries in three different continents (Colombia, Myanmar and South Africa). It shows that, despite challenges, innovative reparation

---

31 S Ratner, 'New Democracies, Old Atrocities: An Inquiry in International Law' (1999) 87 *Geo LJ* 707.

programmes involving the responsibilities of business have been implemented, presenting an interesting avenue for remedy.

While the previous chapters deal with judicial and non-judicial transitional justice mechanisms addressing past corporate abuses, the final chapter of this book looks at institutional reform as a mechanism to prevent future corporate human rights abuses. After a transition to democracy and peace, reform of the institutions that allowed repression and human rights violations to occur is a priority to prevent violations from happening again. Institutional reforms are also of key importance to prevent corporate human rights violations from happening again. Out of the four processes that constitute the core of transitional justice, institutional reform represents the most important to combat corporate impunity. The argument of this chapter is that only by reforming the institutions that have allowed or failed to address corporate human rights abuses – including through vetting, legal and judicial reform, land reform and natural resource governance reform – will it be possible to guarantee the non-reoccurrence of such violations.

This book will show that justice and remedy processes across a number of countries in transitional justice contexts have addressed corporate accountability to different extents and have attempted to provide reparations for victims. But it will also show that corporate accountability is very rarely achieved, that impunity is the norm, and that victims face major obstacles to obtain reparations for past abuses in transitional justice contexts. This book analyzes the normative, practical, economic and political reasons for such failures, compares different transitional justice processes across different countries, and identifies practices within the transitional justice 'toolbox' that can more adequately achieve corporate accountability and redress for victims.

Chapter I

Business and human rights and transitional justice

Early debates on business and human rights focused on the applicability of obligations to business enterprises under international human rights law. Starting in the late 1990s, international law scholars and practitioners argued for the expansion of international human rights law obligations to corporations. In 2000, Saman Zia-Zarifi, the Secretary-General of the International Commission of Jurists, argued that multinational corporations could be held liable under international law.[1] In the realm of core human rights norms, the assertion was that multinational corporations 'are bound by those few rules applicable to all international actors'.[2] Andrew Clapham, a lawyer and international law professor, was among the first to argue that corporations have the capacity to acquire rights and obligations under international law.[3] This early exchange generated a typology that envisaged a division between binding and voluntary approaches in relation to the regulation of corporations when they impact human rights.[4] Whereas proponents of the binding approach argue for

---

1 MT Kamminga and S Zia-Zarifi (eds), *Liability of Multinational Corporations under International Law* (Kluwer Law International 2000).

2 Ibid., 8.

3 A Clapham, *Human Rights Obligations of Non-state Actors* (OUP 2006); 'Extending International Criminal Law Beyond the Individual to Corporations and Armed Opposition Groups' (2008) 6(5) *JIJC* 899.

4 For example, S Deva, 'Human Rights Violations by Multinational Corporations and International Law: Where from Here?' (2003) 19 *Connecticut JIL* 1; N Jägers, *Corporate Human Rights Obligations: In Search of Accountability* (Intersentia 2002), R McCorquodale and P Simons, 'Responsibility Beyond Borders: State Responsibility for Extraterritorial Violations by Corporations of International Human Rights Law' (2007) 70 *Modern L Rev* 559; M Addo, *Human Rights Standards and the Responsibility of Transnational Corporations* (Kluwer 1999); DM Chirwa, 'The Doctrine of State Responsibility as a Potential Means of Holding Private Actors Accountable for Human Rights' (2004) 5 *Melb JIL* 1; JM Woods, 'A Human Rights Framework for Corporate Accountability' (2010) 17 *ILSA J Intl Comp* L 321; L van den Herik and J Letnar Černič, 'Regulating Corporations under International Law: From Human Rights to International Criminal Law and Back Again' (2010) 8 *JICJ* 725; JP Bohoslavsky and V Opgenhaffen, 'The Past and Present of Corporate Complicity: Financing the Argentinean Dictatorship' (2010) 23 *Harvard HRLJ* 157; JW Pitts, 'Corporate Social Responsibility: Current Status and Future Evolution' (2009) 6 *Rutgers JLPP* 348; JH Dunning (ed), *Making Globalization*

the imposition of binding human rights obligations on corporations so they can be directly accountable for human rights at both domestic and international levels,[5] advocates of the voluntary approach maintain that the protection of human rights remains exclusively the responsibility of states, and that business can only assist in their advancement through voluntary means.[6] This academic debate followed the attempts to create a framework of human rights obligations and responsibilities for business enterprises, which, as discussed below, has proved challenging.

International law regulates human rights violations by corporations indirectly, through states.[7] International human rights bodies have affirmed the duty of

Good: The Moral Challenges of Global Capitalism (OUP 2003); LC Backer, 'The Autonomous Global Corporation: On the Role of Organizational Law Beyond Asset Partitioning and Legal Personality' (2006) 41 *TULSA LJ* 541; DG Arnold, 'Corporations and Human Rights Obligations' (2016) 1(2) *BHRJ* 255; J Letnar Černič and T van Ho (eds.), *Human Rights and Business: Direct Corporate Accountability for Human Rights* (Wolf Legal 2015) RM Bratspies, '"Organs of Society": A Plea for Human Rights Accountability for Transnational Enterprises and Other Business Entities' (2005) 13 *Michigan State J Intl L* 9.

5 S Deva and D Bilchitz (eds), *Human Rights Obligations of Business: Beyond the Corporate Responsibility to Respect* (CUP 2013); S Deva, 'Treating Human Rights Lightly: A Critique of the Consensus Rhetoric and Language Employed by the Guiding Principles' in S Deva and D Bilchitz (eds), ibid., 78–104, Deva, 'Human Rights Violations by Multinational Corporations and International Law' (n 4). See also, C Lopez, 'The "Ruggie Process": from Legal Obligations to Corporate Social Responsibility' in S Deva and D Bilchitz (eds), *Human Rights Obligations of Business: Beyond the Corporate Responsibility to Respect* (CUP 2013); Letnar Černič and van Ho (n 4); J Letnar Černič, *Human Rights Law and Business* (Europa Law Publishing 2010) and 'Corporate Human Rights Obligations at the International Level' (2008) 16 *Willamette J Intl L* 130; SR Ratner, 'Corporations and Human Rights: A Theory of Legal Responsibility' (2001) 111 *Yale LJ* 443; PT Muchilinski, *Multinational Enterprises and the Law* (OUP 2007); Clapham, *Human Rights Obligations of Non-state Actors* (n 3); G Chandler, 'The Curse of 'Corporate Social Responsibility' (2003) 2 *New Academy Review* 1; D Kinley and J Tadaki, 'From Talk to Walk: The Emergence of Human Rights Responsibilities for Corporations at International Law' (2004) 44 *Va J Intl L* 931; CM Vasquez, 'Direct vs. Indirect Obligations of Corporations under International Law' (2005) 43 *Columbia J Transnatl L* 927; International Council on Human Rights Policy (ICHRP), *Beyond Voluntarism: Human Rights and the Developing International Legal Obligations of Companies* (ICHRP 2002).

6 For example, JG Ruggie, 'Regulating Multinationals: The UN Guiding Principles, Civil Society, and International Legalization' in C Rodriguez-Garavito (ed.), *Business and Human Rights: Beyond the End of the Beginning* (CUP 2013); R Mayne, 'Regulating TNCs: The Role of Voluntary and Governmental Approaches' in S Picciotto and R Mayne (eds.), *Regulating International Business: Beyond Liberalization* (Mcmillan Press 1999); F Williams, 'Company Norms "Must be on UN Rights Agenda"' (8 April 2004) *Financial Times*, 9; DJ Karp, *Responsibility for Human Rights, Transnational Corporations in Imperfect States* (CUP 2014); JE Alvarez, 'Are Corporations "Subjects" of International Law?' (2011) 9(1) *Santa Clara JIL* 1.

7 C Baez and others, 'Multinational Enterprises and Human Rights' (1999) 8 *U Miami Intl Comp L Rev* 183, 220; D Bilchitz, 'A Chasm Between "Is" and "Ought"? A Critique of the Normative Foundations of the SRSG's Framework and Guiding Principles', in Deva and Bilchitz (n 5).

states to regulate non-state actors, including corporations, in order to ensure that they do not interfere with human rights.[8] For example, the Committee on Economic, Social and Cultural Rights has clarified that protecting rights means that states parties

> effectively safeguard rights holders against infringements of their economic, social and cultural rights involving corporate actors, by establishing appropriate laws, regulations, as well as monitoring, investigation and accountability procedures to set and enforce standards for the performance of corporations.[9]

The regional human rights systems have also affirmed this duty and established similar correlative state requirements to regulate and adjudicate corporate actions.[10] Some UN Special Rapporteurs have interpreted their mandate so as to make recommendations to private actors as well.[11] In 2001, the UN High Commissioner for Human Rights stressed:

> Even though states retain the primary responsibility for ensuring the protection of human rights under the human rights treaties, there is a new awareness that such responsibility entails ensuring that companies operating from or

---

8 For example, UN Human Rights Committee, General Comment No. 31 on the Nature of the General Legal Obligation Imposed on States Parties to the Covenant on Civil and Political Rights (2004) CCPR/C/21/Rev.1/Add.13, which states: 'The positive obligations on States Parties to ensure Covenant rights will only be fully discharged if individuals are protected by the State, not just against violations of Covenant rights by its agents, but also against acts committed by private persons or entities that would impair the enjoyment of Covenant rights', para 8; Committee on Economic, Social and Cultural Rights (ESCR), General Comment No. 12: The Right to Adequate Food (1999) E/C.12/1999/5, para 20, General Comment No. 13: The Right to Education (1999) E/C.12/199/10, General Comment No. 14: The Right to the Highest Attainable Standard of Health (2000) E/C.12/2000/4, General Comment No. 24 on State Obligations under the International Covenant on Economic, Social and Cultural Rights in the Context of Business Activities (2017) E/C.12/GC/2, and Statement on the obligations of States Parties regarding the corporate sector and economic, social and cultural rights (2011) E/C.12/2011/1, para 1; Committee on the Rights of the Child, General Comment No. 16 on State obligations regarding the impact of the business sector on children's rights (2013) CRC/C/GC/16, para 53.
9 Committee ESCR, Statement on the obligations of States Parties regarding the corporate sector and economic, social and cultural rights, E/C.12/2011/1 (12 July 2011), paras 5, 7.
10 For example, European Court of Human Rights, *Autronic AG v Switzerland* (1990) ser A 178, para 47; Inter-American Court on Human Rights, *Velásquez-Rodríguez v Honduras* (1988) ser. C No. 4, 172.
11 For example, UN Human Rights Council, Report of the Special Rapporteur on the right to food Olivier de Schutter, Agribusiness and the Right to Food (22 December 2009) A/HRC/13/33; Special Rapporteur on the Right to Health Paul Hunt, Human Rights Guidelines for Pharmaceutical Companies in relation to Access to Medicines (2008).

within their jurisdiction must not undermine existing human rights obligations or the international rule of law.[12]

Businesses are participants in international life, able to be recipients of international legal norms, without the need to be classed as subjects with full international legal personality.[13] The Preamble of the *Universal Declaration of Human Rights* already embodied this spirit, stating that 'every individual and every organ of society [...] shall strive [...] to promote respect for these rights and freedoms'.[14] As Louis Henkin, an international law professor, emphasized, '[E]very individual includes juridical persons. Every individual and every organ of society excludes no one, no company, no market, no cyberspace. The Universal Declaration applies to them all.'[15] In some specific areas, treaties define international legal obligations that specifically apply to corporations. Earliest among these was the *Apartheid Convention*, which established the international crime of apartheid and declared it a crime when committed by 'organizations, institutions and individuals'.[16] The UN *Convention Against Corruption* is an example of an international treaty that binds corporations with respect to their transnational conduct and the harms they cause.[17] While the claim that corporations have direct human rights obligations remains contentious and there are not yet international treaties that impose direct human rights obligations on corporations, international law in this field is developing.

UN efforts to directly regulate multinational corporations go back to the *Code of Conduct* negotiations that started in the mid-1970s and were abandoned

12 D Weissbrodt and PL Parker, Report of the Seminar to Discuss UN Human Rights
    Guidelines for Companies (29–31 March 2001) E/CN.4/Sub.2/2001/WG.2/
    WP.1/Add.3, paras 11–12.
13 O Martin-Ortega, 'Business and Human Rights in Conflict' (2008) *Carnegie Council
    for Ethics in Intl Affairs* 279.
14 Universal Declaration on Human Rights (UDHR) (10 December 1948) GA Res
    217A (III) A/810, Preamble
15 L Henkin, 'The Universal Declaration at 50 and the Challenge of Global Markets'
    (1999) 25 *Brook JIL* 17, 25.
16 International Convention on the Suppression and Punishment of the Crime of Apartheid
    (entered into force 18 July 1976) A/2645, art 1(2) The Apartheid Convention was
    accompanied by a proposal – never implemented – for an international court to prosecute
    criminal violations of the treaty. According to the proposal, persons, legal entities, groups
    and organizations would all have been subject to the jurisdiction of the court: Draft
    Convention on the Establishment of an International Penal Tribunal for the Suppression
    and Punishment of the Crime of Apartheid and Other International Crimes, reproduced
    in MC Bassiouni, *The Statute of The International Criminal Court: A Documentary
    History* (Transnational Publisher1998). The UN Convention Against Transnational
    Organized Crime, opened for signature in 2000, defined the international crimes of par-
    ticipation in an organized criminal group, money laundering, corruption and obstruction
    of justice, all of which applied to corporations as well as natural persons.
17 UN Convention Against Corruption (entered into force 14 December 2005) 2340
    UNTS 41. For commentary, see A Ramasastry, 'Closing The Governance Gap in the
    Business and Human Rights Arena: Lessons from the Anti-Corruption Movement', in
    Deva and Bilchitz (n 5), 162–90.

a decade later.[18] The next attempt came in 2003 when experts from the UN Sub-Commission on the Promotion and Protection of Human Rights drafted a treaty-like document called the *Norms on the Responsibilities of Transnational Corporations and Other Business Enterprises with Regard to Human Rights* ('the Norms').[19] Intended to become binding, the Norms attributed to companies the 'obligation to promote, secure the fulfilment of, respect, ensure respect of and protect' human rights.[20] This approach faced strong opposition from businesses and was criticized by member states, especially Western countries, which opposed holding corporations directly accountable for human rights violations.[21] When the Norms were submitted to the UN Human Rights Commission in 2004, they were rejected.

In 2005, the UN Secretary-General appointed John Ruggie, an international law professor, as the 'Special Representative on the issue of human rights and transnational corporations and other business enterprises', with a mandate to clarify the existing standards and elaborate on the role of states in regulating businesses.[22] Ruggie was reluctant to accept the idea that companies could have direct obligations under international human rights law and criticized the Norms.[23] He observed:

18 UN Economic and Social Commission, Development and International Economic Cooperation: Transnational Corporations (1990) E/1990/94. See B Stephens, 'The Amorality of Profit: Transnational Corporations and Human Rights' (2002) 20 *Berkeley JIL* 45, 69; SD Murphy, 'Taking Multinational Codes of Conduct to the Next Level' (2005) 43 *Colum J Transnatl L* 403.

19 Sub-commission on Promotion and Protection of Human Rights, Norms on the Responsibilities of Transnational Corporations and Other Business Enterprises with Regard to Human Rights UN Doc. E/CN.4/Sub.2/2003/12/Rev.2.

20 Ibid., Preamble.

21 JG Ruggie, 'Global Governance and "New Governance Theory": Lessons from Business and Human Rights' (2014), 20 *Global Governance* 5, 6; LC Backer, 'Multinational Corporations, Transnational Law: The United Nation's Norms on the Responsibilities of Transnational Corporations as a Harbinger of Corporate Social Responsibility as International Law' (2006) 37 *Columbia HRLR* 287; 'Rights and Accountability in Development ("RAID") v Das Air and Global Witness v Afrimex: Small Steps Toward an Autonomous Transnational Legal System for the Regulation of Multinational Corporations' (2009) 10 *Melbourne JIL* 258; 15; K Lucke, 'States' and Private Actors' Obligations Under International Human Rights Law and the Draft UN Norms', in T Cottier, J Pauwelyn and E Burgi (eds), *Human Rights and International Trade* (OUP 2005), 148, 159–60; D Kinley and R Chambers, 'The UN Human Rights Norms for Corporations: The Private Implications of Public International Law' (2006) *HRLR* 1; Amnesty International, *The UN Human Rights Norms for Business: Towards Legal Accountability* (AI 2004).

22 UN press release, 'Secretary-General Appoints John Ruggie of United States Special Representative on Issue of Human Rights, Transnational Corporations, Other Business Enterprises' (28 July 2005).

23 Interim Report of the UN Special Representative of the Secretary-General on the Issue of Human Rights and Transnational Corporations and Other Business Enterprises John Ruggie, submitted to the Economic and Social Council (2006) E/CN.4/2006/97 [Ruggie Interim Report], para 59, 69. Ruggie, 'Global Governance and "New Governance Theory"' (n 21), 7, 13; JG Ruggie, 'Business and Human Rights: The Evolving International Agenda' (2007) AJIL 101, 125; Backer, 'Multinational Corporations' (n 27), 169–70.

If the Norms merely restate established international legal principles then they cannot also directly bind business because, with the possible exception of certain war crimes and crimes against humanity, there are no generally accepted international legal principles that do so.[24]

Ruggie did, however, identify 'governance gaps' – highlighting that while companies' operations and their economic and political influence reach across borders, international human rights law did not seem able to address them.[25] Ruggie acknowledged that his mandate went beyond the legal realm, and included a 'full range of governmental responsibilities and policy options in relation to business and human rights'.[26] He labelled this approach one of 'principled pragmatism'.[27] By 2008, Ruggie submitted a *Framework for Business and Human Rights* to the UN on the 'different but complementary' responsibilities of states and corporations.[28] The Framework is based upon the 'protect-respect-remedy' three principles, or 'pillars': the duty of the state to protect their citizens against human rights abuses, including those perpetrated by third parties, such as corporations; the responsibility of businesses to respect human rights; and the obligation to provide a more effective remedy for human rights abuses.[29]

In 2011, the Human Rights Council unanimously endorsed the *UN Guiding Principles on business and human rights* ('the Guiding Principles'), which explain how states and corporate entities should implement the Framework.[30] The

24 Ruggie Interim Report (n 23), para 60.
25 Report of the Special Representative to the Secretary General on the issue of transnational corporations and other business enterprises John Ruggie, 'Protect, Respect and Remedy: framework for Business and Human Rights' (2008) A/HRC/8/5 ['Protect, Respect and Remedy' framework]. B Fasterling and G Demuijnck, 'Human Rights in the Void? Due Diligence in the UN Guiding Principles on Business and Human Rights' (2013) 116 *J Business Ethics*, 799.
26 Ruggie Interim Report (n 23). For a discussion, see LC Backer, 'From Institutional Misalignments to Socially Sustainable Governance: The Guiding Principles for the Implementation of the United Nation's "Protect, Respect and Remedy" and the Construction of Inter-systemic Global Governance' (2011) *Pacific McGeorge Global Business and Development LJ*, and 'On the Evolution of the United Nations' "Protect-Respect-Remedy" Project: The State, the Corporation and Human Rights in a Global Governance Context' (2011) 9 *Santa Clara J Intl L* 37, 46–48; Fasterling and Demuijnck (n 25), 800. For opposite view, see D Weissbrodt, 'International Standard-Setting on the Human Rights Responsibilities of Businesses' (2008) 26 *Berkeley J Intl. L* 373 (2008).
27 Ruggie Interim Report (n 23), para 70.
28 'Protect, Respect and Remedy' framework (n 25).
29 Ibid., paras 54, 63.
30 UN Guiding Principles on Business and Human Rights: Implementing the United Nations 'Protect, Respect and Remedy' Framework, annexed to Report of the Special Representative of the Secretary-General on the issue of Human Rights and Transnational Corporations and Business Enterprises, John Ruggie, A/HRC/17/31 (21 March 2011) [Guiding Principles]. UN Doc. A/HRC/17/L.17/Rev.1. The UN Human Rights Council endorsed the Guiding Principles with Resolution A/HRC/RES/17/4 (6 July 2011).

Guiding Principles provided 'for the first time a global standard for preventing and addressing the risk of adverse impacts on human rights linked to business activity'.[31] The principles, however, remain of a persuasive rather than binding nature. Companies are not bound by the principles, which have no provisions for implementation, monitoring or proper enforcement mechanisms. Transitional justice is not mentioned, nor are the specific issues related to post-conflict and transitional contexts, and little research has been done in relation to whether the Guiding Principles could be relevant in transitional justice situations.[32] The Principles briefly mention the issue of business activities in conflict-affected areas, giving some recommendations to states to support business operating in such contexts:

> Because the risk of gross human rights abuses is heightened in conflict-affected areas, States should help ensure that business enterprises operating in those contexts are not involved with such abuses.[33]

With the adoption of the Guiding Principles, a growing body of literature has been generated relating to whether they adequately address the complexities of international law in this area.[34] A significant amount of debate has been dedicated to either defending Ruggie for his pragmatic approach[35] or criticizing him and the Guiding Principles, for not going far enough.[36] In particular, the

31 UN Human Rights Council Resolution A/HRC/RES/17/4 (n 35). After the adoption of the UN Guiding Principles, the UN Human Rights Council appointed a five-member Working Group.

32 G Paul and J Schönsteiner, 'Transitional Justice and the UN Guiding Principles on Business and Human Rights' in S Michalowski (ed.), *Corporate Accountability in the Context of Transitional Justice* (Routledge 2013), 77, 92.

33 Guiding Principles (n 30), principle 7. In 2011, Ruggie also published a brief report on business and human rights in conflict-affected regions. This report recommended state engagement with business enterprises in order to help them meet the challenges of working in conflict situations, in particular to avoid contributing to human rights abuse. Report of the Special Representative of the Secretary-General on the issue of human rights and transnational corporations and other business enterprises, John Ruggie 'Business and human rights in conflict-affected regions: challenges and options towards State responses', A/HRC/17/32, 27 May 2011, para 9.

34 D Bilchitz, 'The Ruggie Framework: An Adequate Rubric for Corporate Human Rights Obligations?' (2010) 12 *IJHR* 199; JM Amerson, '"The End of the Beginning?": A Comprehensive Look at the Business and Human Rights Agenda from a Bystander Perspective' (2012) 17 *Fordham J Corporate Finance L* 871.

35 SA Aaronson and I Higham, '"Re-righting Business": John Ruggie and the Struggle to Develop International Human Rights Standards for Transnational Firms' (2013) 35 *HRQ* 333. For Ruggie's own defence, see e.g. JG Ruggie, *Just Business: Multinational Corporations and Human Rights* (WW Norton 2013); 'Business and Human Rights: The Evolving Agenda' (2007) *AJIL* 101.

36 S Deva, 'Protect, Respect and Remedy? A Critique of the SRSG's Framework for Business and Human Rights' in K Buhmann, L Roseberry and M Morsing (eds) *Corporate Social and Human Rights Responsibilities: Global Legal and Management Perspectives* (Palgrave 2011), 108, 121; RC Blitt, 'Beyond Ruggie's Guiding Principles on Business

principles have been criticized for providing limited provisions related to the role, responsibilities and requirements for companies in conflict, post-conflict and transitional contexts.[37] Some commentators have been critical of the Guiding Principles' remedy 'pillar' due to its strong emphasis on non-judicial and company-based grievance mechanisms – as opposed to judicial mechanisms and impartial administration of justice by independent third parties. For some scholars and activists, the third pillar's over-emphasis on company-based grievance mechanisms poses particular challenges in contexts of transitional justice as it overlooks the complexity of reparations issues, which often take place in large-scale situations and are manageable only on a case-by-case basis.[38] The Guiding Principles appear to misinterpret some fundamental tenets of international law. For instance, the wording of the Guiding Principles suggests that states are neither required to regulate nor prohibited from regulating extraterritorial activity of the enterprises incorporated under their jurisdiction. However, treaty interpretation by authoritative bodies, as well as jurisprudence, indicates that states do indeed have obligations in this area.[39] Within the critical discourse on the Guiding Principles, part of the scholarship pushed for the creation of a binding treaty on business and human rights.[40]

In June 2014, the UN Human Rights Council adopted a resolution establishing an open-ended intergovernmental working group with the mandate to 'elaborate an international legally binding instrument to regulate, in international human rights law, the activities of transnational corporations and other

and Human Rights: Charting an Embracive Approach to Corporate Human Rights Compliance' (2012) 48 *Texas Intl L J* 33; N Jägers, 'UN Guiding Principles on Business and Human Rights: Making Headway Towards Real Corporate Accountability?' (2011) 29 *Netherlands QHR* 159, 160–63; D Weissbrodt, 'U.N. Perspectives on "Business and Humanitarian and Human Rights Obligations"' (2006) 100 *American Society Intl L Proceedings* 135, 138–39; Paul and Schönsteiner (n 32); DG Arnold, 'Transnational Corporations and the Duty to Respect Basic Human Rights' (2010) 20 (3) *Business Ethics Quarterly* 371; W Cragg, 'Ethics, Enlightened Self-interest, and the Corporate Responsibility to Respect Human Rights: A critical Look at the Justificatory Foundations of the UN Framework' (2012) 22(1) *Business Ethics Quarterly* 9; P Muchlinski, 'Implementing the New UN Corporate Human Rights Framework: Implications for Corporate Law, Governance, and Regulation' (2012) 22(1) *Business Ethics Quarterly* 145; JD Bishop, 'The Limits of Corporate Human Rights Obligations and the Rights of For-profit Corporations' (2012) 22(1) *Business Ethics Quarterly* 119; Fasterling and Demuijnck (n 25), 799–800; D Leader, 'Business and Human Rights: Time to Hold Companies to Account' (2008) 8 *ICLR* 447.

37 Paul and Schönsteiner (n 32), 75–84; S Michalowski, 'Due Diligence and Complicity – a Relationship in Need of Clarification' in Deva and Bilchitz (n 11); M Baleza, 'Corporate Complicity in Human Rights Violations. When is it Time to Leave a Country?' (2011) 8 *Información Filosófica*, 55, 65.
38 Paul and Schönsteiner (n 33), 74, 85–91.
39 Ibid., 77.
40 Martin-Ortega (n 13), 282–83; DM Chirwa, 'The Long March to Binding Obligations of Transnational Corporations in International Human Rights Law' (2006) *South African J Human Rights* 76.

business enterprises'.[41] In July 2015, the working group held its first session in Geneva, officially launching the negotiations at the UN towards a binding treaty on business and human rights.[42] Supporters and opponents of such a treaty have been involved in heated debates since.[43] Opponents included Ruggie, who radically concluded that the treaty negotiations 'would represent another dead end, delivering nothing to individuals and communities adversely affected by corporate conduct'.[44] Many scholars, hundreds of civil society organizations and a group of states, however, support this initiative due to their concerns about a lack of balance of rights and obligations of corporations within the current framework.[45] There is growing frustration over the slow pace of implementation of the Guiding Principles and over the apparent inaction of most governments and companies.[46] Companies often operate with impunity, and victims continue to lack access to effective remedy. Therefore, a stronger, legally binding instrument is needed to force companies and states into action.[47] 'Not only is a business and human rights treaty needed, it is doable at this point of time in history', argues Surya Deva, the Chair of the UN Working Group on Business and Human Rights.[48] He refers to the 'springboard' of the Guiding Principles and the growing realization that neither voluntary initiatives alone nor measures merely at national level will ever be adequate to regulate corporate activities.[49]

41 UN Human Rights Council, 'Elaboration of an international legally binding instrument on transnational corporations and other Business Enterprises with respect to human rights, 26 June 2014, UN Doc A/HRC/RES/26/9, para 1.
42 First session of the open-ended intergovernmental working group on transnational corporations and other business enterprises with respect to human rights, 6 to 10 July 2015, Geneva.
43 N Bernaz and I Pietropaoli, 'The Role of NGOs in the Business and Human Rights Treaty Negotiations' (2017) *Oxford J Human Rights Practice* 1.
44 JG Ruggie, 'A UN Business and Human Rights Treaty?' (28 January 2014), 'International Legalization in Business and Human Rights (11 June 2014).
45 Bernaz and Pietropaoli (n 43); International Commission of Jurists, 'Need and Options for a New International Instrument in the Field of Business and Human Rights' (June 2014), 2–8.
46 See e.g. Joint Civil Society Statement on the Draft Guiding Principles on Business and Human Rights (2011) www.fidh.org/IMG/pdf/Joint_CSO_Statement_on_GPs.pdf; S Shetty, 'Corporations Have Rights. Now We Need a Global Treaty on their Responsibility', *The Guardian* (21 January 2015). See also, N Bernaz and I. Pietropaoli, 'The Role of Non-Governmental Organisations in the Business and Human Rights Treaty Negotiations' 9(2) *Journal of Human Rights Practice* (2017) 287.
47 D Bilchitz, 'The Necessity for a Business and Human Rights Treaty' 1(2) *Business and Human Rights Journal* (2016) 203, 209: 'It seems fundamentally unfair that the primary agent which is responsible for a harm is not capable of being held to account: only a treaty has the authority to shift this situation within international fora by recognizing expressly the fact that corporations are bound by international law in this regard.'
48 S Deva, 'The Zero Draft of the Proposed Business and Human Rights Treaty, Part I: The Beginning of an End?', www.business-humanrights.org/en/the-zero-draft-of-the-proposed-business-and-human-rights-treaty-part-i-the-beginning-of-an-end
49 Ibid.

Business and human rights as a field raises questions about the respective areas of responsibility under international law for states and non-state actors. The 'protect, respect, and remedy' framework, and the Guiding Principles implementing the framework, rest on the idea that only states have obligations under international law. Companies, by contrast, have a 'responsibility to respect human rights' in the sense that they are socially expected to do no harm.[50] Many supporters of the business and human rights treaty process believe the treaty must create binding obligations on corporations so as to overcome what they view as the Guiding Principles' deficiencies on this point.[51] Commentators have debated whether this is a good idea and whether it is even feasible.[52]

Ahead of the second session of the working group in October 2017, the third in October 2018, and the fourth, and latest, in October 2019, the chair of the working group released three documents that have formed the basis for negotiations on a treaty text: respectively, the 'Elements' of the treaty,[53] a first 'Zero Draft'[54] and a 'Revised Draft'.[55] The drafts do not include direct obligations for corporations, although the preamble of the Revised Draft highlights that business enterprises 'have the responsibility to respect all human rights', thus mirroring the language of the Guiding Principles.[56]

The revised draft, similarly to previous drafts and following the approach of the Guiding Principles, does not specify any business and human rights measures to consider in times of conflict or for countries in transition, and does not mention transitional justice. Conflict is only mentioned as a situation where 'enhanced' human rights due diligence should be adopted. As such, draft Article 5 provides that state parties should ensure that business enterprises adopt and implement 'enhanced human rights due diligence measures to prevent human rights violations or abuses in occupied or conflict-affected areas, arising from business activities, or from contractual relationships, including with respect to their products and services'.[57] Article 14 also states:

50   Commentary of Guiding Principle 11 states that '[t]he responsibility to respect human rights is a global standard of expected conduct' that 'exists over and above compliance with national laws and regulations protecting human rights'.
51   Bilchitz (n 47), 207.
52   See e.g. L McConnell, 'Assessing the Feasibility of a Business and Human Rights Treaty' (2017) 66 *International and Comparative Law Quarterly* 143.
53   OEIGWG Chairmanship, Elements for the Draft Legally Binding Instrument on Transnational Corporations and Other Business Enterprises with Respect to Human Rights (29 September 2017).
54   OEIGWG Chairmanship, Legally Binding Instrument to Regulate, in International Human Rights Law, the Activities of Transnational Corporations and Other Business Enterprises, Zero Draft (16 July 2018).
55   OEIGWG Chairmanship, Legally Binding Instrument to Regulate, in International Human Rights Law, the Activities of Transnational Corporations and Other Business Enterprises, Revised Draft (16 July 2019).
56   For comments on the revised draft, see C Lopez, 'The Revised Draft of a Treaty on Business and Human Rights: A Big Leap Forward', *Opinio Juris*, 15 August 2019.
57   OEIGWG Chairmanship Revised Draft, Legally Binding Instrument to Regulate, in International Human Rights Law, the Activities of Transnational Corporations and

Special attention shall be undertaken in the cases of business activities in conflict-affected areas including taking action to identify, prevent and mitigate the human rights-related risks of these activities and business relationships and to assess and address the heightened risks of abuses, paying special attention to both gender-based and sexual violence.[58]

Part of the debate on corporate legal accountability focuses on assessing the definition and nature of 'complicity' under international law to determine when a corporation could be held responsible for the actions of a state.[59] Corporate complicity is not a clearly defined notion.[60] In a 2007 report, Ruggie defined corporate complicity as 'an umbrella term for a range of ways in which companies may be liable for their participation in criminal or civil wrong'.[61] The 2008 'protect, respect and remedy' framework elaborates that complicity 'refers to indirect involvement by companies in human rights abuses – where the actual harm is committed by another party, including governments and non-State actors'.[62]

Accusations of direct commission of international crimes or human rights violations against companies as principal perpetrators are rare.[63] Most often corporations are accused of complicity through their assistance in the commission of violations by the principal perpetrator – for example, local police or the armed forces.[64]

Other Business Enterprises (16 July 2019). www.ohchr.org/Documents/HRBodies/HRCouncil/WGTransCorp/OEIGWG_RevisedDraft_LBI.pdf [Revised Draft], Arts 5(2) and 5(3)(e).

58 Ibid., Art 14(3).

59 S Michalowski, 'No Complicity Liability for Funding Gross Human Rights Violations' (2012) 30 *Berkeley J Intl L* 451; CI Keitner, 'Conceptualizing Complicity in Alien Tort Cases' (2008) 60 *Hastings LJ* 61; LJ Dhooge, 'A Modest Proposal to Amend the Alien Tort Statute to Provide Guidance to Transnational Corporations' (2007) 13 U. *C. Davis J Intl L Policy* 119.

60 S Michalowski, 'Due Diligence and Complicity: A Relationship in Need of Clarification' in Deva and Bilchitz (n 5), 218, 220.

61 Report of the Special Representative of the Secretary-General on human rights and transnational corporations and other business enterprises John Ruggie to the UN Human Rights Council, 'Business and human rights: Mapping international standards of responsibility and accountability of corporate acts' (February 2007), A/HRC/4/035 [Ruggie 2007 report], para 31.

62 'Protect, Respect and Remedy' framework (n 25), para 73. An expert panel of the International Commission of Jurists (ICJ) identified three elements that can indicate corporate complicity: causation or contribution; knowledge and foreseeability; and proximity. Report of the International Commission of Jurists Expert Panel on Corporate Complicity and International Crimes, *Corporate Complicity and Legal Accountability* (ICJ 2008) Vol 1–25.

63 An example is the lawsuit against *Blackwater* charged with war crimes committed against civilians in Iraq (e.g. case filed on 10 June 2009 in the US District Court for the Eastern District of Virginia: *Estate of Husain Salih Rabea and Ali Kareem Fakhri v Erik Prince, et al.*, civil action no. 1:09 cv 645).

64 Fafo, *Business and International Crimes. Assessing the Liability of Business Entities for Grave Violations of International Law* (Fafo 2005), 29; International Commission of

Corporations typically aid and abet human rights violations as committed by governments – thus it is crucial to develop a proper complicity standard for establishing corporate liability.[65] Complicity can take different forms. Corporations can facilitate the commission of violations by providing logistical support and by passing on certain information.[66] *Talisman Energy*, for example, was charged with aiding and abetting human rights abuses and international crimes in Sudan for providing logistical support to the military.[67] Another form of direct involvement is providing a regime or armed faction with products and services that are necessary for the execution or the organization of the crimes. The current investigations into allegations of complicity in war crimes against French companies *Amesys* and *Qosmos* over the provision of surveillance systems to Gaddafi's Libya and Assad's Syria respectively are examples of this type of complicity. A more indirect form of involvement occurs when a corporation benefits from the commission of abuses and crimes, without being directly involved in the execution stage of violations.[68] The violent repression of protests against *Chiquita*'s activities by security forces in Colombia is an example. An even more detached form of involvement is that of 'silent' approval: continuing to do business with dictatorial regimes and thus contributing to the political legitimization and economic viability of such regimes. The South African Truth and Reconciliation Commission (TRC), for instance, concluded that the apartheid regime would not have survived without the business support of certain companies, such as *IBM* and *Ford*.[69]

The global civil society movement calling for greater corporate accountability and redress for victims could arguably be traced to the aftermath of the Bhopal disaster, a gas leak incident that occurred on the night of 2–3 December 1984 at the *Union Carbide* pesticide plant in Bhopal, India. It resulted in the death of at least 4,000 people, and permanent injuries to thousands more.[70] But its causes

Jurists (n 62), Vol 1, 1–9; JP Bohoslavsky and MD Torelly, 'Financial Complicity: The Brazilian Dictatorship Under the "Macroscope" in DN Sharp (ed.), *Justice and Economic Violence in Transition* (Springer Science Business Media 2014), 233–59; C Sandoval, L Filippini and R Vidal, 'Linking Transitional Justice and Corporate Accountability' in S Michalowski (ed.), *Corporate Accountability in the Context of Transitional Justice* (Routledge 2013).

65 C Ryngaert, 'Dealing with Organisations and Corporations', in P Malcontent (ed.) *Facing the Past: Amending Historical Injustices through Instruments of Transitional Justice* (Intersentia, 2016).

66 International Commission of Jurists (n 62), 19–20.

67 *Presbyterian Church of Sudan v Talisman Energy Inc* (582 5F.3 244, 259). See also Chapter 3.2.

68 A Clapham and S Jerbi, 'Categories of Corporate Complicity in Human Rights Abuses', 24(3) *Hasting Intl Comp L* 339; W Huisman and E van Sliedregt, 'Rogue Traders: Dutch Businessmen, International Crimes and Corporate Complicity' (2010) 8 *JICJ* 803, 817.

69 South Africa Truth and Reconciliation Commission, Final Report (1998), Vol 4, Chapter 2.

70 DR Varma, 'The Bhopal Disaster of 1984' (2005) *Bulletin of Science, Technology and Society*.

and responsibilities were never fully established. Roughly in parallel with the development of this global movement and of the business and human rights field at the UN level, the field of transitional justice also expanded and gained impetus from political transitions taking place against repressive regimes around the world.

Transitional justice is not uniformly defined. The UN Secretary-General describes transitional justice as 'the full range of processes and mechanisms associated with a society's attempt to come to terms with a legacy of large-scale past abuses, in order to ensure accountability, serve justice and achieve reconciliation'.[71] The International Center for Transitional Justice, an NGO, defines it as a response to systematic or widespread violations of human rights seeking recognition for victims and the promotion of peace, reconciliation and democracy.[72] The classic scholarly definition of transitional justice proposed by Ruti Teitel, a comparative law professor, is 'the conception of justice associated with periods of political change, characterized by legal responses to confront the wrongdoings of repressive predecessor regimes'.[73] Naomi Roht-Arriaza, another law professor, provides another common definition: the 'set of practices, mechanisms and concerns that arise following a period of conflict, civil strife or repression, and that are aimed directly at confronting and dealing with the past violations of human rights and humanitarian law'.[74]

Since the 1980s, when the phrase 'transitional justice' was first used, the field has been extensively researched, with many academic outputs, while also encompassing significant change and evolution through practice.[75] This evolution of

71 Guidance Note of the UN Secretary General, United Nations approach to transitional justice (March 2010).

72 International Center for Transitional Justice (ICTJ), What is transitional justice? www.ictj.org/about/transitional-justice.

73 RG Teitel, *Transitional Justice* (OUP 2000); see also 'Transitional Justice Genealogy' (2003) 16 *Harvard Human* Rights J 69.

74 N Roht-Arriaza, 'The New Landscape of Transitional Justice' in N Roht-Arriaza and J Mariezcurrena (eds), *Transitional Justice in the Twenty-First Century: Beyond Truth Versus Justice* (CUP 2006), 2. For other definitions, see D Gray, 'An Excuse-Centered Approach to Transitional Justice' (2006) 74(5) *Fordham LR* 3, 2621, and 'Devilry, Complicity and Greed: Transitional Justice and Odious Debt' (2007) 70 *L Contemporary Problems* 137; F Haldemann, 'Another Kind of Justice: Transitional Justice as Recognition' (2008) 41 *Cornell Intl LJ* 675.

75 Y Farah, 'Toward a Multi-Directional Approach to Corporate Accountability', in Michalowski (ed.) (n 32); T Olsen, L Payne and A Reiter, *Transitional Justice in Balance* (US Institute for Peace Press 2010); P Arthur, 'How "Transitions" Reshaped Human Rights: A Conceptual History of Transitional Justice' (2009) 31 *HRQ* 321; F Megret, 'Of Shrines, Memorials and Museums: Using the International Criminal Court's Victim Reparation and Assistance Regime to Promote Transitional Justice' (2010) 16 *Buff Hum Rts L Rev* 1; Z Miller, 'Effects of Invisibility' (2008) 2 *Intl J Transitional Justice* 266; UN Secretary General, Report of the Secretary General, 'The rule of law and transitional justice in conflict and post conflict societies' (August 2004) S/2004/616; C Lekha Sriram, 'Transitional Justice Comes of Age: Enduring Lessons and Challenges' (2005) 23(2) *Berkeley J Intl L* 506; AM Gross, 'The Constitution, Reconciliation and Transitional Justice: Lessons from South Africa and Israel' (2004) 40(1) *Stanford J Intl L* 47; BA Leebaw, 'The Irreconcilable Goals of Transitional

transitional justice can be divided into three phases. An initial phase began in 1945 with the post–World War II trials of Nazi war criminals at the International Military Tribunal of Nuremberg, after which the justice discourse changed to take into account new issues of human rights, war crimes, and the possibility of justice through international interventions.[76] A second phase is discernible in the late 1980s, wherein transitional justice emerged as a field of scholarly inquiry in response to dramatic political changes occurring as the Soviet Union collapsed, Eastern Europe underwent shifts in political and economic arrangements, and Latin American democratic regimes replaced authoritarian ones.[77] The third contemporary phase marks the 'expansion and normalization of transitional justice', which moved 'from the exception to the norm'.[78]

Interest in and support for the inclusion of 'economic and social dimensions of transitional justice' has grown over the years. It started with a number of voices calling for transitional justice measures to engage economic, social and cultural rights.[79] In 2006, during a speech at New York University, the then UN High

Justice' (2008) 30(1) *HRQ* 95; J Elster, *Closing the Books: Transitional Justice in Historical Perspective* (CUP 2004).

76 Teitel, 'Transitional Justice Genealogy' (n 73); Roht-Arriaza and J Mariezcurrena (eds), *Transitional Justice in the Twenty-First Century: Beyond Truth Versus Justice* (CUP 2006), 202; R Nagy, 'Transitional Justice as Global Project: Critical Reflections' (2008) 29(2) *ThirdWorld Quarterly*, 276; Elster (n 75); G Bass, *Stay the Hand of Vengeance: The Politics of War Crimes Tribunals* (Princeton University Press 2000).

77 P de Greiff, 'Repairing the Past: Compensation for Victims of Human Rights Violations' in P de Greiff (ed.), *The Handbook of Reparations* (OUP 2006), 1; E Andreevska, 'Transitional Justice And Democratic Change: Key Concepts' (2013) 20 *Lex et Scientia Intl J* 54, 55; Arthur (n 75), 324, 326. Searching in law and political science databases, the first official appearance of the term is in a *Boston Herald* article about the 'Justice in Times of Transition', an international conference held in 1992 in Salzburg: MJ Palumbo, 'New Democracies Debate How to Punish Dictators of Past' (5 April 1992) *Boston Herald*, 16. In 1995, Neil Kritz, the vice-president of the Transitional Justice project at the US Institute of Peace, provided a comprehensive analysis in the three-volume book *Transitional Justice: How Emerging Democracies Reckon with Former Regimes* (US Institute of Peace Press 1995).

78 Teitel, 'Transitional Justice Genealogy' (n 73), 71–72, 89. See also K McEvoy, 'Beyond Legalism: Towards a Thicker Understanding of Transitional Justice' (2007) 34(4) *J Law Society* 412; Andreevska (n 77), 55; D Tutu, *No Future without Forgiveness* (First Image Books 1999); Arthur (n 75), 322–64; Elster (n 75); P Hayner, *Unspeakable Truths: Confronting State Terror and Atrocities* (Routledge 2000); M Mutua, 'What Is the Future of Transitional Justice?' (2015) 9 *Intl J Transitional Justice* 1; Sharp (n 64), 165–201.

79 The earliest such critique came from South African NGOs that regretted the decision of the South African TRC to focus on politically motivated killings, torture and detention and its failure to engage with the widespread socioeconomic aspects of apartheid: University of the Western Cape's Community Law Centre and others, 'Submission to the Truth and Reconciliation Commission Concerning the Relevance of Economic, Social and Cultural Rights to the Commission's Mandate (18 March 1997); R Duthie, 'Toward a Development-sensitive Approach to Transitional Justice' (2008) 2 *Intl J Transitional Justice* 292; P Gready, *The Era of Transitional Justice: The*

Commissioner for Human Rights, Louise Arbour, argued for integrating economic, social and cultural rights into the transitional justice framework, thereby making 'the gigantic leap that would allow justice, in its full sense, to make the contribution that it should to societies in transition'.[80] In 2010, the UN Secretary-General released a *Guidance Note on the United Nations Approach to Transitional Justice* calling on the UN to 'ensure transitional justice processes and mechanisms take account of the root causes of conflict and repressive rule, and address violations of all rights, including economic, social and cultural rights'.[81] Dealing with corporate activities is important to ensure that abuses of economic, social and cultural rights are included in transitional justice discourses and mechanisms:

> Economic, social and cultural rights (such as the prohibition against discrimination and the right to an adequate standard of living, including the rights to adequate food, clothing and housing) are important not only because of frequent abuses by private actors, but also because their violations are often the basis of subsequent infringements of civil and political rights.[82]

Later research showed that in an increasing number of conflicts, alongside atrocities perpetrated on civilians – the traditional subject of transitional justice – a pattern of war economies had emerged, particularly around the exploitation of natural and mineral resources.[83] In the editorial of a 2008 *International Journal of Transitional Justice* special issue on transitional justice and development, Rama

Aftermath of the Truth and Reconciliation Commission in South Africa and Beyond (Routledge 2010); LJ Laplante, 'On the Indivisibility of Rights: Truth Commissions, Reparations, and the Right to Development' (2007) 10 *Yale Human Rights Development LJ* 141; Miller (n 75), 270–72; I Muvingi, 'Sitting on Powder Kegs: Socioeconomic Rights in Transitional Societies' (2009) 3 *Intl J Trans Just* 163; Roht-Arriaza and Mariezcurrena (n 76); E Schmid, *Taking Economic, Social and Cultural Rights Seriously in International Criminal Law* (CUP 2005); A Boraine, 'Transitional Justice: A Holistic Interpretation' (2006) 60 *J Intl Affairs* 18; McEvoy (n 78); R Mani, 'Dilemmas of Expanding Transitional Justice, or Forging the Nexus between Transitional Justice and Development' (2008) 2 *Intl J Trans Just* 253, 257.

80 L Arbour, 'Economic and Social Justice for Societies in Transition' (2007–2008) 40 *Intl JL and Politics* 1.

81 Guidance Note of the Secretary General (n 71).

82 D de Felice, 'Sabine Michalowski (ed.), Corporate Accountability in the Context of Transitional Justice', (2014) 14 *Human Rights Law Review* 576, 578.

83 R Carranza, 'Plunder and Pain: Should Transitional Justice Engage with Corruption and Economic Crimes?' (2008) 2 *Intl J Trans Just* 310; J Cavallaro and S Albuja, 'The Lost Agenda: Economic Crimes and Truth Commissions in Latin America and Beyond' in K McEvoy and L McGregor (eds), *Transitional Justice from Below: Grassroots Activism and the Struggle for Change* (Hart 2008), 121; Bohoslavsky and Opgenhaffen (n 4), 197–201; K Andrieu, 'Dealing with a "New" Grievance: Should Anticorruption Be Part of the Transitional Justice Agenda?' (2012) 11(4) *J Human Rights* 537–57; I Robinson, 'Truth Commissions and Anti-Corruption: Towards a Complementary Framework?' (2015) 9(1) *Intl J Trans Just*, 33; N Roht-Arriaza 'Why Was the Economic Dimension Missing for So Long in Transitional Justice? An

Mani, a scholar, argued that transitional justice 'will lose credibility in the predominantly impoverished and devastated societies where it operates' if it does not tackle social injustice, corruption and resource exploitation.[84] Ruben Carranza, a director at the International Center for Transitional Justice, contended that an impunity gap results when transitional justice measures ignore accountability for large-scale corruption and other 'economic crimes',[85] pointing to the strategic role that such crimes play in maintaining systems of abuse, as well as use of the assets from such crimes to avoid accountability.[86]

Practitioners often 'call for holding responsible those who deliberately contributed to perpetuating a state of mass poverty' and for recovering assets that were wrongly acquired.[87] Practitioners of transitional justice had been initially

Exploratory Essay' in H Verbitsky and JP Bohoslavsky (eds), *The Economic Accomplices to the Argentine Dictatorship* (CUP 2015), 19.

84   Mani (n 79), 235.

85   Economic crimes cover a wide range of offences, from financial crimes committed by banks, tax evasion, money laundering, embezzlement, fraud, bribery and corruption. Economic crimes are not human rights violations as such, but they are linked, especially when dealing with the responsibility of economic actors. International human rights mechanisms, including the Human Rights Council, have paid increasing attention to the negative impact of corruption on the enjoyment of human rights and made numerous recommendations to member states with the aim to prevent and suppress corruption. The UN Office of the High Commissioner for Human Rights (OCHRC) explains that 'Depending on the level, pervasiveness and form of corruption, corruption can have devastating impacts on the availability, quality and accessibility – on the basis of equality – of human rights-related goods and services. Moreover, it undermines the functioning and legitimacy of institutions and processes, the rule of law and ultimately the State itself': OHCHR, 'Corruption and Human Rights' www.ohchr. org/EN/Issues/CorruptionAndHR/Pages/CorruptionAndHRIndex.aspx. In addition, the field of anti-corruption and bribery is a model for future advancement of business and human rights, in particular in relation to the development of international treaties and national legislation. For example, in April 2017, the UK Joint Committee on Human Rights published a report on business and human rights where it proposed that a 'failure to prevent' mechanism, modelled on section 7 of the UK Bribery Act may be 'an appropriate one to apply to business and human rights': Joint Committee on Human Rights (UK), Human Rights and Business 2017, Promoting responsibility and ensuring accountability, Sixth Report of Session 2016–17, 5 April 2017. More generally, see A Ramasastry, 'Closing the Governance Gap in the Business and Human Rights Arena: Lessons from the Anti-Corruption Movement', in S Deva and D Bilchitz (eds), *Human Rights Obligations of Business* (CUP 2013), 162–90; E Schmid, 'War Crimes Related to Violations of Economic, Social and Cultural Rights' (2011) 71(3) *Heidelberg J Intl L* 540; Muvingi (n 79), 180; R Duthie, 'Transitional Justice, Development, and Economic Violence' in Sharp (n 64), 1; Carranza (n 83), 327–28; I Bantekas, 'Corruption as an International Crime and Crime Against Humanity: An Outline of Supplementary Criminal Justice Policies' (2006) 4(3) *J Intl Criminal Justice* 466–84.

86   Carranza (n 83), 314–29. See also D Davitti, *Investment and Human Rights in Armed Conflict. Charting an Elusive Intersection* (Hart Publishing, 2019).

87   L Hecht and S Michalowski, 'The Economic and Social Dimensions of Transitional Justice' (2012) *ETJN Concept Paper* 2.

reluctant to include economic crimes within its scope. This related to legitimate concerns about transitional justice mechanisms, which are often underfunded, facing overly ambitious aspirations and extensive mandates. As such, expanding the mandate of truth commissions or tribunals to include economic crimes may raise unrealistic expectations and make the successful completion of mandates impossible. Contemporary truth commissions, however, established, for example, in Liberia and East Timor, have included economic, social and cultural rights in their investigation mandates.[88]

In parallel to the calls for integration of violations of economic, social and cultural rights, transitional justice practice and scholarship have started to address the role of companies. In 1998, the South Africa TRC found that business had a fundamental role in maintaining the *status quo* of the apartheid society.[89] The Liberian TRC dedicated a chapter of its 2009 final report to the impact of economic activities in prolonging and intensifying the civil war, and urged the aggressive pursuit of proceedings against corporations found to be implicated in the violence.[90] In 2015, the government of Argentina passed a law establishing a new truth commission mandated to investigate economic complicities in the dictatorship.[91] Corporate accountability is part of a broader debate within transitional justice and international criminal law about how economic crimes should be addressed.[92] Economic crimes are deeply intertwined into the narrative of many modern conflicts, as both drivers and sustainers.[93] But transitional justice mechanisms have traditionally focused on acts of physical violence and other civil and political rights violations.[94]

Recently, corporate accountability has begun to overcome its role 'at the periphery of transitional justice work'.[95] Despite the traditional assumption that transitional justice is aimed only at state actors, the most commonly used definition of transitional justice does not limit it in this way.[96] Truth, justice, reparations claims and institutional reform are consistent with examining the role of corporations in past human rights abuses and the prevention of future ones. The next chapters explain why.

---

88 For example, Liberia Truth and Reconciliation Commission, Final Report, Economics Crimes and the Conflict, Exploitation and Abuse (2009), Vol 3.

89 South Africa Truth and Reconciliation Commission (n 69).

90 Liberia Truth and Reconciliation Commission (n 88).

91 Government of Argentina, Ley de Creación de la Comision Bicameral de la Verdad, la Memoria, la Justicia, la Reparación e el Fortalecimiento de las Instituciones de la Democracia (2015).

92 See DN Sharp, 'Addressing Economic Violence in Times of Transition: Toward a Positive-Peace Paradigm for Transitional Justice' (2012) 35 *Fordham Intl LJ Journal* 780.

93 DN Sharp, 'Economic Violence in the Practice of African Truth Commissions and Beyond' in Sharp (n 64), 79.

94 Miller (n 75), 275–76; Cavallaro and Albuja (n 83), 122.

95 Sharp (n 64), 2.

96 LA Payne, 'Corporate Complicity and Transitional Justice: Setting the Scene' in *Peace, Everyone's Business! Corporate Accountability in Transitional Justice: Lessons for Colombia*, PAX (Utrecht, May 2017) 18, 20.

Chapter 2

Nuremberg and international criminal law

Introduction

Judicial processes are a key mechanism to achieving remedies for corporate human rights abuses in transitional justice contexts. This chapter explores the options and limitations of judicial processes at the international level, while the following two chapters analyze the regional and the national level. Because currently there are no mechanisms available to hold corporations legally accountable for human rights violations at the international level, this chapter examines the avenues available through international criminal law. International criminal law deals with the responsibility of individuals (natural persons) for the most serious international crimes. It has a narrow area of application – genocide, crimes against humanity and war crimes. Human rights law, on the other hand, spans a whole array of rights, civil and political rights, economic, social and cultural rights, as well as group rights. But while the theoretical obstacle for corporate human rights obligations is the shift from states to legal persons as subjects of law, in international criminal law a similar shift is not required – instead, the shift is from individuals to corporations, which is less problematic from an international law perspective.[1]

Prosecution initiatives as part of transitional justice aim to ensure that those responsible for committing crimes committed in the context of conflict or repressive rule are tried in accordance with international standards of fair trial and, where appropriate, punished. But states emerging from years of conflict or repressive rule may be unable or unwilling to conduct effective investigations and prosecutions. In such situations, international and hybrid criminal tribunals may exercise concurrent, or 'complementary', jurisdiction. These mechanisms were either never granted jurisdiction over corporations for crimes under international law or never used it. This chapter discusses the normative and political reasons. With the analysis of the post–World War II cases (explored in section 2.1) to the possibility of holding corporate officers and managers criminally responsible before the International Criminal Court (2.2) and the *ad hoc* tribunals (2.3) and the debate of scholars and practitioners in this area, this chapter assesses the limitations of international criminal law in holding

---

1 A Clapham, *Human Rights Obligations of Non-State Actors* (OUP 2006), 3.

corporations accountable for the commission of crimes under international law. It also discusses area of potential future expansion of this avenue.

2.1 Nuremberg and subsequent trials

The debate over the responsibility of corporations under international criminal law has its roots in the Nuremberg trials conducted after World War II.[2] Evidence of the central role of business in the Nazi war effort revealed the extent of crimes committed by companies through the forcible transfer and enslavement of millions of people, the production of arms used to wage aggressive war and the supply of poisonous chemicals for the killing of civilians in concentration camps.[3] The cases against executives and employees of Germany companies, analyzed in the next sections, remain the starting point for any discussion of corporate criminal responsibility in transitional justice contexts.

2.1.1. The International Military Tribunal

The Charter of the International Military Tribunal (IMT) established for the first time the principle of individual criminal accountability for certain crimes under international law.[4] In departing from the notion of state responsibility under international law, where states were the only relevant subjects, responsibility was instead conceptualized along an individual dimension. This conception continues to shape the understanding of individual responsibility and has had a significant impact on the broader scope of transitional justice, including in relation to the prosecution of corporations.[5]

The IMT did not have jurisdiction over legal persons. The Tribunal declared: 'Crimes against international law are committed by men, not by abstract entities, and only by punishing individuals who commit such crimes can the provisions of

---

2 International Military Tribunal, Trials of the Major War Criminals Before the International Military Tribunal, Nuremberg, 14 November 1945–1 October 1946, Vols 1–43 [hereinafter Trial of the Major War Criminals].

3 JA Bush, 'The Prehistory of Corporations and Conspiracy in International Criminal Law: What Nuremberg Really Said' (2009) 109 *Colom LR* 1094, 1105.

4 Charter of the International Military Tribunal, annexed to Agreement for the Prosecution and Punishment of the Major War Criminals of the European Axis, 8 August 1945, 59 Stat. 1544, 82 U.N.T.S. 279 [Charter of the International Military Tribunal], article 6 (granting the Tribunal authority to evaluate the 'individual responsibility' of 'persons' who acted as 'individuals or as members of organizations'). Organizations could be held to be 'criminal', subjecting certain members to prosecution for the crime of membership in a criminal organization, ibid., arts 9, 10. See also Affirmation of the Principles of International Law Recognized by the Charter of the Nuremberg Tribunal, G.A. Res. 95 (I), at 188, A/64/Add.1 (11 December 1946).

5 RG Teitel, 'Globalizing Transitional Justice: Contemporary Essays' (2014) *Oxford Scholarship Online*.

international law be enforced.'[6] The IMT's innovation, however, based on the American law of conspiracy, was in linking up individual and organizational responsibility.[7] A distinctive feature of the Charter of the IMT was the possibility for the Tribunal to declare, in connection with any act for which an individual was convicted, that groups or organizations of which the accused was a member were criminal organizations.[8] Under the Charter, the IMT had jurisdiction for 'the trial and punishment of the major war criminals [...] acting in the interests of the European Axis countries, whether as individuals or as members of organizations'.[9] As such, the Tribunal declared the Gestapo and 55 other Nazi organizations to be criminal in nature.[10] Yet the Tribunal's recognition of the criminal responsibility of these organizations served to provide a legal basis for the prosecution of individuals, and should not be interpreted as recognition of responsibility of legal persons. Such bodies were not analogous to private corporations, as they represented the Nazi state.[11]

Among the 21 people prosecuted at Nuremberg, there were no industrialists who did not also hold an official position in the Nazi regime.[12] One prominent German industrialist, Gustav Krupp, was indicted, but the IMT declared him unfit for trial.[13] Several of those convicted at Nuremberg and subsequent trials were involved in private industry and banking, but also operated as state agents.[14] For example, Walther Funk was the president of the *Reichsbank* and also Minister of Economics and Plenipotentiary General for War Economy. The Tribunal found that Funk agreed with the SS that the *Reichsbank* was to receive personal belongings taken from the victims who had been exterminated in the concentration camps.[15] The aid given to the SS by the bank would render Funk an accessory in the crimes against concentration camp victims.[16] In addition, as president of the

6 Trial of the Major War Criminals (n 2).
7 RH Jackson, 'The Law Under Which Nazi Organizations Are Accused of Being Criminal' (1946) 19 *Temporary L Quarterly* 371.
8 Charter of the International Military Tribunal (n 4), art 9.
9 Ibid., art 6.
10 Counsel for Prosecution of Axis Criminality, Nazi Conspiracy and Aggression: Opinion and Judgment 91, 97,102 (United States Printing Office 1947).
11 P Muchlinski, 'Human Rights and Multinationals: Is there a Problem?' (2001) 77(1) Intl Affairs 31, 39.
12 N Bernaz, 'An Analysis of the ICC Office of the Prosecutor's Policy Paper on Case Selection and Prioritization from the Perspective of Business and Human Rights' (2017) *J Intl Criminal Justice* 527.
13 Ruling of the Tribunal on 15 November 1945 in the matter of the application of Counsel for Krupp Von Bohlen for postponement of the Proceedings against this defendant, Office of the United States Chief of Counsel for Prosecution of Axis Criminality, Vol. I (United States Printing Office 1946), chapter IV, 92.
14 KJ Heller, *The Nuremberg Military Tribunals and the Origins of International Criminal Law* (OUP 2011).
15 Trial of the Major War Criminals (n 2), Vol. 1, 306.
16 T Taylor, *The Anatomy of the Nuremberg Trials: A Personal Memoir* (Knopf Doubleday 1992), 398.

Reichsbank, Funk was indirectly involved in the use of concentration camp labour – the bank set up a credit fund for the SS's construction of factories using concentration camp labourers. Funk was found guilty of war crimes and crimes against humanity.[17]

While the main objective of the trials at Nuremberg was to hold individual high-ranking civilian and military officials accountable for the Nazi regime's crimes, the prosecutors acknowledged that the owners and directors of large German companies played a key role in supporting and facilitating the regime and its crimes.[18] It was alleged before the IMT that, in order to execute a common plan, the defendants undertook acts that included using 'organizations of German business as instruments of economic mobilization for war'.[19] The chief prosecutor at the IMT, Robert Jackson, wrote: 'It has at all times been the position of the United States that the great industrialists of Germany were guilty of the crimes charged in this Indictment quite as much as politicians, diplomats, and soldiers.'[20] Jackson wrote in his first report of his intention to 'accuse a large number of individuals and officials who were in authority in the government, in the military establishment [...] and in the financial, industrial, and economic life of Germany who by all civilized standards are provable to be common criminals'.[21]

In addition to the trial of Nazi officials at the IMT, the Allies envisaged holding at least one other international trial that would target 'businesses or businessmen'.[22] In the end, the plan of holding a second international trial was dropped, and so was the idea of prosecuting corporations.[23] Instead, individual allied countries held their trials in their respective zones of occupation of Germany.

2.1.2. Industrial cases

On 20 December 1945, the Allied Control Council issued *Control Council Law No. 10*, which empowered any of the occupying authorities to try suspected war

17 Trial of the Major War Criminals (n 2), Vol 1, 171, 304–07. For commentary, see S Michalowski, 'No Complicity Liability for Funding Gross Human Rights Violations?' (2002) 30 *Berkeley J Intl L* 451, 476; CR Jakobsen, 'Doing Business with the Devil: The Challenges of Prosecuting Corporate Officials Whose Business Transactions Facilitate War Crimes and Crimes Against Humanity' (2005) 56 *Air Force LR* 176, 196.

18 Bush (n 3); W Kaleck and M Saage-Maab, 'Corporate Accountability for Human Rights Violations Amounting to International Crimes The Status Quo and its Challenges' (2010) 8(3) *J Intl Criminal Justice* 700, 701.

19 Trial of the Major War Criminals (n 2), Vol. 1, 35, 183.

20 Answer of the United States Prosecution to the Motion on Behalf of the Defendant Gustav Krupp von Bohlen, International Military Tribunal Document, 12 November 1945.

21 RH Jackson, Report to the President of the United States (7 June 1945), in The Nuremberg Case 3, 9 (1947).

22 Bush (n 3), 1113.

23 Ibid., 1162.

criminal in their respective occupied areas.[24] Based on this law, the United States Military Tribunal (USMT) held 12 subsequent trials, from 1946 to 1949 after the end of the *Trial of the Major War Criminals* before the IMT. Among these is a series of cases known as the *Industrial* cases, where German industrialists who collaborated with the Nazi regime were indicted for crimes against humanity, war crimes, complicity in the crime of aggression and mass murder, and aiding and abetting murder, torture and other atrocities committed by the Nazis.[25] These business leaders, often working through their companies, had supplied poisonous gas to concentration camps knowing it would be used to exterminate people, sought slave labour for their factories, helped in the deportation, murder and inhumane treatment of slave workers, and made profits by plundering property in occupied Europe.[26]

These cases revealed an underlying implication that the corporations for which the industrialists worked had also committed international crimes.[27] During the trials, even though only individual businessmen were charged, and 'corporate liability formally was not at stake',[28] the tribunals adopted an institutional approach. For example, the prosecution considered 'responsibility on different levels of decision making instead of targeting only the head office'.[29] In practice, corporate and individual liability could not be strictly separated at all times.[30] The idea of the responsibility of the corporations was underlying, and transpires from some of the judgments. For example, in the *Farben* case, the Tribunal remarked:

> While the Farben organization, as a corporation, is not charged under the indictment with committing a crime and is not the subject of prosecution in this case, it is the theory of the prosecution that the defendants individually and collectively used the Farben organization as an instrument by and through which they committed the crimes enumerated in the indictment.[31]

24 Control Council Law No. 10, Punishment of Persons Guilty of War Crimes, Crimes Against Peace and Against Humanity, Berlin, 20 December 1945.

25 Trials of War Criminals Before the Nuremberg Military Tribunals Under Control Council Law No. 10, Nuremberg, October 1946–April 1949 (United States Government Printing Office, 1953).

26 Bush (n 3), 1105, 1113–14; A Ramasastry, 'Corporate Complicity: From Nuremberg to Rangoon, An Examination of Forced Labor Cases and Their Impact on the Liability of Multinational Corporations' (2002) 20 *Berkeley J Intl L* 91.

27 Taylor (n 16).

28 KC Priemel, 'Tales of Totalitarianism: Conflicting Narratives in the Industrialist Cases at Nuremberg' in KC Priemel and A Stiller (eds), *Reassessing the Nuremberg Military Tribunals Transitional Justice, Trial Narratives, and Historiography* (Berghahn Books 2012), 170.

29 Ibid.

30 N Bernaz, 'Corporate Criminal Liability under International Law. The *New TV S.A.L.* and *Akhbar Beirut S.A.L.* Cases at the Special Tribunal for Lebanon' (2015) 13 *JICJ* 313, 321.

31 Trials of War Criminals before the Nuremberg Military Tribunals under Control Council Law No. 10, Vol. VIII [*I.G. Farben* case], 1108.

In 1948, the USMT held five of the directors of I.G. Farben, a major German chemical and pharmaceutical manufacturer, then the largest corporation in Europe, criminally liable for the use of slave labour.[32] This was the first time that a court imposed liability on a group of persons who were collectively in charge of a company.[33] The *I.G. Farben* case represented the first attempt to hold individuals accountable for their business activity under international criminal law.[34] Because the Tribunal did not have jurisdiction over legal persons, it could not render a verdict against *Farben* as a legal entity. But the USMT based much of its findings on the role of *Farben* as a corporate entity. The prosecution was of the opinion that the accused had used *Farben* as a tool to commit crimes against peace, war crimes and crimes against humanity.[35] The Tribunal noted: 'Auschwitz was financed and owned by Farben.'[36] It added, 'If not actually marching with the Wehrmacht, Farben at least was not far behind. But translating the criminal responsibility to personal and individual criminal acts is another matter.'[37]

This consideration points to a key challenge faced in this and other trials against corporate managers: establishing the criminal responsibility of the company itself separately from the responsibility of the individuals managing it. In the *Krupp* case, the Tribunal looked at the actions of the company as opposed to decisions or conduct of any individual director.[38] The case involved the prosecution of 12 employees and officers for the commission of war crimes and crimes against humanity with respect to plunder of factories and other property in occupied Europe, and to the deportation and use of prisoners of war and concentration camp inmates as forced labourers in *Krupp* factories in Germany.[39] Six of the defendants were found guilty. As with the *Farben* decision, the Tribunal focused on the role of the company as such and decided that *Krupp* had violated *The Hague Regulations* in its seizure and confiscation of property in occupied countries.[40] The position of individuals within the company is what determined their liability.[41]

---

32 Ibid. See also F Jessberger, 'On the Origins of Individual Criminal Responsibility under International Law for Business Activity: IG Farben on Trial' (2010) 8(3) *JICJ* 783.
33 Ramasastry (n 26), 104–08.
34 Jessberger (n 32) 784.
35 Ibid.
36 *I.G. Farben* case (n 31), 1183–84.
37 Ibid.
38 Trials of War Criminals before the Nuremberg Military Tribunals under Control Council Law No. 10, Vol. IX *The United States of America v Alfred Krupp et al.*, Military Tribunal IIIA, 9 Trials of War Criminals (1948) [*Krupp* case]. See also, Ramasastry (n 26), 108–13; Bush (n 3), 1111–1112; M Lippman, 'War Crimes Trials of German Industrialists: The "Other Schindlers" (1995) 9 *Temple Intl Comp LJ* 173, 229–49.
39 *Krupp* case (n 38), 467.
40 Ibid., 1351–52. See also Ramasastry (n 26), 108–13.
41 Ramasastry (n 26), 113–14.

The responsibility of individual businessmen was framed both as direct and accomplice liability. The element of knowledge to establish complicity was discussed in detail in the *Industrial* cases and in the trial against Bruno Tesch. He was the owner of *Tesch & Stabenow*, a company that supplied the Auschwitz concentration camps with Zyklon B, a pesticide used by the Nazis in the gas chambers. Tesch was tried in the 1946 *Zyklon B* case by a British Military Tribunal in Hamburg.[42] The charge was that Tesch, 'in violation of the laws and usages of war, did supply poison gas used for the extermination of allied nationals interned in concentration camps, well knowing that the said gas was to be so used'.[43] The co-defendants named included Karl Weinbacher, the company general manager, and gas technician Joachim Drosihn. The crucial question for the Tribunal was whether the accused knew of the purpose of the gas they supplied.[44] According to the Tribunal, the prosecution proved that Tesch and Weinbacher had acted with the requisite knowledge. They were sentenced to death by hanging,[45] while Drosihn was acquitted.

The *Flick* case provides an innovative approach to the liability for financing crimes under international law.[46] The trial was conducted against Friedrich Flick and Otto Steinbrinck, two leading officials of the *Flick Concern*, and members of the 'Himmler's Circle of Friends', a group that 'throughout the period of the Third Reich, worked closely with the [Schutzstaffel (SS)], met frequently and regularly with its leaders, and furnished aid, advice, and support to the SS, financial and otherwise'.[47] Himmler was the commander of the SS and the German Minister of the Interior, and was also responsible for the extermination policy in Germany's concentration camps. Flick and Steinbrink were charged with aiding and abetting criminal activities of the SS, including war crimes and crimes against humanity, and the enslavement and abuse of concentration camp inmates.[48] They were found to have provided 'extensive financial and other support' by profiting from slave labour in the camps.[49] The USMT found both guilty, first observing that 'an organization like the SS that commits war crimes and crimes against humanity on a large scale could be nothing other than criminal'.[50] The Tribunal continued: 'One who knowingly by his influence and money contributes to the support thereof must, under settled legal principles, be deemed to be, if not a principal, certainly an accessory to such crimes.'[51]

---

42 Trial of Bruno Tesch and Two Others in Law Reports of Trials of War Criminals, The United Nations War Crimes Commission, Vol. 1 (HMSO 1947) [*Zyklon B* case].
43 Ibid., 93–103.
44 Ibid., 100.
45 Ibid., 101.
46 Trials of War Criminals Before the Nuremberg Military Tribunals Under Control Council Law No.10, 1952, Vol VI *The United States of America v Friedrich Flick et al.* [*Flick* case].
47 Ibid., 1217–23.
48 Ibid., 103.
49 Ibid.
50 Ibid., 1217.
51 Ibid., 1217–20. See also N Bernaz, 'Establishing Liability for Financial Complicity in International Crimes' in JP Bohoslavsky and J Letnar Cernic (eds), *Making Sovereign Financing & Human Rights Work* (Hart 2014), 61, 69–70.

Part of the discussion on corporate criminal liability is the responsibility of financial entities. Flick and Steinbrinck were convicted even though the prosecution could not show that any part of the money donated by either of them was directly used for criminal activities of the SS.[52] This is an interesting approach to one of the most complex issues in the context of liability for providing funds – that is, whether liability requires establishing a link between a particular loan or donation and specific violations committed by the recipient.[53] The Tribunal showed that in the context of financing, it was not necessary to prove that the contributions made by the defendants were intended for unlawful purposes. Rather, it was sufficient that some part of the receiving fund had such an intended use.[54] Funding that went towards an organization with such clear criminal purposes as the SS was regarded as contributing to maintaining it, eliminating the need to examine the exact use of the funds provided.[55] It is at this point that legal theories related to the liability of financial accomplices started, an area that has received contradictory court decisions and interpretations since then and presents particular challenges in transitional justice contexts, as discussed in Chapter 3.

2.1.3. The Ministries trial

The *Ministries* trial, with 21 defendants, is another important post–World War II decision regarding the liability of bankers.[56] One of the defendants was Emil Puhl, who had been Deputy President of the *German Reichsbank* during the Third Reich and played an active role in arranging 'the receipt, classification, deposit, conversion and disposal of properties taken by the SS from victims exterminated in concentration camps'.[57] He was found guilty for war crimes and crimes against humanity for the administration of concentration and extermination camps.[58] Puhl was also charged with slave labour, including for negotiating a massive loan between the SS and *DEST*, a company specifically designed to utilize concentration camp labour.[59] The Tribunal held that although Puhl had held positions of considerable responsibility and authority, he had not played a decisive role and that it

52 Flick case (n 46), 1221.
53 Michalowski (n 17), 476–78.
54 Flick case (n 46), 1216–17, 1223. But see C Burchard, 'Ancillary and Neutral Business Contributions to "Corporate-Political Core Crime"' (2010) 8 JICJ 919, 936–37, who suggests that the liability of the defendants in the Flick case rests exclusively on their membership in a criminal organization, the SS, and therefore does not provide any guidance as to the standards that apply with regard to liability as an accessory to the crime.
55 Flick case (n 46), 1217. See also Michalowski (n 17), 476–78.
56 Trials of War Criminals Before the Nuremberg Military Tribunals Under Control Council Law No. 10, Vol XIV *The United States of America v Von Weizsaecker*, XIV [Ministries case].
57 Ibid., 609.
58 Ibid., 620–21.
59 Ibid., 850–51.

was doubtful whether Puhl 'did more than act as a conduit in these particular transactions'.[60] Accordingly, the Tribunal dismissed charges against Puhl on the slave labour count.[61]

But it is the case against Karl Rasche that set a precedent about commercial lending not giving rise to liability for gross human rights violations. Rasche was also charged in the *Ministries* trial with different counts of war crimes and crimes against humanity, and with slave labour on the grounds that he had made loans to entities using slave labour.[62] Rasche was a member of the board of managers of *Dresdner Bank*, a private commercial bank in Germany characterized as the bank of the Third Reich.[63] In the report of the Office of Military Government, he was described as 'one of the key liaisons between the Dresdner Bank and the SS, Nazi Party, and government so that the bank might function as an integral part of the Nazi war machine'.[64]

The evidence in the trial established that 'Dresdner Bank loaned very large sums of money to various SS enterprises which employed large numbers of inmates of concentration camps, and also to Reich enterprises and agencies engaged in the so-called resettlement programs'.[65] The Tribunal had to decide whether such loans would give rise to liability for war crimes and crimes against humanity, and first looked at Rasche's criminal responsibility for having been a member of Himmler's Circle of Friends (Freundeskreis der Wirtschaft), and for having approved large annual contributions by *Dresdner Bank* to a fund placed at Himmler's personal disposal.[66] The Tribunal rejected any liability of Rasche related to these contributions on the grounds that there was no evidence that 'Rasche knew that any part of the fund to which the bank made contributions was intended to be or was ever used by Himmler for any unlawful purposes'.[67]

The Tribunal, however, held that Rasche did have the requisite knowledge for the loans *Dresdner Bank* made to SS enterprises, which employed slave labour and otherwise funded the Nazi resettlement programme.[68] The Court reasoned that banks generally seek to learn the purposes of their loans as a matter of practice and found it inconceivable that Rasche did not have the necessary knowledge.[69] In this context, the Tribunal made a statement that has since been interpreted by some courts and commentators as authority for a general rejection

60 Ibid., 852.
61 Michalowski (n 17), 474–75.
62 *Ministries* case (n 56), 852.
63 Ibid., 621–22.
64 C Simpson, War Crimes of the Deutsche Bank and the Dresdner Bank: Office of the Military Government (U.S.) Reports 396 (Holmes & Meier 2002).
65 *Ministries* case (n 56), 621.
66 Ibid., 621–22.
67 Ibid., 622.
68 Ibid.
69 Ibid.

of liability for commercial loans that finance gross human rights violations.[70] It identified 'the real question' as:

> [I]s it a crime to make a loan, knowing or having good reason to believe that the borrower will use the funds in financing enterprises which are employed in using labor in violation of either national or international law? [...] A bank sells money or credit in the same manner as the merchandiser of any other commodity. It does not become a partner in enterprise, and the interest charged is merely the gross profit that the bank realizes from the transaction [...] Loans or sale of commodities to be used in an unlawful enterprise may well be condemned from a moral standpoint [...] but the transaction can hardly be said to be a crime. Our duty is to bring to justice those guilty of violating international law, and we are not prepared to state that such loans constitute a violation of that law.[71]

Sabine Michalowski, a scholar, rightly argues that the general conclusion drawn from this case that commercial loans are always exempt from complicity liability is put into doubt when examining the Tribunal decision in its entirety.[72] Under count seven, Rasche was charged for war crimes and crimes against humanity in the context of slave labour for allegedly having 'participated in the financing of SS enterprises' that used concentration camp labour.[73] Because Rasche testified credibly as to having no knowledge of the slave labour programme, he was found not guilty under this count.[74] The Tribunal rejected Rasche's liability under count seven not because making loans is an activity that is *per se* exempt from liability, but rather because there was not sufficient proof to justify holding Rasche personally criminally liable for the loans.[75]

More contemporary decisions have essentially followed the Tribunal's reasoning in Rasche. For example, the *South African Apartheid Litigation*, discussed in Chapter 4, reached the conclusion that commercial loans and other banking services

---

70 See e.g. *Khulumani v Barclays Nat'l Bank Ltd.*, 504 F.3d 254, 292–93 (2d Cir. 2007); *In re South African Apartheid Litigation*, 617 F. Supp. 2d 228, 258 (S.D.N.Y. 2009); *Doe v Nestle, S.A.*, 748 F. Supp. 2d 1057, 1088–90 (C.D. Cal. 2010); *Presbyterian Church of Sudan v Talisman Energy, Inc.*, 582 F.3d 244, 259 (2d Cir. 2009); *Khulumani*, 504 F.3d at 276. See also, S Bhashyam, 'Knowledge or Purpose? The Khulumani Litigation and the Standard for Aiding and Abetting Liability Under the Alien Tort Claims Act' (2008) 30 *Cardozo L Rev* 245, 269.
71 *Ministries* case (n 56), 622.
72 Michalowski (n 17), 473–74.
73 *Ministries* case (n 56), 853.
74 Ibid., 854–55.
75 Michalowski (n 17), 887–88; K Gallagher, 'Civil Litigation and Transnational Business' (2010) 8 *JICJ* 745, 763; A Mamolea, 'The Future of Corporate Aiding and Abetting Liability Under the Alien Tort Statute: A Roadmap' (2011) 51 *Santa Clara L Rev* 79, 128–29; Ramasastry (n 26), 118.

do not result in complicit liability.[76] In the litigation brought 50 years after Nuremberg by Holocaust survivors against Swiss banks (also in Chapter 4), the defendant banks cited *Rasche* to demonstrate that the mere act of providing money or credit to finance criminal activity does not constitute a violation of customary international law, even where the bank had knowledge of the purpose for such financing.[77]

2.1.4. Lesson from Nuremberg

The Nuremberg and subsequent trials provide important lessons for establishing corporate accountability through judicial processes in a transitional justice context. First, the concept of individual responsibility for crimes under international law was established for the first time. This provided support for the capacity of courts to adjudicate criminal cases whereby corporate officials are accused of committing gross human rights abuses. Although the IMT only prosecuted individuals, it recognized that legal persons can engage in criminal conduct. The Tribunal made clear that norms applicable to 'persons' applied to legal persons as well as individuals.[78]

Second, the involvement of corporate officers was framed in terms of both direct and accomplice criminal liability.[79] The post–World War II trials helped to explain the role that business enterprises have played in times of conflict or repression and to develop criteria of responsibility, in particular in relation to aiding and abetting.[80] Current notions of corporate responsibility for facilitating human rights abuses are indeed backed by legal theories whose origins can be traced back to these trials.[81]

Third, the position of the individual defendants within the corporation, including their decision-making authority, was a crucial factor for establishing liability.[82] For example, the Tribunal found that Funk exercised a sufficiently influential position to be held personally criminally liable for the loans he authorized, whereas it acquitted Puhl and Rasche, finding that although also holding a position of authority, they did not play a decisive role.

Fourth, while only individuals were prosecuted, the *Industrial* cases linked individual and the corporate responsibility, providing the initial jurisprudence for

---

76 *In re South African Apartheid Litigation*, 617 F. Supp. 2d 228, 258 (S.D.N.Y. 2009).
77 A Ramasastry, 'Secrets and Lies? Swiss Banks and International Human Rights' (1998) 31 *V and J Transnatl L* 325.
78 Nuremberg Judgment, The Accused Organizations, 1 October 1946, reprinted in 41 AJIL172 (1947); Charter of the International Military Tribunal (n 4), arts 6.
79 Kaleck and Saage-Maab (n 18), 702.
80 RC Slye, 'Corporations, Veils and International Criminal Liability' (2008) 33 *Brooklyn J Intl L* 955; Bernaz, 'Corporate Criminal Liability under International Law' (n 30).
81 JP Bohoslavsky and V Opgenhaffen, 'The Past and Present of Corporate Complicity: Financing the Argentinean Dictatorship' (2010) 23 *Harvard Human Rights J* 157, 159.
82 Michalowski (n 17), 478–83.

understanding how corporate actors may be held legally accountable.[83] Starting with *Farben*, the trials of German industrialists adopted an 'institutiona.' approach and highlighted the relationship between corporate activities and the commission of war crimes and crimes against humanity.[84] One commentator concludes: 'From the angle of today's international criminal law, the value of the [*Farben*] decision above all lies in having undertaken the attempt to highlight the responsibility of industry and business through the instruments of international criminal law.'[85] Corporate criminal liability was seriously explored, and while it was not adopted, it was never rejected as impermissible under international law. Corporate liability would have added a novel dimension to the emerging legal theory, by broadening the reach and impact of international criminal law and enhancing other features that have emerged from the Nuremberg trials – starting with the idea of an international criminal trial, and the concept of crimes against peace and crimes against humanity.

Fifth, the issue of financial contribution was discussed at length in the *Industrial* cases, but the trials produced different opinions.[86] The notion of complicity for financial actors 'has been confusing to say the least, producing mixed jurisprudence'.[87] The first judicial representations of the idea that financing crimes could trigger responsibility were indeed contradictory, as evidenced by *Flick* and the *Rasche* cases.[88] In *Flick*, Flick and Steinbrinck were convicted because even though the prosecution could not prove that the money they had donated to the SS was directly used for criminal activities, the Tribunal took it for granted that some of it had gone into maintaining this organization, regardless of whether it was spent on salaries or lethal gas.[89] In the *Rasche* case, the Tribunal reached a different opinion – it recognized that money or credit are fungible commodities, which could be used for unlawful enterprises, but did not find it a crime under international law.[90] Nuremberg case law does not draw a clear line between the liability of who committed the crimes and who provided the financial means to make the commission of crimes possible.[91] But beyond the different legal conclusions, both cases recognized the

83 G Skinner, 'Nuremberg's Legacy Continues: The Nuremberg Trials' Influence on Human Rights Litigation in U.S. Courts Under the Alien Tort Statute' (2008) 71 *Alb L Rev* 321, 325, 343, 362; Bush (n 3); Michalowski (n 17), 478–83.
84 *I.G. Farben* case (n 31), 1108.
85 Jessberger (n 32), 802.
86 Bohoslavsky and Opgenhaffen (n 81), 159.
87 JP Bohoslavsky and M Rulli, 'Corporate Complicity and Finance as a "Killing Agent": The Relevance of the Chilean Case' (2010) *JICJ* 8, 829, 834.
88 Bush (n 3), 1094; C Simpson (ed.), *War Crimes of the Deutsche Bank and the Dresdner Bank* (Holmes & Meyer 2002), 1–34.
89 *Flick* case (n 46), 1217–23. See also Bohoslavsky and Opgenhaffen (n 81), 159.
90 *Ministries* case (n 56), 621–22, 1221.
91 Bohoslavsky and Opgenhaffen (n 81), 174; JP Bohoslavsky and S Michalowski, 'Jus Cogens, Transitional Justice and Other Trends of the Debate on Odious Debts – A Response to the World Bank Discussion Paper on Odious Debts' (2010) 48 *Colum J Transnatl L* 61.

substantial effect that money can have over a massive criminal campaign and affirmed the notion that loans can contribute to the commission of international crimes.[92]

Finally, the wider political and economic context within which the post–World War II cases were carried out is of great importance. American foreign policy was undergoing a change in its attitude to German industry. The original goal was the 'industrial disarmament' of Germany. But later on, in 1945–1946, the United States adopted the 'Truman Doctrine', which sought to refrain from severe reprisals against the industrialists.[93] German industry was not to be 'purged'; it was to be recruited against the new communist enemy. The subsequent trials were influenced by the Allies' intention to reintegrate the German economy into the Western system, and the German economic elites into German society. The *Farben* trial may have been 'the expression of a justice that understood the accused to be prospective allies' – the comparatively mild judgment in *Farben* reflected the changed political instructions.[94] Here it is already possible to discern the tension between dealing with the past and shaping the future that confronts any intervention by international criminal law in post-conflict and transitional situations[95] – a point that is addressed also in relation to contemporary cases of domestic criminal liability in Chapter 4.

Indeed, at some point there were discussions about a second international trial being held at Nuremberg that would have targeted German businessmen and corporations.[96] But the appetite for such a trial died out, and the idea was abandoned. The reason was that discussions about whether and how to try big German businesses for their alleged war crimes were part of a broader economic policy in the occupation of Germany.[97] Germany's industrial facilities, its ability to produce and distribute coal and electricity, and its currency were already in suspension. Jonathan Bush, a scholar, articulates the sentiment in relation with *I.G. Farben*: public feeling was centred around the notion that 'the sinister-seeming Farben, a massive octopus of a company with tentacles reaching around the globe, was fully complicit in the crimes of the Nazis'.[98] But,

> [e]ven without counting its tens of thousands of slave labourers at any one time, it had a larger workforce than DuPont, Standard Oil (New Jersey), and Imperial Chemicals combined. It dominated the economic life of entire Latin American countries. Through its factories, patents, and cartel arrangements, it

92 Bohoslavsky and Rulli (n 87), 834.
93 Jessberger (n 32), 798.
94 Ibid., 799.
95 Ibid.
96 Bush (n 3), 1105, 1113–14; D Bloxham, '"The Trial that Never Was": Why There Was No Second International Trial of Major War Criminals at Nuremberg' (2002) 87 *J Hist Assn* 41, 46–47.
97 Bush (n 3), 1117.
98 Ibid., 1114.

supplied vital commodities to the Wehrmacht, and was able to choke their supply to the Allies even during the war.[99]

West German authorities also brought few prosecutions against businessmen. One of the few cases was the prosecution in 1948 of Gerhard Peters, the former general manager of *Degesch*, a distribution company (in which *Farben* had a 42% stake) that manufactured Zyklon B for use at Auschwitz. Peters was first sentenced by a court in Frankfurt to six years in prison for acting as accessory to murder, and finally acquitted in a new trial in 1955.[100] Accountability in West Germany for international crimes committed by corporations and business officials was essentially non-existent. But the reasons for this were political and economic, rather than a matter of international legal theory. Despite having suitable doctrines of principal and accessory liability and complicity within their legal lexicon, Germans authorities decided not to pursue corporate cases. With the political currents running in favour of rebuilding the West German economy, the result was near-total impunity for corporations, which instead had resumed their place as pillars of the West German economy. In his 170-page essay that surveys 'a story of legal energy and optimism in 1946–47, followed by a political about-face around 1948, with accountability yielding to amnesia',[101] Bush concludes:

> [P]erhaps the last lesson of Nuremberg is that innovative doctrines, vigorous trial programs, and a broad impulse toward accountability can, even together, be irrelevant [...] Germany turned out in time to be everything that the wartime Allies hoped for – peace-loving, democratic, prosperous, quiet – very much like Japan, with big industrial firms in both countries a crucial part of that prosperity [...] [S]urely a final, forgotten lesson of Nuremberg has to be that countries can be rebuilt and companies cleansed without legal accountability.[102]

2.2 The International Criminal Court

The International Criminal Court (ICC) has jurisdiction to prosecute individuals for the international crimes of genocide, crimes against humanity, war crimes and aggression. It does not have jurisdiction over corporations. Article 25 of the *Rome Statute of the International Criminal Court* limits the jurisdiction of the ICC to 'natural persons.'[103] There was, however, a proposal to add legal entities to the jurisdiction of the ICC during the negotiations of the Rome Statute. The French

---

99 Ibid., 1117.
100 CF Rüter and others (eds.), *Justiz und NS-Verbrechen. Sammlung deutscher Strafurteile wegen nationalsozialistischer Tötungsverbrechen 1945–1999* (Amsterdam UP 1975), 100–225.
101 Bush (n 3), 1240.
102 Ibid.
103 Rome Statute of the International Criminal Court, 17 July 1998, 2187 U.N.T.S 90, 94 [Rome Statute], Art. 25(1).

delegation proposed a restricted form of corporate criminal liability, limited to private (rather than public) corporations and requiring corporate criminal responsibility to be linked to the individual criminal responsibility of a leading member of a corporation.[104] The 1998 draft statute provided that in addition to natural persons the Court 'shall also have jurisdiction over legal persons, with the exception of States, when the crimes committed were committed on behalf of such legal persons or by their agencies or representatives'.[105] The French delegation believed that this inclusion would make it easier for victims of crimes to sue for restitution and compensation. The proposal was rejected because of a number of concerns – including that the Court would be confronted with overwhelming evidentiary problems when prosecuting corporations, and that there was not yet a recognized standard of criminal liability of corporations, which is still rejected in many national legal orders, and this international disparity would make the principle of complementarily unworkable.[106] No consensus was reached and finally the working group dropped the draft provision.[107] Arguably, expanding the scope of the ICC over corporations may also face the resistance of those worried that this would detract from the focus of the ICC on individual criminal responsibility and about the international criminal justice system being used to punish 'groups' rather that individuals, in conflict with the principle of individual responsibility for criminal offences.

Since the adoption of the Rome Statute, however, there has been persistent support, from scholars and from civil society, for the idea of an international criminal court with jurisdiction over corporations.[108] A special tribunal for international

104   Report of the International Commission of Jurists Expert Panel on Corporate Complicity and International Crimes, *Corporate Complicity and Legal Accountability* (International Commission of Jurists 2008), 56.

105   UN Diplomatic Conference of Plenipotentiaries on the Establishment of an International Criminal Court, Rome, 15 June–17 July 1998 [UN Diplomatic Conference of Plenipotentiaries], Draft Statute for the International Criminal Court and Draft Final Act, UN Doc A/CONF.183/2/Add.1 (1998).

106   UN Diplomatic Conference of Plenipotentiaries, Official Records, Vol. III, Reports and Other Documents [Rome Conference Official Records]. Summary Records of the Meetings of the Committee as a Whole, 26th Meeting, UN Doc. A/CONF.183/C.1/SR.26 (8 July 1998), 10. See also A Clapham, 'The Question of Jurisdiction under International Criminal Law over Legal Persons: Lessons from the Rome Conference' in M Kamminga and S Zia-Zarifi (eds), *Liability of Multinational Corporations under International Law* (Kluwer 2000), 139; WA Schabas, *An Introduction to the International Criminal Court* (Cambridge University Press 2007), 212; WA Schabas, 'Enforcing International Humanitarian Law: Catching the Accomplices' (2001) 83 *IRRC*, 842, 453.

107   Rome Conference Official Records (n 106), Vol. III. See also, P Saland, 'International criminal law principles' in R Lee (ed.), *The International Criminal Court – The Making of the Rome Statute: Issues, Negotiations, Results* (Kluwer Law International 1999), 199.

108   K Haigh, 'Extending the International Criminal Court's Jurisdiction to Corporations' (2008) 14(1) *Australian J Human Rights*, 199–219; J Kyriakakis, 'Corporate Criminal Liability and the ICC Statute: The Comparative Law Challenge' (2006) 56(3) *Netherlands Intl LR* and 'Corporations Before International Criminal Courts:

corporate liability has also been suggested, but the case is most often made to expand the jurisdiction of the ICC in a future amendment of the Rome Statute, given its existing institutional framework, broad geographical coverage and future-oriented mandate.[109]

Currently, the ICC can, in theory, adjudicate corporate involvement in international crimes, when the focus is shifted from the corporation to the individuals acting on behalf of a corporation. Businesspeople, as natural persons, do fall under the ICC personal jurisdiction. Shortly after the adoption of the Rome Statute, an article in the *Financial Times* had already warned that 'the treaty's accomplice liability provision could create international criminal liability for employees, officers and directors of corporations'.[110] The article continued: 'It takes little imagination to jump from complicity with human rights violations to complicity with crimes covered under the ICC Treaty.'[111] As William Schabas, an international criminal law professor, pointed out, the question, then, was how and to what extent these accomplices may be prosecuted by the ICC.[112]

Luis Moreno Ocampo, the first prosecutor of the ICC, observed in 2003 that 'officials of multinational corporations could be held accountable before the ICC for directly or indirectly facilitating conducts that leads to violations of international law'.[113] Moreno Ocampo further noted that he intended 'to investigate these companies to ascertain whether any of them should be brought before the ICC'.[114] Referring to the situation in the civil war in the Democratic Republic of Congo (DRC), Moreno Ocampo stated that clarifying the economic aspects of the alleged crimes was fundamental for preventing future crimes and prosecuting those already committed.[115] He was pointing to the activities of European and American companies exploiting gold, diamonds and oil in the DRC.[116] Ten years later, in 2013, Moreno Ocampo's successor, Fatou Bensouda, reaffirmed the commitment of the Office of the Prosecutor (OTP) to investigate business entities

Implications for the International Criminal Justice' (2017) 30(1) *LJIL*; L Van den Herik, 'Subjecting Corporations to the ICC Regime: Analysing the Legal Counter-arguments' in C Burchard, O Triffterer and J Vogel (eds), *The Review Conference and the Future of the International Criminal Court* (Kluwer 2010), 155–74 and 'Corporations as Future Subjects of the International Criminal Court: An Exploration of the Counterarguments and Consequences' in C Stahn and L van den Herik (eds), *Future Perspectives on International Criminal Justice* (Asser Press 2010), 350.

109 J Sundell, 'Ill-Gotten Gains: The Case for International Corporate Criminal Liability' (2011) 20 *Minn JIL* 648, 675–78; Kyriakakis, 'Corporations before International Criminal Courts' (n 108).

110 M Nyberg, 'At Risk from Complicity with Crimes' *Financial Times* (28 July 1998).

111 Schabas, 'Enforcing International Humanitarian Law' (n 106), 439.

112 Ibid., 441.

113 L. Moreno Ocampo, Presentation by the Chief Prosecutor on the occasion of the press conference of 16 July 2003, ICC-OTP-20030724-28.

114 Ibid.

115 L Moreno Ocampo, 'Communications Received by the Office of the Prosecutor of the ICC', 3, 4.

116 Jessberger (n 32), 801.

responsible for contributing to international crimes.[117] As she put it: 'Conflicts are driven either by financial enrichment or ideology: a thorough investigation of the finances behind a conflict therefore helps to identify suspects and develop a more complete picture of responsibility.'[118]

The threats of the ICC prosecutors to open the door of the Rome Statute to crimes involving economic entities remain unheard to date, with no investigation undertaken so far. A few communications against business people have reached the ICC, but without leading to any prosecution.[119] In October 2014, representatives of Ecuadorian victims sent a communication to the OTP against the 'Chief Executive Officer of Chevron and any other corporate officer' of the company.[120] The heart of the case was *Chevron*'s dumping of toxic waste into Ecuador's Lago Agrio region. Because the ICC cannot look at events that occurred before its establishment on 1 July 2002, the communication focused only on *Chevron*'s strategy to avoid complying with the judgments of Ecuadorian courts on this matter. The communication asserted that *Chevron*, by deliberately refusing to comply with Ecuadorian judgments, had committed 'an attack against the civilian population of the Oriente'.[121] It argued that *Chevron* officers 'deliberately maintained the situation of contamination of the Oriente and the deathly health effects it causes' and that this could constitute a crime against humanity.[122] *Chevron* officers' actions cannot, however, be identified as crimes against humanity within the meaning of Article 7 of the Rome Statute.[123] Crimes against humanity are crimes of context: to establish such crimes, it is necessary to prove that certain criminal acts were 'committed as part of a widespread or systematic attack directed against any civilian population, with knowledge of the attack'.[124] To be held criminally liable, *Chevron* executives would have to have committed certain criminal acts, within that context.[125] The complaint mentions a few such acts, such as murder and persecution, but without explaining how the alleged perpetrators named

---

117 Office of the Prosecutor (OTP), Policy Paper on Case Selection and Prioritisation, 15 September 2016 [OTP Policy Paper]. See also A Batesmith 'Corporate Criminal Responsibility for War Crimes and Other Violations of International Humanitarian Law: The Impact of the Business and Human Rights Movement' in C Harvey, J Summers and ND White (eds), *Contemporary Challenges to the Laws of War: Essay in Honour of Professor Peter Rowe* (CUP 2014), 292.
118 F Bensouda, Keynote address at the Paris Conference on International Corporate Responsibility in Conflict Zones, 21 March 2013, French Ministry of Foreign Affairs.
119 MA Fairlie, 'The Hidden Costs of Strategic Communications for the International Criminal Court' (2016) 51 *Texas Intl LJ* 281.
120 Legal Representative of Victims Mr Pablo Fajardo Mendoza and Mr Eduardo Bernabé Toledo, Communication Situation in Ecuador, October 2014.
121 Ibid.
122 Ibid., 18.
123 N Bernaz, 'Complaint to the International Criminal Court against the CEO of Chevron' 4 November 2014, Rights as Usual, http://rightsasusual.com/?p=895.
124 Rome Statute (n 103), Art 7.
125 Bernaz (n 123).

in the complaint are supposed to have committed them.[126] In March 2015, the ICC decided that there was no basis to proceed in the case.[127]

In May 2017, a coalition of human rights groups submitted a communication to the ICC prosecutor requesting investigation of the complicity of *Chiquita*'s executives in crimes against humanity in Colombia.[128] The communication traces the executives' involvement with payments made to Colombia paramilitaries between 1997 and 2004. 'At the time, Colombian paramilitaries were notorious for targeting civilians, among them banana workers and community leaders', a representative of the victims stated, 'but Chiquita's executives decided to continue giving money to paramilitaries'.[129] *Chiquita* pleaded guilty in a US federal court in 2007 to illegally funding Colombian paramilitaries. But accountability for the executives who oversaw and authorized the payment scheme has been elusive. While civil litigation is pending in US courts against *Chiquita* executives, no criminal prosecution has been attempted and Colombia has not been able to exercise jurisdiction over them. The communication came at a critical time in Colombia, as the country began to implement a peace agreement after nearly half a century of conflict. If the OTP decides to start an investigation into *Chiquita* officials for their payments to the paramilitaries, it would be the first time the Court examines the role of a corporation – through its executives – in international crimes.

Submissions before the ICC are now asking the Court to investigate the role of business activities in facilitating the commission of international crimes committed by the Myanmar military. In September 2018, the OTP announced the opening of a preliminary examination concerning the alleged deportation of Rohingya people from Myanmar to Bangladesh.[130] Myanmar is not a state party to the Rome Statute, but the Pre-Trial Chamber I had decided that the ICC may exercise its jurisdiction as at least one element of the alleged deportation occurred on the territory of Bangladesh, which is a state party.[131] The Rohingya are an ethnic Muslim minority living in Myanmar's Rakhine State. Waves of ethnic and religious violence led in 2017 to the displacement of over 700,000 Rohingya people into Bangladesh and, according to UN investigators, constitute evidence of genocide.[132] In October

126 Communication Situation in Ecuador (n 120), 40–46. See also Bernaz (n 123).
127 International Criminal Court, Ref OTP2014/036752, 16 March 2015.
128 International Human Rights Clinic at Harvard Law School, International Federation for Human Rights (FIDH), and Corporación Colectivo de Abogados José Alvear Restrepo (CAJAR), 'The contribution of Chiquita corporate officials to crimes against humanity in Colombia. Article 15 Communication to the International Criminal Court', May 2017.
129 International Human Rights Clinic at Harvard Law School, 'Human Rights Coalition Call on ICC to Investigate Role of Chiquita Executives in Contributing to Crimes Against Humanity', 18 May 2017.
130 ICC, Press Release: 'ICC Presidency assigns the Situation in Bangladesh/ Myanmar to Pre-Trial Chamber III' case no ICC-CPI-20190626-PR1461, 26 June 2019, https://www.icc-cpi.int/Pages/item.aspx?name=pr1461.
131 Ibid.
132 Report of the independent international fact-finding mission on Myanmar, 12 Set 2018 A/HRC/39/64.

2019, legal representatives of 86 victims from the Tula Toli village in Myanmar filed a submission before the ICC's Pre-Trail Chamber III requesting it to authorize an investigation.[133] Tula Toli was a Rohingya village where hundreds of Rohingya were allegedly killed and raped, during the August 2017 Myanmar military (known in Myanmar as the *Tatmadaw*) offensive against Rohingya civilians. The legal representatives request the ICC to investigate 'other entities involved in facilitating crimes'.[134] They refer to the findings of the Independent International Fact-Finding Mission on Myanmar, set up by the UN Human Rights Council in 2017, which had identified 'a number of companies (Burmese and foreign) whose officers may be liable as accessories, including for knowingly funding criminal activities of the Tatmadaw; supplying weapons or equipment for those activities; or their involvement in construction projects preventing the return of refugees'.[135] Accountability of individuals involved in these activities is in line with the objectives of accountability and deterrence of the ICC.

2.2.1. Thematic prosecutions

Another trend that may have implications for the ICC focus on the business dimensions of conflict are the so-called 'thematic prosecutions'. This term refers to the prosecutorial practice of selecting certain crimes and giving priority to particular phenomena within international criminal indictments, usually for purposes related to the best use of limited resources, but often also due to elevating attention on a given matter of international concern.[136] In September 2016, the OTP released a policy document on the office's selection and prioritization of cases.[137] In relation to assessing the gravity of the crimes, one of the case selection criteria, the document highlights:

> The impact of the crimes may be assessed in light of [...] the social, economic and environmental damage inflicted on the affected communities. In this context, the Office will give particular consideration to prosecuting Rome Statute crimes that are committed by means of, or that result in, inter alia, the destruction of the environment, the illegal exploitation of natural resources or the illegal dispossession of land.[138]

133 Representations of Victims from Tula Toli, Situation in the People's Republic of Bangladesh/Republic of the Union of Myanmar, Pre-Trial Chamber III, No. ICC-01/19, 23 Oct 2019.
134 Ibid., para 76.
135 Ibid. referring to Independent International Fact-Finding Mission on Myanmar, The economic interests of the Myanmar military, 5 Aug 2019, A/HRC/42/CRP.3, esp. paras 6, 105–27, 129–40, 150–65.
136 MM de Guzman, 'An expressive Rationale for the Thematic Prosecution of Sex Crimes', in M Bergsmo (ed.), *Thematic Prosecution of International Sex Crimes* (Torkel Opsahl Academic 2012).
137 OTP Policy Paper (n 117).
138 Ibid., para 41.

The acts described in the policy (environmental destruction, illegal exploitation of natural resources and land confiscation) constitute serious human rights violations for millions of people across the world, especially in countries affected by conflict and poor governance. They often involve multinational corporations, particularly in the extractive and agribusiness sectors. The new policy implies that these could be gateways to the commission of international crimes under the Rome Statute. For this reason, the new policy has attracted the attention of those working in the business and human rights field, who view it as a potential tool to achieve justice for victims in a context of prevalent impunity.[139] *Global Witness*, an NGO, considered the policy a 'landmark shift in international criminal justice' and praised it as a move that 'could reshape how business is done in developing countries'.[140] Others have dismissed it as mere talk unlikely to lead to any real change.[141] Schabas remarks: 'One recalls the excitement when, thirteen years ago, the Prosecutor indicated that he would be looking at the business connections to war crimes and other atrocities. Did anything happen?'[142]

Indeed, nothing happened. The policy shift, however, could at least in theory have important implications in relation to both corporate behaviour and activists' advocacy work.[143] Arguably, it is in relation to crimes against humanity and war crimes that the new policy is most likely to change the practice of the OTP because these two crimes can be committed 'by means of' the conduct referred to in the policy – while the crimes of aggression and genocide cannot.[144] And it is particularly the effect of the policy on the crime of pillaging that could lead to changes in the area of corporate accountability.

The Rome Statute describes the 'war crime of pillaging' as the appropriation of property without the consent of the owner, with intention to deprive the owner of the property in the context of an armed conflict.[145] Although the provisions on pillaging do not mention natural resources, it is reasonable to interpret 'property' as to include natural resources and consider that pillaging of natural resources falls

139 J Vidal and O Bowcott, 'ICC Widens Remit to Include Environmental Destruction Cases', *The Guardian*, 15 September 2016; Bernaz, 'An Analysis of the ICC Office of the Prosecutor's Policy Paper', (n 12); ET Cusato, 'Beyond Symbolism Problems and Prospects with Prosecuting Environmental Destruction before the ICC' (2017).
140 Global Witness, 'Company Executives Could Now be Tried for Land Grabs and Environmental Destruction', 15 September 2016.
141 W Schabas, 'Feeding Time at the Office of the Prosecutor' 23 November 2016 International Criminal Justice Today, American Bar Association's International Criminal Court Project, 23 Nov 2016.
142 Ibid.
143 Bernaz, 'An Analysis of the ICC Office of the Prosecutor's Policy Paper', (n 12); Global Witness (n 140); Vidal and Bowcott (n 139).
144 Bernaz, 'An Analysis of the ICC Office of the Prosecutor's Policy Paper', (n 12).
145 Rome Statute (n 103), Arts 8(2)(b)(xvi) and 8(2)(e)(v), which establish the war crime of 'pillaging a town or place' in international and non-international armed conflicts respectively.

within the remit of the ICC.[146] Different commentators have argued for the prosecution of the crime of pillage for acts that amount to plundering a country's natural resources. Some argue that existing principles of international criminal law ought to be directed to address the illegal exploitation of natural resources during a conflict.[147]

The question of natural resources is increasingly being recognized as a priority in transitional justice processes.[148] Resources are a natural connecting point for post-conflict development and transitional justice. While rarely the single driving cause of conflict, links between conflict and natural resources are present in every conflict. As one scholar points out, 'although the majority of modern conflicts are not fought over natural resources, once the fighting starts all parties tend to consolidate their positions by exploiting the financial opportunities that resource access provides'.[149] Natural resource extraction is also linked to an increased likelihood of authoritarianism.[150] There are a few examples of efforts to hold perpetrators of pillaging crimes legally accountable. A case at the International Court of Justice found that Uganda failed in its obligation to prevent the pillage of natural resources by its armed forces and non-state collaborators in the DRC.[151] Charges against the Revolutionary United Front and Charles Taylor at the Special Court for Sierra Leone included crimes directly associated with efforts to control diamond mines in Sierra Leone.[152] Truth commissions and other investigative bodies across different countries have analyzed the link between natural resource exploitation and conflict to some extent.[153] As detailed

---

146 MA Lundberg, 'The Plunder of Natural Resources During War: a War Crime' (2007–2008) 39 *Georgetown JIL* 495, 507–12.
147 L van den Herik and D Dam-de Jong, 'Revitalizing the Antique War Crime of Pillage: The Potential and Pitfalls of Using International Criminal Law to Address Illegal Resource Exploitation During Armed Conflict' (2011) 15 *Criminal L Forum*, 250.
148 SS Nichols, 'Reimagining Transitional Justice for an Enduring Peace: Accounting for Natural Resources in Conflict' in DN Sharp (ed.), *Justice and Economic Violence in Transition* (Springer 2014), 203, 211; E Harwell and P Le Billon, 'Natural Connections: Linking Transitional Justice and Development Through a Focus on Natural Resources' in P de Greiff and R Duthie (eds), *Transitional Justice and Development: Making Connections* (Social Science Research Council 2009) 282, 283; M Ross, 'What Do We Know About Natural Resources and Civil War?' (2004) 41(3) *J Peace Research* 337.
149 O Martin-Ortega, 'Business and Human Rights in Conflict' (2008) *Carnegie Council for Ethics in Intl Affairs*, 274. See also P Le Billon, *Wars of Plunder* (Columbia University Press 2012); ML Ross, *The Oil Curse* (Princeton University Press 2012).
150 ML Ross, 'Does Oil Hinder Democracy?' (2001) 53(3) *World Politics* 325.
151 International Court of Justice, Armed Activities on the Territory of the Congo (*Democratic Republic of the Congo v Uganda*), Judgment, ICJ Reports 19 December 2005, 168.
152 Special Court of Sierra Leone, *Prosecutor v Charles Ghankay Taylor*, SCSL-03-01, Indictment, 3 March 2003.
153 See e.g. Sierra Leone Truth and Reconciliation Commission, *Witness to Truth: Report of the Sierra Leone Truth and Reconciliation Commission* (October 2004), Vol 2; Commission for Reception, Truth and Reconciliation Timor-Leste, *Chega!* (October 2005), parts 7 and 2, Annex A (esp. paras 128–32). See also Nichols (n 148), 203.

in Chapter 5, a number of those (e.g. in Liberia, East Timor, Sierra Leone and the DRC) have also identified the responsibilities of corporations and businesspeople in their final reports. The current reconsideration and expansion of transitional justice may pave the way for further investigating the role of natural resources in conflicts.[154] Arguably, the new policy paper, which mentions the illegal exploitation of natural resources as a conduct the OTP will pay more attention to, is a step in that direction.[155]

The new policy could influence new communications brought to the ICC. Before the release of the policy paper the OTP had already received at least two communications related to one of the conducts the office had specifically stated it would pay attention to – land confiscation. In 2010 the OTP initiated a preliminary examination of the situation in Honduras in this context.[156] In particular, the situation that arose in the Bajo Aguán region involved the killings of at least 100 civilians and other acts of violence by state and private security forces in land disputes between individual landowners and private corporations on one side and peasant movements on the other side.[157] In 2015, the OTP decided not to proceed because 'in the absence of sufficient information on links and commonality of features between the multiple alleged crimes', it found insufficient evidence to establish the existence of a 'course of conduct' within the meaning of crimes against humanity.[158] In 2014, the OTP received a communication asking for it to investigate allegations that the 'widespread and systematic land grabbing conducted by the Cambodian ruling elite for over a decade amounts to a crime against humanity'.[159] The new policy may lead the OTP to open a preliminary examination of the situation in Cambodia, and, if more evidence is brought concerning events in Honduras, to move the preliminary examination to the next stage.[160]

It is likely that the new policy paper is going to result in an increase of communications filed by civil society organizations on issues related to the illegal exploitation of natural resources and land confiscation. Nadia Bernaz, a scholar, raises the concerns that '[t]he language of the policy paper, coupled with the desire of some organizations to obtain justice, may lead to [...] the erroneous belief that the Court's jurisdiction has changed to encompass land grabbing as a

154 Nichols (n 148), 205.
155 Bernaz, 'An Analysis of the ICC Office of the Prosecutor's Policy Paper' (n 12); PJ Keenan, 'Conflict Minerals and the Law of Pillage' (2013–2014) 14 *Chicago JIL* 524, 535–38.
156 The Office of the Prosecutor, Situation in Honduras Article 5 Report, October 2015.
157 Ibid., 43.
158 Ibid., 49.
159 Global Diligence, 'Communication Under Article 15 of the Rome Statute of the International Criminal Court. The Commission of Crimes Against Humanity in Cambodia. July 2002 to Present', www.fidh.org/IMG/pdf/executive_summary-2. pdf. See also J Embree, 'Criminalizing Land-Grabbing: Arguing for ICC Involvement in the Cambodian Land Concession Crisis' (2015) 27 *Florida JIL* 399.
160 Bernaz, 'An Analysis of the ICC Office of the Prosecutor's Policy Paper' (n 12); Global Diligence, (n 159).

stand-alone offence'.[161] This might encourage the filing of manifestly unfounded communications, which arguably waste the scarce resources of the OTP.[162] 'Strategic communications' can be considered 'highly publicized investigation requests aimed not at securing any ICC-related activity, but at obtaining some non-Court related advantage'.[163] The 'appeal of the technique', arguably, 'is obvious: much good can come from directing international attention to the many unthinkable atrocities taking place around the globe'.[164] Despite this risk, the new policy paper is important for its potential impacts on business behaviour and advocacy work of business and human rights activists. Even an NGO communication with little chance of passing the admissibility stage, if picked up by media, could lead to reputational damage for companies, and increased public awareness of the issue.

II.3 The *ad hoc* tribunals

The two *ad hoc* tribunals, established for the former Yugoslavia and for Rwanda in 1993 and 1994 respectively, expressly provided that they had jurisdiction 'over natural persons', thus excluding prosecution of corporate bodies or organizations.[165] The Security Council resolution establishing the International Criminal Tribunal for the Former Yugoslavia (ICTY) said it was for the purpose of prosecuting 'natural persons' responsible for serious violation of international humanitarian laws. The then UN Secretary-General Boutros-Ghali made a passing reference to the desirability of criminalizing certain juridical persons 'such as an association or organisation' under the Statute of the ICTY, but ultimately rejected this idea in favour of focusing on natural persons.[166] Resolution 955, which established the International Criminal Tribunal for Rwanda (ICTR), said the Tribunal was targeted at 'natural persons' responsible for genocide.[167] Arguably, the exclusion of jurisdiction over legal persons was partly due to crimes in the contexts of the former Yugoslavia and Rwanda not involving businesses to any great extent.

The Special Court for Sierra Leone (SCLS) statute did not specifically refer to natural persons only. Thus it did not explicitly exclude jurisdiction over legal persons, but it did not explicitly provide for it. The report of the Secretary-General on the draft statute did not explain why the limitation to 'natural persons' provision

161 Bernaz, 'An Analysis of the ICC Office of the Prosecutor's Policy Paper' (n 12), 9.
162 Ibid.
163 MA Fairlie, 'The Hidden Costs of Strategic Communications for the International Criminal Court' (2016) 51 *Texas ILJ* 281, 283.
164 Ibid.
165 Statute of the International Tribunal for the Former Yugoslavia, U.N. Doc. S/RES/827 art 6 (1993); Statute of the International Tribunal for Rwanda, U.N. Doc. S/RES/955 art 5 (1994). See also W Schabas, *The UN International Criminal Tribunals* (Cambridge University Press 2006); OK Fauchald and J Stigen, 'Corporate Responsibility Before International Institutions' (2005) 40 Geo Wash Intl L Rev 1025.
166 Report of the Secretary-General Pursuant to Paragraph 2 of Security Council Resolution 808, para 51, 3 May 1993 U.N. Doc. S/25704.
167 Schabas, *The UN International Criminal Tribunals* (n 165), 138.

was not included.[168] This might be a reflection of a specific interest in corporate liability in the Sierra Leone conflict.[169] Theoretically, the SCSL could have prosecuted corporate entities. Despite this possibility, however, SCSL prosecutions have been confined to natural persons.[170]

While international criminal tribunals have not used jurisdiction over corporations for international crimes, they have prosecuted and convicted corporate officials who supported international crimes.[171] Key cases are those at the ICTR involving *Radio Télévision Libre des Mille Collines.*[172] The station broadcasted from July 1993 to July 1994 and it was determined by the Tribunal that its propaganda and vindictive speech incited the Rwandan genocide. In 2003, prosecutors of the ICTR sought life sentences against Ferdinand Nahimana, a director of the radio, and Jean Bosco Barayagwiza, associated with the station. The ICTR also prosecuted Hassan Ngeze, the founder and director of *Kangura* newspaper, known for spreading anti-Tutsi propaganda. The court consolidated the indictment of the three men into a single trial, known as the *Media Case.*[173] This trial was the first time since Nuremberg that the role of the media was examined as a component of international criminal law. Nahimana, Barayagwiza and Ngeze were convicted on counts of genocide, conspiracy to commit genocide, direct and public incitement to commit genocide, and crimes against humanity. Nahimana and Ngeze were sentenced to life imprisonment and Barayagwiza to 35 years. Upon appeal, in 2007, Nahimana and Ngeze's sentences were reduced to 30 and 35 years respectively. Later, in 2009, Valeria Berneriki, a broadcaster, was also found guilty of incitement to genocide by a *gacaca* court (traditional community justice courts of Rwanda, revived in 2001) and sentenced to life imprisonment.[174]

In the case against Alfred Musema, the director of a tea factory, the prosecutor alleged that Musema transported armed attackers, including employees of the factory, to different locations, and ordered them to attack Tutsis seeking refuge there.[175] He exercised legal and financial control over his employees, including the power to appoint or remove them and to prevent or to punish their use of factory equipment that was used in the crimes.[176] He was held responsible for the actions of his employees and convicted of genocide, but the conviction was not directly related to his business activities.

---

168 Security Council Resolution 1385 on the Situation in Sierra Leone, U.N. Doc. S/RES/1385 2001.

169 M Berdal and D Malone, *Greed and Grievance: Economic Agendas in Civil Wars* (International Development Research Centre 2000).

170 Schabas, *The UN International Criminal Tribunals* (n 165) 139.

171 International Commission of Jurists (n 104), Vol 2, 6.

172 *International Criminal Tribunal for Rwanda* (ICTR), *The Prosecutor v Ferdinand Nahimana, Jean-Bosco Barayagwiza and Hassan Ngeze (2003).*

173 Ibid.

174 Ibid.

175 ICTR, *Prosecutor v Alfred Musema* (ICTR-96-13).

176 ICTR, Judgment, *Musema* (ICTR-96-13-T), Trial Chamber, 27 January 2000; Judgment, *Musema* (ICTR-96-13-A), Appeals Chamber, 16 November 2001.

So far, no international criminal tribunal has had jurisdiction over corporations for crimes under international law. In 2014, however, the Special Tribunal for Lebanon decided in two cases, *New TV S.A.L* and *Akhbar Beirut S.A.L.*, that it could assert jurisdiction over corporations for the offence of contempt of court.[177] The Appeals Panel ruling in *New TV* was the first decision by an international criminal tribunal asserting jurisdiction over corporations, although not for human rights violations or international crimes.[178] Its findings were then confirmed in the *Akhbar Beirut* appeal decision. The decision was in relation to the prosecution of *Al-Akhbar* newspaper and *Al-Jadeed TV* as well as two employees, Ibrahim al-Amin and Karma al-Khayat, on charges of contempt of court.[179] The charges were brought against them for publishing information about secret witnesses on whose testimonies the prosecution relied to issue indictments. The STL's Contempt Judge had issued a decision stating that the Tribunal was prosecuting individuals involved in the assassination of former Lebanese Prime Minister, Rafik Hariri, not legal persons, and concluding that the STL had no personal jurisdiction to prosecute *Al-Jadeed TV*.[180] He decided to proceed with the prosecution against Khayat, but not the company for which she worked. But the appeals panel reversed this decision. It expanded the jurisdiction of the Tribunal, reiterating that it was not restricted to the prosecution of individuals, but included the prosecution of legal persons.[181]

The STL relied on the point that even if corporate liability is not included in the Rome Statute, this does not mean that the concept does not exist under international law. The STL elaborated on its decision:

> The omission of legal persons from the Rome Statute should not be interpreted as a concerted exercise that reflected a legal view that legal persons are completely beyond the purview of international criminal law. We thus hold that no definitive legal conclusion can be drawn from the exclusion of legal persons from the jurisdiction *ratione personae* of the ICC. Instead, it is a reflection of the lack of a political (rather than legal) consensus to provide such jurisdiction in the Rome Statute.[182]

The scope of this decision is narrow and it does not represent a breakthrough in terms of corporate accountability for human rights violations or international crimes. It is, nonetheless, important as it establishes for the first time that an international tribunal can exercise jurisdiction over business entities. In this context, the STL decision is of great conceptual importance.[183] Once the precedent is

177 Special Tribunal for Lebanon, *New TV S.A.L* and *Akhbar Beirut S.A.L.*, STL-14-05.
178 Bernaz, 'Corporate Criminal Liability under International Law' (n 30), 313–30.
179 *New TV S.A.L.* Appeal Decision, 66.
180 Ibid., Contempt Judge.
181 Ibid., Appeal Decision, 66.
182 Ibid.
183 Bernaz, 'Corporate Criminal Liability under International Law' (n 30), 313–21.

set, other courts may expand the subject matter to include human rights violations and crimes under international law. The *New TV* case may be relied upon in future business and human rights litigation as evidence that corporations may commit crimes that can be prosecuted at the international level. As such, this decision may have important practical consequences. For example, in *Kiobel*, analyzed in Chapter 4, a US Court of Appeals asserted that 'although international law has sometimes extended the scope of liability for a violation of a given norm to individuals, it has never extended the scope of liability to a corporation'.[184] After the *New TV* decision this is no longer true. It is possible, and probable, that this decision will not remain an isolated one, and that other courts, including domestic courts, may be influenced by this precedent and seek to consolidate it to address the issue of corporate accountability, including in transitional justice contexts.[185]

Conclusion

The motivation for calls to extend international criminal jurisdiction over corporations varies, but most arguments operate on the premise that corporations can, and do, commit or assist in international crimes, and that individual criminal responsibility alone is insufficient to address the realities of corporate crime in modern conflicts.[186] Contemporary conflict studies demonstrate that many wars are rooted in competition over resources and in economic inequality, with the resulting calls for a new generation of international criminal law addressing economic actors and economic crimes.[187] Relatedly, there is the argument that if a goal of international criminal law is to support durable peace, then addressing economic networks that sustain conflicts should be a crucial feature of international criminal practice.[188] Human rights scholars point to the current lacuna in governance, which see corporations enjoying impunity for abuses that overlap with violations of international criminal law.[189] Others point to the prosecutions of industrialists after World War II to claim that contemporary corporate responsibility for international crimes would honour the

184 *Kiobel v Royal Dutch Petroleum* Co. 621 F3d 111, 120 (2d. Cir. 2010).

185 Bernaz, 'Corporate Criminal Liability under International Law' (n 30), 329–30.

186 Kyriakakis, 'Corporations before International Criminal Courts' (n 108), 231; Batesmith (n 117), 286; J Stewart, 'A Pragmatic Critique of Corporate Criminal Theory: Lessons from the Extremity' (2013) 16(2) *New Criminal L Rev* 261.

187 van den Herik and Dam-De Jong (n 147); I Eberechi, 'Armed Conflicts in Africa and Western Complicity: A Disincentive for African Union's Cooperation with the ICC' (2009) 3 *African J Legal Studies* 53.

188 For example, M Delas-Marty, 'Ambiguities and Lacunae: The International Criminal Court Ten Years On' (2013) 11 *JICJ* 553, 557.

189 Kyriakakis, 'Corporations before International Criminal Courts' (n 108), 223; M Ezeudu, 'Revisiting Corporate Violations of Human Rights in Nigeria's Niger Delta Region: Canvassing the Potential Role of the International Criminal Court' (2011) 11 *African Human Rights LJ* 23; L van den Herik and J Letnar Černič, 'Regulating Corporations under International Law: From Human Rights to International Criminal Law and Back Again' (2010) 8 *JICJ* 725.

legacy of Nuremberg.[190] Some advance a legal claim to support calls for institutional competence over corporations committing international crimes: that customary international criminal norms apply equally to corporations as they do to natural persons, with the only distinction lying in the jurisdictional limits of international courts to date.[191]

The pursuit of corporate offenders under international criminal law could have positive implications in at least three areas: (i) in setting a framework that promotes deterrence of such crimes; (ii) in fostering the legitimacy range and effectiveness of the international criminal system; and (iii) in overcoming certain obstacles of international human rights law.[192] First, the deterrent effect of international criminal prosecutions is routinely criticized on the basis that, among other things, it presupposes a psychologically rational actor where such may not exist.[193] However, as some scholars have noted, the ideological presuppositions of criminal law's rational actor may be more accommodating to corporate persons than to human beings.[194] A human rights scholar for example argues that

> [i]n direct contrast to the usual contention that criminal law is necessarily most effective when responsibility is atomized to the human agent, the proposition is that it is potentially more so when directed at legal entities that are constitutionally designed to behave rationally in terms of engaging in emotionally and socially disengaged cost-benefit analysis.[195]

Second, in relation to the legitimacy of the international criminal system, it is the phenomenon of the transnational identity of the corporation that is particularly pertinent. Multinational corporations continue to be primarily headquartered in industrialized countries, while the dynamics that press against corporate accountability for business-related human rights abuses, and where these tend to be most egregious, are most pronounced in developing countries.[196] An international

---

190 For example, T Giannini and S Farbstein, 'Corporate Accountability in Conflict Zones: How Kiobel Undermines the Nuremberg Legacy and Modern Human Rights' (2010) 52 *HILJ* 119.

191 For example, Clapham (n 1), 74–75, 251, 267; V Nerlich, 'Core Crimes and Transnational Business Corporations' (2010) 8 *JICJ* 895, at 896–99.

192 K Cronin-Furman and A Taub, 'Lions and Tigers and Deterrence, Oh My: Evaluating Expectations of International Criminal Justice', in W Schabas, Y McDermott and N Hayes (eds), *The Ashgate Research Companion to International Criminal Law: Critical Perspectives* (Ashgate 2013), 435.

193 N Naffine, 'Who are Law's Persons? From Cheshire Cats to Responsible Subjects' (2003) 66 *Modern L Rev* 346, 365.

194 A Grear, 'Challenging Corporate "Humanity": Legal Disembodiment, Embodiment and Human Rights' (2007) 7(3) *Human Rights L Rev* 511, 524; Kyriakakis, 'Corporations before International Criminal Courts' (n 108), 236

195 Kyriakakis, 'Corporations before International Criminal Courts' (n 108), 237.

196 B Roach, 'A Primer on Multinational Corporations' in AD Chandler and B Mazlish (eds), *Leviathans: Multinational Corporations and the New Global History* (Cambridge University Press 2005), 19, 24–28; O De Schutter, 'The Accountability of Multinationals for

criminal court addressing this phenomenon through appropriate prosecutions 'provides the opportunity for international criminal jurisprudence to construct more complete narratives of power, law and responsibility for otherwise apparently localized conflicts'.[197] Another scholar notes:

> Local populations, if they notice the proceedings at all, often view international tribunals' brand of justice as distinctly Western. In the case of corporate offenses, however, the target audience is not the local population, but rather multinational corporations. An international trial in such a situation would not go unnoticed by the relevant actors. Nor would it generally be perceived as Occidental bias or victor's justice since a large percentage of multinational corporations come from the developed world.[198]

Third, international criminal law may also overcome certain obstacles of human rights law. While it is still largely debated whether non-state actors, and in particular corporations, are bound by international human rights law, from a normative point of view there are no obstacles for an international criminal tribunal to have jurisdiction over corporations.[199] Conceptually, corporations are bound, as individuals are, by the prohibitions underlying the core crime of international law. Ingrid Gubbay, a human rights litigator, rejects the idea that the international criminal tribunals' limitation of jurisdiction over natural persons means that corporate liability for international crimes does not exist under international law.[200] The fact that these institutions' jurisdiction is limited to individual criminal liability and does not extend to corporate liability 'says nothing about the existence or non-existence of a norm'.[201] This concept, as seen above, was the basis of the reasoning of the STL. As a 2007 report by the Special Representative on business and human rights concluded, corporations can be held liable under similar principles that are used to hold individuals liable for genocide, crimes against humanity and war crimes.[202]

Andrew Clapham, an international law professor, writing in 2008, said that it was imaginable that the jurisdiction of the international criminal tribunals could be

Human Rights Violations in European Law' in P Alston (ed.), *Non-State Actors and Human Rights* (OUP 2005), 227, 238–39; D Spar and D Yoffie, 'Multinational Enterprises and the Prospects for Justice' (1999) 52(2) *J Intl Affairs* 557.
197 Kyriakakis, 'Corporations before International Criminal Courts' (n 108), 231.
198 J Sundell, 'Ill-Gotten Gains: The Case for International Corporate Criminal Liability' (2011) 20 *Minnesota JIL* 648.
199 Clapham (n 1), 25–57; van den Herik and Letnar Černič (n 189).
200 Lecture by I Gubbay, Hausfeld & Co LLP, at Institute of Advanced Legal Studies in London, 19 February 2013.
201 Ibid.
202 Report of the Special Representative of the Secretary-General on human rights and transnational corporations and other business enterprises John Ruggie, 'Business and human rights: Mapping international standards of responsibility and accountability of corporate acts' (February 2007), A/HRC/4/035, para 28.

expanded to include corporations, arguing that the exclusion of legal persons could be seen as 'the consequence of a rule of procedure rather than the inevitable result of application of international criminal law'.[203] Ten years later, the only international tribunal taking on new cases is the ICC, and while it does not appear likely that there will be an imminent expansion of its jurisdiction to include corporations, there are arguably no conceptual reasons why corporations should be immune from liability under international criminal law.[204] The idea has never been clearly rejected.[205] Instead, 'a closer look at both the law and the practice from a historical perspective reveals a mixed picture when it comes to the idea of corporate liability under international criminal law'.[206]

Complementarity concerns have also increasingly lost relevance.[207] The growing trend in legal systems across different jurisdictions to incorporate extraterritorial corporate liability for international crimes 'is likely function as a catalyst for courts to construe international criminal law so as to apply to corporations as non-state actors, or even bring the issue of corporate liability back to the agenda of the states parties to the ICC'.[208] Moreover, the extraterritorial exercise of jurisdiction is more accepted in international criminal law than it is under human rights law.[209] Many state parties to the Rome Statute have vested their courts with universal jurisdiction upon the implementation of the Statute in their domestic codes. By contrast, these same countries are hesitant about regulating corporations headquartered in their territory for extraterritorial corporate activities. The acceptance of corporate responsibility under international criminal law may have beneficial effects on the human rights discussion in terms of recognizing the legal personality of corporations under international law.[210]

Current notions of corporate responsibility for facilitating human rights abuses are backed by legal theories that originated in Nuremberg. As seen above, although the IMT only prosecuted individuals, it recognized that legal persons can engage in criminal conduct, labelling the Nazi leadership corps, the SS and the Gestapo as 'criminal'.[211] In the trials of German industrialists, the idea of the responsibility of

---

203 A Clapham, 'Extending International Criminal Law beyond the Individuals to Corporations and Armed Opposition Groups' (2008) 5(4) *JICJ* 902.
204 RM Bratspies, '"Organs of Society": A Plea for Human Rights Accountability for Transnational Enterprises and Other Business Entities' (2005) 13 *Michigan State JIL* 9; Bernaz, 'Corporate Criminal Liability under International Law' (n 30), 329–30.
205 Bernaz, 'Corporate Criminal Liability under International Law' (n 30), 329–30.
206 Ibid.
207 C Kaeb, 'The Shifting Sands of Corporate Liability under International Criminal Law' (2016) 49 *George Washington International Law Review* 351.
208 Ibid., 352.
209 E Engle, 'Extraterritorial Corporate Criminal Liability: A Remedy for Human Rights Violations?' (2006) 20 *St John's J Legal Commentary* 291.
210 van den Herik and Letnar Černič (n 189), 726–27.
211 International Military Tribunal, Judgement and Sentences (1 October 1946), reprinted in (1947) 41 AJIL 172.

the corporations was an underlying element in some of the judgments.[212] In May 2019, the International Law Commission released the *Draft Articles on the Prevention and Punishment of Crimes against Humanity*.[213] Article 6(8) states that each state shall take measures 'to establish the liability of legal persons' for crimes against humanity – such liability of legal persons may be criminal, civil or administrative. This provision seems to suggest that the international legal system is gradually moving toward a broader acceptance of corporate liability for international crimes.

Some scholars have suggested that concerns over the extension of the ICC jurisdiction are far from insurmountable and they do not preclude states parties to the ICC from extending personal jurisdiction of the Court to legal persons in a future amendment of the Rome Statute.[214] The international criminal law framework, however, cannot serve as an adequate enforcement tool of human rights law.[215] International criminal law only covers the most serious human rights violations: genocide, crimes against humanity and war crimes.[216] Even if corporations were in the future accepted as subjects of the ICC, and even considering the focus of the OTP thematic prosecution over natural resources exploitation and land grabs, corporations remain unlikely to become the primary focus of an ICC prosecutor. The contextual element of war crimes and crimes against humanity and the specific intent required for genocide limit the scope of application of international crimes at least in practical terms. Thus, while international criminal law could address crimes attributable to corporations, it would intervene only in extraordinary circumstances.[217]

Despite prosecutions on accomplice liability grounds, international courts concentrate on prosecuting people who were directly involved in committing crimes, in particular military or political officials.[218] By contrast, individual businesspeople often only play a supportive role in the commission of international crimes. The priority is to prosecute the 'most serious crimes of concern to the international

---

212 *I.G. Farben* case (n 31), 1108.
213 International Law Commission, Crimes against humanity, Texts and titles of the draft preamble, the draft articles and the draft annex provisionally adopted by the Drafting Committee on second reading, Prevention and punishment of crimes against humanity A/CN.4/L.935, 19 May 2019.
214 J Kyriakakis, 'Corporations and the International Criminal Court: The Complementary Objection Stripped Bare' (2008) 19 *Criminal L Forum* 115, 120–21, 151.
215 Ibid.
216 Ibid., 742–43.
217 N Farrell, 'Attributing Criminal Liability to Corporate Actors Some Lessons from the International Tribunals' (2010) 8(3) *JICJ* 872.
218 A Marston Danner and JS Martinez, 'Guilty Associations: Joint Criminal Enterprise, Command Responsibility and the Development of International Criminal Law' (2005) 93 *California L Rev* 75; JD Ohlin, 'Joint Intentions to Commit International Crimes' (2011) 11 *Chicago JIL* 721–25; MJ Kelly, 'Grafting the Command Responsibility Doctrine onto Corporate Criminal Liability for Atrocities' (2010) 24 *Emory Intl L Rev* 671.

community as a whole'.[219] The ICC prosecutorial strategy is to 'select for prosecution those situated at the highest echelons of responsibility'.[220] Businesspeople and corporations would rarely meet the criteria for ICC prosecution as in most cases they are not among those masterminding international crimes, but rather they, for the most part, benefit from a given situation and exploit the financial opportunities. Investigations initiated, or not initiated, by the OTP may hint that business responsibility may not be 'of sufficient gravity to justify further action'.[221] Too broad a swathe of prosecutions for a variety of crimes may conflict with the ICC's focus on a small number of perpetrators of the most notorious offences. Therefore, the responsibility of corporations for their involvement in international crimes has been of marginal interest in international prosecution efforts.[222] This is arguably a necessary limitation of international criminal law that remains unlikely to be overcome.

In November 2019, the ICC Prosecutor Fatou Bensouda released a statement addressing the individual liability for business involvement in international crimes, which she describes as 'a cutting edge topic of great importance for any effort aimed at ending impunity for atrocity crimes':

> The ICC personal jurisdiction is not limited to political or military leaders. Accordingly, under certain circumstances, the ICC may exercise jurisdiction over individuals, who through business activities either contribute or directly commit international crimes under the Rome Statute – for instance [...] by providing armed groups the means to commit [international] crimes, such as weapons, ammunitions, communications, and other equipment. Individuals may also provide incentives, financial or otherwise, to the main perpetrators of the crimes, or may even be the main perpetrators themselves. [...] Business activities can directly impact human lives. In some cases, the degree of the impact of business activities on human lives may be sufficiently serious for those activities to reach the threshold of constituting Rome Statute crimes. As an example certain organised industrial activities [...] may force people to leave their land, thereby depending on the facts and circumstances could potentially amount to crimes against humanity under Article 7 of the Rome Statute [...] Certain business practices result in serious human harm [...] The ICC can play a role in addressing the conduct causing this harm and, when appropriate, in calling it for what it is: an international crime. [...] The ICC is, of course, not a panacea and, even in the best of circumstances, it is able to only address a few instances that require a legal response. The investigation

---

219 Rome Statute (n 103), Art 25.
220 Prosecutorial Strategy 2009–2012, The Hague, 1 February 2010, 19.
221 H Vest, 'Business Leaders and the Modes of Individual Criminal Responsibility under International Law' (2010) 8(3) *JICJ* 852.
222 Jessberger (n 32), 801; Kaleck and Saage-Maab (n 18), 710.

and prosecution of these crimes at the national level is therefore critically important.[223]

Despite these promising statement, international criminal law does not currently offer an effective avenue to seek remedy for corporate human rights abuses in transitional justice contexts. The next chapters assess whether the regional human rights systems and national law may offer a suitable option.

223 Statement of ICC Prosecutor Fatou Bensouda at International Association of Penal Law (AIDP) XX International Congress of Penal Law 'Criminal Justice and Corporate Business' (Rome, 13–16 November 2019). Shortly after this statement, on 11 December 2019, a group of NGOs submitted a communication to the ICC asking for the opening of a preliminary examination into the conduct of several European companies supplying weapons to the Saudi/UAE-led coalition engaged in the armed conflict in Yemen since March 2015. The communication alleges that these companies supplied fighter jets and other military equipment, which were used in indiscriminate attacks against civilians and may constitute war crimes under Article 8 of the Rome Statute. See M Aksenova and L Bryk, 'Extraterritorial Obligations of Arms Exporting Corporations: New Communication to the ICC', *OpinioJuris*, 14 January 2020, http://opiniojuris.org/2020/01/14/extraterritorial-obligations-of-arms-exporting-corporations-new-communication-to-the-icc

Chapter 3

Regional human rights systems

Introduction

After the assessment of the limitations of international criminal law as a remedy for corporate human rights abuses in the previous chapter, this chapter turns to the analysis of the potential of the regional human rights systems in this area. The European, Inter-American and African regional human rights systems have developed judicial, legislative and administrative mechanisms to provide remedies to people who have suffered human rights violations within states party to the respective regional human rights conventions.[1] Arguably, the regional systems also contribute to providing remedies in transitional justice contexts, as they order and supervise national prosecutions and reparations measures when states emerging from conflict or repression have been unable or unwilling to act.[2] These mechanisms can in some instances also remedy violations involving business activities through scrutiny of complaints made against states that fail to prevent, investigate or redress human rights violations related to corporate activities. Bodies set up to monitor the implementation of the regional treaties can, for example, order new investigations into corporate abuses and can contribute to shape reparations programmes at national level.

The Inter-American Court of Human Rights, in particular, has provided important contributions to the analysis of evidence of corporate abuses and the provision of remedy and reparations for victims, including in transitional justice contexts.[3] A decision of the African Commission of August 2017 ordering the

---

1 Convention for the Protection of Human Rights and Fundamental Freedoms, adopted 4 November 1950, entered into force 3 September 1953; American Convention on Human Rights, signed 22 November 1969, entered into force 18 July 1978, O.A.S. Doc. OEA/Ser.L/V/II.23, doc. 21, rev. 6 (1979), O.A.S.T.S. No. 36, 1144 U.N.T.S. 143; African Charter on Human and Peoples' Rights, adopted 27 June 1981, entered into force 21 October 1986.

2 A Huneeus, 'International Criminal Law by Other Means: The Quasi-Criminal Jurisdiction of the Human Rights Courts' (2013) 107 *AJIL* 1.

3 For example, Inter-American Court of Human Rights (IACtHR), *Santo Domingo Massacre v Colombia* (2012), 135; *Afro-Descendant Communities Displaced from the Cacarica River Basin (Operation Genesis) v Colombia* (2013).

Democratic Republic of the Congo (DRC) to investigate the role of an Australian mining company in a village massacre during the 1998 civil war also provides innovative precedents in this area.[4] This chapter shows that while the regional systems are not mandated to directly investigate corporate human rights abuses (they investigate violations by states parties, or circumstances where state parties have failed to provide adequate remedies to violations that occur on their territory), they can offer a complementary avenue for victims who have failed to obtain justice and reparations at the national level. This is particularly important in transitional justice contexts where, for a number of reasons detailed in the next chapter, national litigation is rarely an effective option. This chapter examines the jurisprudence of the Inter-American (3.1), the African (3.2) and the European systems (3.2).

3.1 The Inter-American system

The Inter-American Court, established by the Organization of American States in 1979, is an independent judicial institution with jurisdiction over the states that are party to the *American Convention on Human Rights* ('American Convention') and have accepted its jurisdiction for alleged violations of the obligations included in the convention. The Court has adjudicated on several cases involving large-scale abuses that occurred during conflict or repression. Such cases often arrived at the Court when the state concerned had undergone or was undergoing a transition. The Inter-American Court is not a criminal court and cannot adjudicate on individual responsibility. However, in a creative interpretation of its remedial powers, it regularly orders states to investigate, try and punish those responsible for human rights violations and to provide different forms of reparation to victims.[5] The Court was, from its first contentious case, confronted with mass state-sponsored violations of human rights, whose dynamics came to shape the Court's remedial

---

4 African Commission on Human and Peoples' Rights (ACHPR), *Institute for Human Rights and Development in Africa and Others v Democratic Republic of Congo*, Communication 393/10, 9 June 2016 [*IHRDA v DRC*].

5 For example, IACtHR, *Ituango Massacres v Colombia*, 1 July 2006, Series C, No. 148. See also Huneeus (n 2), 2, 11; DC Baluarte, 'Strategizing for Compliance: The Evolution of a Compliance Phase of Inter-American Court Litigation and the Strategic Imperative for Victims' Representatives' (2012) 27 *Am Univ Intl L Rev* 263; V Abramovich, 'From Massive Violations to Structural Patterns: New Approaches and Classic Tensions in the Inter-American Human Rights System' (2009) 6 *Sur Intl J Human Rights* 7 (2009); C Binder, 'The Prohibition of Amnesties by the Inter-American Court of Human Rights' (2011) 12 *German LJ* 1203; LJ Laplante, 'Outlawing Amnesty: The Return of Criminal Justice in Transitional Justice Schemes' (2009) 49 *Va J Intl L* 915; FF Basch, 'The Doctrine of the Inter-American Court of Human Rights Regarding States' Duty to Punish Human Rights Violations and Its Dangers' (2007) 23 *Am Univ Intl L Rev* 195; TM Antkowiak, 'An Emerging Mandate for International Courts: Victim-Centered Remedies and Restorative Justice' (2001) 4(7) *Stan J Intl L* 279 (2011).

practice.[6] The *Velasquez-Rodriguez* case, which dealt with enforced disappearances in Honduras, established new ground rules with respect to reparations that were 'manifestly transitional'.[7] The decision had an enormous impact on the processes of political transformation on-going in various Latin American countries.

The Inter-American Court only has jurisdiction over states that have ratified the American Convention, clearly not over companies. Arguably, however, the Court's decisions can have an indirect impact on corporate accountability and can determine effective remedies for victims when investigating states' conduct related to the regulation of business activities. In this sense, the Court has begun to refine its guidance on state obligations, including the duty to regulate and supervise corporations.[8] The Court recognizes that there are instances when certain acts or omissions by private actors can be directly treated as state acts – and therefore they amount to a violation of state duties to protect people from human rights abuses and to provide victims with a meaningful remedy. This occurs when such actors are 'empowered to act in state capacity' (such as through a contract) and they act with the 'acquiescence, collaboration, support or tolerance of state agents'.[9] State responsibility can also result when there is a failure to prevent, investigate and punish rights violations.

Most cases brought before the Inter-American system involving corporate activities concern environmental harms and indigenous communities.[10] While not relevant for transitional justice as such, they are, however, important in setting

---

6   For example, IACtHR, *El Amparo v Venezuela*, Ser. C, No. 19, 18 January 1995. See also Huneeus (n 2), 5; V Krsticevic, 'Reparations in the Inter-American System: A Comparative Approach' (2007) 56 *Am Univ L Rev* 1375; Antkowiak (n 5).

7   IACtHR, *Velasquez-Rodriguez v Honduras*, Ser C No. 4, 29 June 1988.

8   IACtHR, *Ximenes-Lopes v Brazil*, I. No .149 (2006), 141, *Gonzales Lluy et al. v Ecuador*, No. 298 (2015). See also C Anicama, 'State Responsibilities to Regulate and Adjudicate Corporate Activities under the Inter-American Human Rights System. Report on the American Convention on Human Rights to inform the mandate of the Special Representative of the UN Secretary-General (SRSG) on Business and Human Rights' (April 2008). In November 2029, the IACHR published a report on 'Business and Human Rights: Inter-American Standards'. The report is based on the identification of the international obligations of states in cases in which businesses are involved in the violation of human rights. It compiles various pronouncements made within the inter-American system in relation to the issue of business and human rights. Comisión Interamericana de Derechos Humanos, Relatoría Especial sobre Derechos Económicos Sociales Culturales y Ambientales *Informe Empresas y Derechos Humanos: Estándares Interamericanos* OEA/Ser.L/V/II CIDH/REDESCA/INF.1/19 1 November 2019, www.oas.org/es/cidh/informes/pdfs/EmpresasDDHH.pdf

9   IACtHR, *Ximenes-Lopes v Brazil* (n 8), 87; *Gonzales Lluy et al. v Ecuador* (n 8); *Mapiripán Massacre v Colombia*, No. 134 (2005), 162.

10   IACtHR, *Kichwa Indigenous People of Sarayaku v Ecuador*, No. 245 (2012); *Mayagna (Sumo) Awas Tingi Community v Nicaragua*, Ser C No. 79; *Kaliña and Lokono Peoples v Suriname*, No. 309, (2015); *Saramaka People v Suriname*, No. 172 (2007); *Yakye Axa Indigenous Community v Paraguay*, No. 125 (2005); *Sawhoyamaxa Indigenous Community v Paraguay*, No. 146 (2006); *Xákmok Kásek Indigenous Community v Paraguay*, No. 214 (2010). See also A Gonza, 'Integrating Business and Human Rights in the Inter-American Human Rights System' (2016) 1 *Business Human Rights J* 357; TM Antkowiak,

precedents, especially in relation to reparations standards for victims of human rights abuses. Indigenous peoples have routinely confronted the consequences of economic interests in their ancestral lands and natural resources, which often take the form of extractive projects conducted by corporate actors with the permission of governments. These abusive practices have led to a number of social, legal and political disputes, many of which have resulted in violence.[11] The Inter-American Court has played a prominent role in delimitating indigenous property rights in connection to business operations. For example, in *Sarayaku v Ecuador*, the Court found that the Ecuadorian government violated the American Convention because it failed to protect and respect the Sarayaku indigenous peoples' community property rights and their cultural identity, when it granted oil concessions in the community's ancestral lands without consultation.[12] The Court awarded the Sarayaku people a total of US$1.3 million in damages. Only a few months after the *Sarayaku* case was presented, the *State Oil Company* of Ecuador and *Compañía General de Combustibles* signed a deed of termination of the partnership contract for the exploration and exploitation of crude oil in Sarayaku lands, but with the agreement that there was 'no environmental liability'.[13]

The Inter-American Court cannot assign specific obligations to corporations through its award of remedies. As a consequence, the remedies ordered (to states), while substantial and often including full land restitution, removal of explosives and reforestation of the affected territories, usually neglect a full consideration of the violations at issue and their connection to corporate accountability.[14] For example, Nicaragua, in compliance with the Court's order in *Mayagna (Sumo) Awas Tingni Community v Nicaragua*, suspended the logging concession on Awas Tingni community's ancestral land that had been granted to *SOLCARSA*, a Korean lumber company.[15] The ending of such contractual relationships, however, came without any obligation for corporations to pay reparations to affected communities.

In the *Kaliña and Lokono Peoples v Suriname* judgment, the Court did not order the review and revocation of mining concessions, as requested by petitioners, only requiring that the government institute a consultation process for awarding future concessions.[16] The Court required Suriname to establish 'the necessary mechanisms

'Rights, Resources, and Rhetoric: Indigenous Peoples and the Inter-American Court' (2013) 35 *Univ Pennsylvania J Intl L* 113.

11 N Reguart-Segarra, 'Business, Indigenous Peoples' Rights and Security in the Case Law of the Inter-American Court of Human Rights' (2019) 4(1) *Business and Human Rights Journal* 109.

12 *Sarayaku* (n 10). See also L Brunner and K Quintana, 'The Duty to Consult in the Inter-American System: Legal Standards after Sarayaku' 2012 16(35) *Insights*.

13 *Sarayaku* (n 10), 123.

14 For example, ibid. See also Gonza (n 10); TM Antkowiak, 'A Dark Side of Virtue: The Inter-American Court and Reparations for Indigenous Peoples' (2015) 25 *Duke J Comp Intl L* 1.

15 Mayagna (Sumo) Awas Tingni Community (n 10).

16 Kaliña and Lokono Peoples (n 10), 224, 287, 299.

to monitor and supervise the execution of the rehabilitation by the company'.[17] Even without a full development of corporations' obligations, the *Kaliña* case is significant as it represents the first time that the Court designed specific reparations to restore the indigenous territories, placing the obligation not only on the state but 'in conjunction with the company'.[18] Alejandra Gonza, a former lawyer at the Inter-American Court, argues that this tentative first step indicates that the Court might require in the future stronger substantiation of remedies by petitioners.[19]

The Inter-American Court has also adjudicated and ordered reparations in cases associated with business activities in the context of armed conflicts. For example, in *Santo Domingo Massacre v Colombia*, the representatives of the victims asked the Court to establish the participation of private security agents acting to supervise and protect the property of *Occidental Petroleum* (*Oxy*), as well as the financial and arms collaboration between *Oxy* and the Colombian National Army.[20] In 2003, residents of Santo Domingo had filed a lawsuit against *Oxy* and its security contractor, *Airscan*, in US federal court under the Alien Tort Statute. The plaintiffs claimed that in 1998 *Oxy* and *Airscan*, in a bid to secure *Oxy*'s pipeline in Caño Limón, helped the Colombian Air Force (CAF) to conduct an aerial bombing attack on Santo Domingo. The raid led to 17 people dead, 25 injured and the destruction of homes and properties. Plaintiffs alleged that *Oxy* and *Airscan* provided key strategic information, as well as ground and air support to the CAF in the bombing raid, and thus they were complicit in extrajudicial killings, torture, crimes against humanity and war crimes.[21] In the case before the Inter-American Court, the representatives argued that Colombia 'did not have an adequate legislative framework that truly developed the obligation to protect human rights in relation to the activities of multinational corporations on its territory' and that the contribution to the Santo Domingo massacre by *Oxy* and *Airscan* was evident.[22] The Court found that there was 'no dispute that the armed conflict in Arauca is closely related to the revenue derived from the oil and the location of the Caño Limón-Coveñas pipeline' and that this 'resulted in the establishment of illegal armed groups since the 1980s'.[23]

A particularly relevant case in the context of transitional justice is the *Afro-Descendant Communities Displaced from the Cacarica River Basin (Operation Genesis) v Colombia*, which arose from fighting in the Colombia's Urabá region.[24] The area

---

17 Ibid., 224.
18 Ibid.
19 Gonza (n 10), 361–64.
20 Santo Domingo Massacre (n 3), 135.
21 In 2014, after years of proceedings, the Court of Appeals dismissed the case, finding that it had insufficient ties with the United States to be heard in US courts.
22 Santo Domingo Massacre (n 3), 185.
23 Ibid., 55, 56, 59.
24 *Afro-Descendant Communities* (n 3). See also T van Ho, 'Is it Already Too Late for Colombia's Land Restitution Process? The Impact of International Investment Law on Transitional Justice Initiatives' (2016) 5 *Intl Human Rights LR* 60.

was 'of major geostrategic importance in the armed conflict, in particular for the illegal armed groups', who used the passage to Panama to traffic arms and drugs.[25] The public administration in the region was corrupt, 'also owing to the award of permits or the corruption of public officials by logging companies'.[26] When illegal armed groups exerted pressure on the Afro-Descendant communities, which were 'firmly established' in the region, the communities attempted 'to maintain their autonomy'.[27] In response, armed groups threatened, murdered and disappeared community members.[28] The case before the Inter-American Court raised several claims, including in relation to the forced displacement and allegations of illegal logging by the Colombian company *Madarién*.[29]

Legal recognition of land rights for the Afro-Descendant communities of the Cacarica River basin took a long time and, as a result, *Madarién* was able to gain government approval for logging rights on the territory claimed by the communities.[30] In 1992, government agencies granted *Madarién* several permits, which were met by complaints by the public and finally a constitutional court decision to suspend the logging activities.[31] In 1996, after the courts revoked the order allowing *Madarién* to proceed, but before the logging operations were suspended, paramilitary groups launched attacks against the Revolutionary Armed Forces of Colombia (*Fuerzas Armadas Revolucionarias de Colombia* – FARC).[32] Communities were attacked and members of a Colombian military and paramilitary group 'told the leaders of the Afro-Descendant communities that they had to evacuate'.[33] The communities, and their 3,500 members, remained displaced until 2001.[34] They alleged that *Madarién*, which continued logging in the area, unlawfully benefitted from and was complicit in their forced displacement.[35] Clearly, the Inter-American Court could not establish whether *Madarién* was complicit in the forced displacements. The *Afro-Descendant Communities* case process, nonetheless, represented an avenue for the communities, which did allege *Madarién*'s complicity,[36] to launch their grievance against the company and against the state's actions. The Inter-American Court heard the complaint and found that the 'logging activities ignored the Law concerning the black communities' and that the state was responsible for the failure of administrative and judicial bodies to protect the communities' property rights.[37]

---

25 Afro-Descendant Communities (n 3), 89.
26 Ibid., 87.
27 Ibid., 85, 87, 93, 94.
28 Ibid., 93.
29 Ibid.
30 Ibid., 132, 137, 347.
31 Ibid., 132.
32 Ibid., 91, 92, 95
33 Ibid., 105, 108.
34 Ibid., 111, 125.
35 Ibid., 140, 142, 341, 378.
36 Ibid., 341, 374.
37 Ibid., 355–58. See also van Ho (n 24), 69.

The Inter-American Court also dealt with a case involving *Urapalma*, a Colombian palm oil company. In the midst of the 50-year internal armed conflict in the Pacific region of Colombia, Afro-Colombian communities, paramilitaries and corporations have coexisted and disputed control over land. Palm oil companies have been accused of associating with the *Autodefensas Unidas de Colombia* (AUC), a right-wing paramilitary and drug-trafficking group, to forcibly displace the members of the Afro-Colombian communities of Curvaradó and Jiguamiandó.[38] The struggle started for these communities in 1997 when the Colombian army and the AUC joined forces to expel the leftist FARC guerrilla group from the area, resulting in the forced displacement of 3,500 peasants.[39] After an agreement with the paramilitary group to allow access to land for palm oil production, in 2000, several palm oil companies started acquiring these lands – *Urapalma* in particular used threats and legal strategies to obtain legal titles to the lands, paying derisory prices.[40] Members of the communities who tried to return to their land were threatened and harassed. The case moved all the way to the Inter-American Court, which ordered a number of provisional measures requiring the government of Colombia to investigate the abuses against the communities, guarantee the restitution of lands and 'address the issue of palm oil plantation'.[41] In 2005, the Colombian Public Prosecutor Office filed a criminal complaint against several executives of the palm oil companies that were occupying the lands. The Court decided to sentence 12 businessmen, four of them former employees of *Urapalma*, to ten years in prison and a high fine. The Court ordered the defendants to pay compensation of approximately 20 million pesos to each victim of forced displacement and the restitution of lands to the communities of Curvaradó and Jiguamiandó.[42]

Another relevant case is *Río Negro Massacres v Guatemala*, which involves the construction of the Chixoy dam in Guatemala.[43] The dam, financed by the World Bank and the Inter-American Development Bank, was constructed in the early

38 Juzgado Quinto Penal del Circuito Especializado de Medellín. Sentencia Rad. No. 201101799, 30 Oct 2014.
39 G Gallón, "Operación Génesis' al desnudo,' *El Espectador*, 9 Jan 2014.
40 Defensoría del Pueblo, 'Resolución Defensorial No. 39 – Violación de los Derechos Humanos por Siembra de Palma Africana en Territorios Colectivos de Jiguamiandó y Curvaradó – Chocó'; Juzgado Quinto Penal del Circuito Especializado de Medellín. Sentencia Rad., 165.
41 Inter-American Court of Human Rights, Provisional Measures Regarding Colombia, Matter of the Communities of Jiguamiandó and Curbaradó, 7 Feb 2006, para 23. Previous orders were given on 6 March 2003, 17 Nov 2004, and 15 March 2005.
42 Juzgado Quinto Penal del Circuito Especializado de Medellin, 'Sentencia Condenatoria', 349–56. For comments, see NC Sánchez León and D Marín López, 'Corporate Accountability in Transitional Justice in Colombia', in *Peace, Everyone's Business! Corporate Accountability in Transitional Justice: Lessons for Colombia*, PAX (Utrecht, May 2017), 141–47.
43 IACtHR, *Rio Negro Massacres v Guatemala* Ser C, No. 250 (2012). See also N Roht-Arriaza, 'Reparations and Economic, Social, and Cultural Rights' in DN Sharp (ed.), *Justice and Economic Violence in Transition* (Springer Science Business Media 2014) 109, 132.

1980s during the civil war in Guatemala by the state-owned *National Electricity Institute (INDE)*. The project forcibly displaced more than 3,500 Achi Maya people. The damages caused by the project were extensive and included pollution of the rivers and loss of land, livestock, crops, fishing grounds and religious sites. When community members from the village of Río Negro protested that the alternative land offered to them was unsuitable and the compensation inadequate, they were massacred by paramilitary civil patrols acting under army orders; more than 400 people were killed.[44] The massacre took place during the height of the genocide campaign of the 1980s, and it was the subject of the National Reparations Programme as well as several domestic criminal cases against the perpetrators.[45] Eventually, a case against the Guatemalan government reached the Inter-American Court. In 2012, the Court found the government responsible for violations of the American Convention including freedom of movement and residence, as a result of the forced displacement of the population during the internal armed conflict and the impossibility of returning to their ancestral lands due to construction of the dam and reservoir.[46] In relation to reparations, the Court ordered Guatemala, among other things, to build basic infrastructure and services for the Río Negro community, implement a project to rescue the culture of the Maya Achi, provide medical and psychological treatment to the victims, and provide compensation for material and immaterial damages.[47]

The novel strategy of this case was that the victims worked on redress at the Inter-American and national levels simultaneously, focusing on the banks that had financed the Chixoy project. They argued that the banks, as well as the Guatemalan government, knew that the dam was being constructed by a murderous regime that would be unlikely to make adequate provision for the people being displaced. In 1996, the World Bank investigated the claims and found that *INDE* had only partially compensated the community. For example, titles to alternative land were never granted, not all those eligible received land, and the land was of poor quality.[48] While it was impossible to sue the banks directly before any administrative or legal body due to immunities, the banks agreed to finance a solution by the government as a result of pressure from international and national civil society organizations.[49] In 2010, the 'Reparations Plan for Damages Suffered by the Communities Affected by the Construction of the Chixoy Dam' was signed and agreed by all parties.[50] The

---

44 Rio Negro Massacres (n 43), 65–74.
45 Ibid.
46 Ibid., 172–82.
47 Ibid.
48 Center for Political Ecology, 'Reparations and the Right to Remedy' (World Commission on Dams Briefing Paper 2000).
49 S Herz, 'Rethinking International Financial Institution Immunities' in D Bradlow and Da Hunter (eds), *International Financial Institutions and International Law* (Kluwer 2010), 137.
50 Plan de Reparación de Daños y Perjuicios Sufridos por las Comunidades Afectadas por la Construcción de la Hidroeléctrica Chixoy, April 2010.

plan included provisions to compensate community members up to US$154.5 million for material and non-material damages and losses, construct and repair homes, and improve roads, water and sewage systems. The government, however, did not sign the local agreement that would have made the reparation plan binding, and as a consequence this still remains to be implemented.

3.2 The African system

Cases alleging the liability of states for violations of human rights by private actors have rarely been brought before the African Commission.[51] But a recent successful case may change the trend. In June 2016, the African Commission found the government of the DRC responsible for the 2004 massacre of more than 70 people in Kilwa, in the southeast of the country, and granted unprecedented compensation of US$2.5 million to the victims and their families.[52] *Anvil Mining*, an Australian–Canadian mining company who operated a copper and silver mine near Kilwa, was publicly criticized for its role in the violations, which included providing logistical support to soldiers who indiscriminately shelled civilians, summarily executed at least 28 people and disappeared many others. The decision in *Institute for Human Rights and Development in Africa (IHRDA) and Others v Democratic Republic of Congo* followed a 13-year legal battle for justice by the victims and their families.

On 14 October 2004, a small group of lightly armed rebels tried to take control of Kilwa. In retaliation, the Congolese army (*Forces Armées de la République Démocratique de Congo* – FARDC) bombarded the town and, searching for rebels, arbitrarily detained, tortured and killed civilians. Over two days, at least 73 civilians were killed, including an estimated 28 people who were arbitrarily arrested and summarily executed. Others were brutally tortured, some dying from their injuries in the weeks and months that followed. A week after the events, the UN peacekeeping mission based in Congo (*Mission des Nations Unies au Congo* – MONUC) conducted an investigation and accused the FARDC of war crimes.[53]

The massacre in Kilwa was part of the second of two consecutive wars in DRC, from 1998 to 2003. The exploitation of the DRC's vast mineral wealth was an important feature in the wars. *Anvil* won the licence to mine the copper and silver

---

51 In *Human Rights NGO Forum v Zimbabwe*, No. 145/02 (2006), the African Commission, for the first time, held that the state duty to protect human rights applies to protecting against abuse by all non-state actors, including corporations. See also South African Institute for Advanced Constitutional, Public, Human Rights and International Law, 'Obligations and Extra-territorial Application in the African Regional Human Rights System' 17 February 2010, 30.

52 *IHRDA v DRC* (n 4). Victims were notified on 7 August 2017.

53 Mission des Nations Unies au Congo (MONUC), 'Report on the conclusions of the Special Investigation concerning allegations of summary executions and other human rights violations perpetrated by the Armed Forces of the Democratic Republic of Congo (FARDC) in Kilwa (Katanga Province)', 15 October 2004.

at Dikulushi, 50 kilometres from Kilwa, in 1998, during the DRC's second war. It began mining operations in 2002.[54] According to the UN investigation, *Anvil* provided substantial logistical support to the military action by the FARDC in Kilwa.[55] An airplane chartered by *Anvil* was used to transport an estimated 150 troops from Pweto to Kilwa on 14 and 15 October.[56] The FARDC used the company's vehicles, driven by *Anvil* employees, to transport soldiers.[57] The vehicles also transported looted goods, corpses and people arbitrarily detained by the soldiers.[58] As noted by MONUC:

> In October 2004, the Commander of the 6th military region in Lubumbashi informed MONUC that the intervention of the FARDC to bring safety back to Kilwa was made possible thanks to the logistical assistance given by Anvil Mining. On another occasion, during an interview made with an Australian television channel (ABC) on 6 June 2005, the President and CEO of Anvil Mining, M. Bill Turner, responded to a question concerning the use of Anvil Mining vehicles by saying 'so what?'. He acknowledged that Anvil Mining had provided logistic [*sic*] to the army, following a 'request from the army of a legitimate government'. He also added: 'We helped the military to get to Kilwa and then we were gone. Whatever they did there, that's an internal issue.'[59]

In 2006, after two years of pressure by human rights groups, a Congolese military prosecutor recommended that nine soldiers and three serving and former *Anvil* employees stand trial for war crimes or complicity in war crimes.[60] In March 2007, just before the trial was due to start, the prosecutor was removed from the case and replaced by a close associate of President Kabila, who had also been an adviser to a former *Anvil* board member.[61] A few months later, all the defendants were acquitted.[62] A higher military court refused to hear the appeal against the acquittals.

Survivors and their families continued to pursue justice in Canada and Australia, where *Anvil* had offices. In 2005, the Australian Minister of Justice instructed the federal police to open an investigation into *Anvil*'s role in the Kilwa massacre.[63] The inquiry was flawed by personnel changes: in the space of two years the case

---

54 In 2010, the Dikulushi mine was sold to Mawson West, a small Australian mining company. In January 2015, Mawson West stopped industrial production at Dikulushi, stating the mine was no longer economically viable.
55 MONUC (n 53), VI.
56 Ibid., para 36.
57 Ibid.
58 Ibid.
59 Ibid., para 37.
60 Rights and Accountability in Development (RAID) and others, 'Kilwa Trial: a Denial of Justice – a chronology, October 2004–July 2007' 17 July 2007.
61 UN News Centre, 'DR Congo: UN's top rights official concerned at acquittal in military trial', 4 July 2017.
62 Ibid.
63 *Pierre v Anvil Mining Management NL* (2008), SCWA 30.

was assigned to six different officers.[64] In October 2006, just before the start of the Congolese trial, the police recommended the investigation be closed because of insufficient evidence.[65] Following the verdict in the Congolese Military Court in June 2007, the Australian police ended its investigation. It brought no charges. In March 2007, human rights NGOs requested the Canadian Minister of Justice to open an investigation into the Canadian entity of *Anvil*.[66] The War Crimes Unit of the Canadian Mounted Police began to investigate, but its efforts were slow and appeared to languish after a number of years. In March 2010, the Canadian Association against Impunity, a coalition of six NGOs, filed a class action suit in Quebec, where *Anvil* had its Canadian office, in an effort to obtain justice and compensation for the victims.[67] Finally, the Court of Appeal ruled that the Quebec courts did not have jurisdiction to hear the case.[68] An appeal to the Supreme Court by the victims was unsuccessful.

Following the failure to obtain justice in the DRC, Canada or Australia, the victims and the human rights groups supporting them decided to seek justice before the African Commission. In 2010, they submitted a complaint.[69] The Commission found that the Congolese government had violated nine human rights provisions of the *African Charter on Human and Peoples' Rights* ('African Charter'), including extrajudicial executions, torture, arbitrary arrests, disappearances and forced displacement.[70] It awarded the eight victims named in the complaint US$2.5 million, the highest ever award by the African Commission.[71] The decision sets new precedents.

First, it specifies the exact sum to be paid to each individual victim – the Commission does not usually indicate the sum of compensation to be paid, but rather recommends that the state provide 'adequate compensation'. Second, the Commission's decision not only covers compensation for the direct violation the victims suffered, but also acknowledges the needs of the larger Kilwa community. It urged the DRC government to identify and compensate other victims and their families not party to the complaint who were also directly affected by the attack.[72] The Commission said the government should formally apologize to the people of Kilwa, exhume and re-bury the bodies dumped in a mass grave, construct a memorial, provide trauma counselling for those affected and rebuild the schools,

---

64 RAID (n 60), 5–7.
65 Ibid., 7–10.
66 Ibid., 11–25.
67 Canadian Association against Impunity, 'Significant step forward in holding Anvil Mining to account' 29 April 2011.
68 Canadian Association against Impunity, 'No justice in Canada for Congolese massacre victims as Canada's Supreme Court dismisses leave to appeal' 1 November 2012.
69 *IHRDA v DRC* (n 4).
70 Ibid., para 154. The Commission found that DRC violated articles 1, 4, 5, 6, 7, 14, 22 and 26 of the African Charter.
71 Ibid., para 154(ii)(iii)(iv).
72 Ibid., para 154(v).

hospital and other structures destroyed during the attack.[73] These collective and restorative reparations benefit the Kilwa community as a whole and recognize the wrongs done to both the individuals and the affected community.

Third, the Commission urged the government to launch a new criminal investigation and 'take all due measures to prosecute and punish agents of the state and Anvil Mining Company staff'.[74] The Commission publicly criticized *Anvil* by stressing that extractive industry companies are also legally required to carry out their activities with due regard to the rights of the host communities: 'At a minimum, [extractive industry companies] should avoid engaging in actions that violate the rights of communities in their zones of operation. This includes not participating in, or supporting, violations of human and peoples' rights.'[75]

Finally, the collection of evidence immediately after the attack was key in this case. The African Commission cannot directly investigate the actions of companies, but it can request the complainant to present evidence substantiating the allegations, including reports by international organizations. In this decision, the report by MONUC was key to establishing the facts. The UN investigation team was able to interview eyewitnesses, speak with *Anvil* and collect other evidence just a week after the attack, and the African Commission used this material in its criticism of the company.[76]

Despite the importance of this decision and the precedents it sets for future cases, however, remedy for victims will now depend on the willingness of the DRC government. The Commission recommended the establishment of a monitoring committee to supervise the implementation of its decision, which is another innovation.[77] But the African Charter contains no provision for enforcement of the Commission's findings and recommendations, which are not formally binding. The Commission can refer cases to the African Court on Human and Peoples' Rights if a state is a member, but the DRC is not.[78]

Until the decision in *HRDA*, the Commission's most comprehensive decision concerning the involvement of a corporation in human rights violations was the *Social and Economic Rights Action Centre (SERAC) v Nigeria* case.[79] The case alleged that, in the process of oil production, the Nigeria military government, through a consortium formed by the state oil company *Nigerian National Petroleum Company* (*NNPC*) and *Shell*, caused environmental contamination and health problems to the Ogoni people living in the oil areas, and thus violated several rights in the African

---

73 Ibid.
74 Ibid., para 154(i).
75 Ibid, para 101.
76 Ibid., para 73.
77 Ibid., para 154(vi).
78 As at July 2017, only eight of the 30 states parties to the Protocol had made the declaration recognizing the competence of the Court to receive cases from NGOs and individuals.
79 ACHPR, *Social and Economic Rights Action Centre (SERAC) and Center for Economic and Social Rights (CESR) v Nigeria* (2001) AHRLR 60 [*SERAC v Nigeria*].

Charter.[80] It also alleged that Nigerian security forces attacked, burned and destroyed several Ogoni villages and homes in response to the Movement of the Survival of Ogoni People's campaign against the oil companies. Many Ogoni people became displaced as a result.

The *SERAC* case is significant as the African Commission affirmed the state duty under the African Charter to protect human rights against abuses perpetrated by private parties.[81] In 1996, the Commission ruled that the Nigerian government violated the rights to life, to health and to clean environment, among others. The Commission also held that the state's failure to monitor oil activities and involve local communities in decisions violated the right of the Ogoni people to freely dispose of their wealth and natural resources.[82] The direct role of the Nigerian government included 'placing the legal and military powers of the State at the disposal of the oil companies'.[83] The Commission found that the Nigerian government gave 'the green light to private actors, and the oil companies in particular, to devastatingly affect the well-being of the Ogonis'.[84] As remedial measures, the Commission called the government of Nigeria to conduct 'an investigation into the human rights violations' and to 'prosecut[e] officials of the security forces, NNPC and relevant agencies involved in human rights violations'.[85] It also recommended cleaning the land and rivers affected, ensuring adequate compensation to victims and the provision of information to exposed communities.[86]

Some additional developments in the African system might led to further cases scrutinizing the role of corporations in human rights abuses. In 2014, the African Union adopted a Protocol that, should it come into operation, would create a new international criminal law section of the African Court of Justice and Human and People's Rights[87] with jurisdiction over international and certain transnational crimes, as well as competence to hear cases against corporations.[88] Should it come into

---

80 Articles 2, 4, 14, 16, 18(1), 21, and 24 of the African Charter.
81 *SERAC v Nigeria* (n 79). See also D Aguirre, 'Corporate Social Responsibility and Human Rights Law in Africa' 2005 5(2) *African Human Rights LJ*, 239, 263.
82 Article 21 of the African Charter. *SERAC v Nigeria* (n 79), paras 55–58.
83 *SERAC v Nigeria* (n 79), para 58.
84 Ibid.
85 *SERAC v Nigeria* (n 79), para 71(2).
86 South African Institute (n 51), 32; J Oloka-Onyango, 'Reinforcing Marginalized Rights in an Age of Globalization: International Mechanisms, Non-State Actors, and The Struggle for People's Rights in Africa' (2003) *American Univ Intl Law Rev* 852; R Murray, *The African Commission on Human and People's Rights and International Law* (Hart 2000), 37–38; E Druigbo 'Multinational Corporations and Compliance with International Regulations Relating to Petroleum Industry' (2001) *Annual Survey of Intl Comp L* 101, 139.
87 The African Court of Justice and Human Rights was founded in 2004 by a merger of the African Court on Human and Peoples' Rights and the Court of Justice of the African Union.
88 Statute of the African Court of Justice and Human and Peoples' Rights, Annex to the Protocol on Amendments to the Protocol on the Statute of the African Court of Justice and Human Rights, adopted 27 June 2014 (Malabo Protocol). See in particular

operation, the new criminal chambers of the African Court would have the potential to hear cases against corporations doing business in Africa, whether or not they are also headquartered or incorporated in states that are party to the African Charter.[89]

In 2015, the African Commission adopted *General Comment No. 3 on the Right to Life*.[90] This is the first time that a treaty body mentions the direct responsibility of corporations operating an entirely private business without performing state-like activities.[91] Paragraph 18 reads:

> States must hold to account private individuals and corporations, including private military and security companies that are responsible for causing or contributing to arbitrary deprivations of life in the State's territory or jurisdiction. Home States also should ensure accountability for any extra-territorial violations of the right to life, including those committed or contributed to by their nationals or by businesses domiciled in their territory or jurisdiction.[92]

3.3 The European system

The European Court of Human Rights has also dealt with cases alleging the responsibility of the states in relation to activities of corporations.[93] Of some relevance to transitional justice is the case related to the operations in Colombia of the Swiss multinational company *Nestlé*. Over the last 30 years, almost 3,000 trade unionists have been murdered in Colombia, including 13 workers at *Nestlé*. In 2005, Luciano Romero, a trade unionist and former employee at *Nestlé* factory *Cicolac* was kidnapped, tortured and murdered by members of a paramilitary group. His murder came after a number of death threats in the context of a long-standing labour dispute between the trade union Sinaltrainal and *Cicolac*. Criminal proceedings were launched in Colombia resulting in the conviction of the direct perpetrators of the murder. In his verdict, the Colombian judge stated that *Nestlé*'s role in the crime was of particular relevance and ordered an investigation to look into the matter in more detail. Ultimately, however, the Colombian prosecution authorities failed to look into the issue. In 2012, the European Center for

Art 28A (international criminal jurisdiction of the Court) and Art 46C (corporate criminal liability).
89 It will only come into operation when it is ratified by 15 member states. Malabo Protocol, Art 11.
90 ACHPR, General Comment No. 3 on the African Charter on Human and Peoples' Rights: The Right to Life (Article 4), 18 Nov 2015.
91 N Bernaz, 'Corporate Accountability in Draft General Comment on Right to Life by African Commission on Human and Peoples' Rights' 24 Aug 2015, www.rightsasusual.com/?p=989.
92 General Comment No. 3 (n 90), para 18.
93 For example, ECtHR, *Guerra v Italy* (1998)1 210, 26 EHRR 357, 228, 360; *López Ostra v Spain*, (1994) 303-C (ser A) 41, 20 EHRR 277, 56, 297. See also A Clapham, 'The "Drittwirkung" of the Convention' (2004) *Melbourne J Intl L* 23.

Constitutional and Human Rights (ECCHR) and Sinaltrainal filed a criminal complaint in Switzerland against *Nestlé* and some of its managers. The complaint alleged that *Nestlé* was complicit in the murder of Luciano Romero, for failing to take precautionary measures to prevent the crime. The prosecution rejected the claim and closed the proceedings on the basis that the crimes were statute-barred, and the Swiss Federal Supreme Court finally dismissed the case in 2014. Having exhausted all domestic remedies, the ECCHR filed a complaint against Switzerland, on behalf of Luciano Romero's widow, before the European Court. In 2015, the Court dismissed this complaint, without giving explanation, exhausting all legal avenues in Europe.[94]

Conclusion

Although they are not a transitional justice mechanism as such, regional human rights courts, and in particular the Inter-American Court and the African Commission, have at times examined material related to companies when deciding on a state's violation of human rights during times of conflict or repression. These courts are only mandated to establish the responsibility of states, but their judgments provide useful elements to understand the role of business in contributing to human rights violations during conflict or under the rule of authoritarian governments. The jurisprudence of the regional systems usually seeks to describe the context in which violations took place and in doing so they also contribute to establishing facts related to corporate involvement in human rights abuses. In some cases this may lead to further investigations at the national level or to payment of reparations, but at the very least this contributes to the establishment of a more truthful and accurate picture of the facts.

Arguably, precedents set by the regional systems may become particularly relevant if a future business and human rights treaty is adopted. Although negotiations are still under way, it is likely that such treaty will follow the classic UN treaty model: it will only bind states that have ratified it (i.e. it will not directly bind corporations). Possibly, if a UN business and human rights treaty is adopted, this will include obligations for the states that ratify it to regulate the operations of corporations headquartered in their territory and to investigate business-related human rights abuses.[95] As such, the jurisprudence being developed by the regional system may set precedent for cases that could be adjudicated under a potential future monitoring body of the business and human rights treaty.

Despite the theory that human rights systems ought to present an important avenue for victims of corporate human rights abuses when domestic remedies have

---

94 ECtHR, *European Center for Constitutional and Human Rights v Switzerland* (2015).
95 N Bernaz and I Pietropaoli, 'The Role of NGOs in the Business and Human Rights Treaty Negotiations' (2017) *Oxford J Human Rights Practice* 1; International Commission of Jurists (ICJ), 'Need and Options for a New International Instrument in the Field of Business and Human Rights' (June 2014).

failed, this chapter shows that their effectiveness is curtailed by a number of limitations. Proceedings are extremely lengthy, as the *HRDA* case demonstrates: the facts transpired in 2004; the complaint before the African Commission was filed in 2010, after a number of unsuccessful attempts in different jurisdictions; the Commission took six years to reach the decision and more than one year after that to release the judgment and notify the parties. Now is up to the DRC government to pay reparations to victims and reopen an investigation against *Anvil*. The decisions of the regional systems have the potential to recommend that national governments implement reparations measures addressing corporate activities. Ultimately, however, the national governments have to implement those recommendations. As discussed in this chapter, to date they have done so only to a limited extent. An additional avenue to seek remedy for corporate human rights abuses, including in transitional contexts, is litigation at the national level, which the next chapter analyzes.

Chapter 4

Domestic criminal and civil liability

Introduction

The previous two chapters have assessed the potential and limitations of international criminal tribunals and regional human rights systems in providing remedies in cases of corporate human rights abuses. This chapter moves to the analysis of domestic jurisdictions, which currently afford the only viable option to directly prosecute corporations for human rights violations and provide reparations to victims. Enjoying legal personality under domestic law, corporations are subject not only to the national regulations but also to the international obligations incorporated into domestic law, among which are those of international human rights law and international criminal law.[1] This has led to a dynamic development of law – a search for how different branches of national law can be adapted to hold business enterprises accountable for violations of human rights and international criminal law norms.[2] These types of judicial processes are not specifically transitional justice mechanisms, but they have provided, at times, the only opportunity for remedies to victims of corporate-related abuses in a transitional justice context. The Guiding Principles recognize:

> Some operating environments, such as conflict-affected areas, may increase the risks of enterprises being complicit in gross human rights abuses committed by other actors (security forces, for example). Business enterprises should treat this risk as a legal compliance issue, given the expanding web of potential corporate legal liability arising from extraterritorial civil claims, and from the incorporation of the provisions of the Rome Statute of the International Criminal Court in jurisdictions that provide for corporate criminal responsibility. In addition,

---

1 R Bismuth, 'Mapping a Responsibility of Corporations for Violations of International Humanitarian Law Sailing Between International and Domestic Legal Orders' (2009/2010) 38 *Denver J Intl L Policy* 203, 205.
2 International Commission of Jurists, *Report of the Expert Legal Panel on Corporate Complicity in International Crime* (International Commission of Jurists 16 Sep 2008), vol 1, 2; PC Zumbasen, 'Transnational Legal Pluralism' (2010) 10(2) *Transnational Legal Theory* 141.

corporate directors, officers and employees may be subject to individual liability for acts that amount to gross human rights abuses.[3]

The integration of international obligations in domestic legal orders has created two channels of liability of corporations: criminal and civil. Actually, establishing a strict distinction between the two remains a questionable point. In both cases, the liability of corporations is sought for the same violations and stems from similar international obligations, and similar standards of corporate complicity are used. The enforceability comes directly from international norms, through national laws. But while the distinction between civil and criminal liability of corporations is blurred from a substantive perspective, the two channels of liability are procedurally different and present distinct challenges, which the next sections seek to analyze.[4]

This chapter starts with the analysis of corporate criminal liability in transitional justice contexts (Section 4.1) and then turns to the issue of civil liability (4.2), looking in particular at cases under the Unites States' Alien Tort Statute. Cases are selected on the basis of their relevance in transitional justice contexts – in other words, all the cases selected concern alleged corporate abuses that occurred in a country in conflict or governed by a repressive regime. Examples of cases discussed here are those against *Unocal, Talisman Energy, ExxonMobil* and *Chiquita*, where complicity in gross human rights violations was levelled against these corporations in Myanmar, Sudan, Indonesia and Colombia respectively. The *South Africa Apartheid Reparation* litigation is another key lawsuit discussed in Section 4.2. This chapter engages in an analysis of the normative, economic and practical obstacles to achieving legal corporate accountability and reparations for victims through domestic litigation in a transitional justice context.

4.1 Criminal liability

In some cases, the nature and extent of wrongful conduct in which corporations are being implicated include slavery, crimes against humanity, war crimes, genocide and torture, and can be classified as international crimes.[5] There are three potential venues at the domestic level for prosecuting companies or executives alleged to have committed, or been complicit in, human rights violations or international crimes: the 'host' state on whose territory the crimes were committed; the 'home' state in whose territory the executive lives or the corporation is legally domiciled (through

---

3 Guiding Principles on Business and Human Rights: Implementing the United Nations 'Protect, Respect and Remedy' Framework, annexed to Report of the Special Representative of the Secretary-General on the issue of Human Rights and Transnational Corporations and Business Enterprises, John Ruggie, A/HRC/17/31 (21 March 2011) [Guiding Principles], principle 23, commentary.

4 Bismuth (n 1), 218.

5 J Kyriakakis, 'Prosecuting Corporations for International Crimes: The Role for Domestic Criminal Law', in L May and Z Hoskins (eds), *International Criminal Law and Philosophy* (Cambridge University Press, 2010), 108–37.

the use of extraterritorial jurisdiction); or any state exercising universal jurisdiction over the crimes considered to be of concern to the entire international community. Proceedings may be directed against corporations or against individual corporate officers.

4.1.1. The prosecution of corporations

Corporate criminal liability was common in continental Europe in the 17th and 18th centuries and was reflected in great detail, for example, in the French Criminal Code of 1670.[6] The concept fell into disfavour after the French Revolution, when corporate-style associations were disbanded and individualism dominated.[7] There are two key problems with the criminal liability of corporations from a theoretical legal perspective. First, the existence of a moral dimension of corporations – and therefore the existence of the *mens rea* in the commission of a criminal act.[8] 'Corporations have neither bodies to be punished, nor souls to be condemned; they therefore do as they like', said Edward Thurlow, first Baron Thurlow, in the 18th century.[9] It is difficult for some to conceptualize the moral culpability of companies and the nature of any punishment they may receive.[10] Second, the consideration of corporate criminal liability as a form of 'collective punishment' and therefore incompatible with criminal law. Criminal law has traditionally focused on individual, rather than collective, guilt.[11] There has been an understandable reluctance to impose on a group what might be seen as collective punishment for the wrongdoing of an individual.[12] The concern is also that sanctioning the corporation could in some cases unjustly hurt its stakeholders (shareholders, employees), who would pay an unjust price for past actions of the corporation. Theoretical arguments on the merits of corporate guilt are outside the remit of this research, as is a comparative assessment of how the concept of corporate criminality is realized, or not, in

6 G Stessens, 'Corporate Criminal Liability: A Comparative Perspective' (1994) 43 *Intl Comp LQ* 493, 494.
7 Ibid.
8 S Neumann Vu, 'Corporate Criminal Liability: Patchwork Verdicts and the Problem of Locating a Guilty Agent' (2004) 104 *Columbia LR* 459.
9 Edward, First Baron Thurlow, *Oxford Dictionary of Quotation* (OUP 1989) 550: 32.
10 AW Altschuller, 'Two Ways to Think about the Punishment of Corporations' (2009) 46 *American Criminal L Rev* 1359; J Clough and C Mulhern, *The Prosecution of Corporations* (OUP 2002), 4–5; KF Brickey, 'Corporate Criminal Accountability: A Brief History and an Observation' (1982) 60 *Wash Univ LQ* 393; VS Khanna, 'Corporate Criminal Liability: What Purpose Does It Serve?' (1996) 109 *Harv L Rev* 1477, 1479–81; J Hill, 'Corporate Criminal Liability in Australia: An Evolving Corporate Governance Technique?' (2003) J Business L 3. See also *United States v Sam*, 141 F.3d 463, 474 (3d Cir. 1998) reviewing nature of a corporation as separate legal entity, capable of suing and of being sued.
11 M Pieth and R Ivory, *Corporate Criminal Liability: Emergence, Convergence and Risk, Ius Gentium: Comparative Perspectives on Law and Justice* (Springer 2011), 4.
12 J Hasnas, 'The Centenary of a Mistake: One Hundred Years of Corporate Criminal Liability' (2009) 46 *American Criminal LR* 1329.

different jurisdictions.[13] What is important is that most countries now permit corporations to be prosecuted for criminal offences.[14]

Today, the principle of corporate criminal liability is typically recognized in common law countries, and is increasingly accepted in civil law systems – Australia, Canada, the United States, Japan, the United Kingdom and many countries in Europe, led by the Netherlands in the 1920s.[15] These countries consider that a corporation is an entity that can exercise autonomous will, and commit a crime, distinct from the individual intentions of its directors, representatives and employees, and therefore can be held criminally accountable.[16] The Council of Europe gave additional impetus to this movement in 1988, when it recommended that member states adapt their laws to permit corporate criminal prosecutions.[17] Across jurisdictions, however, different corporate criminal liability laws apply and the field is continuing to develop unevenly under different legal orders.[18]

Importantly from a transitional justice perspective, an increasing number of states have incorporated international criminal law into their domestic criminal legislation.[19] States parties of the Rome Statute have amended their domestic criminal laws to include international crimes among those that may be prosecuted in national courts.[20] Consequently, there is a basis for finding companies liable for

---

13 Pieth and Ivory (n 11); Hasnas (n 12); Altschuler (n 10); Fafo, *Business and International Crimes. Assessing the Liability of Business Entities for Grave Violations of International Law* (Fafo 2005); J Kyriakakis, 'Corporate Criminal Liability and the ICC Statute. The Comparative Law Challenge' (2006) 56(3) *Netherlands Intl LR*, 340.

14 The United States, Canada, Australia, Japan, the United Kingdom, and a number of EU countries (Austria, Belgium, Denmark, Estonia, Finland, France, Ireland, Norway, the Netherlands, Poland, Portugal, Romania, Luxembourg and Spain, but notably not Germany).

15 Fafo (n 13); Kyriakakis 'Corporate Criminal Liability and the ICC Statute' (n 13), 342; International Commission of Jurists (n 2), 31–32; H de Doelder and K Tiedemann (eds), *Criminal Liability of Corporations* (Brill 1996); C Wells, *Corporations and Criminal Responsibility* (OUP 1993); LH Leigh, 'The Criminal Liability of Corporations and Other Groups: A Comparative View' (1982) 80 *Mich L Rev* 1508 (1982); Stessens (n 6).

16 M Kremnitzer and H Genaim, 'The Criminal Liability of a Corporation' in A Barak (ed.) *Shamgar Rook* (Israel Bar Association 2003), 33, 67–68; R Slye, 'Corporations, Veils and International Criminal Liability' (2008) 33 *Brooklyn J Intl L* 955, 960–61; S Beale and A Safwat, 'What Developments in Western Europe Tell Us about American Critique of Corporate Criminal Liability' (2005) 8 *Buffalo Criminal L Rev* 89, 110–15; M Kremnitzer, 'A Possible Case for Imposing Criminal Liability on Corporations in International Criminal Law' (2010) 8(3) *J Intl Criminal Justice* 913.

17 Council of Europe, Recommendation No. R(88)18. Vol 20:45 20.

18 International Commission of Jurists (n 2), vol II, 57; Bismuth (n 1), 203.

19 For example, Australia, Belgium, Canada, France, India, Japan, the Netherlands, Norway, Slovenia, South Korea, South Africa, the UK and the US have introduced legislation that extends domestic legislation on international crimes to legal persons. See Max Planck Institute, National Prosecution of International Crimes, www.mpicc.de/en/research/projects/national-prosecution-of-international-crimes.

20 A Ramasastry and RC Thompson, *Commerce, Crime and Conflict: Legal Remedies for Private Sector Liability for Grave Breaches of International Law* (Fafo 2006).

international crimes within most domestic legal systems.[21] As David Scheffer, the diplomat at the Rome Conference who led the US delegation, underlined: 'Rather than witnessing a retreat from corporate liability in international practice since 1998, there has been a marked progression towards adoption of corporate criminal liability among nations joining the International Criminal Court.'[22]

Anita Ramasastry, a member of the UN Working Group on Business and Human Rights, argues that 'since most of the countries that have incorporated [international criminal law] into their domestic statutes also do not make a distinction between natural and legal persons [...] these jurisdictions include corporations and other legal persons in their web of liability'.[23] Arguably, the growing recognition of the criminal liability of corporations in national legal orders, added to the domestic incorporation of international crimes, can be a vehicle for liability of corporations for violations of international criminal law.[24]

Further, the jurisdiction of the ICC is limited *ratione personae* not only to individuals but also by provisions stipulating that persons covered by the ICC jurisdiction must either be nationals of a state party to the Rome Statute or have perpetrated their criminal conduct on the territory of a state party. Domestic criminal legislation does not include such limitations and makes possible, under certain conditions, the prosecution of a legal person of any nationality and even for a conduct occurring abroad.[25] The extended jurisdictional basis of domestic laws may 'fill the impunity gap left by the ICC's focused jurisdictional approach [and] we should expect national courts to cast a wider prosecutorial net than the ICC'.[26] Prosecutions at the national level may become increasingly possible as more states incorporate all or some aspects of gross human rights abuses amounting to crimes under international law into their domestic laws.[27]

---

21 A Batesmith, 'Corporate Criminal Responsibility for War Crimes and Other Violations of International Humanitarian Law: The Impact of the Business and Human Rights Movement' in C Harvey, J Summers and N White (eds), *Contemporary Challenges to the Laws of War: Essays in Honour of Professor Peter Rowe* (Cambridge University Press 2014), 296.

22 Ambassador DJ Sheffer, *Amicus Curiae* in support of the petitioners in *Joseph Jesner et al v Arab Bank, Plc*, 26 June 2017, 19.

23 Ramasastry and Thompson (n 20), 15.

24 In addition, some international treaties on financial, economic and transnational crimes require states which are party to introduce criminal liability of legal persons into domestic law. See in particular Article 10 of the UN Convention against Transnational Organized Crime, which calls for legal persons to be subject to civil, administrative or criminal sanctions.

25 Bismuth (n 1), 219–22.

26 WC Wanless, 'Corporate Liability for International Crimes under Canada's Crimes Against Humanity and War Crimes Act' (2009) 7(1) *JICJ*, 201, 205–06. Ruggie also observed, in 2008, an 'expanding web of potential corporate liability for international crimes'. Special Representative of the UN Secretary-General on the Issue of Human Rights and Transnational Corporations and Other Business Enterprises, Protect, respect and remedy: A framework for business and human rights, U.N. Doc. A/HRC/8/5, 7 April 2008, 20.

27 International Commission of Jurists (n 2), vol II, 8.

While prosecution in the 'host' state where the abuses have been committed is in theory the most effective – as victims, evidence and witnesses are located there – in a transitional justice context the reality of most countries emerging from conflict or repression makes this avenue difficult to pursue. Indeed, the majority of cases dealing with the responsibility of companies for human rights violations have been litigated in a different country from the place where the violations have occurred, usually invoking the home state's use of its extraterritorial jurisdiction. There is an vast body of national, regional and international frameworks and case law, decisions of UN Committees and scholarship regarding the applicability of human rights beyond borders.[28] Several international bodies have been encouraging states to take extraterritorial measures to exercise control over the overseas activities of companies registered in their territories.[29] For example, the Committee on Economic, Social

28 For example, Committee on Economic, Social and Cultural Rights (CESCR), *General Comment 14: The right to the highest attainable standard of health*, UN Doc E/C.12/2000/4, para 39 (11 August 2000); *General Comment 15 on the right to water*, UN Doc. E/C.12/2002/1 para 31 (January 2003); Committee on the Rights of the Child, *General Comment 16 on State obligations regarding the impact of the business sector on children's rights*, UN Doc. CRC/C/ GC/16, paras 43 and 44 (April 2013); Committee on the Elimination of Discrimination against Women, *General Recommendation No. 28 on the core obligations of States parties under article 2 of the Convention on the Elimination of All Forms of Discrimination against Women*, UN Doc. CEDAW/C/GC/28 para 36 (December 2010). See also SL Seck, 'Home State Responsibility and Local Communities: The Case of Global Mining' (2008) 11 *Yale Hum Rts Dev LJ* 177; W Vandenhole, 'Economic, Social and Cultural Rights in the CRC: Is There a Legal Obligation to Cooperate Internationally for Development' (2009) 17 *Intl J Children Rts* 23; R McCorquodale and P Simons, 'Responsibility Beyond Borders: State Responsibility for Extraterritorial Violations by Corporations of International Human Rights Law' (2007) 70 *Modern L Rev* 618; DM Chirwa, 'The Doctrine of State Responsibility as a Potential Means of Holding Private Actors Accountable for Human Rights' (2004) 5 *Melb J Intl L* 1, 4–5, 36.

29 For example, the Committee on Economic, Social and Cultural Rights affirms that states parties should prevent third parties from violating the rights protected under the Covenant in other countries, if they are able to influence these third parties. CESCR, General Comment No. 14 (2000), The right to the highest attainable standard of health (article 12 of the Covenant), E/C.12/2000/4, 11 August 2000, para 39, General Comment No. 15 (2003), The right to water (arts 11 and 12 of the Covenant), E/C.12/2002/11, 20 Jan 2003, para 33 which reads: 'Steps should be taken by States parties to prevent their own citizens and companies from violating the right to water of individuals and communities in other countries.' In regard to corporations, the Committee has stated that States parties should 'take steps to prevent human rights contraventions abroad by corporations that have their main seat under their jurisdiction', CESCR, Statement on the Obligations of States Parties regarding the corporate sector and economic, social and cultural rights. The Committee on the Elimination of Racial Discrimination has also called upon States to regulate the extraterritorial actions of third parties registered in their territory. For example, Concluding observations of the Committee on the Elimination of Racial Discrimination, Canada, CERD/C/CAN/CO/18, 25 May 2007, para 17; CERD/C/CAN/CO/19–20, 9 March 2012, para 14; CERD/C/GBR/CO/18–20, 14 Sep. 2011, para 29. The first example of the affirmation by an international body encouraging states to ensure that

and Cultural Rights has repeatedly emphasized that states parties 'are required to take the necessary steps to prevent human rights violations abroad by corporations domiciled in their territory and/or jurisdiction'.[30] Victims of corporate human rights abuses have increasingly turned to courts using extraterritorial criminal or civil jurisdiction to hold companies responsible for such abuses accountable and to seek remedies and reparations.[31] At times, the use of extraterritorial jurisdiction is presented as a 'magic potion' to address the challenges of corporate accountability, in particular because of its use in transnational civil litigation.[32]

The use of extraterritorial jurisdiction for corporate criminal liability is important in a post-conflict transitional context as victims in the host country may be unable to seek redress, the courts may be unable or ill-equipped to handle their cases or the host government may not pursue enforcement against the perpetrators.[33] But extraterritorial application of these pieces of domestic criminal legislation varies from country to country, and some national judicial systems do not have jurisdiction over crimes committed by their companies in other countries.[34] This often means impunity for companies when they are involved in criminal activity abroad and lack of reparations for victims. Amnesty International and the International Corporate Accountability Roundtable have documented more than

companies registered on their territories do not violate, while operating overseas, human rights contained in the UDHR is a 1970 resolution by the Security Council. In relation of the South African occupation of Namibia, the resolution called 'upon all states to discourage their nationals or companies of their nationalities not under direct governmental control from investing or obtaining concessions in Namibia', UN SC Res 283, 29 July 1970 Situation in Namibia para 7. In 1972, in the context of the strike of African contract workers, the Security Council adopted a resolution in which it called 'upon all states whose nationals and corporations are operating in Namibia [...] to use all available means to ensure that such nationals and corporations conform in their policies of hiring Namibian workers, to the basic provisions of the UDHR.' UN SC Res 310, 4 Feb 1972, Situation in Namibia, para 5. Report by the Secretary-General on the Implementation of Security Council Resolution 301 (1972), S/10752, 31 July 1972, p. 14.

30 CESCR, Statement on the obligations of States parties regarding the corporate sector and economic, social and cultural rights, E/C.12/2011/1, paras 5–6; General Comment No. 24 on State Obligations under the International Covenant on Economic, Social and Cultural Rights in the Context of Business Activities E/C.12/GC/2, 23 June 2017, paras 25–28.

31 IPIS, The Adverse Human Rights Risks and Impacts of European Companies: Getting a glimpse of the pictures (2014).

32 B Stephens, *Corporate Accountability: International Human Rights Litigation against Corporations in US Courts* (Martinus Nijhoff Publishers 2008); PI Blumberg, 'Asserting Human Rights against Multinational Corporations under United States Law: Conceptual and Procedural Problems' (2002) 50 *American J Comp L* 493.

33 A Ramasastry, 'Corporate Complicity: From Nuremberg to Rangoon – An Examination of Forced Labor Cases and Their Impact on the Liability of Multinational Corporations' (2002) 20 *Berkeley J Intl L* 91, 92.

34 W Kaleck and M Saage-Maab, 'Corporate Accountability for Human Rights Violations Amounting to International Crimes' (2010) 8 *J Intl Criminal Justice* 699, 714–15.

20 examples where authorities have not prosecuted multinational companies, despite being provided with evidence of illegal conduct linked to serious human rights abuses in other countries.[35] Many of the documented cases implicate Western companies in serious human rights abuses in fragile or war-torn areas. For example, as discussed in Chapter 3, no national government did an adequate investigation into the involvement of Australian–Canadian *Anvil Mining* in the DRC's Kilwa massacre.[36]

Some criminal complaints against companies have, however, been filed on the basis of extraterritorial jurisdiction. In particular, French authorities have opened investigations into at least six cases involving French companies accused of complicity of torture with Gaddafi's regime in Libya and Assad's in Syria, and genocide in Sudan. These cases are all at an initial stage and no corporation has been charged yet. Thus, while an assessment of the success of the cases from a victim point of view is not yet possible, the mere starting of the proceedings is significant. 'As the notion of corporate criminal liability for international crimes is still at its infancy in international law', Nadia Bernaz argues, 'these domestic cases are of paramount importance'[37] in the area of corporate accountability and remedy.

The first of such legal complaints was lodged in November 2009 by four NGOs before the French Public Prosecutor against *Dalhoff, Larsen and Horneman* (*DLH*). The complaint alleged that during the Liberian civil war, from 2002 to 2003, *DLH* bought timber from Liberian companies that provided support to Charles Taylor's government. The group claims that revenues from the timber industry were used to fuel the civil war by being a major source of funding for the Liberian government's extra-budgetary unofficial activities such as procurement of arms and ammunition in breach of UN sanctions. *DLH* allegedly continued to buy timber from Liberian suppliers despite strong evidence of their involvement in corruption, tax evasion, environmental degradation, UN arms sanctions violations and human rights abuses. The complainants further charged that *DLH*'s suppliers were not legally entitled to fell the timber sold to the company, and that *DLH* therefore was guilty of '*recel*' (the handling of and profiting from goods obtained illegally, which is a crime under French law). In 2013, the prosecutor dismissed the case and required 'no further action'.

A second complaint was filed in 2011 against *Amesys*, a French subsidiary of the *Bull* group.[38] The complaint alleged that in 2007 *Amesys* had entered into an agreement with the Libyan government to provide and assist with the development of a communication surveillance network, which the authorities used to intercept private Internet communications and to identify opponents of Gaddafi – who were then detained and tortured. FIDH and the *Ligue française des droits de*

---

35 Amnesty International and International Corporate Accountability Roundtable, 'Corporate Human Rights Principles', 2016, http://www.commercecrimehumanrights.org.

36 See Chapter 3.2.

37 N Bernaz, 'Complicity of War Crimes: Criminal Complaint against a French Technology Company' 30 June 2016, http://rightsasusual.com/?p=1057.

38 FIDH, *The Amesys Case* (FIDH 2013).

l'Homme, two NGOs, lodged the complaint in France on the basis of the principle of extraterritorial jurisdiction, alleging the complicity of *Amesys* and its executive managers in acts of torture. The application of the UN *Convention against Torture*, and the principle of extraterritorial jurisdiction enshrined therein, gives French judges jurisdiction over crimes committed outside of France, regardless of the nationality of the perpetrator or the victim.[39] In this instance, however, the fact that *Amesys* had its headquarters in France at the time that the alleged crimes were perpetrated was enough to give the French courts jurisdiction over acts of torture committed outside France where the main perpetrators were non-French nationals – namely, agents of the Libyan state.[40] The opening of a criminal investigation was met with opposition from the Prosecutor of the Paris Tribunal, who asked that the case be closed. In 2013, the Criminal Investigations Tribunal of the Paris Appeals Court denied the Prosecutor's request, thus confirming the opening of an investigation.[41] The case is on-going.

A third similar complaint was filed in 2012 by two NGOs which urged the French courts to investigate the complicity of French companies in human rights violations in Syria. The complaint alleged that *Qosmos*, a French software company, provided the Bashar El-Assad government with surveillance equipment, which was used to monitor and target dissidents later arrested and tortured.[42] As in the *Amesys* case, the French courts asserted their jurisdiction based on *Qosmos*'s being headquartered in France. In April 2015, the investigative judge declared *Qosmos* an 'assisted witness', which means that there was evidence showing it was plausible that the company could have taken part in the commission of the offences.[43] This case is also on-going.

The complaint against French company *Exxelia Technologies*, an electronic manufacturer, is the fourth of its kind in France. In June 2016, a Palestinian family, with the support of *Action des Chrétiens pour l'Abolition de la Torture* (ACAT) and represented by the law firm *Ancile-avocats*, filed a criminal complaint against *Exxelia*.[44] They claim that the company is guilty of manslaughter and possibly complicit in a war crime. In July 2014, a missile, probably dropped from a drone, landed on the Palestinian family house's roof where several children were feeding birds. A little girl and two boys were killed in the attack. Two other children were severely injured. As the house was not a legitimate military target, the attack may constitute a war crime. A component with the mark '*Eurofarad France*' was

---

39 Article 7 of the Convention against Torture and Other Cruel, Inhuman or Degrading Treatment, ratified by France on 18 February 1986.
40 FIDH, *The Amesys Case* (n 38).
41 Ibid.
42 FIDH, 'France: Opening of a judicial investigation targeting Qosmos for complicity in acts of torture in Syria', 4 November 2014.
43 FIDH, 'Designation of Qosmos as "assisted witness" constitutes an important step forward in case underway', 20 April 2015.
44 Middle East Monitor, 'Palestinian family sues French technology company for complicity in war crimes', 30 June 2016.

found in the debris. Experts have since determined that it is an effect sensor made by *Exxelia*. The core of the complaint is that the company sold the component to the Israeli government with knowledge that it would be part of a missile, which was likely to be used to commit a war crime. *Exxelia* has not yet been charged.

Further, in November 2016, Sherpa and the European Center for Constitutional and Human Rights, two NGOs, filed a criminal complaint against French–Swiss company *LafargeHolcim*, the world's largest cement producer, on behalf of 11 employees, accusing the company of complicity in war crimes in Syria. At issue is the activity of *Lafarge* before merging with *Holcim*, in 2015. In 2010, *Lafarge* had built a cement factory of 240 workers near Kobane, a northern Syria town. Operations there continued until 2014, long after the violence began in 2011. While fighting among Syrian rebels, the Syrian army and the terrorist group Islamic State (IS) drove other foreign companies out of the country, the plant operated by *Lafarge* was 'curiously' able to operate from its opening in 2010 through to 2014.[45] The criminal complaint alleged that *Lafarge* paid, via third parties, local armed groups, including IS, to keep the plant open, despite sanctions by the UN on the terrorist group.[46] It argued that *Lafarge* and its subsidiary *Lafarge Cement Syria* should be investigated on charges of complicity in crimes against humanity, financing of a terrorist enterprise, deliberate endangerment of people's lives and working conditions incompatible with human dignity. In an exceptional move, the French investigative judges issued a series of indictments between December 2017 and June 2018, thereby acknowledging the seriousness of the allegations and bringing the inquiry closer to a possible trial. Eight of *Lafarge*'s former executives, including two former CEOs, have been charged with criminal offences.[47] In June 2018, three investigative judges indicted *Lafarge* on charges of complicity in crimes against humanity, financing of a terrorist enterprise, and endangerment of people's lives.[48] This is the first time a parent company has been indicted for complicity in crimes against humanity. In November 2019, the French

---

45 EECHR, 'Case Report. Lafarge in Syria: accusation of complicity in war crimes and crimes against humanity', November 2016.
46 Ibid.
47 *Lafarge*'s executives indicted include Bruno Lafont, the company's chief executive from 2007 to 2015, Christian Herrault, the former director general, who was responsible for *Lafarge*'s operations in Syria, Frédéric Jolibois, Syria plant's director from 2014 to 2016, Bruno Pescheux, who oversaw the plant from 2009 to 2014, and Jean-Claude Veillard, *Lafarge*'s former security director. *The New York Times*, 'France investigate Lafarge executives for terrorist financing', 8 Dec 2017.
48 See ECCHR, 'Landmark decision in Lafarge case', 28 June 2018, www.ecchr.eu/en/case/lafarge-in-syria-accusations-of-complicity-in-grave-human-rights-violations; Le Monde, 'Syrie: l'entreprise Lafarge mise en examen pour complicité de crimes contre l'humanité ', 28 June 2018. In November 2019 the case was dismissed; see J Crawford, 'Corporate Responsibility in War Crimes, A New Legal Battlefield', *JusticeInfo*, 15 November 2019, www.justiceinfo.net/en/tribunals/national-tribunals/42906-corporate-responsibility-war-crimes-new-legal-battlefield.html

court dismissed the case against *Lafarge* – nevertheless, the case is important for a number of reasons.

First, an asset in this case was the overwhelming evidence implicating *Lafarge* senior executives in illegal activities in Syria. *Lafarge* reportedly pressured local Syrian employees to continue coming to work, threatening that they would be dismissed without compensation should they not show up – which happened to some. Kidnappings of employees started in August 2012 and peaked when nine of them were abducted for a month on their commute to work – for a ransom *Lafarge* ended up paying. Documents obtained by Syrian and French newspapers involving communication between *Lafarge* directors and their subsidiary's staff provided clear evidence. They indicated that the company had hired intermediaries to negotiate with and finance local armed groups, including IS – revelations have brought the amount of the payments *Lafarge* made to various armed groups to an alleged €13 million.[49]

Second, at the time *Lafarge* financed IS, the murders, widespread sexualized violence, kidnappings and other atrocities that the armed group perpetrated in Syria constituted crimes against humanity. They were systematic planned attacks against specific groups of the civilian population – as concluded in the EU Parliament resolution of 15 March 2018. While *Lafarge* may argue that it never had the intention to contribute to such crimes, this is not necessarily a decisive factor in the proceedings. In the Nazi collaborator '*Papon*' case of 1997, the French Supreme Court's judgment established that complicity in crimes against humanity does not require supporting the ideology of the principal perpetrators, nor is it necessary for the accomplice to know that the specific crime was being planned and actually perpetrated.[50] What matters is knowledge that crimes are being carried out and that one's conduct would contribute to these crimes being committed.[51]

Third, human rights cases against corporations are rarely a question of law alone; they are about power and politics. On the legal front, the complaint argued that French law, which provides for corporations to be held criminally liable, had been violated. But the scandal surrounding *Lafarge*'s financing of IS, a group put on a terrorist list – and one that claimed responsibility for the November 2015 attacks in Paris – meant the case gathered exceptional attention from the media and French politicians. The French Minister of Economy filed a complaint against *Lafarge* for violating the EU sanctions against Syria.[52] The financing of terrorism

49 C Tixeire, European Center for Constitutional and Human Rights, 'Can the Lafarge case be a game changer? French multinational company indicted for international crimes in Syria' for Business & Human Rights Resource Centre, www.business-huma nrights.org/en/can-the-lafarge-case-be-a-game-changer-french-multinational-compa ny-indicted-for-international-crimes-in-syria?utm_content=buffer43a79&utm_m edium=social&utm_source=twitter.com&utm_campaign=buffer
50 Cour de Cassation, Chambre criminelle, 23 Jan 1997, 96-84.822.
51 Tixeire (n 49).
52 Ibid.; *The New York Times*, 'Lafarge scandal points to difficulty in business in war zone', 4 April 2017.

became the driving force of the case. Yet it would be a setback for the legal case to stay locked within the counter-terrorism paradigm. Counter-terrorism legislation usually prioritizes national security over human rights. As such, it is important for reaffirming the fundamental superiority of human rights norms over the fluctuating counter-terrorism political agenda that the former directors were indicted not just for financing of terrorism but also for endangering the lives of their employees and for work conditions that are incompatible with human dignity.[53]

Lastly, in September 2019, nine Sudanese victims filed a criminal complaint in the French courts alleging that *BNP Paribas*, a French bank, was an accomplice in crimes against humanity, torture and genocide that took place in Sudan.[54] Another on-going criminal lawsuit against *BNP* alleges the bank's complicity in the Rwanda genocide. In June 2017, three human rights groups submitted a complaint to a French judge accusing *BNP* of war crimes and complicity in genocide in Rwanda in 1994.[55] The groups claim that *BNP* transferred US$1.3 million from the Rwandan national bank to a Swiss account belonging to a South African arms dealer in June 1994, a month after the UN had implemented an arms embargo.[56] According to the complaint, the alleged transfer of funds allowed for 80 tonnes of weapons to be sold to Hutu colonel Théoneste Bagosora, a key player in the genocide. The ICTR found him guilty of genocide and other crimes in 2008.[57] This complaint represents a first against a bank in France.[58]

France is not alone in attempting the use of extraterritorial jurisdiction to prosecute companies for crimes under international law. For example, in the United Kingdom, as a result of a lawsuit filed on behalf of 142 Sierra Leonean claimants, investigations are under way against the mining firm *Tonkolili Iron Ore* and its parent company *African Minerals*, alleging complicity in police crackdowns in Sierra Leone in 2010 and 2012.

In the Netherlands, a criminal case was filed against *Riwal Group*, a Dutch company that rents out construction equipment, concerning its involvement in the Occupied Palestinian Territory (OPT). In 2006, *Riwal* rented mobile cranes and aerial platforms for use in construction of the wall around West Bank villages in the OPT. A criminal complaint was submitted to the Dutch public prosecutor alleging that *Riwal* was complicit in the commission of war crimes and crimes against humanity in relation to the construction of the wall and illegal settlements in the occupied West Bank. *Riwal* was also accused of complicity in the crimes of

---

53 Tixeire (n 49).
54 FIDH, 'Sudanese victims ask French judges to investigate BNP Paribas' role in atrocities', 26 Sept 2019, www.fidh.org/en/region/Africa/sudan/sudanese-victims-a sk-french-judges-to-investigate-bnp-paribas-role-in
55 *The Economist*, 'BNP Paribas faces accusation over the Rwanda genocide', 8 July 2017.
56 Ibid.
57 ICTR, *The Prosecutor v Bagosora et al.*, 18 December 2008, Case no. ICTR-98-41-T, para 2266, part 3.1, 571.
58 Ibid.

persecution and apartheid, and of being responsible for acts that were part of widespread and systematic violations of international law committed by Israel against the civilian population. The *International Crimes Act* in the Netherlands prohibits the commission of war crimes and crimes against humanity by Dutch nationals, including companies.[59] Acts that amount to complicity in crimes, such as the facilitation or the aiding or abetting of crimes, are also criminalized. In 2013, after three years of investigations, the Dutch public prosecutor dismissed the case – *Riwal*'s contribution to the entire settlement enterprise including the wall was deemed to be minor.[60] The Dutch prosecutor was not able to obtain the necessary evidence for a conviction, much of which was located in the OPT and Israel, as their collection required cooperation from the relevant authorities.[61]

Despite the dismissal of the case, company executives came under legal and political scrutiny. The publicity and public pressure surrounding the case meant that *Riwal* took steps to disassociate itself from its subsidiary and its operations in the OPT.[62] Similarly, in March 2017, after an internal independent inquiry into possible dealings with armed groups, the *LafargeHolcim* board said the investigation had found that measures taken by staff had been 'unacceptable' and described 'significant errors of judgment'.[63] In response to the criminal complaint, coupled with mounting pressure in the press, *LafargeHolcim* conducted an internal investigation and in March 2017 issued a statement accepting that it had indirectly funded illegal armed groups in Syria in order to continue its operations there and allow safe passage for staff.[64] In April, the company announced that its chief executive, Eric Olsen, would resign.[65]

4.1.2. Universal jurisdiction

Under the principle of universal jurisdiction, any state has the authority to investigate, prosecute and punish certain serious crimes under international law, regardless of the location in which crimes are committed and the nationality of perpetrators or victims of crimes.[66] In the absence of any connection to the prosecuting state,

59 International Crimes Act 2003, article 2(2). See also International Commission of Jurists, *Access to Justice: Human Rights Abuses Involving Corporations. The Netherlands* (ICJ 2010), 7.
60 International Commission of Jurists, *Corporate Complicity in International Crime* (n 2).
61 Ibid.
62 Al-Haq, 'Prosecutor dismisses war crimes against Riwal', 14 May 2013.
63 *The Economist*, 'A giant cement firm may have unwittingly funded Islamic State', 29 Apr 2017.
64 LafargeHolcim, 'Lafarge responds to Syria Review', 3 Feb 2017, www.lafargeholcim. com/LafargeHolcim-responds-syria-review.
65 Ibid.
66 International Court of Justice, Arrest Warrant Case (*Congo v Belgium*), Case No. 121, 14 Feb 2002. See also A Addis, 'Imagining the International Community: The Constitutive Dimension of Universal Jurisdiction' (2009) 31 *HRQ* 129; J Zerk, 'Extraterritorial Jurisdiction: Lessons for the Business and Human Rights Sphere From Six

universal jurisdiction is asserted over 'the most serious crimes of concern to the international community'.[67] The source of this jurisdiction lies in the nature of the crimes: they are so serious that they are universally condemned and are of concern to the international community as a whole. In such instances, no connection is needed between the prosecuting state and the perpetrator. These crimes include war crimes, crimes against humanity, enforced disappearance, slavery, genocide and torture. Several international conventions provide for universal jurisdiction.[68] National legislation enabling the exercise of universal jurisdiction for international crimes exists in a number of both common and civil law countries, including Australia, Canada, the Netherlands and the United Kingdom.[69]

The principle of universal jurisdiction creates a possibility for victims of serious violations of human rights or international crimes committed by companies to lodge a complaint in any state invested with such jurisdiction. In 2001, William Schabas argued that the lacunae related to the liability of corporations under international criminal law may possibly be partially corrected by national legal systems exercising universal jurisdiction: 'those that allow for corporate criminal liability will be in a position to prosecute, as they would prosecute individuals'.[70] While there are no conceptual obstacles to the exercise of universal jurisdiction to prosecute corporations involved in serious international crimes, to date only one case has been pursued.

In 2002, four Myanmar refugees in Belgium filed a lawsuit in Brussels against *Total*, the chairman and the former director of *Total*'s Myanmar operations over human rights abuses linked to the operation of the Yadana pipeline.[71] The Myanmar refugees brought the lawsuit pursuant to a 1993 Belgian law on universal jurisdiction. This case was the first to be brought under this law against a company rather than an individual. The plaintiffs alleged that *Total* and its managers were complicit in crimes against humanity, such as torture and forced labour, committed by the Myanmar military junta in the course of the construction and operation of the pipeline. The

Regulatory Areas', Working Paper 59 of the Corporate Social Responsibility Initiative, June 2010.

67 Rome Statute of the International Criminal Court, Preamble. For a list of examples of domestic prosecutions using universal jurisdiction, see J Rikhof, 'Fewer Places to Hide? The Impact of Domestic War Crimes Prosecutions on International Impunity' (2009) 20 *Criminal L Forum* 1.

68 For example, the four Geneva Conventions, the Convention against Torture and Other Cruel, Inhuman or Degrading Treatment, and the International Convention for the Protection of All Persons against Enforced Disappearances.

69 International Commission of Jurists, *Corporate Complicity in International Crime* (n 2), vol II, 53.

70 W Schabas, 'Enforcing International Humanitarian Law: Catching the Accomplices' (2001) 83(842) *RICR* 439, 454.

71 Actions Birmanie, Civil action for Crimes against humanity and complicity in Crimes against humanity committed in Burma (Myanmar) lodged on 25 April 2002 in the Brussels magistrates court against X, the company Totalfinaelf S.A., Thierry Desmarest and Herve Madeo (2007).

plaintiffs alleged that *Total* provided moral and financial support to the Myanmar military government with knowledge that its support resulted in human rights abuses. A procedural issue arose as to whether the plaintiffs had standing to bring the lawsuit under the law of universal jurisdiction because they were not Belgian citizens. Following a number of procedural hurdles, the case was closed in 2008, without the merits of the allegations being addressed.[72] *Total* is the only example of an attempt to use universal jurisdiction to prosecute companies for crimes under international law.

The criminal prosecution of corporations for crimes under international law is an avenue, still at an early stage of development, which could potentially become more relevant for victims. If the cases opened in France are successful, the judgments may provide important precedents and standards that may be replicated in other countries, especially in other European countries with similar criminal provisions. At the moment, however, no corporation in its own right has yet been found criminally responsible by a national court for crimes under international law. While criminal prosecutions for gross human rights abuses and crimes under international law are under way against both businesspeople and corporations, successful criminal actions are rare. Most of the successful outcomes of the domestic cases globally involve civil courts.

4.1.3. The prosecution of businesspeople

In addition to corporations, individual businesspeople have also been prosecuted both at 'home' and abroad over allegations of having committed, or having been complicit in, crimes under international criminal law related to the activities of their companies.[73] For example, Frans van Anraat is a Dutch businessman who was accused of complicity in war crimes and genocide for having sold chemicals used in the fabrication of mustard gas, with knowledge of what the chemicals would be used for, to the Iraqi government under Saddam Hussein's rule. The gas, made with the chemicals that van Anraat sold, was later used in the massacres of Kurdish minorities in the Kurdish-Iraqi town of Halabja and in Iran in 1988 in the context of the Iran–Iraq war.[74] In 2005, the District Court of The Hague

---

72 For a summary of the case, see Business & Human Rights Resource Centre, 'Total lawsuit in Belgium (re Myanmar)', http://business-humanrights.org/en/total-lawsuit-in-belgium-re-myanmar.

73 International Commission of Jurists (n 2), vol II, 53. Kaleck and Saage-Maab (n 34), 716; W Huisman and E van Sliedregt, 'Rogue Traders: Dutch Businessmen, International Crimes and Corporate Complicity' (2010) 8 *J Intl Criminal Justice* 803; Kremnitzer (n 16), 911; H Vest, 'Business Leaders and the Modes of Individual Criminal Responsibility under International Law' (2010) 8 *J Intl Criminal Justice* 851, 853; Wells (n 15); TL van Ho, 'Transnational Civil and Criminal Litigation' in S Michalowski (ed.), *Corporate Accountability in the Context of Transitional Justice* (Routledge 2013), 55.

74 District Court of The Hague, 23 December 2005, Case No. AX6406 [*van Anraat* case].

found van Anraat guilty of aiding and abetting war crimes and sentenced him to 15 years in prison, a sentence that was increased to 17 years by the Appeals Court in 2007.[75] The court found that he was aware that his product could be used for producing poison gas and that there was a reasonable chance it would be used for chemical attacks. The court found that van Anraat 'consciously and solely acting in pursuit of gain, has made an essential contribution to the chemical warfare program of Iraq [...] which enabled, or at least facilitated, a great number of attacks with mustard gas on defenceless civilians'.[76]

The Dutch Supreme Court upheld van Anraat's conviction for being an accessory to war crimes.[77] It found that the accused knew that the chemicals he was supplying to the Hussein regime were being used for the production of poison gas and, in the context of a long-standing war in which this gas was being used in the attacks, van Anraat's conduct constituted 'deliberate contribution' to the offences. In other words, he was found to have provided the opportunity and the means for the gas attacks.[78] He was, however, acquitted of the charges of complicity in genocide because there was insufficient evidence that he had known of the Iraqi regime's genocide intent towards the Kurdish minorities.[79]

Guus Kouwenhoven is another Dutch businessman accused of complicity in war crimes. Kouwenhoven was the director of *Firestone and Oriental* and *Royal Timber*, two major timber companies in Liberia, and it was alleged that he supplied the former President of Liberia Charles Taylor's forces with weapons and illegally traded in timber to finance Taylor's conflicts in Liberia and Sierra Leone.[80] *Oriental Timber* gained trading concessions from Taylor at a time when conflict between rival militia spilled over to Sierra Leone.[81] As discussed in Chapter 5, the Truth and Reconciliation Commission of Liberia also discusses the involvement of these timber companies in the conflict. The Dutch prosecution indicted Kouwenhoven with aiding and abetting war crimes committed by Liberian militias and with the violation of an UN arms embargo. According to the prosecution: 'the militias hired by the former timber companies belonging to this Dutchman, are accused of

---

75 Ibid. See also M Zwanenburg and G den Dekker, 'Prosecutor v. Frans van Anraat, case No. 07/10742' (2011) 104 *AJIL* 86; R van Rossum, 'Adjudication of International Crime in the Netherlands' (2011) 39 *Intl J Legal Information* 202; Huisman and van Sliedregt (n 73), 805, 807.
76 *van Anraat* case (n 74), para 17.
77 *van Anraat* case (n 74), Dutch Supreme Court, 30 June 2009, Case No. BG4822.
78 Ibid., Court of Appeal of The Hague, 9 May 2007, Case No. BA6734, para 12.5.
79 Ibid., para 17. See also Huisman and van Sliedregt (n 73), 808–09; H van der Wilt, 'Genocide v. War Crimes in the Van Anraat appeal' (2008) 6 *J Intl Criminal Justice* 557, 558–59; *New York Times*, 'Vendor Tied to Gas Attack Is Convicted', 24 December 2005, A5; *New York Times*, 'World Briefing Europe: The Netherlands: Stiffer Sentence for Iraq Poison Gas', 10 May 2007, A14.
80 Huisman and van Sliedregt (n 73), 810–12
81 *The Guardian*, 'Dutch arms trafficker to Liberia given war crimes conviction', 22 April 2017.

participating in the massacre of civilians [...] Guus Kouwenhoven is accused of having supplied the arms to the militias to enable them to carry out these crimes.'[82]

In 2006, Kouwenhoven was acquitted by the District Court of The Hague of complicity in war crimes due to lack of evidence, but convicted for illegal arms supplies to Taylor.[83] The conviction was overturned by the Court of Appeal, which acquitted Kouwenhoven of all charges.[84] In 2010, the Supreme Court quashed the judgment of the Appeal Court and ordered a retrial.[85] In April 2017, the Appeal Court convicted Kouwenhoven as an accessory of war crimes and arms trafficking and sentenced him to 19 years in prison. *Global Witness*, a campaign group that gathered evidence against *Oriental Timber* cited by the Dutch prosecutors, said that the case is 'the first war crimes conviction for a businessman profiting from conflict resources'.[86] The court found that shipments for Kouwenhoven's timber operation in Liberia carried caches of hidden weapons, used by Taylor in an armed conflict with rebels where 'countless civilians' died.[87] Kouwenhoven's conviction, the Dutch judges said in a written summary of their ruling, will serve as an example to others that do business with repressive governments 'that they can thereby become involved in serious war crimes'.[88] Both cases were centred on theories of indirect perpetration as a mechanism to establish criminal responsibility and were able to proceed with the use of extraterritorial jurisdiction.

The case against *Danzer Group*, a Swiss–German timber manufacturer, involves criminal prosecution attempts in both the home and host countries. In May 2011, the village of Bongulu in northern DRC was attacked by Congolese police and military, who committed rape, arbitrary arrests and other human rights violations. Senior staff of *Danzer* allegedly aided and abetted these abuses by failing to prevent these crimes from being committed. In addition, Congolese security forces reportedly received financial and logistical help from *Danzer*'s former subsidiary, *SIFORCO*. A group of Bongulu villagers filed a complaint in DRC against 60 Congolese military and police officers allegedly involved in the attack. The plaintiffs also claimed there was evidence that some *SIFORCO* employees participated in its planning and preparation. In addition, an NGO filed a complaint against *SIFORCO* for civil responsibility and against two *SIFORCO* employees for criminal responsibility for alleged complicity in the incident. The DRC Military Prosecutor's office conducted investigations, with the joint participation of the UN. In December 2015, a military court ruled that the accused were guilty of 'torture' and issued a

---

82 District Court of The Hague, 7 June 2006, Case No. AY5160, Rechtbank's-Gravenhage, 09/750001-05.
83 Ibid. See also Huisman and van Sliedregt (n 73) 811.
84 Dutch Court of Appeals, Case No. BC7373.
85 Dutch Supreme Court, 20 April 2010, Case No. BK8132.
86 *The Guardian* (n 81).
87 Ibid.
88 *New York Times*, '8-Year Sentence for Businessman Who Smuggled Arms to Liberia', 8 June 2006, A8; *New York Times*, 'Arms Ruling Overturned by Dutch', 11 March 2008, A10.

prison sentence; *SIFORCO* was found not guilty. The *European Center for Constitutional and Human Rights* and *Global Witness*, two NGOs, filed a criminal complaint in Germany against Olof von Gagern, a senior manager of *Danzer Group*. The complaint alleges that von Gagern was complicit in human rights abuses committed during the attack on the village of Bongulu by failing to prevent it. Under German law, corporations cannot be prosecuted for crimes. Senior managers may, however, have criminal responsibility arising from a duty of care towards those affected by the actions of their employees. In March 2015, the Public prosecutor's office in Tübingen discontinued the investigations.

A further case resulted in a different outcome. In October 2018, the Swedish government authorized the Swedish Prosecution Authority to proceed in a case regarding activities of two corporate directors of Swedish oil companies *Lundin Oil* and *Lundin Petroleum*, in South Sudan (Sudan at the time) between 1998 and 2003.[89] Sudan was ravaged by an internal armed conflict that lasted from 1983 until 2005 between the government of Sudan and the Sudanese People's Liberation Army. Beginning with the signing of contracts in 1997, *Lundin* formed a consortium that carried out oil exploration and production in an oil concession area called Block 5A in the southern part of the country. According to a report by the *European Commission on Oil in Sudan (ECOS)*, the oil exploration 'brought exacerbated conditions while setting off a battle for control of the disputed region, leading to thousands of deaths and the forced displacement of local population'.[90] The consortium's interaction with local counterparts came under criminal investigation after *ECOS*'s report was submitted to Swedish prosecutors in 2010.[91] The company directors could be charged with aiding and abetting gross crimes against international law in accordance with the Swedish Penal Code.[92] Such charges carry a sentence of up to life imprisonment. Shortly after the indictment, in November 2018, *Lundin Petroleum* announced that the company had been notified by the prosecutor of a potential corporate fine and forfeiture of economic benefits in relation to the operations in Sudan.[93] A corporate fine is considered 'an extraordinary legal remedy serving as a repressive sanction supplanting corporate criminal liability'.[94] The corporate fine and forfeiture 'would likely be tried alongside any

---

89 In the United States, a case comprised of a similar set of facts was brought against *Talisman Energy*, a Canadian oil company, which commenced its activities in the area one year after *Lundin*.

90 ECOS, Unpaid Debt, 2010, www.ecosonline.org/reports/2010/UNPAID_DEBT_fullreportweb.pdf

91 Reuters, 'Lundin Petroleum CEO, chairman to be questioned on possible Sudan crimes', 21 Oct 2006.

92 Chapter 22, Section 6.

93 Lundin Petroleum, 'Lundin Petroleum receives information regarding a potential corporate fine and forfeiture of economic benefits in relation to past operations in Sudan', 1 Nov 2018, www.lundin-petroleum.com/media-centre/?cp_press_release=4

94 M Ingeson and AL Kather, 'The Road Less Travelled: How Corporate Directors Could be Held Individually Liable in Sweden for Corporate Atrocity Crimes Abroad', 13 Nov 2018, *EJIL: Talk! Blog of the European Journal of International Law*, www.ejiltalk.org/

future individual indictment, placing the corporation next to its directors in the courtroom'.[95] As mentioned above, it is a rule of customary international humanitarian law that states should exercise their criminal jurisdiction over war crimes.[96] The crimes can be prosecuted on the basis of universal jurisdiction as provided for in the Penal Code, regardless of the nationality of the perpetrators or victims and the place where the crimes were committed.[97] If the prosecutor decides to proceed with prosecution, other legal issues remain, such as how to adequately assess individual liability within corporations for the crimes concerned. Crimes against international law have only ever been tried in a handful of cases in Sweden and never in a corporate setting. The theory of individual liability for crimes – particularly for the crimes under international criminal law – within corporations is in need of conceptual development in Swedish law, as elsewhere.[98] The contribution of the *Lundin* case could be substantial as a starting point for discussions around corporate criminal liability in Swedish law, regardless of the outcome.[99]

Italian criminal law is also being tested. In October 2016, an airstrike allegedly by the Saudi-led military coalition struck the village of Deir Al-Hajari in northwest Yemen. The airstrike killed a family of six. At the site of the airstrike bomb remnants were found, including a suspension lug manufactured by *RWM Italia*, a subsidiary of the German arms manufacturer *Rheinmetall*. All parties to the Yemen conflict have repeatedly violated human rights of the civilian population. Numerous airstrikes by the Saudi-led military coalition have been found by the UN to be in violation of international humanitarian law. In April 2018, three NGOs submitted a criminal complaint to the Italian Public Prosecutor's Office in Rome.[100] The legal intervention calls for an investigation into the criminal liability of Italian authority *Unità per le Autorizzazioni dei Materiali di Armamento* (UAMA) which authorizes Italy's armament exports, and of *RWM Italia*'s directors for armament exports to members of the Saudi-led military coalition involved in the conflict in Yemen.

The cases discussed above involve the use of extraterritorial jurisdiction to prosecute corporations in their home state for crimes allegedly committed abroad. Argentina offers a rare example of a country that, decades after the transition, has

    the-road-less-traveled-how-corporate-directors-could-be-held-individually-liable-in-swe den-for-corporate-atrocity-crimes-abroad.

95 Ibid.
96 ICRC, Rule 158. Prosecution of War Crimes. States must investigate war crimes allegedly committed by their nationals or armed forces, or on their territory, and, if appropriate, prosecute the suspects. They must also investigate other war crimes over which they have jurisdiction and, if appropriate, prosecute the suspects.
97 Chapter 2, Section 3 (6).
98 Ingeson and Kather (n 94).
99 Ibid.
100 European Center for Constitutional and Human Rights (ECCHR), 'Are Arms Manufacturer A and Italian Authorities Complicit In Deadly Saudi-Coalition Airstrike In Yemen?', 16 Apr 2018, www.ecchr.eu/nc/en/press-release/are-arms-manufacturer-a nd-italian-authorities-complicit-in-deadly-saudi-coalition-airstrike-in-yemen

used its national laws to prosecute businesspeople responsible for human rights violations. The process of memory, truth and justice in relation to crimes committed in Argentina during the military dictatorship (1976–1983) can be considered the birthplace of contemporary transitional justice. The reckoning of the crimes perpetrated by those in power in Argentina started with the report issued by National Commission on the Disappearance of Persons (*Comisión Nacional sobre la Desaparición de Personas* – CONADEP) in 1984, entitled '*Nunca Más*', and the so-called 'Trial of the Military Juntas' in 1985. This process included times of impunity, achieved first by laws restricting the legal process during the 1980s and later by presidential executive pardons. The process regained strength in 2001 with a judiciary decision reopening the trials, backed by the Supreme Court of Justice in 2005.

Now Argentinian prosecutors are also taking innovative steps to address the criminal responsibility of business.[101] Argentinian law does not allow the prosecution of companies, so only business executives have been charged. Since the end of the dictatorship, researchers, activists and lawyers have collected strong evidence showing that several factories had been territories of labour repression and proving that workers and union leaders were primary targets of repression, with military and business participation. CONADEP found that almost half of the disappeared were part of the country's organized labour force.[102] For example, the majority of the 5,000 detainees at Campo de Mayo, the country's biggest prison, most of who were later executed, had been active in the labour movement. About a hundred unionists and dozens of the work council members of car manufacturers *Ford* and *Mercedes-Benz* were detained there.[103] When the judiciary process reopened, one of the issues under scrutiny was the level of responsibility of corporations and business executives in human rights violations. The theme of the yearly march in Buenos Aires on the 24 March 2012 anniversary of the military coup was the connection of 'economic groups' to the *coup d'état* and the regime it installed. At the end of the event, on the stage where the final speeches were broadcast, a screen projected the names of companies allegedly complicit in the dictatorship. Investigations of such complicity, and in particular of the role of banks in financing the military junta, took off in the aftermath of the march.[104] 'The quest to end impunity in Argentina continues with renewed fervour [...] motivated by a

---

101 LA Payne and G Pereira, 'Accountability for Corporate Complicity in Human Rights Violations: Argentina's Transitional Justice Innovation?' in H Verbitsky and J Bohoslavsky (eds), *The Economic Accomplices to the Argentine Dictatorship* (CUP 2015), 29–44; 'Corporate Complicity in International Human Rights Violations' (2016) 12 *Annual Rev L Social Science* 63.
102 Comisión Nacional sobre la Desaparición de Personas (CONADEP), *Nunca Más* (20 September 1984).
103 W Kaleck, 'International Criminal Law and Transnational Businesses: Cases from Argentina and Colombia' in Michalowski (n 73), 178.
104 JP Bohoslavsky and V Opgenhaffen, 'The Past and Present of Bank Responsibility for Financing the Argentinean Dictatorship' (2009) 23 *Harvard Human Rights J* 157.

widespread sense that justice has not yet been achieved', writes Juan Pablo Bohoslavky, the UN Independent Expert on the effects of foreign debt.[105]

In 2006, three decades after the *coup* of 1976, a paper by historian Victoria Basualdo addressing corporate complicity shed light on the role played by business leaders during the dictatorship.[106] Its publication opened the door to investigations to explore the issue further. In 2015, the Ministry of Justice and Human Rights published an exhaustive study that investigated 'business responsibility in crimes against humanity'.[107] The investigation analyzed 25 companies across different sectors, including *FIAT, Ford Motor* and *Mercedes-Benz.* The report found that in the majority of cases, directors and managers had played an active role in the arrest, kidnapping, torture and enforced disappearances of 900 workers.[108] Even more common was the vast deployment of military and security forces on factory grounds; some corporate officials explicitly sought this military intervention and provided logistical or financial support.[109] The report indicates the installation of clandestine detention and torture centres on company premises as the 'most extreme manifestation of the widespread militarization of factories during the dictatorship'.[110]

Criminal prosecutions against corporate officers followed.[111] An emblematic case involves the trial of the corporate leaders of the *Ledesma* sugar mill, accused of cooperating with the death squads that abducted dozens of people in Jujuy in the mid-1970s. In 2012, the Federal Court in Jujuy prosecuted the director of *Ledesma*, Pedro Blaquier, and former manager, Alberto Lemos, over complicity in arbitrary arrests and enforced disappearances. The prosecution was related to their suspected involvement in the so-called *noche de apagón* (night of the blackout). Allegedly, on the night of 21 July 1976, with technical assistance from *Ledesma*, electrical power was cut off in the entire municipality. Using military and company vehicles, members of the military arrested about 400 people, mainly unionists and employees of *Ledesma* – 55 people are still missing.[112] A raid of the company revealed intelligence reports compiled for *Ledesma* on trade unionists, who

105 Ibid., 197–201.
106 V Basualdo, 'Complicidad patronal-militar en la última dictadura argentina: Los casos de Acindar, Astarsa, Dálmine Siderca, Ford, Ledesma y Mercedes Benz' (March 2006) 5 Revista Engranajes de la Federación de Trabajadores de la Industria y Afines.
107 Argentina Justice Ministry's Truth and Justice Programme and the Human Rights Secretariat, Latin-American School for Social Sciences, and the Center for Legal and Social Studies, 'Business Responsibility in Crimes Against Humanity: The Repression of Workers During State Terrorism', December 2015.
108 UN Office of the High Commissioner for Human Rights (OHCHR), 'Argentina Dictatorship: UN Experts Back Creation of Commission on Role Business People Played', 10 November 2015.
109 Ibid.
110 Argentina Justice Ministry (n 107).
111 In addition to Ledesma, Mercedes-Benz and Ford Motor Company discussed here, senior officers from the following companies are being currently prosecuted for direct involvement in human rights abuses: Techint; Atarsa, Minera Aguilar S.A., Loma Negra, La Veloz del Norte, and Acindar.
112 Kaleck (n 103), 178–79.

subsequently disappeared.[113] In addition, *Ledesma* allegedly allowed the armed forces to set up a clandestine detention centre, *Escuadrón 20*, on its grounds. In 2015, the Federal Court dismissed the charges against Blaquier and Lemos, concluding that there was no evidence of the involvement of the two directors in the crimes.[114] Further, in March 2016 a criminal guilty verdict was rendered by an Argentine court against Marcos Levin, owner of the *Veloz del Norte*. Levin was sentenced to 12 years in prison for crimes against humanity involving the illegal detention and torture of a company employee, Victor Cobos.

Another particularly important case sought to determine the responsibility of a military leader and of *Ford Motor Argentina*'s executives in the kidnapping, torture and illegal detention of 24 former *Ford* workers (some of them also trade union representatives) between 1976 and 1977. This judiciary process started in 2002. It derived from an investigation focused on military chief Santiago Omar Riveros, who was, between 1976 and 1978, in charge of the defence zone 'Campo de Mayo' where the *Ford* plant is located. The *Ford* case took more than 11 years to get to trial stage, which finally began in December 2017. The criminal complaint filed against *Ford* executives alleged that they conspired with the regime in political repression, abductions and mistreatment of *Ford*'s workers and union organizers. The public prosecutor charged that the military operated a detention centre within *Ford*'s factory complex in Buenos Aires and that company officials gave names, ID numbers, pictures and home addresses to security forces who arrested 24 *Ford* trade union leaders, and illegally detained and tortured them. Four company executives had allegedly been involved in the events. Two of them could not be prosecuted because they died before the proceedings begun. Only two executives stood trial: Pedro Müller, manager of production of the plant, and Héctor Francisco Jesús Sibilla, the Chief of Security at the time. After a year of trial hearings, 42 years after the events and 16 years after the case was initiated, a panel of three judges found the three accused guilty, and sentenced Sibilla to 12 years in prison and Müller to ten years.[115] The closing statements of the prosecution underlined that the criminal acts, which began the same day as the military junta seized power, on 24 March 1976, can only be understood when taking into account the shared concern by the armed forces and the company's leadership about trade union activity. They emphasized that the kidnappings between March and August 1976 happened in a context of increasing presence of military personnel inside the *Ford* plant. Corporate participation was crucial in the commission of the crimes.[116]

---

113 ECCHR, 'Corporations supported the Argentinian military dictatorship', www.ecchr. eu/en/our_work/business-and-human-rights/corporations-and-dictatorships.html.
114 Ibid.
115 Case no. 4012/3, 20 May 2013.
116 Victoria Basualdo, 'The Ford Case, 40 Years Later', JusticeInfo.net, 18 Feb 2019, www. justiceinfo.net/en/justiceinfo-comment-and-debate/opinion/40348-the-ford-case-40-years-later.html; Victoria Basualdo, The Ford Trail in Argentina, A Workers' Victory, JusticeInfo.net, 1 Apr 2019, www.justiceinfo.net/en/justiceinfo-comment-and-debate/opinion/40813-the-ford-trial-in-argentina-a-workers-victory.html

A similar lawsuit against the manager of *Mercedes-Benz* involves the company's creation of a 'blacklist' of workers who were subsequently kidnapped.[117] The case concerned 16 union activists working at the *Mercedes-Benz* plant in Buenos Aires, who were arrested by the military police in 1976 and disappeared. Journalist Gaby Weber, who investigated the case, described her motivation: 'I wanted to research where the real power was concentrated. And this is not the military and its retired generals [...] I was looking for a German company [...] that had a skeleton in the cupboard.'[118]

Based on her research, in 1999 a criminal complaint was filed in Germany against Juan Tasselkraut, a senior manager at *Mercedes-Benz Argentina*. It was alleged that he facilitated the arrest, torture and disappearance of a union worker by giving military personnel access to him in the workplace and by passing on the private addresses of other workers. In 2003, the public prosecution discontinued these proceedings because of insufficient evidence, as the murder of the unionist was not proved.[119] Because the case was filed before the entry into force of the Rome Statute, crimes against humanity, including enforced disappearance, did not constitute a crime in German law, and therefore the charges were only of murder. In addition, because German law does not provide for corporate liability, the case was filed only against the manager of *Mercedes-Benz*, not against the corporate entity.[120] A significant side effect of the litigation in Germany was the formation in Argentina of a group of former *Mercedes-Benz* unionists – which shows how important legal proceedings can be, regardless of their outcome.[121]

Cases targeting businesspeople, either under the national law of the country where they committed abuses or through the use of extraterritorial jurisdiction, are an important remedy for victims of violations. Individual liability should be seen as complementary to corporate liability: even if the liability of individuals associated with the company such as directors or managers is established, this does not preclude corporate criminal liability.[122] While under certain circumstances and depending on the underlying sentencing purposes, targeting individual businessmen may be an effective option, both avenues of criminal prosecution should be left open to a prosecutor.

Despite being conceptually possible, however, the criminal prosecution of corporations at the domestic level for violations under international human rights law or crimes under international criminal law still represent the exception and have been largely unsuccessful. The recent 'French cases' against *Amesys, Qosmos, LafargeHolcim* and *BNP Paribas*, described above, represent an interesting development, but they are all still pending and their outcome remains unclear. Another possible avenue to provide accountability for corporate violations in the context of

117 ECCHR (n 113).
118 G Weber, *Die Verschwundenen von Mercedes Benz* (Verlag Assoziation 2001).
119 ECCHR (n 113).
120 Kaleck (n 103), 180–83.
121 Ibid., 182.
122 Clough and Mulhern (n 10), 8.

transitional justice lies in an expansion of domestic civil liability, which the next section examines.

4.2 Civil litigation

Under domestic civil liability law, a company may be held responsible and be required to pay compensatory or punitive damages to an aggrieved party if found guilty of violation of a civil law, tort or breach of contract.[123] Although the law of civil remedies does not use the terminology of human rights law, in all jurisdictions it protects 'interests' such as life, liberty, dignity, physical and mental integrity, and property. In countries that do not recognize the criminal liability of corporations, the law of civil remedies provides victims with their only domestic venue to seek corporate accountability. Civil liability is an important means of assuring legal accountability when a company is complicit in gross human rights abuses.[124] Civil liability gives more latitude than criminal liability for several reasons. First, compared with criminal prosecution, establishing a tortious act requires a lower burden of proof, and proving both liability and causation in a tortious suit may be easier than attributing criminal liability and causation.[125] Second, victims do not have to wait for the decision of a state prosecutor for the case to commence. Third, across jurisdictions, there are similar principles of civil liability for companies – the law of civil remedies always has the ability to deal with the conduct of companies, as well as of individuals and state authorities.[126]

There are, however, some important drawbacks too. *Ratione temporis*, civil liability is generally restricted in time and does not benefit from the absence of statutes of limitations attaching to the commission of international crimes in domestic criminal law, which is important considering the frequent long time lapses between the perpetration of the crimes and the moment when victims are able to seek remedy in a transitional justice context.[127] Further, in criminal liability, the impact on the reputation of the corporation is arguably more serious, which may make future deterrence more likely.[128] In addition, the negligent or intentional conduct of the company involved in human rights abuses is not necessarily assessed against

---

123 B Stephens, 'The Amorality of Profit: Transnational Corporations and Human Rights' (2002) 20 *Berkeley J Intl L* 45; JE Malamud-Goti and LS Grosman, 'Reparations and Civil Litigation: Compensation for Human Rights Violations in Transitional Democracies' in P de Greiff (ed.), *The Handbook of Reparations* (OUP 2006), 539; R Meeran, 'Tort Litigation Against Multinational Corporations for Violation of Human Rights: A View of the Position Outside the United States' (2001) 3(1) *City Univ Hong Kong L Rev* 1, 3.
124 International Commission of Jurists, *Corporate Complicity in International Crime* (n 2), vol III, 4–5.
125 Fafo (n 13), 24.
126 Ramasastry, 'Corporate Complicity' (n 33), 151–53; International Commission of Jurists, *Corporate Complicity in International Crime* (n 2), Vol III, 4–5.
127 Bismuth (n 1), 221–22.
128 Kremnitzer (n 16), 915; T Weigend, 'Societas delinquere non potest? A German Perspective' (2008) 6 *J Intl Criminal Justice* 927, 931.

the standards of international human rights law and international criminal law. Arguably, when non-criminal liability is imposed for serious crimes, this may put the severity of the crime and the importance of the protected value in doubt.[129]

Extraterritorial civil liability has provided an important avenue in a post-conflict transitional context where victims often face obstacles to access to justice in the country where the harm was inflicted.[130] Tort claims against the parent corporation of a multinational group brought in civil courts of the home state test the extra-territorial limits of civil litigation rules.[131] This is a practice sometimes referred as 'foreign direct liability' – a term intended to reflect the flip side of foreign direct investment.[132] The United States, the United Kingdom, the Netherlands and Canada, among others, have examined civil claims against companies for complicity in human rights violations committed in other countries in times of conflict or repression. While jurisdictions outside the United States have been used,[133] the literature and practice on transnational civil claims has principally focused on US law.[134] In particular, a great deal of attention has been paid to high-profile litigation against multinational corporations under the US Alien Tort Statute (ATS), also called Alien Tort Claims Act (ATCA),[135] the largest body of domestic jurisprudence regarding corporate responsibility for violations of international law.

Occasionally, cases under the ATS have alleged the direct commission of violations by a company as the principal perpetrator – for example, the private military company *Blackwater* as well as several of its private contractors were accused of war crimes committed against civilians in Iraq.[136] For the most part, however, cases against companies under ATS have involved claims of complicity, where the direct perpetrators of human rights violations were public or private security

---

129 Ibid.
130 International Commission of Jurists, *Corporate Complicity in International Crime* (n 2), vol III, 50–51.
131 J Kyriakakis, 'Corporations Before International Criminal Courts: Implications for the International Criminal Justice Project' (2017) 30(1) *Leiden J Intl L* 221, 233.
132 P Muchlinski, 'The Changing Face of Transnational Business Governance: Private Corporate Law Liability and Accountability of Transnational Groups in a Post Financial Crisis World' (2011) 18(2) *Indiana J Global Legal Studies* 665, 685–90; Kyriakakis (n 131), 232.
133 For example, UK (e.g. *Bodo v Shell*), Netherlands (e.g. *Oruma v Shell*), and Canada (e.g. *Anvil Mining* case).
134 van Ho (n 73); MV Hristova, 'The Alien Tort Statute: A Vehicle for Implementing the United Nations Guiding Principles for Business and Human Rights and Promoting Corporate Social Responsibility' (2012) 47 *Univ San Francisco L Rev* 89.
135 SH Cleveland, 'The Alien Tort Statute, Civil Society, and Corporate Responsibility' (2004) 56 *Rutgers L Rev* 971; B Stephens, 'Corporate Liability Before and After Sosa v. Alvarez-Machain' (2004) 56 *Rutgers L Rev* 995; RL Herz, 'The Liberalizing Effects of Tort: How Corporate Complicity Liability under the Alien Tort Statute Advances Constructive Engagement' (2008) 21 *Harvard Human Rights J* 207.
136 A suit was filed under the ATS on behalf of an injured survivor and three families of men killed in the incident.

forces, other government agents, or armed factions in civil conflicts.[137] These cases have produced a range of solutions.[138] Some courts that have dealt with ATS claims for company complicity in human rights abuses have referred to and applied the international criminal law standards of aiding and abetting.[139] Some federal courts cited the Nuremberg *Industrial* cases, which demonstrate how certain corporations could be an 'instrumentality of cohesion in the name of which the enumerated acts [...] were committed'.[140] Relying on this precedent, which did not recognize the actual criminal liability of corporations, the court, however, considered that 'limitations on criminal liability of corporations do not necessarily apply to civil liability of corporations', thus exploiting the civil aspect of the ATS to extend its reach to corporations.[141] The next sections discuss ATS cases most relevant in transitional justice contexts.

4.2.1. Litigation under the US Alien Tort Statute

Enacted in 1789, the ATS reads as follows: 'The District Courts shall have original jurisdiction of any civil action by an alien for a tort only, committed in violation of the law of nations or a treaty of the United States.'[142] In other words, it allows US courts to adjudicate civil actions involving breaches of international law.[143] Originally, the ATS was intended to protect against 'violation of safe conducts, infringement on the rights of ambassadors, and piracy' and the statute remained dormant for almost two centuries. In 1980, it was revived when it was successfully invoked in a claim on behalf of two Paraguayan nationals against a former Paraguayan police officer, based in New York at the time of the case, for having tortured to death a member of their family in Paraguay.[144] Although the ATS makes no reference to human rights, the claim led to the landmark decision *Filartiga v Pena-Irala*, which enabled victims of certain international human

---

137 For example, *Unocal* case, *Talisman* case (n 146). See also Special Representative of the Secretary-General on the Issue of Human Rights and Transnational Corporations and other Business Enterprises, John Ruggie, 'Clarifying the Concepts of "Sphere of influence" and "Complicity"' 15 May 2008, para 29; van Ho (n 73), 64; S Bhashyam, 'Knowledge or Purpose? The Khulumani Litigation and the Standard for Aiding and Abetting Liability Under Alien Tort Claims Act' (2008) 30 *Cardozo L Rev* 245, 248.

138 Y Farah, 'Toward a Multi-Directional Approach to Corporate Accountability', in Michalowski (n 73), 42.

139 For example, *Khulumani v Barclays National Bank*, 504 F.3d 254, 276 (2d Cir., 2007) [*Khulumani*]; *Almog v Arab Bank, PLC*, 471 F. Supp. 2d 257, 285–286 & n.33 (E.D.N.Y. 2007) [*Almog v Arab Bank*]; *Talisman* case (n 146).

140 Trials of War Criminals before the Nuremberg Military Tribunals under Control Council Law No. 10, Vol VIII.

141 Bismuth (n 1), 222–25.

142 Alien Tort Claims Act, 28 U.S.C. para 1350 (2000), a section of the Judiciary Act of 1789.

143 'Well-established, universally recognized norms of international law', as explained in *Kadic v Karadzic*, 70 F.3d 232, 239 (2d Cir. 1995).

144 *Filártiga v Peña-Irala* 630 F.2d 876 (2d Cir. 1980).

rights abuses to bring civil actions in US federal courts.[145] Access to judicial remedies in Paraguay had been denied by the dictatorship of General Alfredo Stroessner, and the ATS made it possible for victims to find a form of justice.

Following the *Filartiga* decision, a wave of human rights cases was filed under the ATS, and from the 1990s human rights advocates began to use the law against corporations for a wide range of activities, including complicity in torture, extra-judicial killings, enforced disappearances, arbitrary arrests and forced labour committed during times of conflict or repression.[146] Indeed, before the round of cases in the US courts, no corporation had ever been charged with or convicted for an international crime.[147] Occasional suggestions to the contrary by human rights scholars are mistaken.[148] This trend continued despite controversy about whether the original meaning of the ATS would allow such claims. Anthony Bellia and Bradford Clark explain that the ATS, taken in its original historical and legal context, is best understood as giving federal courts jurisdiction only to hear claims by aliens against American citizens for intentional acts of violence.[149] The law of nations required the United States to redress acts of violence by its own citizens against citizens of foreign nations by imposing criminal punishment, extraditing the offender or providing a civil remedy. Failure to redress such violence in one of these ways gave the offended nation just cause to retaliate against the United States, including through war. Because of this obligation under the law of nations, acts of violence by a citizen of one nation against a citizen of another were referred to as violations of the law of nations. As discussed by Bellia and Clark, the language of the ATS – 'where an

145 Ibid. See also B Stephens, 'Translating Filartiga: A Comparative and International Law Analysis of Domestic Remedies for International Human Rights Violations' (2002) 27 *Yale J Intl L* 1.

146 For example, *Doe v Unocal Corp.*, 963 F. Supp. 880 (C.D. Cal. 1997), 27 F. Supp. 2D 1174, 1184 (C.D. Cal. 1998), 110 F.Supp.2d 1294 (C.D. California, 2000), 248 F.3d 915 (9th Circuit, 2001), 395 F.3d 932 (9th Circuit, 2002) [*Unocal* case]; *Wiwa v Royal Dutch Petroleum Co.*, 225 F.3d 88 (2nd Circuit, 2000) [*Wiwa v Shell* case]; *Doe v Exxon Mobil Corp.*, 393 F. Supp. 2d 20 (D.D.C. 2005). 80 [*ExxonMobil* case]; *Presbyterian Church of Sudan v Talisman Energy, Inc.*, 2006 U.S. Dist. LEXIS 86609 (S.D.N.Y. Dec. 4, 2006). 82 [*Talisman* case]; *Mujica v Occidental Petroleum Co.*, 381 F. Supp. 2d 1164 (C.D.Cal. 2005) [*Occidental* case]. See also S Coliver and others, 'Holding Human Rights Violators Accountable by Using International Law in U.S. Courts: Advocacy Efforts and Complementary Strategies' (2005) 19 *Emory Intl L Rev* 169.

147 J Bush, 'The Prehistory of Corporations and Conspiracy in International Criminal Law: What Nuremberg Really Said' (2009) 109 *Columbia L Rev* 1098.

148 H Hongju Koh, 'Separating Myth from Reality About Corporate Responsibility Litigation' (2004) 7 *J Intl Econ L* 263, 266 (confusing Nuremberg tribunals that tried Flick, Krupp and I.G. Farben officials with Nuremberg tribunal that was permitted by 'the Nuremberg Charter' to designate groups or organizations as criminal, but that did not adjudge any corporations or firms); Stephens (n 145), 76 (confusing court's finding of Farben's offenses, for which evidence was abundant, with legal finding of corporate guilt as an entity).

149 AJ Bellia and BR Clark, 'The Alien Tort Statute and the Law of Nations' (2011) 78 *U Chi L Rev* 445; and 'Two Myths About the Alien Tort Statute' (2014) 18(1609) *Notre Dame L Rev*.

alien sues for a tort only in violation of the law of nations' – referred to just such violations.[150]

The following sections analyze tort actions under the ATS that have pursued compensation from corporations accused of complicity in abuses of regimes in Myanmar, Sudan, Indonesia and the Philippines, for their profits from the Holocaust and its victims, and for their involvement in the apartheid regime.[151] Tort litigation is not a transitional justice mechanism as such, but at times it has been used for the purpose of obtaining justice in times of transitions.

Unocal (re Myanmar)

In *Doe v Unocal*, the first ATS case brought against a corporation in 1996, a group of Myanmar nationals alleged that US-based *Unocal* (since bought by *Chevron*), aided and abetted the Myanmar military in the commission of human rights abuses such as forced labour, murder, rape and torture during the construction of a gas pipeline that runs across Myanmar into Thailand.[152] *Unocal* and Myanmar's military government were in a consortium for the pipeline's construction. The same charges were brought against the French oil company *Total*, the actual operating company of the joint venture with *Unocal*, but they were dismissed because *Total* lacked a sufficient business presence in the United States for US courts to exercise jurisdiction.[153] The trial court held that there was no evidence that the company desired the military's violation; as a result, *Unocal* could not be held liable. The court held that in order to be liable, *Unocal* must have taken active steps in cooperating or participating in forced labour activities. Mere knowledge that someone else might commit abuses was not sufficient.[154]

The court of appeals reversed the trial court's decision, setting a precedent by agreeing to hear cases whereby corporations are charged with human rights violations committed abroad. The court noted that for certain violations of international law private actors might be liable absent state action.[155] In relation to whether the ATS applies to corporations (*ratione personae*), it was established in *Karadzic* that some violations of the law of nations, including war crimes and violations of international humanitarian law, could be committed by non-state actors.[156] Citing the *Karadzic* decision, the court observed that participation in the slave trade 'violates the law of nations whether undertaken by those acting under the auspices of a state or only as private individuals'.[157] Just prior to a hearing by the court of appeals in 2004, the parties reached an out-of-court settlement, in which *Unocal* denied any

150 Ibid.
151 For example, *Unocal, ExxonMobil, Talisman* cases (n 146).
152 *Unocal* case (n 146).
153 The criminal case against *Total* in Belgium is discussed above.
154 Ramasastry, 'Corporate Complicity' (n 33), 130–39.
155 *Unocal* case (n 146).
156 *Kadić v Karadzić* (n 143).
157 Ibid., 891.

complicity but agreed to compensate the plaintiffs and provide funds for programmes in Myanmar to improve living conditions and protect the rights of people from the pipeline region – the exact terms of the settlement are confidential.[158]

Unocal is to this day the only decision under the ATS that regarded it as sufficient that the corporations should have been aware of the consequences of its acts. Relying on the *Furundzija* decision of the ICTY, the court set the *mens rea* standard to be one of 'actual or constructive (i.e. "reasonable") knowledge that [the accomplice's] actions will assist the perpetrator in the commission of the crime'.[159] Applying this to the facts of the case, the court regarded it as sufficient that 'Unocal knew or should reasonably have known that its conduct – including the payments and the instructions where to provide security and build infrastructure – would assist or encourage the Myanmar Military to subject the Plaintiffs to forced labour'.[160]

Talisman Energy (re South Sudan)

The extension of the ATS to corporations, expressly acknowledged in *Unocal*, was then explained in greater detail in *Presbyterian Church of Sudan v Talisman Energy* where the court considered that 'corporations may also be held liable under international law, at least for gross human rights violations'.[161] Canadian oil producer *Talisman*, which operated in the same South Sudan region as *Lundin*, above, was sued for supporting the Sudanese military during the civil war. The plaintiffs alleged that the Sudanese government was engaged in an armed campaign of ethnic cleansing against the non-Muslim Sudanese, which included massive displacement, extrajudicial killing, torture and rape. They alleged that *Talisman* was complicit in such crimes against people living in the area of *Talisman*'s oil concession and that these abuses amounted to genocide. The case was dismissed because of insufficient admissible evidence, and later the Court of Appeals found that to determine liability under the ATS the plaintiffs needed to show that the defendant 'purposefully' aided and abetted a violation of international law.[162] The Court of Appeals for the Second Circuit held that the claimants had failed to establish that *Talisman* 'acted with the purpose to support the Government's offences'.[163] Under the ATS the plaintiffs needed to show that 'Talisman acted with the purpose to advance the Government's human rights abuses'.[164] Arguably such *mens rea* standard has been set unreasonably high.

---

158 *Unocal* case (n 146).
159 *Unocal* case (n 146), 395 F.3d 932 (9th Cir. 2002), 950 (quoting *Prosecutor v Furundzija*, para 245).
160 Ibid., 953.
161 *Talisman* case (n 146).
162 Ibid.
163 *The Presbyterian Church of Sudan et al. v Talisman Energy, Inc. and Republic of The Sudan*, 2 Oct 2009.
164 The Supreme Court declined to grant certiorari and respectively to hear the appeal in this case.

Ingrid Gubbay criticizes the 'purpose test' established in the *Talisman* ruling, according to which a company is only liable for aiding and abetting violations of international law where it has provided substantial assistance *with the specific aim* of furthering the violation.[165] In *Talisman* the application of this test led to the conclusion that by letting the Sudanese regime use their airstrips, the company had not aided and abetted the international crimes of the regime because they did not share the intent of furthering the crimes. Arguably, it would have been more accurate to apply a looser test, known as the 'knowledge' test, whereby aiding and abetting is established if the company knew or should have known about the violations, without necessarily aiming to further the crimes.[166] The 'knowledge' element generally translates into the question: Did the business entity know, or should it have known, that the business activities contributed to international crimes or gross human rights violations?[167]

ExxonMobil (re Indonesia)

Another relevant ATS case concerns *ExxonMobil's* role in employing the Indonesian military forces (*Tentara Nasional Indonesia* – TNI) to protect its natural gas facilities in Aceh, Indonesia. In 2001, the International Labor Rights Fund brought a case in the US Federal Court under the ATS on behalf of 11 surviving family members of victims of human rights abuses, including torture, rape and killings, allegedly committed by members of the TNI. Following the discovery of vast natural gas fields, *ExxonMobil* helped build one of the largest and most profitable natural gas facilities in the world in Arun, north Aceh, in 1971. Very little of the profit that flowed from these operations remained in Aceh, and this inequality contributed to the formation of the Free Aceh Movement (*Gerakan Aceh Merdeka* – GAM) in 1976. In its initial contract with Suharto, the president of Indonesia from 1967 to 1998, *Mobil* (which later merged with *Exxon*) agreed to hire members of the TNI as private security personnel. As the security situation in Aceh deteriorated, *ExxonMobil* increased its reliance on the TNI.

According to the plaintiffs' claims, by 2000 *ExxonMobil* was paying more than US$500,000 a month to the TNI.[168] The lawsuit alleged that *ExxonMobil* helped to equip and train TNI members who provided private security to its Aceh operations.[169] The Indonesian government used the threat to the immense revenue generated at the Arun facility to justify its increased militarization of Aceh. This in turn led to escalation of the conflict between the TNI and GAM. Fighting

---

165 Lecture by I Gubbay, Hausfeld & Co LLP, at Institute of Advanced Legal Studies in London, 19 Feb 2013.
166 Ibid.
167 International Commission of Jurists, *Corporate Complicity in International Crime* (n 2), 18–20.
168 *ExxonMobil* case (n 146).
169 Ibid.

between GAM and the TNI had a severe impact on civilians, especially those who lived near the *ExxonMobil* facility. The plaintiffs argued that *ExxonMobil* should have been aware of the high degree of risk that TNI security personnel might commit human rights abuses.[170] The corporation should have taken appropriate measures after it became aware that Indonesian military forces acting as its agents were committing serious violations.

In 2015, after *Kiobel*, a US federal court ruled that the plaintiffs' claims sufficiently 'touch[ed] and concern[ed]' the Unites States and therefore could proceed in US courts.[171] The court accepted 'as true for purposes of this motion' the assertion that *ExxonMobil* exercised substantial control over the activities of the soldiers.[172] The significance of the *ExxonMobil* case in Aceh is that it provided a strong contribution to transitional justice processes in Indonesia. The *ExxonMobil* case represents an opportunity to investigate the conflict in Aceh and to give acknowledgment to the victims of the Indonesian military and indirectly the actions of multinational corporations. To date, there has been limited judicial accountability for crimes committed by the TNI in Aceh despite evidence of their involvement in mass crimes. Commitments that were part of the 2005 *Helsinki Memorandum of Understanding*, to establish a truth and reconciliation commission and a human rights court, have not been fulfilled.[173] Although this case does not examine every aspect of the Aceh conflict and represents the claims of only a small number of victims, it is important in achieving some degree of accountability for human rights abuses committed in Aceh. The case has dragged on for more than 16 years and victims are still waiting for justice.

Closing of the ATS door after Kiobel and Jesner decisions

Since the *South Africa Apartheid Litigation* judgment (analyzed below), whereby Judge Korman in his minority opinion raised the objection that multinational corporations might not be sued under the ATS as they are not subjects of international law, multinational corporations summoned in ATS litigations for violation of international human rights norms have started to include such an objection among their defence strategies.

In September 2010, this theory was upheld by the Court of Appeals for the Second Circuit in the *Kiobel v Royal Dutch Petroleum Co* case.[174] The Second Circuit dismissed *Kiobel*, with a divided opinion holding that the ATS did not

---

170 Ibid.
171 Ibid.
172 Ibid.
173 International Center for Transitional Justice, A Matter of Complicity? Exxon Mobil on Trial for its Role in Human Rights Violations in Aceh (ICTJ 2008), 3.
174 *Kiobel v Royal Dutch Petro. Co.*, 621 F.3d 111 (2d Cir. 2010), 642 F.3d 379 (2d Cir. 2011), 2011 WL 2326721 (U.S. June 6, 2011), 79 U.S.L.W. 3728 (U.S. Oct. 17, 2011) (No. 10–1491), 133 S.Ct. 1659 (2013) [*Kiobel* case].

apply to corporations.[175] The foundational premise relied upon by *Kiobel* is that the actors in international law are almost exclusively states – therefore, private corporations do not have obligations under international law and thus cannot have liability under the ATS.[176] *Sarei v Rio Tinto* had relied on dissolution of *I. G. Farben* after War World II and of jurisprudence of the International Court of Justice to find that prohibition against genocide extends to corporations.[177] But the Second Circuit in *Kiobel* relied on the fact that no international criminal tribunal has ever prosecuted a company.[178] The *Kiobel* majority asserted that the fact that only individuals were charged at Nuremberg definitively demonstrated that there was no accountability mechanism under international law for pursuing *I.G. Farben* as a juristic entity.[179] Tyler Giannini and Susan Farbstein rightly contend that 'this argument misses the mark': the lack of charges against the corporation does not indicate anything about corporate liability under international law.[180] The lack of criminal prosecution of corporations at Nuremberg does not support the conclusion in *Kiobel* that international law excludes juristic entities from liability. It only means that criminal prosecution was not chosen in that particular instance.[181]

In February 2012, during the Supreme Court oral arguments in the appeal, the focus shifted to the ATS's extraterritorial reach. Justice Kennedy questioned whether any other jurisdiction in the world 'permits its courts to exercise universal civil jurisdiction over alleged extraterritorial human rights abuses to which the nation has no connection'.[182] Thus, the Court ordered the parties to reargue the case on this question: 'Whether and under what circumstances the Alien Tort Statute

---

175 Ibid., 79 U.S.L.W. 3728 (U.S. Oct. 17, 2011) (No. 10–1491) (Leval, J. Concurring). See also, I Wuerth, 'The Supreme Court and the Alien Tort Statute: Kiobel v. Royal Dutch Petroleum Co.' (2013) 107 AJIL; A Colengelo, 'A Unified Approach to Extraterritoriality' (2011) 97 Virginia L Rev 1019 (2011).
176 *Kiobel* case (n 174), 621 F.3d, 122.
177 *Sarei v Rio Tinto*, US Court of Appeals, 9th circuit, nos. 02-5656, 0256390, 16 December 2008, 760–61.
178 *Kiobel* case (n 174), 132–45. See also van Ho (n 73), 62–63; O Murray, D Kinley and C Pitts, 'Exaggerated Rumors of the Death of an Alien Tort? Corporations, Human Rights and the Remarkable Case of Kiobel' (2011) 12 *Melb J Intl L* 57, 80–81; A Mamolea, 'The Future of Corporate Aiding and Abetting Liability Under the Alien Tort Statute: A Roadmap' (2011) 51 *Santa Clara L Rev* 79, 100–01.
179 *Kiobel* case (n 174), 2010 U.S. App. 19382, 32–33. See also *Khulumani* (n 139), Korman, J., dissenting.
180 T Giannini and S Farbstein, 'Corporate Accountability in Conflict Zones: How Kiobel Undermines the Nuremberg Legacy and Modern Human Rights' (2010) 52 *HILJ* 130.
181 Ibid., 131.
182 Justice Alito added: '[T]here's no particular connection between the events here and the United States [...] What business does a case like that have in the courts of the United States?' Chief Justice Roberts further added: 'If there is no other country where this suit could have been brought, regardless of what American domestic law provides, isn't it a legitimate concern that the suit itself contravenes international law?' *Kiobel* case (n 146), Transcript of Oral Argument, 3, 7, 8.

allows courts to recognize a cause of action for violation of the law of nations occurring within the territory of a sovereign other than the United States.'[183]

In April 2013, the Supreme Court dismissed the case for lack of jurisdiction under the ATS.[184] The ruling stated that the ATS could not be invoked for cases where the conduct did not 'touch and concern' the territory of the United States with sufficient force as to displace the 'presumption against extraterritorial application' (i.e. that the ATS does not apply to conducts outside the United States).[185] *Kiobel*'s denial of corporate liability in the ATS context generated a split of circuit authority[186] and divided scholarship,[187] including on whether corporations have direct human rights obligations under customary international law.[188] Arguments have been made to consider multinational corporations as 'modern day pirates'. Justice Breyer in a separate opinion considered 'pirates' in their modern form to include international violators such as 'torturers or perpetrators of genocide'.[189] This suggests that if multinational companies are alleged to be involved in such violations, they should be held accountable just like the pirates of the past.[190]

In April 2017, the US Supreme Court agreed to hear a new ATS case, *Jesner v Arab Bank*.[191] The sole question for consideration was whether the ATS

183 JG Ruggie, 'Kiobel and Corporate Social Responsibility. An Issues Brief', 4 September 2012.
184 Affaire Association France-Palestine Solidarité AFPS c/ Société Alstom Transport SA, Cour d'Appel de Versailles, 22 March 2013.
185 *Kiobel* (n 146), Case No 10-1491, 2013 (U.S. Apr. 17, 2013), 1669.
186 Compare *Kiobel* (n 146), 621 F.3d 111 2d Cir. 2010 (holding that private corporations cannot have liability) with *Doe v Exxon*, 654 F.3d 11 (D.C. Cir. 2011) (corporations can have liability).
187 B Thompson, 'Was Kiobel Detrimental to Corporate Social Responsibility: Applying Lessons Learnt from American Exceptionalism' (2014) 30 *Utrecht J Intl Europ L* 82; R McCorquodale, 'Waving Not Drowning: Kiobel Outside the United States' (2013) 107 *AJIL* 846; 'Debate: The Alien Tort Statute and Corporate Liability' (2011) 160 *Univ Pennsylvania L Rev* 99; U Kohl, 'Corporate Human Rights Accountability: the Objections of Western Governments to the Alien Tort Statute' (2014) 63 *Intl Comp L Quarterly* 665; B Stephens, 'The Curious History of the Alien Tort Statute' (2014) 89 *Notre Dame L Rev* 1467; R Alford, 'The Future of Human Rights Litigation After Kiobel' (2014) 89 *Notre Dame L Rev* 1749; J Ku, 'The Curious Case of Corporate Liability under the Alien Tort Statute: A Flawed System of Judicial Lawmaking' (2011) 51 *Va J Intl L* 353 (2011); Giannini and Farbstein (n 180); E Engle, 'Kiobel v. Royal Dutch Petroleum Co.: Corporate Liability Under The Alien Tort Statute' (2012) 34 *Hous J Intl L* 499.
188 Ku (n 187).
189 Ibid., Separate opinion by Justice Breyer, 5.
190 A Tamo, 'Corporate Complicity for Human Rights Violations in Africa Post-Kiobel Case', in J Letnar Černič and T van Ho (eds), *Human Rights and Business: Direct Corporate Accountability for Human Rights Abuses* (Wolf Legal Publishers 2015), 447, 470.
191 *Jesner v Arab Bank PLC*, No. 16-499. US-citizen plaintiffs sued under the Anti-terrorism Act (ATA), while non-US-citizen plaintiffs sued under the ATS. In the ATA suit, the district court found that *Arab Bank* knowingly provided financial services to persons that it knew to be terrorists. In the ATS suit, the district court dismissed, and

'categorically forecloses corporate liability.'[192] The case concerned *Arab Bank*, a Jordanian financial institutions, accused of processing financial transactions through its New York branch for Hamas and other groups linked to terrorism. The plaintiffs in the case, non-US citizens who were victims of terrorist attacks that occurred over a ten-year period in Israel and in the Palestinian territories, alleged that the bank maintained accounts for known terrorists and distributed millions of dollars to families of suicide bombers.[193] They said the bank facilitated acts of terrorism in the Middle East as it had 'served as the "paymaster" for Hamas and other terrorist organizations, helping them identify and pay the families of suicide bombers and other terrorists'.[194] While most of the claimants' allegations concerned conduct that occurred outside the United States, the claim sought to impose liability on *Arab Bank* for using its New York branch to clear dollar-denominated transactions that benefitted terrorists through a system known as 'Clearing House Interbank Payments System'.

The *Kiobel* decision has limited the claims that can be brought under the ATS for victims of corporate abuses, including in a transitional justice context. The Second Circuit majority, in the words of concurring Judge Leval, dealt 'a substantial blow to international law and its undertaking to protect fundamental human rights'.[195] In rejecting corporate liability under the ATS, the Second Circuit embraced a statist approach to international law. The decision in *Kiobel* contributed directly to the dismissal of at least three such cases: against *Chiquita*, against *Drummond* and in the *Apartheid Litigation* case.

In *Chiquita*, the first such case to reach the Supreme Court after *Kiobel*, in April 2015, the court declined to hear the case because all the relevant conduct occurred outside the United States. The case had been on-going since 2007. It concerned more than 4,000 plaintiffs who contended that the funds that *Chiquita* paid to Colombian paramilitary organizations, from the 1990s to 2004, made the company complicit in extrajudicial killings, torture, forced disappearances, crimes against humanity and war crimes committed in *Chiquita*'s Colombian banana-growing region.[196]

Several cases were also filed under the ATS against *Drummond*, a coal-mining company headquartered in the United States and operating in Colombia.[197] In 2002, the families of three deceased Colombian labour leaders, and the union they belonged to, filed a suit in US federal court against *Drummond* and its subsidiary in

---

the Second Circuit affirmed the dismissal, on the sole ground that under circuit precedent ATS cannot be brought against corporations.
192 Ibid.
193 Ibid.
194 Ibid.
195 *Kiobel* case (n 146), 2010 U.S. App. LEXIS 19382, at 113 (Leval, J., concurring). Judge Leval disagreed with the majority's position that corporate liability does not exist under customary international law, ibid., 113.
196 *In re: Chiquita Brands International, Inc.*, Alien Tort Statute and Shareholders Derivative Litigation, Transfer Order, Feb. 20, 2008.
197 *Romero v Drummond Company, Inc.*, 430 F.3d 1234, 1243 (11 Cir. 2007); *Estate of Rodriguez v Drummond Company, Inc*, 256 F Supp 2d 1250, 1257 (N.D. Ala. 2003).

Colombia. The plaintiffs alleged that *Drummond* hired Colombian paramilitaries to kill and torture the three labour leaders in 2001.[198] In 2009, the children of the three union leaders filed new lawsuits in the US alleging *Drummond's* complicity in the killings, and that the company had made payments to the paramilitary group *Autodefensas Unidas de Colombia* (AUC) to kill labour leaders. Those cases were dismissed on similar grounds: the courts found they no longer had jurisdiction to hear the case, citing the decision in *Kiobel*.[199]

The question then moves to what standard is necessary to provide a sufficient connection to the United States, to disprove the presumption against extra-territoriality. The *South Africa Apartheid Litigation*, detailed below, provides some elements to answer this question. In 2013, the Court of Appeal recommended dismissing the *Apartheid Litigation*, citing the limitation on extraterritorial application of the ATS in *Kiobel*. The lower court ruled that the plaintiffs could amend their complaints against two of the defendants to provide evidence that the companies' activities 'touch and concern' the territory of the United States.[200] The judge said that in order to overcome the presumption against extraterritoriality set forth in *Kiobel*, the plaintiffs must show corporate presence, in addition to other factors. In 2014, the lower court judge dismissed the case, finding that the plaintiffs had not shown a sufficient connection with the United States to warrant the case being heard in US courts.

While *Kiobel* has clearly narrowed the options under the ATS, it has not eliminated them. For example, in the case against *ExxonMobil*, examined above, a US federal court decided in 2015 that the claims sufficiently 'touch and concern[ed]' the United States as to overcome the presumption against extraterritoriality that has applied to ATS since *Kiobel*, and allowed the case to proceed. Noting that the 'primary inquiry in deciding whether the presumption against extraterritoriality is displaced is the location of the conduct at issue', the court found that plaintiffs had made 'numerous and detailed allegations' that *ExxonMobil* executives based in the United States had made decisions regarding the deployment of military security personnel in Indonesia. As federal courts continue to determine the parameters of the 'touch and concern' standard set forth in *Kiobel*, this decision is likely to be a key reference point for victims seeking remedies in transitional contexts.[201] As Austen Parrish notes: '*Kiobel* should not mark the end of human rights litigation [...] [rather, it] is time to rebuild the legitimacy of international law, and to reclaim international law and its institutions as primary methods for global governance'.[202] A later judgment, however, seems to have completely closed the doors to corporate liability under the ATS.

198 Ibid.
199 Ibid., on the basis that the 'allegations and evidence [...] do not show conduct focused in the United States'.
200 *Khulumani* (n 139).
201 *ExxonMobil* case (n 146).
202 A Parrish, 'Kiobel Insta-Symposium: A More Positive Outlook for International Law' (24 April 2013) Opinio Juris.

In *Kiobel*, the Supreme Court did not answer the question it had initially agreed to consider: whether corporations are categorically excluded from the law. The *Jesner* case produced that answer. The arguments in *Jesner* fell into three categories: (i) whether customary international law allows corporate liability; (ii) whether, as a matter of US domestic law, the ATS cause of action should be interpreted as allowing corporate liability; and (iii) whether the case against *Arab Bank* should be dismissed on other grounds. Whether customary international law permits corporate liability is the threshold question. In *Kiobel*, the Second Circuit held that corporations could never be held liable under the ATS because there is no 'norm of corporate liability under customary international law'. The Second Circuit relied heavily on international criminal tribunals from Nuremberg to the ICC only being given jurisdiction over natural persons. A number of *amici curiae*, however, contradict this point. Nuremberg Scholars' *amicus* brief, for example, shows it was understood at Nuremberg that judicial persons could violate international law and be held legal accountable for doing so.[203] The *amicus* brief filed by Ambassador David Scheffer, who led the US delegation in the negotiations that established the ICC, explains that corporations were excluded from the Rome Statute because of a lack of consensus on criminal, rather than civil liability, which, as detailed in Chapter 1.1, posed problems under the ICC's principle of complementarity.[204] On 11 October 2017, the Supreme Court heart oral arguments in the case.[205] The Supreme Court was divided. After the oral arguments, several of the justices appeared to be ready to hold that the ATS does not allow lawsuits against corporations, while others seemed to be trying to salvage a ruling that might eventually end the *Arab Bank* lawsuit while leaving the door open for future lawsuits against corporations.[206]

In April 2018, the Supreme Court rendered its judgment.[207] The ruling, decided by a 5-to-4 vote, upheld the decision of the Court of Appeals for the Second Circuit, according to which foreign corporations cannot be sued under the ATS. The decision in *Jesner* largely relied on the two-tier test set in the *Sosa v Alvarez-Machain* decision.[208] The first part of the *Sosa* test starts from the assumption that the ATS is strictly jurisdictional and does not itself provide causes of action for

---

203 Ibid., Nuremberg Scholars, On writ of certiorari to the United States Court of Appeals for the Second Circuit, Brief of Amici Curiae in support of petitioners.

204 Ibid., Ambassador David J. Sheffer, On writ of certiorari to the United States Court of Appeals for the Second Circuit, Brief of Amici Curiae in support of petitioners.

205 *Jesner v Arab Bank PLC*, No. 16-499.

206 A Howe, Supreme Court of the United States blog, 'Argument Analysis: Corporate liability for violations of international law on shaky ground', 11 Oct 2017, www.scotusblog.com/2017/10/argument-analysis-corporate-liability-violations-international-law-shaky-ground.

207 Jesner, 584 U.S. Supreme Court of the United States Syllabus Jesner et al. v Arab Bank, Plc Certiorari to the United States Court of Appeals for the Second Circuit No. 16-499, decided 24 April 2018.

208 Sosa, 542 U.S., 692. Supreme Court of the United States Syllabus Sosa v Alvarez-Machain et al. Certiorari to the United States Court of Appeals for the Ninth Circuit No. 03-339, decided 29 June 2004.

international law violations. Federal courts might allow new causes of action only for violations of rules that are 'specific, universal, and obligatory'.[209] The Court in *Jesner* applied the *Sosa* requirement to ask whether a rule of international law exists that establishes liability of corporations for human rights violations. While acknowledging that corporate liability might be permissible under international law in some circumstances, the Court affirmed that the claimants fell short of demonstrating the existence of a specific, universal and obligatory norm on liability for corporations.[210] As to the second part of the *Sosa* test, which bears on whether allowing a particular case to proceed is an appropriate exercise of judicial discretion, the Court asked whether federal courts have the authority to impose liability on foreign corporations under the ATS. The majority emphasized the perils of extending the scope of ATS liability to foreign multinational corporations, such as *Arab Bank*.[211] There are at least three different aspects of the ruling that deserve criticism.

First, the case could have been dismissed on *forum non conveniens* grounds or on the basis of non-justiciability concerns such as the act of state, political question and comity doctrines.[212] Instead, the Court went for an absolute ban of business and human rights ATS litigation against non-US companies. In the words of Justice Sotomayor writing for the dissenting minority, the decision amounts to 'us[ing] a sledgehammer to crack a nut'. The dissent of Justice Sotomayor blamed the reasoning and conclusion of the majority for 'absolving corporations from responsibility under the ATS for conscience-shocking behaviour'.[213] She concluded that '[f]oreclosing foreign corporate liability in all ATS actions, irrespective of circumstances or norm, is simply too broad a response to case-specific concerns that can be addressed via other means'. Requiring the plaintiff to prove the existence of a rule on corporate liability 'fundamentally misconceives how international law works'.[214]

209 542 U.S., 732.
210 L Chiussi, 'Jesner et al. v. Arab Bank, Plc: Closing the Door to Litigation Against Foreign Corporations Under the Alien Tort Statute?', *SIDIBlog*, 12 Sept 2018, www.sidiblog.org/2018/09/12/jesner-et-al-v-arab-bank-plc-closing-the-door-to-litigation-against-foreign-corporations-under-the-alien-tort-statute.
211 It was recalled that the purpose of the ATS was 'to promote harmony in international relations by ensuring foreign plaintiffs a remedy for international-law violations when the absence of such a remedy might provoke foreign nations to hold the United States accountable', 584 U.S., 25. In his concurring opinion, Justice Alito stressed that extending the scope of the ATS would precipitate exactly the sort of diplomatic strife that the law was enacted to prevent (Justice Alito, concurring in part and concurring in judgment U.S. 584, 1).
212 N Bernaz, 'Unnecessary, Wrong, and Misguided – the US Supreme Court's Blanket Ban on All ATS Suits against Foreign Corporations in Jesner v Arab Bank', *Rights as Usual*, 25 April 2018, www.rightsasusual.com/?p=1202.
213 Justice Sotomayor, with whom Justice Ginsburg, Breyer, and Kagan, dissenting, 584 U.S, 1.
214 584 U.S., Justice Sotomayor, Dissenting, 2.

Second, assessing the existence of a given rule is not to be confused with the question of whether an international institution exists to enforce such rule.[215] Justice Kennedy emphasized that there are no international criminal courts and tribunals with jurisdiction over corporate violations of international law.[2-6] Yet this only tells us that states have not, so far, agreed on an international mechanism to address corporate violations. In other words, a rule on corporate liability may very well exist regardless of the mechanism chosen by states to enforce it.[217] In fact, the great majority of legal systems in the world recognize corporate liability in some forms.[218] This could have led the Court to enquire whether corporate liability has evolved into a general principle of law.

Third, foreign policy concerns weighed in *Jesner*. A cause of concern for the Court was the possibility that allowing to sue foreign corporations under the ATS 'could subject American corporations to an immediate, constant risk of claims seeking to impose massive liability for the alleged conduct of their employees and subsidiaries around the world, all as determined in foreign courts'.[219] Jordan considered the suit against *Arab Bank* 'a direct affront' to its sovereignty and one that 'risk[ed] destabilizing Jordan's economy and undercutting one of the most stable and productive alliances the United States has in the Middle East'.[220] But the utilitarian approach adopted by Justice Alito, according to which 'unless corporate liability would actively decrease diplomatic disputes, we have no authority to act', finds no support in the text of the ATS.[221] Dissenting with the majority, Justice Sotomayor noted that 'nothing about the corporate form in itself raises foreign policy concerns that require the Court, as a matter of common law discretion, to immunize all foreign corporations from liability under the ATS'.[222] To think that the mere possibility of an ATS lawsuit against foreign corporations could 'discourage' US corporations from investing abroad seems misguided. Such lawsuits were possible before the decision in *Jesner* and US corporations had not refrained from investing abroad for that reason.[223]

The South Africa Apartheid Litigation

South Africa's transition from apartheid to democracy in 1994 is emblematic of the complex challenges that make corporate accountability and reparations for

215 Chiussi (n 210); Bernaz (n 212).
216 584, Justice Kennedy, 14–15.
217 Chiussi (n 210).
218 No. 16-499 in the Supreme Court of the United States Joseph Jesner et al., Petitioners, v Arab Bank, Plc., Respondent. on a Writ of Certiorari to the United States Court of Appeals for the Second Circuit Brief of Amici Curiae of Comparative Law Scholars and Practitioners in Support of Petitioners, 27 June 2017.
219 584 U.S., 24.
220 Brief for Hashemite Kingdom of Jordan as Amicus Curiae, 4.
221 Chiussi (n 210).
222 Ibid, 1.
223 Bernaz (n 212).

victims a difficult issue for transitional justice.[224] This is particularly clear in the way in which South Africa's TRC dealt with the issue of corporate involvement with apartheid (examined in Chapter 5). It also shows the potential and problems of using the courts to hold corporations liable to redress the shortcomings of the TRC's approach and the government's implementation of the TRC's recommendations. The payment of reparations was described as the 'unfinished legacy' of the TRC. To the extent that the ATS facilitated the payment of reparations, it can be considered a mechanism of transitional justice.[225]

As detailed in Chapter 5, in its final report, the South Africa TRC extensively documented the central role businesses played in sustaining the economy during apartheid.[226] The TRC recommended a number of reparation measures for business, including, for example, a one-off 'wealth tax' on businesses that profited from apartheid. The South Africa government, however, did not implement any of the TRC's recommendations concerning business, leaving victims unsatisfied.[227] As a consequence, in 2002, four years after the publication of the TRC report, lawsuits were filed in the United States on behalf of South African victims against several multinationals corporations for aiding and abetting or otherwise participating in violations committed by the apartheid regime. The *South Africa Apartheid Litigation* addresses two cases in its 2009 consolidated amendment: the *Khulumani v Barclays* case and the *Ntsebeza v Daimler* case.[228]

In 2002, a group of South Africans, represented by the Khulumani Support Group, sued 20 banks and corporations that did business in South Africa during apartheid in US federal courts.[229] The case alleged that from the 1960s to the demise of apartheid in the early 1990s these corporations made it possible for key areas of apartheid to continue to operate despite a mounting worldwide campaign to isolate the South African government.[230] The plaintiffs alleged that the participation of the defendant companies in key industries during the apartheid era was influential in

---

224 P Clark and others, 'Justice for Apartheid Crimes: Corporations, States, and Human Rights' (2009) Oxford Transitional Justice Research.

225 M Swart, 'The Khulumani Litigation: Complementing The Work of the South African Truth and Reconciliation Commission' (2011) 16 *Tilburg L Rev* 30; C Abrahams, 'Lessons from the South African Experience' in Michalowski (n 73), 153.

226 Truth and Reconciliation Commission of South Africa, *Final Report* (29 October 1998), Volume IV, Chapter II, 140.

227 E Daly, 'Reparations in South Africa: A Cautionary Tale' (2003) 33 *U Mem L Rev* 367, 383–87.

228 *In re South African Apartheid Litigation*, 617 F. Supp. 2d 228 (S.D.N.Y. 2009) [*South African Apartheid Litigation*]. For commentary on the case, see D Fig, 'Manufacturing Amnesia: Corporate Social Responsibility in South Africa' (2005) 81(3) *Intl Affairs* 599; Swart (n 225); S Michalowski, 'No Complicity Liability for Funding Gross Human Rights Violations?' (2012) 30 *Berkeley J Intl L* 451, 454–70; Abrahams (n 225); I Gubbay, 'Towards Making Blood Money Visible: Lessons Drawn from the Apartheid Litigation' in JP Bohoslavsky and J Letnar Černič (eds) *Making Sovereign Financing & Human Rights Work* (Hart 2014).

229 *South African Apartheid Litigation* (n 228).

230 Ibid.

encouraging and furthering abuses against black Africans. The plaintiffs were victims or relatives of victims of human rights abuses such as extrajudicial killings, torture and rape, and they alleged that the companies' activities in South Africa during the apartheid era made them complicit in the commission of those abuses.[231] The claimants relied on the legal theory of secondary liability for aiding and abetting crimes, arguing that banks and corporations aided and abetted the apartheid regime in the commission of international crimes. The original complaint argued:

> The participation of the defendants, companies in the key industries of oil, armaments, banking, transportation, technology, and mining, was instrumental in encouraging and furthering the abuses. Defendants' conduct was so integrally connected to the abuses that apartheid would not have occurred in the same way without their participation.[232]

The *Apartheid Litigation* received a wide array of criticism.[233] The issue of apartheid, some critics said, had already been resolved domestically by South Africa; the TRC ran its course, and it achieved the peaceful transition to democracy that it was intended to achieve.[234] Digging the issues back up, as a scholar suggested, would 'subvert what the Truth and Reconciliation Commission sought to achieve'.[235] John Bellinger, a Legal Adviser to the US Secretary of State, remarked in 2008:

> Imagine what the U.S. reaction would be if a Swiss court sought to adjudicate claims brought against U.S. government officials or businesses for Jim Crow-era racial restrictions, or [...] even for slavery [...] The United States has come to terms with and sought to remedy the effects of slavery and Jim Crow laws through domestic measures. From the South African perspective, the apartheid case must look very similar.[236]

The South African government initially opposed the lawsuit, and it filed documentation with both the district court and appeals court urging to dismiss the case.[237] The main argument of the so-called 'Maduna declaration' was that litigation in the United States interfered with South Africa's sovereignty.[238] The government officially

231 Ibid.
232 Ibid. See also, Abrahams (n 225), 162–72.
233 JB Bellinger, Former Legal Advisor to US Secretary of State, 'Enforcing Human Rights in US. Courts and Abroad: The Alien Tort Statute and Other Approaches', Remarks at 2008 Jonathan I. Charney Lecture in International Law (2008).
234 J Simcock 'Unfinished Business: Reconciling The Apartheid Reparation Litigation With South Africa's Truth and Reconciliation Commission' (2011) 47 *Stan J Intl L* 239, 240–41.
235 Ibid.
236 Bellinger (n 233).
237 PM Maduna, 'Declaration by Justice Minister Pennell Maduna on Apartheid Litigation in the United States', 11 July 2003 [Maduna declaration].
238 Ibid., para 2.

justified their opposition to the *Apartheid Litigation* with the concern that such a lawsuit could discourage foreign investment in South Africa and therefore be detrimental to the country's economic development.[239] The government attention focused on economic growth as a remedy to the apartheid legacy, which resulted in a policy of non-confrontation toward corporations and a lack of political will to follow the TRC recommendations regarding the accountability of corporations for their role in apartheid.[240] The government approach to the recommendations of the TRC was influenced by its 'Growth, Employment, and Redistribution' policy, which acknowledged the importance of 'fast economic growth and job creation as the only way out of poverty, inequality, and unemployment'.[241] Foreign and local private sector investment was regarded as crucial to achieve these goals. This is a common trend in transitional justice countries – for example, as discussed in the next three chapters, the governments of Liberia and Myanmar have taken similar approaches.

The government said that South Africa deliberately avoided a 'victors' justice' approach to the crimes of apartheid and opted instead for a transitional justice process based on 'reconciliation, reconstruction, reparation and goodwill'.[242] It considered the remedies claimed before the US courts to be inconsistent with the government strategy of achieving reconciliation and social transformation through economic growth in partnership with private actors, including corporations.[243] The government feared that the litigation could have a negative effect on foreign investment so 'undermining economic stability'.[244] Alex Boraine, the vice-chairman of the TRC, argued that the lawsuit 'could damage investment and new jobs just when we need business to come here'.[245] The avoidance of confrontation with the legacy of corporations by the South African government, however, is inconsistent with the aim of achieving justice for victims of their complicit behaviour. By focusing on growth, the government confused the rights of victims with the constitutionally guaranteed socioeconomic rights of all disadvantaged citizens. For example, claims of victims of torture or killing of family members should not be confused with general claims of all victims of apartheid to be lifted out of poverty and social exclusion.

The government claims were contested by Archbishop Desmond Tutu, the TRC's chairman, and by other commissioners, who filed *amici curiae* in support of the litigation, which they considered 'entirely consistent' with the findings of the TRC.[246] They argued that the litigation was unlikely to affect investment

---

239 Ibid.
240 Abrahams (n 225), 158–62.
241 Maduna declaration (n 237).
242 Ibid., para 3.2.1.
243 Ibid., para 10.
244 Ibid., para 12.
245 Cited in I Evans, 'Multinationals face damages claim from victims of apartheid', *The Observer*, 18 May 2008.
246 Brief of Amici Curiae Commissioners and Committee Members of South Africa's Truth and Reconciliation in Support of Appellants, United States Court of Appeal for the Second Circuit, 30 August 2005, 1–2.

decisions and instead would have a positive effect of deterring threats to 'inequitable economic growth in South Africa'.[247] They pointed out that the TRC proceedings precluded litigation only against perpetrators who had been granted amnesties, which none of the defendant companies had received. 'There was absolutely nothing in the TRC process, its goals, or the pursuit of the overarching goal of reconciliation, linked with the truth, that would be impeded by this litigation', the commissioners said.[248] They further added that litigation was in line with the goals of transitional justice: 'by giving voice to those harmed by multinational corporations aiding and abetting apartheid, it assists the healing of the reconciliation process'.[249] Archbishop Tutu had already concluded after the business hearings that these 'did not mean the end of the process, as there was the question of restitution and repairing the wrongs done'.[250]

The TRC process 'did not put an end to the pursuit of accountability for human rights violations committed under apartheid (but) in fact started it'.[251] The TRC expressly recognized bases for civil and criminal liability of certain business for their actions, including aiding and abetting crimes committed by the apartheid regime. Serious findings were made against specific corporations.[252] The TRC also suggested the existence of legal grounds for instituting a claim for reparations based on the enforceability of contracts that had been contrary to public policy.[253] The TRC report stated that, going forward, there were 'legal grounds for instituting claims for reparations against banks and other corporations'.[254] Although the TRC provided little clarification of the type of legal mechanisms it was referring to, it appeared clear that some form of legal proceedings was considered valid.[255] The Commission acknowledged that the scope of its findings regarding business involvement was limited, and left the door open for future proceedings. The *Apartheid Litigation* drew significantly on the work of the TRC in terms of the factual findings made against companies and the Commission's articulation of legal responsibility.[256] Indeed, the *Apartheid Litigation* needs to be understood as 'a logical continuation

247 Ibid., 16.
248 Ibid., 14.
249 Ibid., 15–16.
250 Cited in South African Press Association, 'Some Glaring Absences in Business Submissions to TRC: Tutu', 11 November 1997.
251 International Center for Transitional Justice, Brief of *Amicus Curiae* in the United States Court of Appeals for the Second Circuit, 30 November 2009.
252 TRC of South Africa (n 226), Volume IV, Chapter II, 144, 151–155.
253 Ibid., 146–47.
254 Ibid. See also M Seekoe, 'Reparations', in C Villa-Vicencio and F du Toit (eds), *Truth and Reconciliation in South Africa: 10 Years On* (New Africa Books 2006), 36.
255 TRC of South Africa (n 226). See also,Abrahams (n 225), 158–62.
256 AR Chapman and H van der Werwe, 'Reflections on the South African Experience' in AR Chapman and Hugo van der Werwe (eds), *Truth and Reconciliation in South Africa; Did the TRC Deliver?* (University of Pennsylvania Press 2008), 286.

of the outcome of the TRC'.[257] With it, victims extended efforts to hold corporations accountable beyond the truth-seeking process – which, as discussed in the next chapter, suffered from a number of limitations.

In 2009, after the decision in the district court, the government changed its view and announced its support of the lawsuit, withdrawing its previous opposition. The South African Justice Minister sent a letter to the district court judge informing her that the government believed the court to be the appropriate forum to decide this case.[258] This change was also linked with a new economic policy based on state-led development, and not only on free market practices.[259] The *Apartheid Litigation* illustrates the consequences of the political tensions between justice and reconciliation with regard to corporations.[260] The failure of transitional justice in South Africa to hold corporations accountable was inherent in the design of the South African transitional justice model, animated as it was by a spirit of 'reconciliation'.[261] Some scholars saw the *Apartheid Litigation* as an opportunity for some companies to prove that they were not complicit in apartheid, and to be free of any such stigma in the international community.[262] In this regard, however, the litigation did little in terms of establishing the role of business in apartheid.[263]

After years of proceedings, the claims were first narrowed to proceed only against *Daimler, Ford, General Motors, IBM* and *Rheinmetall*, and then allowed only against *IBM* and *Ford*.[264] The court dismissed aiding and abetting claims against the banks. It dismissed, for example, the claims against *Barclays* and *UBS* for loaning money to the South African government.[265] It based its decision on the grounds that commercial loans were too far removed from human rights violations carried out by their recipients for a legally relevant link to exist.[266] The court considered that 'simply doing business with a state or individual who violate the law of nations is insufficient to create liability under customary international law'.[267] As a consequence, the only claims that remained were those where the court found that the goods and services provided by the defendant corporation

---

257 C Abrahams, 'The TRC's Unfinished Business: Reparations', in Villa-Vicencio and du Toit (eds), *Truth and Reconciliation in South Africa: 10 Years On* (New Africa Books 2006), 34, 36.
258 Minister Justice and Constitutional Development, 'Re South African Apartheid Litigation' (MDL 1499).
259 Abrahams (n 225), 176–80.
260 Abrahams, 'The TRC's Unfinished Business' (n 257), Abrahams (n 225), 158–62.
261 R Carranza, 'Transitional Justice, Corporate Responsibility and Learning from the Global South', 28 April 2015, http://jamesgstewart.com/transitional-justice-corporate-resp onsibility-and-learning-from-the-global-south/?subscribe=success#blog_subscription-2.
262 Simcock (n 234), 242, 249–53.
263 Abrahams (n 225).
264 *South African Apartheid Litigation* (n 228).
265 Ibid., Judge Scheinlin.
266 Ibid., 269.
267 Ibid., 257, Judge Sprizzo.

had provided the direct means for carrying out the violations, such as the sale of vehicles with military specifications or the design of computer software to implement the policy of geographical segregation and racial discrimination.[268] For example, the court allowed the case to go forward and be heard against IBM for providing computers and software to the apartheid regime, charging that it had helped to implement a 'de-nationalization' policy against black South Africans.[269] The plaintiffs later reached a settlement with *General Motors*. In 2015, the case was dismissed because, after the decision in *Kiobel*, the connection with the United States was not sufficient to warrant the case being heard in US courts.[270]

The issue of corporate complicity was discussed during the litigation. On appeal to the Second Circuit, Judge Korman (dissenting) regarded the complaints as being about nothing other than condemning the defendants for having done business with the apartheid regime,[271] something that in itself would not be sufficient to trigger legal liability for complicity:

> [I]t is (or should be) undisputed that simply doing business with a state or individual who violates the law of nations is insufficient to create liability under customary international law. International law does not impose liability for declining to boycott a pariah state or to shun a war criminal. Aiding a criminal 'is not the same thing as aiding and abetting [his or her] alleged human rights abuses'.[272]

The original complaints in the *Apartheid Litigation* requested damages and also sought broad equitable relief – for example, the institution of affirmative action education and training programmes.[273] But because of the nature of the ATS, the *Apartheid Litigation* aimed to provide exclusively monetary reparations to victims seeking punitive as well as compensatory damages. To that end, the litigation was aligned with the TRC's desire to leave civil obligations intact, and also with the Committee's ultimate decision to provide monetary compensation to victims, as the preferred form of reparation.[274] The South African government originally opposed the litigation, asserting that reparations should be addressed through a broad programme of socioeconomic transformation.[275]

In the end, the *Apartheid Litigation* did not compensate the victims in the way they hoped. As seen, the claims were dismissed and only one of the corporations involved, *General Motors*, agreed to a settlement in 2012, ten years after the

268 Ibid., 264–66. See also Abrahams (n 225), 162–67; Michalowski (n 228).
269 *South African Apartheid Litigation* (n 228), 265.
270 Ibid.
271 Ibid., 294, Judge Korman (dissenting).
272 Ibid., 257.
273 Gubbay (n 228), 345.
274 Simcock (n 234), 259–60.
275 Hausfeld LLP, 'South African Government withdraws opposition to apartheid lawsuits pending in US federal court', 3 Sept 2009.

beginning of the litigation. It agreed to pay US$1.5 million in shares in the company without acknowledging responsibility for apartheid crimes. The shares were to be placed into a trust fund and converted into money to be shared between the 25 plaintiffs and the Khulumani Support Group. The positive aspect of this approach is that the beneficiaries were not limited to the plaintiffs in the case, but also included victims more generally, such as those who may have been equally harmed but did not meet the requirements to qualify as plaintiffs in the lawsuit.[276] There are important lessons from this case, in particular in relation to the debate on the role of financial actors and their potential responsibility for complicity in gross human rights violation.

4.2.2. Financial complicity

Authoritarian regimes need money to obtain minimal support and make the repressive machinery work. In case of fiscal deficit and a deteriorating national economy, external financiers (be they aid agencies or private banks) play a fundamental role. The *Apartheid Litigation* decision draws a distinction between the provision of goods or commodities and the provisions of loans or financial contributions. Without doing an analysis of the concrete effect of the loans, the ruling established that funds could never be sufficiently connected to the crimes, because they are not 'lethal commodities'.[277] For some, the decision of the *Apartheid Litigation* to narrow the claims is in line with the TRC's 'closed list' approach, when it established the requirements for reparation eligibility, and that limiting complicity liability to instances in which the corporation contributed some form of substantial assistance is also in line with the TRC's efforts to stratify degrees of corporate involvement.[278] According to Juan Pablo Bohoslavky, this differentiation, which focuses on the intrinsic qualities of the goods rather than assessing the provisions' use and impacts, instead used a confusing rationale:

> On one hand, it accepted that the computers provided by IBM to the apartheid regime were 'sufficiently risky' commodities in their connection to aiding in the denationalization of black South Africans, thus contributing to the State's crimes. Simultaneously, however, the court asserted that even lethal gas could be used in some cases for so-called legitimate purposes.[279]

The *Apartheid Litigation* ruling, which denied that financial assistance could contribute to or facilitate human rights abuses, represents a conservative and narrow interpretation of previous developments in international law with regard to

---

276 C Sandoval and G Surfleet, 'Corporations and Redress in Transitional Justice Processes' in Michalowski (n 73), 107.
277 *South African Apartheid Litigation* (n 228).
278 Simcock (n 234), 254–55, 257.
279 Bohoslavky and Opgenhaffen (n 104), 177.

corporate complicity, particularly for financing *ius cogens* violations.[280] The view of the court was that money is inherently neutral and loans are always too far removed from the violations carried out by their recipients. In its decision, the court, using the 'inherent quality' of the commodities as its criterion, made a distinction between an agent such as poison gas being provided to a regime (referring to the post–War World II *Zyklon B* case analyzed in Chapter 1) and a fungible resource, such as finance or investment (referring to the *Ministries* case), which it felt did not meet the legal standards for responsibility in this case.[281] The court decided when analyzing the *actus reus* component that loans could not empirically be sufficiently connected to the crimes in question.[282]

The criterion of 'inherent quality' seems to ignore the very definition of money as a good that acts as a medium of exchange in transactions, a unit of account and a store of value.[283] Money allows its holder to do something by virtue of its purchasing power. Therefore, what is crucial is what the holder will do with it and this is the point where the foreseeable consequences of giving money to someone enter into play. By dismissing the claims against the banks, the *Apartheid Litigation* implies immunity for banks from the consequences of their actions.[284] The decision creates an exemption for commercial lenders from complicity liability, without the requirement of a case-by-case analysis or an examination of the lender's *mens rea*.

The court relied on the *Ministries* case as the sole authority in support of the rejection of complicity liability for commercial loans, but developments in international law do not justify such a conclusion.[285] Since the Nuremberg trials, the notion of accomplice liability in international criminal law has developed considerably and financing human rights abuses has been increasingly denounced.[286] Particularly instructive in this respect is the decision in *Almog v Arab Bank*.[287] The plaintiffs alleged that *Arab Bank* 'aided and abetted, was complicit in, intentionally facilitated, and participated in a joint venture to engage in acts of genocide in violation of the laws of nations by providing financial and other practical assistance [...] to HAMAS'.[288] With regard to the question of whether routine

280 JP Bohoslavsky and M Rulli, 'Corporate Complicity and Finance as a "Killing Agent": The Relevance of the Chilean Case' (2010) 8 *JICJ* 8 829, 830, 836, 838, 840, 847.
281 S Michalowski and JP Bohoslavsky, 'Ius Cogens, Transitional Justice and other Trends of the Debate on Odious Debts. A Response to the World Bank Discussion Paper on Odious Debts' (2010) 48 *Columbia J Transnatl L* 61.
282 *South African Apartheid Litigation* (n 228), 70.
283 Bohoslavsky and Rulli (n 281), 835.
284 Bohoslavky and Opgenhaffenv (n 104), 159.
285 Trials of War Criminals Before the Nurenberg Military Tribunals Under Control Council Law No. 10, 478 (Nurenberg Military Tribunals 1950).
286 For example, *Unocal* case (n 146), 395 F.3d 932 (9th Cir. 2002); *Burnett v Al Baraka Inv. & Dev. Corp.*, 274 F. Supp. 2d 86 (D.D.C. 2003). See also SW Scott, 'Taking Riggs Seriously: The ATCA Case Against a Corporate Abettor of Pinochet Atrocities' (2005) 89 *Minn L Rev* 1497, 1533–34.
287 *Almog v Arab Bank* (n 139) 471 F. Supp. 2d 257 (E.D.N.Y. 2007).
288 Ibid.

banking activities can give rise to complicity liability, the Court maintained that 'acts which in themselves may be benign, if done for a benign purpose, may be actionable if done with the knowledge that they are supporting unlawful acts'.[289]

In March 2005, a US Senate's report found that the former Chilean dictator Augusto Pinochet and his family hid US$15 million in more than 125 accounts at banks that included *Riggs* and *Citigroup*.[290] Pinochet, whose regime killed more than 3,000 people and tortured about 28,000 between 1983 and 2000, used the accounts to move funds from offshore holding companies to personal accounts in the US and to transfer cash to Chile. According to a member of the sub-committee: 'Some banks actively helped him hide his funds; others failed to comply with US regulations requiring banks to know their customers.' In January 2005, *Riggs* had already admitted to failing to report suspicious transactions, pleaded guilty to US money laundering charges, and agreed to pay US$8 million to the victims of the Chilean dictatorship.

Already in 1978, Antonio Cassese, a public international law jurist, had pre-pared a report, commissioned by the then UN Commission on Human Rights, on the role played by lenders in Chile during the Pinochet dictatorship.[291] The 'Cassese Report' explained in detail how the financial aid received by the regime facilitated human rights abuses in Chile.[292] In his 260-page report, Cassese developed a sophisticated methodology to evaluate the impact of the financial aid on the human rights situation, concluding:

> As foreign economic assistance largely serves to strengthen and prop up the economic system adopted by the Chilean authorities, which in its turn needs to be based on the repression of civil and political rights, the conclusions warranted that the bulk of present economic assistance is instrumental in consolidating and perpetuating the present repression of those rights.[293]

But the Cassese Report was 'inexplicably ignored for decades by those engaging in the corporate complicity debate'.[294] The commission of international crimes, which by definition are large scale, requires finance to pay for the equipment and human resources that crimes of that magnitude entail.[295] Lenders that provide funds used to finance international crimes are often banks and other private financial entities,

289 Ibid., 471 F. Supp. 2d 291-92 (E.D.N.Y. 2007).
290 US Senate Permanent Subcommittee on Investigations.
291 A Cassese, 'Study on the impact of foreign Economic Aid and Assistance on Respect for Human Rights in Chile', E/CN.4/Sub.2/412, 1978 (Vol I–IV).
292 Ibid., Vol I, 3, 18.
293 Ibid., Vol IV, 24.
294 A Cassese, 'Foreign Economic Assistance and Respect for Civil and Political Rights: Chile – A Case Study' (1979) 14 *Texas Intl LJ* 251, 251–53. See also Bohoslavsky and Rulli (n 281), 830, 836, 838, 840, 847.
295 N Bernaz, 'Establishing Liability for Financial Complicity in International Crimes' in Bohoslavsky and Letnar Černič (n 228), 61.

and gains from those crimes are often deposited in private banks.[296] As Anita
Ramasastry puts it, 'What do Hitler and Marcos have in common? Their bankers.
Both leaders used numbered Swiss accounts in order to deposit ill-gotten gains.'[297]
But financial complicity in international crimes and gross human rights abuses is
extremely difficult to establish. Establishing liability in law, civil or criminal, requires
a careful examination of causation and other key elements such as knowledge or
foreseeability, and proximity.[298] Even if it is recognized that corporations can be
held accountable for complicity, there remains confusion about the scope of this
responsibility and its broader implications.[299]

For example, one question that may arise is whether investors may bear secondary responsibility for human rights violations committed using funds they have
provided. The challenge in specific cases is to determine when neutral business
activities, such as providing goods or financial resources, have turned into legally
relevant behaviour and thus become an act of complicity with the perpetrator. In
the context of financing, there is a need for analysis of the *actus reus* and causation
elements of complicity liability.[300] The international standard defining the *actus
reus* of liability in international law,[301] which is consistently applied by US courts
in the context of corporate complicity liability[302] and widely accepted in the relevant academic literature,[303] is that of 'practical assistance, encouragement, or
moral support which has a substantial effect on the perpetration of the crime'.[304]
The assistance 'need not constitute an indispensable element, that is, a *conditio
sine qua non* for the acts of the principal'.[305] Instead, it is sufficient that the acts of
the accomplice make a significant difference to the commission of the criminal act
by the principal. Further, *Mastafa v Australian Wheat Board Limited and Banque*

296 See e.g. on-going lawsuits against *BNP Paribas* alleging the bank's complicity in war
crimes in Sudan and Rwanda in the section 'BNP Paribas' below.
297 A Ramasastry, 'Secrets and Lies? Swiss Banks and International Human Rights' (1998)
31 *V and J Transnatl L* 325, 328
298 International Commission of Jurists, *Corporate Complicity and Legal Accountability*
(n 2), Vol I, 8.
299 Bohoslavky and Opgenhaffenv (n 104), 159.
300 Michalowski, 'No Complicity Liability' (n 228).
301 Report of the International Law Commission, Article 2(3)(d) of Draft Code of Crimes
against the Peace and Security of Mankind, U.N. GAOR, 48th Sess., Supp. No. 10,
U.N. Doc. A/51/10 (1996).
302 See e.g. *Khulumani* (n 39); *Talisman* case (n 146), 324; *Almog v Arab Bank* (n 139),
287; *South African Apartheid Litigation* (n 228), 257.
303 A Clapham and S Jerbi, 'Categories of Corporate Complicity in Human Rights
Abuses' (2011) 24 *Hastings Intl Comp L Rev* 339, 344; D Cassel, 'Corporate Aiding
and Abetting of Human Rights Violations: Confusion in the Courts' (2008) 6
Northwestern Univ J Intl Human Rights 304, 16; Ramasastry, 'Corporate Complicity'
(n 33), 143. International Commission of Jurists, *Corporate Complicity and Legal
Accountability* (n 2), Vol II, 17.
304 *Prosecutor v Furundzija* (Case No: IT-95-17/1-T), 235.
305 Ibid., 209.

Nationale de Paris Paribas, a case on corporate complicity brought under the ATS, describes the relevant standard as follows:

> It is not enough that a defendant provides substantial assistance to a tortfeasor; the 'substantial assistance' must also 'advance the [tort's] commission' [...] [P]roviding the Hussein regime with funds – even substantial funds – does not aid and abet its human rights abuses if the money did not advance the commission of the alleged human rights abuses. This does not mean that plaintiffs must allege that the particular funds provided were used to commit the abuses, or that without the funds the Hussein regime would not have been able to commit such abuses, so long as the assistance is 'a substantial factor in causing the resulting tort'.[306]

The International Commission of Jurists has developed some helpful criteria to distinguish corporate complicity in international crimes from neutral business activity.[307] It considered that the 'liability of a financier will depend on what he or she knows about how his or her services and loans will be utilised and the degree to which these services actually affect the commission of a crime'.[308] This distinction becomes relevant when companies facilitate state-sponsored human rights abuses by providing the means to commit these violations. A similar principle has been expressed by a US court in *Almog v Arab Bank*.[309]

Some scholars argue that in cases that concern neutral business actions, a line must be drawn between the morally condemnable behaviour of 'doing business with the devil' and criminally relevant contributions to another actor's international crimes.[310] Arguably, it is necessary to make the distinction between the supply of goods that are dangerous *per se*, such as weapons, and the supply of goods that may only contribute, in a certain scenario, to the commission of international crimes, such as computer programmes or certain chemicals.[311] Talking about the liability of the funders of international crimes, such as banks and other financial institutions, Ingrid Gubbay recognizes that 'the legal theory about financing human rights violations is still in its early days'.[312] Indeed, there are many unresolved questions in this area, including how to distinguish between 'doing business' and 'being complicit', and whether the purpose for which the loan was granted should make a difference.

---

306 *Mastafa v Australian Wheat Board Limited and Banque Nationale de Paris Paribas* 2008 WL 4378443 (S.D.N.Y.).
307 International Commission of Jurists, *Corporate Complicity in International Crime* (n 2), Vol I, 9.
308 Ibid., 39–40.
309 *Almog v Arab Bank* (n 139).
310 *Kaleck and Saage-Maab* (n 34), 719–21.
311 Ibid.
312 Lecture by I Gubbay (n 165).

A number of scholars have made a solid case for reconsidering the complicity liability of lenders in gross human rights violations.[313] In particular, Juan Pablo Bohoslavsky strongly argues for the liability of those who grant loans, despite being aware that this money would contribute to the commission of human rights abuses and crimes under international law.[314] Bohoslavsky's book *Cuentas Pendientes* ('Outstanding Debts') examines the role of foreign financial institutions and their potential complicity in supporting Argentina's regime.[315] The authors advocate a national truth commission to investigate corporate financial support of the dictatorship, arguing that the dictatorship could not have existed or carried out the repression without corporations' direct and indirect involvement.[316] They suggest that the assistance provided by private financial institutions played a role in the dictatorship significant enough to warrant possible future legal action on the basis of complicity in crimes against humanity.[317] Chapter 5 analyzes this proposal and its outcomes.

There are several factors that render the act of scrutinizing company responsibility relevant. For example, if it is determined that the banks are liable, this could provide an additional source of funding for reparations to victims and their families.[318] Further, according to Bohoslavsky:

> A thorough examination of the banks' behaviour would create recognition of the idea that financial support can be as powerful a legitimating and strengthening tool as other types of assistance to regimes known to violate human rights. This could create precedent to subject other financial institutions to the same kind of scrutiny in the future, which may serve as an overall deterrent effect on corporate behaviour.[319]

While there is no international case law and no consensus on mechanisms to hold financial backers of international criminals liable for their role, there are at least three options to legally address the consequences of financing gross human rights violations or crimes under international law.[320] The first option is to prove the

---

313 Michalowski (n 228), 453–54; Bohoslavsky and Opgenhaffen (n 104), Bohoslavsky and Rulli (n 281); Z Miller 'Effects of Invisibility: In Search of the "Economic" in Transitional Justice' (2008) 2 *Intl J Trans J* 266–91; C Acuña, 'Transitional Justice in Argentina and Chile: A Never Ending Story?' in J Elster (ed.), *Reparation and Retribution in the Transition to Democracy* (Columbia University Press 2006), 223.
314 Bohoslavsky and Opgenhaffen (n 104), 175.
315 JP Bohoslavsky and H Verbitsky, *Cuentas Pendientes: Los cómplices económicos de la dictadura* (Siglo Ventiuno Editores 2015).
316 Ibid.
317 Bohoslavsky and Verbitsky (n 316). See also Bohoslavsky and Opgenhaffen (n 104), 185.
318 Bohoslavsky and Opgenhaffen (n 104).
319 Ibid., 197–201.
320 Bernaz (n 296), 62–63.

criminal responsibility of the financial accomplices.[321] Rare examples are the lawsuits filed in September 2019 against *BNP Paribas* in France alleging complicity in war crimes in Sudan and Rwanda.[322]

A second option is to challenge the validity of the loan, which is related to the 'odious debt' debate.[323] 'Odious debt' is a private law doctrine whose core addresses debts incurred by despots, without the consent of their subjects, for corrupt purposes that are not in the interests of the population.[324] These debts are 'odious' because they are secured by the resources of subjugated people who enjoy no benefit from the financial commitments made by illegitimate leaders.[325] Despite this, the rules of state succession require a new state to repay debts incurred by its predecessor, even if they were used to perpetuate oppression. The sense of moral indignation that such result inspires is the driving force behind the doctrine of odious debt. Thus, principles of contract and agency prevent the burden of the debt from falling on those who did not consent or did not receive consideration.[326]

While few authors expressly refer to concepts of transitional justice when discussing this particular feature of odious debts,[327] the issue of odious debts frequently arises in transitional situations. To investigate the history of these debts and their role in contributing to the commission of human rights violations may contribute to achieving some of the goals of transitional justice.[328] The ability of a state in transition to void debts associated with past atrocities also appears to promise a number of benefits in relation to the governments being able to free resources for reparation, reform, reconstruction and restitution.[329] Arguably, accepting the

---

321 C Chiomenti, 'Corporations and the International Court', in O de Schutter (ed.), *Transnational Corporations and Human Rights* (Hart 2006), 287.
322 See section 4.1.1 above.
323 S Michalowski, *Unconstitutional Regimes and the Validity of Sovereign Debt: A Legal Perspective* (Routledge 2007); LC Buchheit, G Mitu Gulati, and RB Thompson, 'The Dilemma of Odious Debts' (2007) 56 *Duke LJ* 1201; A Ramasastry, 'Odious Debt or Odious Payments? Using Anti-Corruption Measures to Prevent Odious Debt' (2007) 32 *NC J Intl L Com Reg* 819.
324 A Sack, 'Les Effets Des Transformations Des Etats Sur Leurs Dettes Publiques Et Autres Obligations Financières' (1927) Recueil Sirey 157.
325 D Gray, 'Devilry, Complicity, and Greed: Transitional Justice and Odious Debt' (2007) 70 *Law Contemp Probs* 137, 150.
326 Sack (n 325).
327 Gray, 'Devilry, Complicity, and Greed' (n 326), 137; Michalowski and Bohoslavsky (n 282), 92; A Gelpern, 'Sovereign Debt Restructuring: What Iraq and Argentina Might Learn from Each Other' (2005) 6 *Chi J Intl L* 391.
328 L Laplante, 'Transitional Justice and Peace Building: Diagnosing and Addressing the Socioeconomic Roots of Violence through a Human Rights Framework' (2008) 2 *Intl J Transitional Just* 331; R Carranza, 'Plunder and Pain: Should Transitional Justice Engage with Corruption and Economic Crimes?' (2008) 2 *Intl J Transitional Just* 310; Miller (n 314).
329 D Gray, 'An Excuse-Centered Approach to Transitional Justice' (2006) 74 *Ford L Rev* 2621, 2624–29.

responsibility of business for human rights violations may provide a basis for a theory of 'odious profit', which borrows from the concept of odious debt: business should account for profits accumulated through their relationships with illegitimate regimes.[330]

Scholar David Gray argues that, in many circumstances, full faith in truth and accountability will require that transitional regimes accept the burden of financial obligations incurred by an odious predecessor.[331] He argues that this would reinforce assignments of liability to international investors and debtors who supply financial support to odious regimes.[332] His central claim is that expansion of the odious debt doctrine to cover all debts of an odious regime fails to account for the full truth about the past, and compromises transitional justice priorities of accountability.[333] Gray argues:

> Voiding a debt as odious effectively puts all the blame for past wrongs on the shoulders of a few elites who are made to bear as personal both the weight of the debts and the weight of blame for past wrongs, providing a free pass for those whose complicity is ignored and for corporations, banks, and other investors who have a share of the responsibility.[334]

By contrast, Michalowski and Bohoslavsky put forward the argument that debts can be void if they violate *ius cogens* norms.[335] Lender awareness is clearly relevant, as the purpose of preventing *ius cogens* violations by deterring lenders from making money available to this effect can only be achieved where creditors have a clear idea of the situations in which this consequence might arise, and which they therefore need to avoid.[336] It is, however, sufficient, according to Michalowski and Bohoslavsky, that lenders could or should have known of the use of the loan by the borrowing regime, whereas it is irrelevant whether they shared this purpose.[337]

An example of how the *ius cogens* approach can be applied in practice is that of the debts taken up by Argentina's military regime. An argument for a partial repudiation of Argentina's debt is that the loans were made to a regime that violated *ius cogens* norms, and that the incoming funds contributed to the growing expenditures of the military apparatus that perpetrated these violations.[338]

Finally, a third option to legally address the consequences of financing gross human rights violations or crimes under international law is to demonstrate civil

---

330 BS Lyons, 'Getting to Accountability: Business, Apartheid and Human Rights' (1999) 17 *Neth Q Hum Rts* 135, 159–60
331 Gray, 'Devilry, Complicity, and Greed' (n 326), 137.
332 Ibid., 138, 145, 147, 150.
333 Ibid., 155, 160, 164.
334 Ibid., 161
335 Michalowski and Bohoslavsky (n 282), 69.
336 Ibid.
337 Ibid., 80.
338 Ibid., 83.

responsibility for financial complicity.[339] Claims for civil remedies presented in a federal court in Buenos Aires against financial institutions because of their complicity with the crimes committed by the junta might shed more light on these issues, as they raise some of the questions that are essential in the context of a *ius cogens*-based odious debts doctrine.[340] In 2009, a civil suit was filed in Buenos Aires on behalf of five victims of Argentina's dictatorship against a number of banks accused of complicity in human rights abuses for financing the military junta.[341] The *Ibañez Manuel Leandro and others v Undetermined financial institutions* case is a rare example of a civil claim over financial complicity filed in the country where abused allegedly occurred.

Between March 1976 and December 1983, several commercial banks lent funds to the regime in Argentina. The claim alleged that the financing of the regime facilitated the commission of grave human rights violations, characterized as crimes against humanity, against the civil population, including the plaintiffs.[342] The claim argued that due to the public character of the human rights abuses in Argentina, banks were aware of the potential and foreseeable consequences of lending money to the regime.[343] An *amicus curiae*, filed in support of the plaintiffs argued that while the defendant banks did not directly participate in the crimes, they met the requirements of liability, in that they participated as accomplices in the crimes committed by the regime and that caused harm to the plaintiff with the requisite *mens rea*, and their contribution was not too remote.[344]

In line with the international standard defining the *actus reus* of liability in international law,[345] it is not necessary that without the contribution of the banks, the regime could not have committed the violations, but rather simply that the banks played an influential role and that without the loans, the military regime would not have been able to carry out its human rights violations in the same way – for example, with the same intensity and over the same period of time. Applying the relevant provisions of Argentinian law in light of international principles and standards, it appears that the banks were complicit in the crimes committed by Argentina's military junta.

The question of corporate complicity liability in gross human rights violations has arisen mainly in litigation before the ATS and a number of cases have defined

---

339 Bohoslavsky and Opgenhaffen (n 104), at 159–85.
340 For example, *Ibañez Manuel Leandro and others v Undetermined financial institutions*, Juzgado Civil y Comercial Federal no. 7 Sec 14, Buenos Aires.
341 Ibid.
342 Ibid.
343 Ibid.
344 Essex University and Centro de Estudios Legales y Sociales, *Amicus Curiae* presented before the Juzgado Civil y Comercial Federal n 7 Sec 14, in the case of *Ibañez Manuel Leandro and others v Undetermined financial institutions*, 26 March 2010, 1–26.
345 Report of the International Law Commission, Article 2(3)(d) of Draft Code of Crimes against the Peace and Security of Mankind, U.N. GAOR, 48th Sess., Supp. No. 10, U.N. Doc. A/51/10 (1996).

the *mens rea* standard of such liability.[346] The Marcos and Holocaust cases in particular are important in that they attempt to challenge the role that commercial banks play with respect to international human rights. In both instances, plaintiffs challenge the assertions that banks are always neutral actors engaged in purely commercial activities.[347]

Marcos litigation

In 1986, eight Filipinos resident in the United States filed a lawsuit in Hawaii over abuses committed by the Marcos government.[348] The suit was filed while Marcos and his entourage were fleeing Manila and were en route to Hawaii after a democratic uprising forced them to leave the Philippines.[349] The plaintiffs sought compensation for torture, summary execution, disappearance and arbitrary detention.[350] Marcos died in Hawaii in 1989, but the litigation continued against his estate. In 1995, after receiving a US$1.9 billion judgment, the plaintiffs tried to gain access to an estimated US$475 million that Marcos had deposited in Swiss accounts.[351] At that point the plaintiffs, who had not initially named the Swiss banks as defendants, alleged that the banks had done more than accept funds: they had actively helped Marcos conceal his wealth.

In 1996, the court ordered the Swiss banks to hand over the Marcos accounts in partial satisfaction of the US$1.9 billion judgment.[352] The court found the Swiss banks to be 'agents and representatives' of the Marcos estate and authorized a permanent injunction in respect of the assets held by the banks.[353] The Marcos

346 *Talisman* case (n 146) (suggesting a move from a mens rea standard of knowledge to one of primary purpose, which would considerably reduce the possibility of successful litigation against corporations); *ExxonMobil* case (n 146) (holding that Talisman was wrongly decided and that the mens rea standard in international law is that of knowledge); *Kiobel* case (n 146) (2d Cir. 2010). See also V Nerlich, 'Core Crimes and International Business Corporations' (2010) 8 *JICJ* 895; Ku (n 187); LJ Dhooge, 'Accessorial Liability of Transnational Corporations Pursuant to the Alien Tort Statute: The South African Apartheid Litigation and the Lessons of Central Bank' (2009) 18 *Transnatl L Contemp Probs* 247, 280–81.
347 Ramasastry, 'Secrets and Lies?' (n 298), 449.
348 *In re Ferdinand Estate of Marcos Human Rights Litigation*, 25 F.3d 1467, 1469 (9th Cir. 1994), 94 F.3d 539, 542 (9th Cir. 1996) [*Marcos Litigation*]. Five cases were filed against Marcos and were eventually consolidated: *Clemente v Marcos*, 878 F.2d 1438 (9th Cir. 1989); *Hilao v Marcos*, 878 F.2d 1438 (9th Cir. 1989); *Ortigas v Marcos*, 878 F.2d 1439 (9th Cir. 1989); *Sison v Marcos*, 878 F.2d 1438 (9th Cir. 1989); *Trajano v Marcos*, 878 F.2d 1439 (9th Cir. 1989). See also RG Steinhardt, 'Fulfilling the Promise of Filartiga: Litigating Human Rights Claims Against the Estate of Ferdinand Marcos' (195) 20 *Yale J Intl L* 65 (1995).
349 *Marcos Litigation* (n 349).
350 Ibid., 94 F.3d 539, 542.
351 Ramasastry, 'Secrets and Lies?' (n 298), 430–33.
352 *Marcos Litigation* (n 349), 910 F. Supp. 1470, 1473 (D. Haw. 1995).
353 Ibid. The Ninth Circuit, while acknowledging the district court judge's characterization of the banks as 'agents' of Marcos, reversed the decision because the banks were not parties in the original lawsuits, *Hilao v Estate of Marcos*, 95 F.3d 848, 855 (9th Cir. 1996).

litigation does not contain detailed accounts of the role of the Swiss banks because the banks were not initially named as defendants. The litigation is instructive, nonetheless, because it is the first to characterize Swiss banks as agents and facilitators in an ATS lawsuit.[354] The decision to subject the banks to the worldwide injunction demonstrates a view that the banks were not just repositories of wealth, but entities that had played a more active role for their client.[355]

Holocaust reparation lawsuits

After World War II, the Allies had agreed not only to punish war criminals but also to implement reparations.[356] The Allied Control Council ordered the dissolution of certain corporations and the seizure of their assets.[357] For example, *I. G. Farben* received the ultimate administrative sanction when the Control Council ordered its dissolution, 'the equivalent of the corporate death penalty'.[358] *Control Council Law No. 9* ordered that important *I.G. Farben* assets, including some plants, be destroyed.[359] The Council also included provisions related to the distribution and payment of reparations.[360] In the end, however, the tensions between the goals of reconstruction, reparations, securing political alliances and unification were incompatible, and reparation efforts ended.[361] By mid-1946, when decisions about war crimes, in which business played a role, were being reached, the Allies had concluded that political and economic stability could only be achieved with the participation of German industry run by the same managers, regardless of culpability.[362] Companies had long rejected legal claims by slave labourers, insisting that the German government, as successor to the Third Reich, should pay any damages.[363] While the government paid out over DM80 billion to

354 Ramasastry, 'Secrets and Lies?' (n 298), 430–35.
355 Ibid., 449–50.
356 Bush (n 147), 1119.
357 Control Council Law No. 9, art I, 225 (ordering dismantling of I.G. Farben as well as seizure of its assets: 'All plants, properties and assets of any nature situated in Germany which were, on or after 8 May, 1945, owned or controlled by I.G. Farbenindustrie A. G., are hereby seized by and the legal title thereto is vested in the Control Council'); Control Council Law No. 57, Dissolution and Liquidation of Insurance Companies Connected with the German Labor Front (Aug. 30, 1947), in VIII Enactments and Approved Papers of the Control Council and Coordinating Committee 1 (ordering seizure of insurance company assets).
358 T Giannini and S Farbstein, 'Corporate Accountability in Conflict Zones: How Kiobel Undermines the Nuremberg Legacy and Modern Human Rights' (2010) 52 *HILJ* 129.
359 Control Council Law No. 9, art III(b), 226 (providing for 'destruction of certain plants').
360 Ibid., art III, III(a), at 225–26.
361 Bush (n 147), 1120.
362 Ibid., 1122.
363 BB Ferencz, *Less Than Slaves: Jewish Forced Labor And The Quest For Compensation* (Indiana University Press 1979), xvii; MJ Bazyler, 'Nuremberg in America: Litigating the Holocaust in United States Courts' (2000) 34 *U Rich L Rev* 1, 31–39, 191–92; *The Economist*, 'Companies and the Holocaust: Industrial Actions', 14 November

victims of the Nazis, German companies paid almost nothing.[364] Only a few – most significantly *Farben* – paid small reparations amounts.[365] Monies and assets that had been seized in the United States during the war were returned to the companies in whole or part, notably in the high-profile settlement involving *GAF*, the *Farben* successor *Interhandel* and the United States government. Flick, described as one of the two richest men in Germany and the owner of hundreds of companies, paid nothing. The richest man, Alfried Krupp, with his property restored in full, was instructed to pay an average of US$825 per slave labourer to a small percentage of his former labour pool.[366]

In the 1990s, the issue of reparation for slave labour practices in Nazi Germany gained momentum with a series of lawsuits brought in the United States.[367] Hundreds of Holocaust survivors and relatives of Holocaust victims filed several class action lawsuits in US federal courts against Swiss banks in an effort to recover money deposited in bank accounts prior to and during World War II.[368] Joined in these lawsuits were Holocaust survivors who were forced by the Nazis to engage in slave labour, and survivors and the heirs of Holocaust victims who had property looted by the Nazis.[369] Plaintiffs alleged that Swiss banks knowingly accepted profits derived from slave labour as well as looted assets, and claimed that the banks actively financed such efforts.[370] The Swiss banks were alleged to have

1998, 75; E Black, *IBM and The Holocaust: The Strategic Alliance Between Nazi Germany and America's Most Powerful Corporation* (Crown Books 2001).

364 J Authers, 'Making Good Again: German Compensation for Forced and Slave Laborers' in de Greiff (n 123), 420.

365 After almost two decades of congressional and courtroom battles, the valuable Farben assets that were held in the United States by the Alien Property Custodian were returned to the German or Swiss claimants, J Borkin, *The Crime and the Punishment of I.G. Farben* (The Free Press 1978), 200–22.

366 The provisions of Control Council Law No. 27, under whose terms the Krupp empire would be split, were renegotiated and suspended. A Home, *Return to Power: A Report on the New Germany* (F.A. Praeger, 1956), 106–19.

367 See C Goschler, 'German Compensation to Jewish Nazi Victims after 1945' in P Hayes and JM Diefendorf (eds), *Lessons and Legacies VI: New Currents in Holocaust Research* (2004), 373; A Colonomos and A Armstrong, 'German Reparations for the Jews after World War II: A Turning Point in the History of Reparations' in de Greiff (n 123), 390; Bazyler (n 3164), 31–39 (2000).

368 *Weisshaus v Union Bank of Switz.*, No. 96-CV-4849 (E.D.N.Y. Oct. 3, 1996) (Am. Compl. Jan. 24, 1997); *Friedman v Union Bank of Switz.*, No. 96-CV-5161 (E.D.N.Y. Oct. 21, 1996) (Am. Compl. 1997); *World Council of Orthodox Jewish Communities, Inc. v Union Bank of Switz.*, No. 97-CV-0461 (E.D.N.Y. Jan. 29, 1997) (Am. Comp. July 1997) [*Holocaust Litigation*]. See also L Bilsky, 'Transnational Holocaust Litigation' (2012) 23(2) *Eur J Int Law* (2012) 349; Black (n 364); Ferencz (n 364), xvii; Bazyler (n 364), 191–92, 207, 249–55.

369 *Holocaust Litigation* (n 369).

370 Ibid. See also C Simpson (ed.), *War Crimes of the Deutsche Bank and the Dresdner Bank* (Holmes & Meyer 2002), 1–34. *Friedman v Union Bank of Switz.*, No. 96-CV-5161 (E.D.N.Y. Oct. 21, 1996); Bazyler (n 364) 31–39, 93–136, 237–49.

violated 'international treaties, customary international laws, and fundamental human rights laws'.[371]

The Holocaust claims evoked a number of criticisms specifically as to the characterization of banks as collaborators. Walter Rockler, an American prosecutor at Nuremberg responsible for prosecuting the two German bankers Karl Rasche and Emil Puhl, asked:

> The charge that Swiss banks accepted moneys looted by the Nazis is probably true. So did French banks, Italian banks, Swedish banks. And so would any other banks, including American and British banks, were these countries not at war with the Nazis. A substantial aspect of the business of banking for profit is acceptance of deposits without regard to the history of the money being deposited. Swiss bankers are not unusual in this practice [...] [I]n the matter of the claims of survivors to deposits of the murdered persons in Swiss banks, the Swiss bankers seem to have behaved badly, but like bankers. They would not part with the money except upon strict proofs – proofs that of course were not available anywhere. As to many of these accounts, there were and are no claimants and that undoubtedly has pleased the bankers [...] [H]ave they been insensitive and glad to profit? Of course. Why would anyone expect otherwise?[372]

Rockler's comments emphasize the problem of drawing lines with respect to the activities of a commercial bank.[373] Holocaust restitution claims had to overcome considerable formal barriers. The claims were filed over 50 years after the fact and were often instigated by descendants of victims who had either perished during the Holocaust or passed away in the following years. They initiated proceedings outside the jurisdictions where the acts were committed, and where the corporate defendants were incorporated.[374] In the end, the validity of the claims was never fully adjudicated. The parties reached a settlement agreement in 1998, whereby the Swiss banks agreed to pay an unprecedented US$1.25 billion to the Holocaust plaintiffs in exchange for a release of claims by the plaintiffs relating to the Holocaust, World War II and targets of Nazi persecution.[375] These lawsuits attracted some criticism. In relation to the calculation of reparations due by companies that benefitted from slavery, Lord Anthony Gifford, a senior British barrister, conceded:

> Such an approach would create more problems than it solved: Enormous research would be needed to identify the companies and the families, to determine how much money was made by their ancestors, and to calculate

371 *Friedman v Union Bank of Switz*, No. 96-CV-5161, 215 (E.D.N.Y. Oct. 21, 1996). See also, Ramasastry, 'Secrets and Lies?' (n 298), 350–72.
372 WJ Rockler, 'Bankers Not Collaborators', *Washington Post*, 22 July 1997, A15.
373 Ramasastry, 'Secrets and Lies?' (n 298), 393.
374 Bilsky (n 369), 349–75.
375 *In re Holocaust Victim Assets Litig.*, 105 F. Supp. 2d 139, 142 (E.D.N.Y. 2000).

how much should be forfeited by the present shareholders or family members. The process would inevitably be somewhat arbitrary, and potentially oppressive, and it would be rejected both by the targets themselves and their governments.[376]

Lawsuits in US courts were almost always dismissed or denied.[377] For example, plaintiffs in the lawsuit against *Ford Motor* sought disgorgement of profits accumulated over more than 50 years, alleging that the US-based *Ford* parent company profited from the rapid growth of its German subsidiary.[378] This amount was in practice almost impossible to quantify, but lawyers initially requested US$37 billion. The suit against *Ford* was finally dismissed because the claims exceeded time limits imposed under German and US laws.[379] In a separate ruling on four cases involving *Degussa* and *Siemens*, two German companies, the US district judge decided that the matter was a subject of international treaties and not civil law – the question of payments to victims was left to states, not courts, to decide.[380]

But the threat of lawsuits in the United States contributed to the pressure to negotiate reparations with the surviving labourers and their representatives.[381] Despite lawsuits being dismissed, any German company with a subsidiary in the United States was potentially liable under US law.[382] Although companies admitted no legal obligation, they started talking of their 'moral responsibility' to former labourers. *Volkswagen* set aside DM45 million for 'humanitarian projects'. *Siemens*, which had tried to document its innocence within months of the war's end, offered up to US$1,250 per slave labourer – but with a written insistence that it was not under 'any legal or moral obligation' to do so. The company placed advertisements in East European newspapers to track down its former labourers, but it declined to increase its offer when additional claimants came forward, causing the actual average payment to shrink to US$825 – in total *Siemens* paid out DM20 million.[383] After the US$1.25 billion settlement with the Swiss banks, other claims were made against German and Austrian firms accused of profiting

---

376 A Gifford, 'The Legal Basis of the Claim for Reparations', paper presented to the first Pan-African Congress on Reparations, Abuja, Nigeria, 27–29 April 1993.
377 For the Farben settlement, see *Kelberine v Societe Internationale*, Interhandel, 363 F.2d 989 (D.C. Cir. 1966). See also Borkin (n 366), 205–22.
378 *Iwanowa v Ford Motor Co.*, 67 F. Supp. 2d 424, 432–34 (D.N.J. 1999) (discussing allegations about Ford's use of slave labour and the impact of that labour on the company's profitability).
379 Stephens (n 145), 46–51.
380 M du Plessis, 'Reparations and International Law: How Are Reparations to Be Determined (Past Wrong or Current Effects), Against Whom, and What Form Should They Take?' (2003) 22 *Windsor YB Access Just* 44.
381 Authers (n 365), 431–32.
382 Ibid., 431.
383 Bazyler (n 364), 31–39.

from slave labour.[384] These cases were also settled and led to the establishment of a US$5 billion fund to which the German government and corporations contributed in equal shares.[385]

BNP Paribas (re Sudan)

As mentioned above, in September 2019, Sudanese victims filed a criminal complaint in French courts alleging that *BNP Paribas* was an accomplice in crimes against humanity, torture and genocide in Sudan.[386] Based on the same acts, a tort lawsuit is under way in the United States. In May 2019, the US Second Circuit Court of Appeals ruled that a lawsuit brought by victims of genocide in Sudan against French bank *BNP* can proceed.[387] The named plaintiffs, who reside in the United States, sued on behalf of a class of similarly situated victims.[388] The victims allege that they were tortured, detained, raped or displaced or had family members killed by militia forces who were armed and dispatched using resources made available by virtue of *BNP*'s violation of US sanctions. Although the alleged conduct violates international law, all the causes of action were framed in terms of New York state tort law (e.g. negligence, intentional infliction of emotional distress, battery, false arrest and wrongful death). Plaintiffs contend that the bank is either directly liable for these acts (e.g. negligence) or indirectly liable for the conduct of Sudanese forces under theories of conspiracy and aiding and abetting. Originally, the district court had dismissed the suit on the basis of the act of state doctrine (a common law rule holding that courts cannot adjudicate the lawfulness of the acts of a foreign state committed within that state's territory) and the expiration of the statute of limitations.[389] In its opinion, the Second Circuit unanimously reversed the district court's decision. The three-judge panel reasoned that the act of state doctrine cannot shield a defendant's conduct from scrutiny when the state's own laws and 'a universal international consensus' prohibit the

384 According to claims filed against Ford, for example, the Ford affiliate in Germany operated with as much as half of its workforce composed of forced labourers, *Iwanowa v Ford Motor Co.*, 67 F. Supp.2d 424, 432–33 (D.N.J. 1999). See also Bazyler (n 364), *The Economist* (n 364), 75; Stephens (n 145), 46–51.
385 Bilsky (n 369), 349–75; B Neuborne, 'Holocaust Reparations Litigation: Lessons for the Slavery Reparations Movement' (2003) 58 *New York Univ Annual Survey American L* 615; Bohoslavsky and Rulli (n 281), 834.
386 See section 4.1.1 above.
387 *Entesar Osman Kashef, et al. v BNP Paribas et al.*, Appeal from the United States District Court for the Southern District of New York No. 16-cv-3228, 22 May 2019. See also Jonathan Stempel, 'Paribas must face revived lawsuit over Sudanese genocide – U.S. appeals court', Reuters, 22 May 2019, www.reuters.com/article/bnp-paribas-sudan-lawsuit/update-1-bnp-paribas-must-face-revived-lawsuit-over-sudanese-genocide-u-s-appeals-court-id USL2N22Y0XR
388 *US District Court Southern District of New York, Entesar Osman Kashef, et al. v BNP Paribas et al.*, Second Amendment Complaint Case 1:16-Cv-03228-Ajn., 20 Jan. 2017.
389 Ibid., Motion to dismiss, 20 March 2018.

acts in question. In other words, genocide and crimes against humanity cannot, as a matter of law, be 'official acts' of Sudan.[390] In addition, the Second Circuit confirmed that US courts are prohibited from deeming violations of *jus cogens* norms to be valid acts of a foreign sovereign.

The criminal action in question has its origins in US human rights and counter-terrorism sanctions against Sudan and the determination by the US government that a genocide was underway in Darfur.[391] In an earlier criminal suit settled in 2014, *BNP* admitted to evading those sanctions and providing Sudanese banks with access to the US financial system, all with the knowledge that the regime of Omar al-Bashir was a sponsor of terrorism and was committing genocide and crimes against humanity.[392] According to US authorities, *BNP* was essentially acting as 'the central bank for the government of Sudan'.[393] The criminal suit resulted in close to US$9 billion in fines and forfeiture penalties, the largest financial penalty ever awarded.[394] Some of those funds, which include the proceeds of criminal activity, were supposed to go to people who had been harmed.[395] But Sudanese victims did not ultimately receive any compensation as the US Congress diverted the funds to victims of domestic terrorist attacks.

The lawsuit exemplifies the potential of tort law to provide justice for human rights violations, given the limitations of the ATS. As discussed above, in *Jesner* the Supreme Court limited the ability of human rights victims to sue foreign corporations for violations of international law in US federal courts under the ATS. The opinion left open the possibility of suing US corporations under the ATS, and several such suits are proceeding, including one against defence contractor *CACI* for its role in the US torture programme.[396] The *BNP* suit demonstrates the viability of a legal strategy focusing on ordinary state tort law.[397]

390 B Van Schaack, 'Understanding the Decision to Revive the Sudanese Genocide Lawsuit against BNP Paribas', Just Security, 30 May 2019, www.justsecurity.org/64335/under standing-the-decision-to-revive-the-sudanese-genocide-lawsuit-against-bnp-paribas

391 US Department of the Treasury, Sudan and Darfur Sanctions, www.treasury.gov/ resource-center/sanctions/Programs/pages/sudan.aspx

392 *USA v BNP Paribas S.A.*, Docket No. 1_14-cr-00460 (S.D.N.Y. Jul 09, 2014), Court Docket, 12. See also, US Department of Justice, 'BNP Paribas Agrees to Plead Guilty and to Pay $8.9 Billion for Illegally Processing Financial Transactions for Countries Subject to U.S. Economic Sanctions', 30 June 2014, www.justice.gov/opa/pr/bnp -paribas-agrees-plead-guilty-and-pay-89-billion-illegally-processing-financial

393 Nate Raymond, 'BNP Paribas sentenced in $8.9 billion accord over sanctions violations', Reuters, 1 May 2015, www.reuters.com/article/us-bnp-paribas-settlem ent-sentencing-idUSKBN0NM41K20150501

394 US Department of Justice (n 393).

395 *United States of America v BNP Paribas*, Consent Preliminary Order of Forfeiture/ Money Judgment.

396 WS. Dodge, 'Jesner v. Arab Bank: The Supreme Court Preserves the Possibility of Human Rights Suits Against U.S. Corporations', Just Security, 26 April 2018, www. justsecurity.org/55404/jesner-v-arab-bank-supreme-court-preserves-possibility-human -rights-suits-u-s-corporations

397 Van Schaack (n 391).

4.2.3. Civil litigation in other jurisdictions

The ATS legislation is unique to the United States, but it has arguably motivated lawyers in other countries to explore the feasibility of their jurisdictions in establishing civil liability of corporations involved in human rights abuses. At the European level, corporate accountability for international crimes and gross human rights violations is beginning to gain traction.[398] There is a small, but growing number of civil claims being brought in different jurisdictions seeking such liability.[399] These developments are creating a network of avenues to accountability and justice that is slowly establishing opportunities for victims to obtain civil redress after times of conflict or repression.[400] For example, in 1997, five South Africans suffering from asbestos-related diseases brought a suit against *Cape*, a British energy company, in the English High Court, seeking compensation.[401] The plaintiffs, former *Cape* workers and people living in the vicinity of *Cape*'s asbestos mining and milling operations in South Africa, alleged that *Cape* exposed its workers to 30 times the British legal limit of asbestos dust. More victims joined the case, which ended in 2003 with an out-of-court settlement with the 7,500 claimants for £7.5 million.[402] *Cape* benefitted financially by operating in an apartheid state where the health and safety of black workers was of little value and tort law was used to complement the reparations owned by the state to the victims.[403]

The apartheid legacy led also to litigation against mining companies in South Africa.[404] South Africa's TRC had indicated that the gold mining industry had been critical in designing and benefitting from the exploitative migrant labour system.[405] In 2012, lawyers started to test the courts in South Africa for silicosis-related compensation claims for 4,365 mine workers against South African mining companies *Anglo American* and *AngloGold Ashanti*. The case was set for arbitration in April 2016, but a month before the mining companies announced they had reached an out-of-court settlement worth up to R464 million.[406] Also in 2012, attorneys filed a motion in the South African courts seeking class certification for 17,000 former

---

398 C Kaeb, 'The Shifting Sands of Corporate Liability under International Criminal Law' (2016) 49 *George Washington International Law Review* 351; W Kaleck and P Kroker, 'Syrian Torture Investigations in Germany and Beyond: Breathing New Life into Universal Jurisdiction in Europe?' 2018 16(1) *Journal of International Criminal Justice* 165.
399 Meeran (n 123).
400 International Commission of Jurists, *Corporate Complicity in International Crime* (n 2), vol III, 5–6.
401 *Chandler v Cape Plc* (2012) EWCA Civ 525.
402 *Lubbe and others v Cape*.
403 Farah (n 138), 48.
404 *Mankayi v AngloGold Ashanti*, Constitutional Court of South Africa, 3 March 2011.
405 TRC of South Africa (n 226), Volume IV, Chapter II, 144, 151–55.
406 Leigh Day, 'Victory at last for South African gold miners as Anglo American and AngloGold agree landmark silicosis compensation scheme' 5 March 2016, www. leighday.co.uk/News/News-2016/March-2016/Victory-at-last-for-South-Africa n-gold-miners-as-A.

gold miners suffering from the lung disease silicosis. The proposed class action named 30 gold mining companies as defendants.[407] The plaintiffs allege that the companies knew of the dangers posed to the miners by exposing them to silica dust but failed to take adequate measures to protect the workers from this exposure. In May 2016, South Africa's High Court allowed the class action lawsuit.[408]

In January 2013, a Dutch court in The Hague issued a ruling against *Royal Dutch Shell* and its subsidiary *Shell Nigeria* for pollution in Nigeria's Niger Delta.[409] It was the first time that a Dutch multinational corporation had appeared in a civil court in the Netherlands to answer for violations committed overseas. Although all claims against the parent company were dismissed, its foreign subsidiary *Shell Nigeria* was held liable to pay compensation to one of the plaintiffs for environmental damages caused by oil spills.[410] In most cases, human rights violations are committed by foreign subsidiary companies in countries affected by conflict or authoritarian regimes where human rights laws are poorly enforced. In these situations, holding multinational companies accountable for abuses committed in the host state is often impossible for the victims.[411] Lawsuits brought in Nigeria are a case in point. Despite the number of litigations pending in front of Nigerian courts, very few cases have ever awarded compensation to the victims of corporate human rights violations. After *Kiobel* and *Jesner*, the United States no longer provides an accessible avenue for justice for victims of violations committed overseas. Therefore, questions as to whether European jurisdictions may constitute an alternative for holding multinational corporations accountable have gained greater importance. The underlying issues are the competence of European jurisdictions to hold multinational companies accountable in Europe for violations committed abroad, and the task of establishing the law applicable to these specific cases.[412]

From a normative point of view, for a case against a multinational company over human rights abuses committed abroad to proceed, first the national court must establish its jurisdiction over the company's conduct or facts abroad and effectively

---

407 Including African Rainbow Minerals, AngloGold Ashanti, Gold Fields, and Harmony Gold.

408 *Mankayi v AngloGold Ashanti* (n 405).

409 *Oguru, Efanga, Milieudefensie v Royal Dutch Shell Plc and Shell Petroleum Development Co Nigeria Ltd*, District Court of The Hague, case no. C/09/330891/ HAZA09-0579, 2013; *Friday Alfred Akpan v Royal Dutch Shell Plc and Shell Petroleum Development Co Nigeria Ltd*, District Court of The Hague, case no. 337050/ HAZA09-1580, 2013; *Barizaa Manson TeteDooh v Royal Dutch Shell Plc and Shell Petroleum Development Co Nigeria Ltd*, District Court of The Hague, case no C/09/ 337058/HAZA09-1581, 2013. See also D Cambou, 'The Dutch Shell Case: Foreign Direct Liability Claims as an Avenue for Holding Multinational Corporations Accountable for Human Rights Violations' in Černič and van Ho (n 190), 347–65.

410 *Friday Alfred Akpan v Shell* (n 410), 5.1.

411 M Anderson, 'Transnational Corporations and Environmental Damage: Is Tort Law an Answer?' (2002) 41 *Washburn L J* 405; Cambou (n 410), 348.

412 Cambou (n 410), 350.

exercise it. In the United States, and other common law countries (but not in European Union countries), courts may invoke the doctrine of *forum non conveniens* to abstain on the grounds that the jurisdiction would be more appropriately exercised by the courts of another country, such as the host state where the wrongful conduct occurred.[413] This doctrine presents a major hurdle to litigants in cases where the witnesses, other evidence and the subsidiary are all located in another country.[414]

Further, when a parent company is allegedly complicit in human rights abuses alongside its subsidiary, the ability to establish the liability of the parent company may be necessary in ensuring proper redress for the victims and their rights to remedy and reparation. However, establishing jurisdiction over a parent company for the conduct of its subsidiaries remains a complex issue. In legal terms, each company has a separate legal personality and is deemed to be a distinct entity from all other legal and natural persons.[415] This legal separation, or 'corporate veil', between different corporate entities affects whether or not a parent company can be held legally responsible in situations where its subsidiary has become involved in human rights abuses. Only in exceptional cases can the corporate veil be effectively 'pierced'. As a result, in most cases parent companies manage to escape liability even though they effectively control their subsidiaries. The use of subsidiaries in host countries and the limited liability enjoyed by corporate entities means that the harms caused by multinational companies often cannot be traced back to solvent parent companies located in home states.[416]

Until recently, the responsibility of multinational corporations for human rights violations was not a matter of concern in Europe. Very few tort cases had been brought in national courts in the European Union (EU), even though many national courts appeared to have jurisdictions over corporations operating abroad.[417] An explanation for this lack of action lies in the legal culture of EU states, which, in

413 International Commission of Jurists, *Corporate Complicity in International Crime* (n 2), vol III, 50–51. For countries in the European Union, Brussels Regulation I stipulates that a defendant shall be sued in its domicile, and that the domicile of a company is in the location of its corporate headquarters or its registered office. Brussels Regulation on Jurisdiction and the Recognition and Enforcement of Judgments in Civil and Commercial Matters (*Brussels I Regulation*), Council Regulation (EC) No 44/2001 of 22 December 2000, art 2.

414 S Deva, 'Human Rights Violations by Multinational Corporations and International Law: Where from Here?' (2003) 19 *Connectiut JIL* 1, 9.

415 Under the principle of 'corporate entity' an incorporated company has a legal personality that is separated from its members. B Petter, *Company Law* (Pearson Longman 2005), 23–25.

416 P Muchlinski, 'Limited Liability and Multinational Enterprises: A Case for Reform?' (2010) 34(5) *Cambridge J Economics*, 915; Sandoval and Surfleet (n 277).

417 J Wouters and C Ryngaert, 'Litigation for Overseas Corporate Human Rights Abuses in the European Union: The Challenge of Jurisdiction' (2009) 40 *George Washington Intl L Rev* 939.

comparison to the United States, is far less favourable to this type of litigation.[418] In Europe, public issues such as transnational human rights violations generally tend to be addressed on the basis on government intervention rather than litigation.[419]

Since the 1999 *Brussels I Regulation*, civil law jurisdictions have entertained foreign direct liability.[420] Regardless of the nationality of the victim and of the place where the damage occurred, European multinational companies can be sued in the national courts of EU member states for abuses they committed overseas. In other words, courts can no longer make use of the *forum non conveniens* doctrine to refuse judicial competence, even if the competing *forum* would be in a non-EU member state. This conclusion could already be implied from the European Court of Justice (ECJ) judgment in the *Group Josi Reinsurance* case, which stated that the rules on jurisdiction that are now reflected in *Brussels I* are 'applicable where the defendant has its domicile or seat in a Contracting State, even if the plaintiff is domiciled in a non-member country'.[421] This was also the conclusion reached by some commentators.[422] The ECJ later explicitly confirmed the non-applicability of the *forum non conveniens* doctrine in the case of *Andrew Owusu v N.B. Jackson.*[423]

In the Dutch litigation, *Shell* did not contest the competence of the Dutch court over the parent company but opposed the competence over its Nigerian subsidiary. In the Netherlands, the Dutch procedural civil code provides that a foreign subsidiary can be sued in front of the Dutch civil court by means of joint hearing when the court already has competence over the parent company, provided that the claims are connected to such extent to justify a joint hearing.[424] The decision of the

---

418 L Enneking, *Foreign Direct Liability and Beyond* (Eleven International Publishing 2009), 194–95.

419 Cambou (n 410), 352.

420 Parliament Resolution on EU Standards for European Enterprises Operating in Developing Countries: Towards a European Code of Conduct, 14 April 1999, Preamble, Recital 18, 1999 O.J. (C 104), 180. Replaced by EU Council Regulation (EC) 44/2001 on jurisdictions and the recognition and enforcement of judgments in civil and commercial matters 2001 OJ L 012/1.

421 ECJ, Case C-412/98, Group Josi Reinsurance Company SA v Universal General Insurance Company (UGIC), 2000 E.C.R. I-5925, para 61.

422 O de Schutter 'The Accountability of Multinationals for Human Rights Violations in European Law' in Alston (ed.), Non-State Actors and Human Rights (OUP 2005), 227, 271–72; J Wouters and L Chanet, 'Corporate Human Rights Responsibility: A European Perspective' (2008) 6(2) *Northwestern J Intl Human Rights* 3, 292.

423 ECJ, Case C-281/02, *Andrew Owusu v N.B. Jackson*, 2005 E.C. R. OJ C 106. As a general principle, after the passing of the *Rome II* Regulation, for any future foreign liability claim related to events that occurred after 11 January 2009, the applicable law is the law of the country where the damage occurs. In other words, the law applied to foreign liability cases is the law of the host state. As an exception, however, it is possible to apply the law of a state that has 'manifestly closer connection' with the case. Regulation (EC) No 864/2007 of the European Parliament and of the Council of 11 July 2007 on the law applicable to non-contractual obligations (*Rome II*), Arts 4.3 and 15.

424 Dutch Code of Civil Procedure, Art 7, sub 1.

Dutch court that a sufficient connection existed and therefore that the case could be tried in the Netherlands is a major step forward for litigation in the area of corporate accountability because it supports the concept that parent companies and their subsidiaries can be held accountable in the home state of the parent companies for abuses committed overseas.[425] The decision also confirms the existence of a nascent trend to adjudicate foreign direct liability in the EU. This decision, however, still remains an isolated success case and underlines the legal difficulties that plaintiffs may face in the course of future proceedings.

Claims by alleged victims of harm caused by the operations of UK-head-quartered multinational corporations have enjoyed an increasing successful track record in British courts.[426] Cases against corporations have been pursued on the basis of tort or negligence – alleging harm caused by negligence arising from a breach of a duty of care, rather than, for example, torture or violation of the right to life. Since they involve claims for compensation and are invariably costly, these cases may serve to achieve critical elements of corporate accountability, namely monetary redress for victims and deterrence against future human rights violations.[427] Although it is not related to transitional justice, the case against UK mining company *Vedanta* represents an important development as it establishes the duty of care of the parent company – a principle that could have important consequences when applied to companies operating in countries affected by conflict or repression.

In April 2019, the UK Supreme Court handed down the final judgment in *Lungowe v Vedanta*.[428] The claimants, some 1,800 Zambian citizens, allege that *Vedanta* and its Zambian subsidiary *Konkola Copper Mines* (*KCM*), are responsible for the discharge of toxic waste from the Nchanga Mine operated by *KCM*, which caused severe damage to the vishealth and livelihood of local communities.[429] The most consequential finding is in relation to the duties and responsibilities of the parent company *Vedanta vis-à-vis* the communities living in the vicinity of its subsidiary operations in Zambia. To avoid UK courts' jurisdiction over the claim, both *Vedanta* and *KCM* asserted that there was no real triable issue against *Vedanta*, which was, they said, 'merely an indirect owner of *KCM*, and no more than

---

425 Cambou (n 410), 353.
426 R Meeran, 'Access to Remedy: The UK Experience of MNC Tort Litigation for Human Rights Violations' in S Deva and D Bilchitz (eds), *Human Rights Obligations of Business: Beyond the Corporate Responsibility to Respect* (CUP 2013), 378, 379.
427 Ibid.
428 *Lungowe & Others v Vedanta Resources Plc & Konkola Copper Mines* [2019] UKSC 20 [*Lungowe v Vedanta*], Judgment given on 10 April 2019.
429 For summary and analysis see the claimants' law firm Leigh Day legal briefing, Leigh Day, Legal Briefing April 2019, 'Lungowe & Others v Vedanta and KCM Parent company liability clarified'10 April 2019 www.leighday.co.uk/LeighDay/media/LeighDay/documents/Zambia/Supreme-Court-final-brief-Zambia.pdf; Carlos Lopez, 'Symposium on Vedanta Resources Plc vs Lungowe', *OpinioJuris*, 17 April 2019, https://opiniojuris.org/2019/04/17/symposium-on-vedanta-resources-plc-vs-lungowe-judgment-of-the-united-kingdom-supreme-court/

that'.[430] But the Supreme Court held that there was an arguable case against Vedanta, which rested on the application of an old principle involving the duty of care, where *Vedanta* could be shown to have intervened in or controlled relevant activities of *KCM*.[431] The Court found that there was sufficient evidence deriving from Vedanta's own reporting on its implementation of group-wide policies on environmental management. The duty-of-care standard so formulated may put an end to a long-standing dispute on its applicability regarding communities impacted by subsidiaries' operations. But its implications, including its impact on encouraging – or not – parent companies' 'hands off' approach in respect to the operations of subsidiaries, are not entirely clear.[432]

A second important aspect of the decision is the Court's findings about the 'proper forum' for the claim and the likelihood that claimants will have access to substantial justice in Zambia. The Court found that the proper place for the claims would be Zambia, but the risk that claimants would not have access to substantial justice in that forum convinced the Court to decide finally that the United Kingdom was the proper forum. The Supreme Court found that Zambia, in principle, would have been the proper place for the claim to be tried due to the many connections that existed between *KCM*, claimants and events and that forum. But the Court found that there would be insufficient resources for the claimants to bring and prove their claims in a group legal action in Zambia. Although the final outcome was favourable to the claimants, the path of analysis undertaken by the Court may generate some concern. Carlos Lopez, a jurist, argues: 'The Court certainly had to consider the position of KCM as a foreign defendant over which UK jurisdiction is not, in principle, clear. But its reasoning suggests the doctrine of *forum conveniens* is back through the back door – as applicable to foreign defendants.'[433]

Some issue may arise in relation to the implementation of mandatory human rights due diligence, recently established in France and under negotiation in other jurisdictions. Take the situation of executives of a French extractive company which decides to invest in a post-conflict state. The company fulfils its responsibilities under the 2017 French Duty of Vigilance Law and ensures that there is a robust human rights vigilance plan and due diligence process for its operations.[434] In circumstances where the conflict resumes and the state commits a crime under international law, the information derived from the process could be used to substantiate an allegation that the executive team had the requisite knowledge for complicity in the crime. This may not be a problem if the ICC's 'purpose of facilitating' standard is applied, but certain states exercising universal jurisdiction may proceed on the basis of a much lower 'knowledge' or 'indifference' standard.

---

430 *Lungowe v Vedanta* (n 429), para 17.
431 Lopez (n 430).
432 Ibid.
433 Ibid.
434 Loi n 2017–399 du 27 mars 2017 relative au devoir de vigilance des sociétés mères et des entreprises donneuses d'ordre (1).

In Europe the development of foreign liability claims as a means to hold multinational companies liable for human rights abuses abroad is only in its infancy.[435] Victims of corporate human rights abuses overseas are likely to encounter many obstacles. Questions about the competence of the jurisdiction and the law applicable, in addition to the burden of proof and the cost of litigation, may seriously limit the ability of victims to seek redress in Europe.

Canada is also seeing interesting developments. In November 2014, three Eritreans filed a lawsuit against *Nevsun Resources* in Vancouver, British Columbia, Canada. They allege the company was complicit in the use of forced labour by *Nevsun*'s local sub-contractor, *Segen Construction* (owned by Eritrea's ruling party), at the Bisha mine in Eritrea. This lawsuit is the first in Canada where claims are based directly on violations of international law. The plaintiffs claim that they worked at the Bisha mine against their will and were subject to 'cruel, inhuman and degrading treatment'. They allege that they were forced to work long hours and lived in constant fear of threats of torture and intimidation. The plaintiffs seek damages on behalf of all Eritreans forced to work at the mine from September 2008. Their claims are based on alleged breaches of *jus cogens* customary international law (including prohibitions against slavery, torture and crimes against humanity).[436] Thus, the Supreme Court of British Colombia considered whether breaches of customary international law may form the basis of a civil proceeding in British Columbia. *Nevsun* argued that customary international law claims are barred by the act of state doctrine. Given the uncertainty surrounding the scope and application of the doctrine (it has yet to form the basis of a decision by any Canadian court), the Court was not prepared to dismiss the plaintiffs' claims on a preliminary application. *Nevsun* also argued that the plaintiffs' claims have no reasonable prospect of success because customary international law does not apply to corporations and cannot form the basis of a private law action. Again, the Court disagreed, noting the uncertain state of the law in this area.[437] In November 2017, the British Columbia Court of Appeal rejected *Nevsun*'s appeal to dismiss the suit, thereby allowing the case to proceed in Canadian courts.[438] The court also allowed claims of crimes against humanity, slavery, forced labour and torture to go forward against *Nevsun*. This decision marked the first time an appellate court in Canada permitted a mass tort claim for modern slavery. The case is on-going.

---

435 Cambou (n 410), 364.
436 *Araya v Nevsun Resources Ltd.*, 2016 BCSC 1856 (CanLII).
437 See M Lam and R Gifford, 'Araya v. Nevsun Resources Ltd., 2016 BCSC 1856: British Columbia Supreme Court refuses to allow a "common law class action" alleging human rights violations at Eritrean mine', *McCarthy Tetrault*, 2 November 2016, www.mccarthy. ca/en/insights/blogs/canadian-class-actions-monitor/araya-v-nevsun-resources-ltd-2016 -bcsc-1856-british-columbia-supreme-court-refuses-allow-common-law-class-action-alle ging-human-rights-violations-eritrean-mine
438 *Araya v Nevsun Resources Ltd.*, 2017 BCCA 401 (CanLII).

4.2.4. Out-of-court financial settlements

Civil litigation is irremediably linked to settlement as a dispute-resolution mechanism, and settlement, by definition, undermines the attempt to determine legal and historical responsibility, as it allows the defendant to pay without the issue of liability being determined.[439] In March 2016, for example, *Anglo American* and *AngloGold Ashanti* reached an out-of-court settlement with 4,365 mine workers worth up to R464 million to be paid into an independent trust.[440] *Wiwa v Shell*, which was initiated on the accusation that *Shell* was complicit in human rights violations in Nigeria by funding the military to suppress civilians living in *Shell*'s operational area, also reached closure through an out-of-court settlement.[441] This settlement may have implicitly acknowledged *Shell*'s role in contributing to violations, but it kept issues around the alleged violations from receiving formal legal treatment.[442] Further, in 2004, just one day before a hearing by the court of appeals in the long-running *Unocal* litigation, the parties reached an out-of-court settlement. In the settlement, the exact terms of which are confidential, *Unocal* agreed to compensate the plaintiffs and provide funds for programmes in Myanmar's pipeline region, but denied any complicity in human rights abuses with the Myanmar military junta.[443] Although the outcome of the case could arguably be considered a success, the settlement signified no further judicial scrutiny of the circumstances of the case.

As seen above, none of the Holocaust restitution cases was ultimately resolved on the merits. To avoid reputational damage and the monetary costs of litigation, corporations preferred to settle cases outside the courts without any formal acknowledgment of legal responsibility.[444] The settlements reached between the parties avoided any clear ruling on the legal responsibility of the corporations. Some legal scholars and historians have criticized this litigation, raising doubts as to the measure of redress achieved for Holocaust victims. For example, for legal historian Michael Marrus, the litigation not only failed to contribute to historical understanding, but it also distorted the historical picture of the involvement of corporations in the Holocaust.[445] He argues that the focus on monetary gains shifted attention away from the gravest crime committed during World War II to theft. '[The law] gets the history wrong', Marrus claims.[446] The legal pressure,

---

439 Bilsky (n 369).
440 Leigh Day (n 407).
441 *Wiwa v Shell* case (n 46).
442 Bohoslavsky and Opgenhaffen (n 104), 159.
443 *Unocal case* (n 146).
444 MR Marrus, *Some Measure of Justice: The Holocaust Era Restitution Campaign of the 1990s* (University of Wisconsin Press 2009), 32; EG Korman, 'Rewriting the Holocaust History of the Swiss Banks: A Growing Scandal' in MG Bazyler and R Alford (eds), *Holocasut Restitution: Perspectives on the Litigation and Its Legacy* (NYU Press 2006), 115.
445 Marrus (n 445).
446 Ibid.

however, did yield some historical findings. Swiss banks agreed to a comprehensive audit, and German corporations established historical committees and opened their archives to historians to investigate their involvement in the Holocaust.[447] Although the courts did not make any pronouncement of liability, they were actively involved in the negotiation process as well as in the implementation of the Swiss bank settlement, issuing numerous rulings as to the proper categorization of claims and allocation of funds.[448] In addition, by making claims of economic and property rights under the ATS, the Holocaust plaintiffs helped further an expansion of the substantive human rights recognized by international law.[449]

Settlements are a double-edged sword. By accepting a settlement, victims effectively renounce a final decision on the case and the potential granting of any different form of reparation.[450] The out-of-court settlements of cases is frustrating for academics and activists because they impede the development of a much-needed jurisprudence, and limit the goal of achieving corporate accountability and finding the truth about corporate involvement. But they reflect the financial realities and risks to corporations and to the claimants of not settling. Unless a company is confident of a resounding victory and reassured that no significant evidence damaging to its reputation will emerge at trial, the risk of going to trial usually makes little commercial sense. Settlements also provide the quickest way for victims to obtain compensation.[451] Litigation against corporations often takes a long time and involves high costs. Prolonged litigation works to the disadvantage of the victims, in particular where their need for a remedy is immediate. For the South African miners, whose legal battle against *Anglo American* and *AngloGold Ashanti* began in 2004, the agreement was probably a relief. Likewise, the settlement in *Unocal* was a relief for Myanmar victims.[452]

Further, settlements may also lay the ground for the production of new historical narratives. The process of the *Unocal* litigation, for example, did shine some light on the evidence against the company. In its decision granting summary judgment, the court described the history of *Unocal*'s presence in Myanmar and its knowledge of the forced labour problem.[453] The court concluded thta 'the evidence does suggest that Unocal knew that forced labour was being utilized and it [...] benefited from the practice'.[454] Similarly, despite failed attempts to litigate under the ATS the role of companies such as *Chiquita* and *Drummond*

447 E Barkan, The Guilt of Nations: Restitution and Negotiating Historical Injustices (WW Norton 2001), 88–111.
448 Bergier Committee, Final Report of the Independent Commission of Experts, Switzerland. Second World War (2002), 276–77.
449 KL Boyd, 'Collective Rights Adjudication in U.S. Courts: Enforcing Human Rights at the Corporate Level' (1999) *Byu L Rev* 1139, 1179.
450 Sandoval and Surfleet (n 277), 106.
451 Meeran (n 123), 10.
452 Deva (n 415), 8.
453 *Unocal* case (n 146), 1297–98.
454 Ramasastry, 'Corporate Complicity' (n 33), 130–39.

in the conflict in Colombia, the information retrieved in these lawsuits has shed some light on the material and economic aid companies provided to paramilitary groups.[455]

In addition to serving the punitive goals of justice, another function of judicial processes against corporations after periods of mass atrocity is to help to understand the systems that worked together to make these crimes possible, serving to discourage similar behaviour in the future and authenticating an historical record about a given regime's functioning.[456] While the unprecedented sums paid in the *Holocaust Litigation* settlement made particularly salient the goal of reparation, the actions also brought about a certain degree of truth and reform of the corporate culture. Despite the absence of any court decision determining the degree of their liability, following the lawsuit the defendant Swiss banks agreed to extensive audits, and many German companies established internal historical committees charged with examining their involvement in the Holocaust, opened their archives to historians and published their findings.[457] These archives were private and would not have been opened if not for the lawsuit.[458] Indeed, 'the lack of adjudication transferred the question of the defendants' responsibility from the legal to the moral level'.[459] Leora Bilsky, a scholar, argues that the class actions shifted attention from the individual perpetrator to the organization, and specifically to the complicity of private corporations in the plunder of victims of the Nazis, and put unprecedented pressure on the corporations to cooperate with the plaintiffs' representatives.[460] The civil action lawsuit allowed the financial story behind the Holocaust and the story of corporations' involvement and contribution to the Nazi regime to be told.[461]

The clarification of the historical narrative continued after the settlement was reached. At that point, the entitlements of individual survivors and their families had to be ascertained.[462] Thus, following the settlement, questionnaires were sent to approximately one million survivors and their families, seeking to allow potential class members to express support or opposition to the settlement, as well as to gather information to assist the court in designing a fair scheme of allocation of the settlement funds.[463] A central reason for bringing the cases was 'to speak to history – to build a historical record that could never be denied'.[464] Thus, in

---

455 NC Sánchez León, 'Corporate Accountability, Reparations, and Distributive Justice in Post Conflict Societies' in Michalowski (n 73), 114, 127.
456 Bohoslavsky and Opgenhaffen (n 104), 197–201.
457 Bilsky (n 369), 349–75.
458 Ibid.
459 G Feldman, 'The Historian and Holocaust Restitution: Personal Experiences and Reflections' (2005) 23 *Berkeley J Intl L* 347.
460 Bilsky (n 369), 349–75.
461 Ibid.
462 B Neuborne, 'Preliminary Reflections on Aspects of Holocaust-Era Litigation in American Courts' (2002) 80 *Washington U LQ* 795, 801.
463 Ibid., 795, 801, 827, 828, 830.
464 Ibid., 830.

parallel to the opening of the defendants' archives, the lawsuit produced a large repository of oral history consisting of testimonies by survivors.[465]

Claims against Swiss banks were brought by Holocaust survivors who were denied access in the name of banking secrecy. Faced with the prospect of reputation damage and high litigation costs, German companies eventually signed the Berlin Accords in 2000 with the plaintiffs, and eight 'interested states', ending litigation and making clear that the companies do not accept any legal responsibility. In exchange, the companies and the German government agreed to pay DM10 billion to a specially created German foundation. Both series of claims led to criticism, and were viewed as being 'about the money', and thus as 'a cynical manipulation of the memory of the Holocaust'.[466] Bilsky uses the claims filed on behalf of Holocaust survivors, which resulted in unprecedented settlements of US$1.25 billion and US $5 billion respectively, to defend the position that settlements actually empower victims and advance norm creation on corporate accountability.[467] Settlements do not deny justice, she argues; instead, 'transnational class action settlement offers a new mode of accountability that adequately addresses the bureaucratic nature of business involvement in atrocities'.[468] She concludes that the Swiss settlement 'produced narratives of accountability similar to those produced by courts adjudicating legal liability', by relying, for example, on historical research.[469] By contrast, the German settlement 'can be characterized as a denial of responsibility'.[470] In doing so, she solidifies one of the book's arguments which is that we need to move from the question of 'whether or not settlement' to 'what kind of settlements'.[471] Arguably, the right type of settlement can contribute to fact-finding and novel historical research. Historians have frequently criticized how legal processes, particularly criminal trials, produce inaccurate historical narratives. In a criminal trial, facts are relevant to the extent that they demonstrate guilt or innocence, which can lead to imprecision. By contrast, settlement led corporations to open their archives, triggering the production of invaluable historical research that better reflected the historical truth: 'from a normative perspective, the findings of the historical commissions should be considered a gold mine for researchers trying to understand the motivations and modus operandi of corporations in relation to repressive regimes'.[472]

One consequence of corporate involvement in human rights violations is an increase of foreign direct liability cases, which have been filed with increased

---

465 Bilsky (n 369).
466 Ibid., 36.
467 L Bilsky, *The Holocaust, Corporations, and the Law. Unfinished Business* (University of Michigan Press, 2017).
468 Ibid., 4.
469 Ibid., 118.
470 Ibid., 118.
471 Ibid., 115.
472 Ibid., 164. See also N Bernaz, 'Book Reviews: Leora Bilsky, *The Holocaust, Corporations, and the Law. Unfinished Business*' (2019) 21 *Journal of the History of International Law* 1.

frequency since the 1990s.[473] The result has been 'rather disillusioning' so far: most cases are dismissed, and compensation is rarely achieved.[474] To date, with the exception of the Shell's Nigerian subsidiary conviction by a Dutch court in 2014, no company has been found guilty of human rights violations in a foreign direct liability case. But beside the limited judicial success, human rights litigation has the potential of 'non-judicial side effects'.[475] Beyond its primary judicial purpose, human rights litigation serves two additional functions – one educational and one regulatory.[476] First, most companies introduced or adjusted their human rights policies during or shortly after the litigation. Second, the threat of litigation is likely to drive other corporations, especially in the same sector, to adopt or amend human rights policies.[477]

Conclusion

Ensuring the legal accountability of business enterprises and access to effective remedy for rights holders affected by corporate abuses is a vital part of a state's duty to protect against business-related human rights abuse.[478] State-based judicial mechanisms are not the only means of achieving accountability and access to remedy, but they are 'at the core of ensuring access to remedy'.[479] At present, however, accountability and remedy is often elusive. The UN Office of the High Commissioner for Human Rights points out:

> Although causing or contributing to severe human rights abuses would amount to a crime in many jurisdictions, business enterprises are seldom the subject of law enforcement and criminal sanctions. Human rights impacts caused by business activities give rise to causes of action in many jurisdictions, yet private claims often fail to proceed to judgment and, where a legal remedy is obtained, it frequently does not meet the international standard of 'adequate, effective and prompt reparation for harm suffered'.[480]

473 JD Drimmer and SR Lamoree, 'Think Globally, Sue Globally: Trends in Out of Courts Tactics in Transnational Tort Actions' (2011) 29(2) *Berkeley J Intl L* 456; LF Enneking, 'The Future of Foreign Direct Liability? Exploring the International Relevance of the Dutch Shell Nigeria Case' (2014) 10(1) *Utrecht L Rev* 44.
474 J Schrempf-Stirling and F Wettstein, 'Beyond Guilty Verdicts: Human Rights Litigation and Its Impacts on Corporations' Human Rights Policies' (2017) 145 *J Bus Ethics* 545, 546.
475 Ibid.
476 Ibid.
477 Ibid.
478 Guiding Principles, principle 25 and commentary; OHCHR, 'Improving accountability and access to remedy for victims of business-related human rights abuse', A/ HRC/32/19, 10 May 2016, para 1.
479 Guiding Principles, principle 26 and commentary.
480 OHCHR, 'Improving accountability' (n 479), para 2 quoting article I.2 (b) and VII of the Basic Principles and Guidelines on the Right to a Remedy and Reparation for

In recent years, domestic courts have begun adopting innovative measures to overcome the blockages posed by business veto power, unsettled international law and reliance on voluntary principles. These innovations creatively combine domestic law and international human rights law in ways that might become models for overcoming impunity. Lawsuits against corporations at the domestic level have provided alternative justifications for enforcement of international law through domestic courts' interpretation and a clarification of multinational corporations' obligations under international law and the extraterritorial enforcement of human rights law.[481]

Despite the occasional out-of-court financial settlement, however, no case to date has resulted in adequate remedies for victims. The obstacles faced by victims seeking to hold companies legally accountable in a transitional context are inevitably more complex. Some of these problems, common to many jurisdictions, are exacerbated in transitional justice contexts due to the prevalence of weak rule of law, dysfunctional judicial systems, corruption and logistical difficulties. Those problems have all contributed to a system of domestic law remedies that is 'patchy, unpredictable, often ineffective and fragile'.[482] Persistent challenges, of normative, practical and political nature, include: (i) the inability or unwillingness of host states to prosecute corporations; (ii) the difficulty in establishing jurisdiction in the home state; (iii) practical problems related to the investigation of corporate crimes; (iv) procedural difficulties that result in most civil lawsuits being dismissed or, at best, ending in out-of-court financial settlements; and (v) the urgent need to encourage investment.

First, the positive obligation to address corporate abuse lies principally with host states, as the violations are committed on their territory. There are several advantages of conducting legal proceedings in the host state – above all, to ensure better access to evidence and witness testimonies. There are, however, normative and practical challenges for domestic authorities in host states conducting investigations against companies, especially multinational corporations. Relying on the human rights obligations of the host state presents two preliminary problems: first, whether the state has such an obligation (whether it has ratified the relevant international human rights treaty);[483] and, second, whether the host state has the will and capacity to sanction the corporate actor – especially in a transitional justice

Victims of Gross Violations of International Human Rights Law and Serious Violations of International Humanitarian Law (General Assembly resolution 60/147, annex).

481 Tamo (n 190), 464; Farah (n 138), 42–43; *Kaleck and Saage-Maab* (n 34), 709.

482 J Zerk, 'Corporate liability for gross human rights abuses: towards a fairer and more effective system of domestic law remedies', Feb 2014, www.ohchr.org/Documents/Issues/Business/DomesticLawRemedies/StudyDomesticeLawRemedies.pdf, 7. See also OHCHR, 'Improving accountability and access to remedy for victims of business-related human rights abuse', A/HRC/32/19, 10 May 2016, para 4.

483 O Martin-Ortega 'Business and Human Rights in Conflict' (2008) *Carnegie Council for Ethics in International Affairs*.

context where the host state's economy may be heavily dependent on either a specific corporation or the need to reassure corporate entities in general that their activities and revenues are relatively safe. In addition, in transitional justice contexts the legal systems and means of enforcement are often deficient, and the state may lack *de facto* control over relevant areas, or may be the principal perpetrator of the violations in the first place.[484] The worst human rights violations are often committed during armed conflict where the rule of law is severely compromised, if not totally absent. Many wars are fought in countries with a weak police and judicial infrastructure, where there is limited physical capacity to undertake even the most basic prosecutions. Systematic flaws in the domestic regulation and the judicial system due to the lack of institutional capacity and resources are likely to be prominent in host states in a transitional context.[485] In addition, in cases where the company is complicit in the abuses with an authoritarian or repressive government that may be the main perpetrator, victims face further difficulties in obtaining justice before that very state's judicial system. Because the avenues offered by transitional justice mechanisms to address corporate accountability in the host state are limited, victims may be forced to turn to litigation in other courts.[486] Another challenge to litigation is the risk of exposure to Investor State Dispute Settlement arbitration and the unknown extent to which the tribunals would take past corporate complicity in human rights abuses into account in the determination of responsibility and of awards.

Second, the home state's use of extraterritorial jurisdiction over corporations incorporated in its territory is a useful tool in a transitional justice context where the host state may be unwilling or unable to prosecute. But home states remain equally reluctant to hold multinational companies accountable, a factor Ruggie blames, in part, on 'the permissible scope of national regulation with extraterritorial effect remain[ing] poorly understood'.[487] The civil remedies system across different jurisdictions remains a possible avenue of redress for victims of corporate human rights abuses seeking justice in a transitional context. The jurisprudence developed so far has addressed issues related to transitional justice – for example, which human rights violations are severe enough to justify litigation against corporations for complicity in actions taken by a foreign state, or how courts should address competing claims by a society where specific transitional justice processes are in place. The ATS litigation appears as part of different responses to prosecution in the absence of full political or legal transition.[488] But attempts to achieve legal accountability of corporations through extraterritorial jurisdiction face serious obstacles as the complicated history of the *South Africa*

484 Ibid., 280.
485 L van den Herik and J Letnar Černič, 'Regulating Corporations under International Law. From Human Rights to International Criminal Law and Back Again' (2010) 8 *JICJ* 725, 728–29; de Schutter (n 423), 237–40.
486 Martin-Ortega (n 484), 282.
487 'Protect, Respect and Remedy framework' (n 26), para 14.
488 R Teitel, *Globalizing Transitional Justice* (OUP 2014), 169–75.

Apartheid Litigation and the recent narrowing of the exercise of extraterritorial jurisdiction by the *Kiobel* decision demonstrate.[489] In addition, civil litigation in foreign courts has intrinsic limitations: it can only address a small number of cases, it can offer compensation but no other forms of reparations, and it might be insensitive to local contexts and needs.

Third, in more practical terms, 'extraterritorial international investigations can be a real headache'.[490] Because the corporate actors involved in crimes are often located in multiple jurisdictions, investigations of such activities become expensive, time-consuming and therefore daunting. It is often difficult for victims in proceedings against corporations to satisfy the necessary standard of proof, because the company retains control over the requisite documents and evidence.[491] The capacity and willingness of law enforcement agencies to investigate such extraterritorial cases creates a further major obstacle.[492] Even when they do investigate, law enforcement officials often lack the expertise and resources to pursue this type of offence, and face difficulties and language barriers in taking statements from witnesses and collecting other evidence from abroad. Ensuring adequate protection and support for such witnesses through such a complicated process may prove particularly troublesome, particularly where the home authorities are uncooperative. The political instability in post-conflict and transitional contexts adds to the challenge. Other challenges related to extraterritorial litigation include language translation (which makes the process more cumbersome, slow and complex), ways of delineating the state and corporate roles in the harms caused, and the limitations of financial remedies in the context of confiscation and damage caused to land and resources that form the basis for livelihoods.

Fourth, most human rights lawsuits against corporations are dismissed on procedural grounds in the early stages of litigation.[493] Complex jurisdictional and procedural difficulties have prevented most cases against corporations from being considered on the merits.[494] Binding legal precedents in this area are generally limited to procedural issues that, in spite of tangential relevance to the substance of a case, are frequently decisive.[495] Where cases survive inevitable legal procedural challenges and are not dismissed, corporate cases to date have been settled before trial, as has been demonstrated in key cases in this chapter. For example, the

489 Abrahams (n 225), 153–54.
490 Batesmith (n 21), 293.
491 *Kaleck and Saage-Maab* (n 34), 715–16; International Commission of Jurists, *Corporate Complicity in International Crime* (n 2), Vol II, 40; Farah (n 138), 48–49.
492 W Kaleck, 'From Pinochet to Rumsfeld: Universal Jurisdiction in Europe 1998–2008' (2009) 30 *Michigan J Intl L* 931, 961–64.
493 K Gallagher, 'Civil Litigation and Transnational Business: An Alien Tort Statute Primer' (2010) 8 *JICJ* 745, 751; S Joseph, *Corporations and Transnational Human Rights Litigation* (Hart 2004).
494 For example, *Sarei v Rio Tinto* (n 177), *In re Union Carbide Corp Gas Plant Disaster at Bhopal*, 634 F. Supp 842, 850–51 (S.D.N.Y. 1986), *Flores v Southern Peru Copper Corp.*, 253 F. Supp. 2d 510, 526 (S.D.N.Y. 2002).
495 Meeran (n 123).

majority of cases against corporations under the ATS ended in dismissal, while a significant minority resulted in out-of-court financial settlements, before the dispute was determined in a final judgment.

Finally, the investment and economic activity that a corporation (especially a multinational corporation) could bring, and particularly its scale, may be more appealing to a post-conflict state than the need to provide redress for individual or groups of citizens, for violations committed by the company – or potentially other companies.[496] Transitional governments thus have a vested interest in not investigating or prosecuting foreign companies for fear of jeopardizing overseas investment and development.[497] State authorities, often reliant on revenues generated by corporate entities, are less likely to prioritize the investigation and prosecution of corporate crimes.[498] Makau Mutua, a law professor, explains that transitional justice concepts comprise a two-step process of change.[499] The first seeks to stabilize a post-conflict society through temporary measures that signal a commitment to addressing past abuses and building the public's confidence in a process of reconstruction. In the second phase, those who have been aggrieved must find justice, but the place of the perpetrators of the abusive past in the future of the society is equally important. 'While justice needs to be done, concessions must be made by each side in order to move forward to a shared and common future', says Mutua.[500] A basic precondition for the intervention of judicial processes in a transitional justice context is that the system or regime to which the accused belonged has changed – that is, that the transition has actually happened.[501] As a rule in such processes, it is the political or the military elites that change first.[502] As a result, situations of transition after conflicts and repression often lead to the prosecution of political elites.

By contrast, industry and business activities constitute a continuum in most societies, which may explain why there is often no drive for a determined legal remedy for these cases.[503] Economic elites are often seen as key actors in rebuilding a society as it goes through a political transition. Should corporations be brought to justice for

---

496 van den Herik and Letnar Černič (n 486), 728–29.
497 Batesmith (n 21), 293.
498 E Harwell and P Le Billon, 'Natural Connections: Linking Transitional Justice and Development Trough a Focus on Natural Resources' in P de Greiff and R Duthie, *Transitional Justice and Development: Making Connections* (Social Science Research Council 2009), 282, 290–99.
499 M Mutua, 'What Is the Future of Transitional Justice?' (2015) 9 *Intl J Trans Just*, 1, 2.
500 Ibid.
501 F Jessberger, 'On the Origins of Individual Criminal Responsibility under International Law for Business Activity: IG Farben on Trial' (2010) 8(3) *JICJ* 783, 800.
502 In many post-transition societies these efforts are tokenistic and in reality the same groups continue to maintain power – e.g. the Fujimori family in Peru are still major players in the political world, the Marcos family in the Philippines are still major players in the mining sector, the President of Colombia was an actor in the conflict with the FARC, etc.
503 Ibid.

complicity in human rights violations, or should they receive absolution to generate growth and economic activity in order to further national economic development? A state emerging from conflict or oppressive regimes is often less likely and perhaps even reluctant to pursue claims against corporations – especially foreign companies – during a time when it needs foreign direct investment, economic growth and development, and jobs.[504] Countries in transition are often in a state of economic collapse, and in this scenario corporations are often viewed as critical for economic progress. They face increased pressure to reduce corporate regulations in an attempt to attract investment.[505] As a result, even if economic actors have substantially contributed to the systemic injustice, they may not be held accountable, in a tacit promise to continue to contribute to the economic recovery. This tendency can be observed in the post–World War II cases, later in the South African truth and reconciliation process and the initial position of the South African government towards claims of the *Apartheid Litigation*, and more recently in Myanmar.[506]

No case against a corporation for human rights violations has yet been determined on the merits. But judicial processes are not the only type of remedy available for victims of corporate abuses: in transitional justice contexts, truth-seeking mechanisms can also recommend measures related to the responsibilities of companies and reparations for victims. The next chapter analyzes this aspect.

504 de Schutter (n 423), 237–40; Carranza (n 329).
505 T Van Ho, 'Due Diligence in Transitional Justice States: An Obligation For Greater Transparency?' in Letner Černič and van Ho (n 190), 229, 236.
506 *Kaleck and Saage-Maab* (n 34), 718–19.

Chapter 5

Truth-seeking processes

Introduction

After the assessment of the limitations, and potentials, of international, regional and national courts to establish corporate accountability and provide reparations for victims, the analysis turns to the work of truth-seeking processes, in particular truth commissions. Truth commissions are a typical transitional justice mechanism, with widespread use across the world, seeking to enable societies to come to terms with the human rights violations perpetrated during the period of strife from which they are emerging. The UN Secretary-General describes truth commissions as 'official, temporary, non-judicial fact-finding bodies that investigate a pattern of abuses of human rights or humanitarian law committed over a number of years'.[1] State practice of truth commissions varies: in some cases truth commissions are considered complementary to criminal trials; in others they may even form an alternative to criminal justice, where trials are unlikely because of an overwhelming number of perpetrators, a destroyed justice system, or political deals involving amnesties.[2] Although described as 'non-judicial' bodies, truth commissions are, in effect, official bodies, usually established by legislation and often conferred with a wide range of legal powers, including compelling powers such as the ability to subpoena, search and seize.[3] Each truth commission is a unique institution, but their core activities usually include collecting statements from victims and witnesses, conducting thematic research, organizing public hearings and publishing a report outlining findings and recommendations.[4] Some commentators believe that a state's duty to investigate and provide effective remedies, especially in the

1 Report of the UN Secretary-General, 'The Rule of Law and Transitional Justice in Conflict and Post-conflict Societies', UN Doc. S/2004/616, 3 August 2004, 17.
2 W Schabas and S Darcy (eds), *Truth Commissions and Courts: The Tension between Criminal Justice and the Search for Truth* (Kluwer 2005).
3 M Freeman, Truth Commissions and Procedural Fairness (CUP 2007), 188.
4 Ibid.; PB Hayner, *Unspeakable Truths: Confronting State Terror and Atrocity* (Routledge 2001), 251; S Darcy 'Truth Commissions, the European Union and Reparations from Business' in F Medjouba (ed.), *Building Peace in Post-Conflict Situations: British Institute of International and Comparative Law* (BIICL 2011) 43, 43; E Wiebelhaus-Brahm, 'Truth Commissions and Other Investigative Bodies' in CM Bassiouni (ed.), *The Pursuit*

absence of a functioning judiciary system, mandates the creation of a truth commission to examine a repressive past.[5]

Priscilla Hayner, a scholar who undertook comprehensive research on the work on truth commissions, specifies that truth commissions are usually focused on the past, rather than on on-going events, and will often investigate a pattern of events that took place over a period of time.[6] Because truth commissions generally seek to address systemic patterns of human rights violations, rather than those that may occur solely against specific individuals, they usually have the mandate to examine the underlying causes, consequences and nature of gross human rights violations that other processes are often restricted from engaging with, not least due to statutory time limitations.[7] As part of their varied mandates, TRCs have started to pay more attention to the range of different actors involved in perpetrating violations or part of the state infrastructure that tolerated violations, including corporations.[8] While the majority of truth commissions have focused on the state's responsibility for human rights violations, an emerging number of commissions have also recognized business responsibility in their final reports.[9] In this sense,

  of International Criminal Justice: A World Study on Conflicts, Victimization, and Post-Conflict Justice (Intersentia 2010), Vol I, 477.

5 J Pasqualucci, 'The Whole Truth and Nothing but the Truth: Truth Commissions, Impunity and the Inter-American Human Rights System' (1994) 12 *BU Intl LJ* 333; P Clark, 'Establishing a Conceptual Framework: Six Key Transitional Justice Themes' in P Clark and Z Kaufman (eds), *After Genocide: Transitional Justice, Post-Conflict Reconstruction and Reconciliation in Rwanda and Beyond* (Hurst 2009), 203. Hayner (n 4), 25, 26; W Lambourne, 'Transformative Justice, Reconciliation and Peace-building' in S Buckley-Zistel and others (eds), *Transitional Justice Theories* (Routledge 2013), 25, 26–28; Freeman (n 3), 34; Darcy (n 4), 43–46.

6 Hayner (n 4), 11–12.

7 For example, the Liberia TRC was mandated to establish 'the antecedents, circumstances, factors and context of violations and abuses', *An Act to Establish the Truth and Reconciliation Commission of Liberia* (2005) art IV, Section 4(a). See also Hayner (n 4), 77; R Carranza, 'Plunder and Pain: Should Transitional Justice Engage with Corruption and Economic Crimes?' (2008) 2 *Intl J Trans Just* 310, 319–21.

8 See e.g. Commission for Reception, Truth and Reconciliation in East Timor (CAVR), *Chega!* (2006) [CAVR East Timor, *Chega!*], Part 3, 6–13; Truth and Reconciliation Commission of South Africa, *Final Report* (1998), Vol II, Ch 7, 694; Volume V, Ch 6, 228, 278, 445 [TRC South Africa report]; Truth and Reconciliation Commission of Liberia, *Consolidated Final* Report, 30 June 2009 [TRC Liberia report], Vol III, title III. See also, BS Lyons, 'Getting to Accountability: Business, Apartheid and Human Rights' (1999) 17 *Neth Q Hum Rts* 135; N Nattrass, 'The Truth and Reconciliation Commission on Business and Apartheid: A Critical Evaluation' (1999) 98 *African Affairs* 373. A study by the University of Oxford reveals that over half of truth commissions that issued final reports recognized business involvement in gross violations of human rights during dictatorships and armed conflicts (in Argentina, Brazil, Chile, Cote D'Ivoire, East Timor, Ecuador, Ghana, Guatemala, Haiti, Honduras, Kenya, Liberia, Nigeria, Paraguay, Peru, Sierra Leone, South Africa, South Korea, Zambia).

9 For example, CAVR East Timor, *Chega!* (n 8); TRC South African report (n 8); TRC Liberia report (n 8). See also G Koska, 'Corporate Accountability in Times of

they play the unique role of establishing an official record of corporations' involvement in past abuses.[10]

In addition to truth commissions, UN-mandated commissions of inquiry, fact-finding missions and other investigative bodies are increasingly being used to respond to situations of serious violations of international humanitarian law and international human rights law, often in times of conflict and transition.[11] Normally, these are mandated to determine the facts surrounding the human rights violations, to make recommendations and, in the case of commissions of inquiry – the highest level of investigation – also to identify alleged perpetrators. While doing so, at times, they have also reported on the involvement of companies and businesspeople, and have framed recommendations to address their responsibilities.[12] This chapter addresses this aspect as part of the attempt to identify a remedy-oriented architecture that can effectively address corporate human rights violations in transitional justice contexts.

This chapter first describes the investigations and finding of the truth and reconciliation commissions (TRCs) and other bodies, and then assesses their limitations in relation to corporate accountability. It looks in particular at the work of TRCs, starting with the South Africa's TRC, whose findings represent the first and one of the most important contributions in the area of corporate accountability (5.1). This section is followed by an exploration of the work of truth commissions established in Liberia, East Timor, Sierra Leone, Guatemala, Brazil and Argentina (5.2), alongside the contributions made by UN investigative bodies (5.3). The objective of this section is to describe emerging state practice in a variety of different settings. This chapter seeks to show that, as a complement or alternative to judicial processes, truth-seeking initiatives can recommend important measures for the accountability of companies involved in abuses during times of conflict or repression and for reparation measures for victims. Often, however, mainly for economic and political reasons, governments have failed to implement such recommendations.

Transition: The Role of Restorative Justice in the South African Truth and Reconciliation Commission' (2016) 4(1) *Restorative Justice* 41–67.

10 Darcy (n 4); MP Scharf, 'The Case for a Permanent International Truth Commission' (1997) 7(2) Duke *J Comp Intl Law* 375; Carranza (n 7), 319–21.

11 The UN has established 63 International Commission of Inquiry and other fact-finding missions – the first was the 1963 UN fact-finding mission to Vietnam and the last the fact-finding mission to Myanmar established in March 2017. UN, Research Guide, http://libraryresources.unog.ch/factfinding.

12 An example is the fact-finding mission established by the Human Rights Council in 2012 (resolution 19/17) to investigate the implications of the Israeli settlements on the human rights of the Palestinian people throughout the Occupied Palestinian Territory. The mission found that business enterprises, directly and indirectly, enabled, facilitated and profited from the construction and growth of the settlements. Report of the Independent International Fact-finding Mission to investigate the implications of the Israeli settlements on the civil, political, economic, social and cultural rights of the Palestinian people throughout the Occupied Palestinian Territory, including East Jerusalem, 7 Feb 2013, A/HRC/22/63, paras 96, 97, 117.

V.1 South Africa's Truth and Reconciliation Commission

When Nelson Mandela became the first black president of South Africa in 1994, the government established a TRC to investigate and document human rights violations committed during the apartheid regime between 1960 and 1994.[13] The South African TRC was the first such commission to examine the role of different sectors of society during the previous authoritarian regime, and also the first to investigate business involvement in human rights abuses.[14] The TRC Act recognized the systemic nature of the gross violations of human rights, and that both individuals and collective entities were involved in those violations.[15] Under its comprehensive mandate, the TRC investigated systemic patterns of human rights violations through public hearings on legislated apartheid, and the roles of different sectors of society – the health, media, legal and business sectors.[16] The sectoral hearings at the South Africa's TRC aimed to address the issue of apartheid as part of a systemic phenomenon.

5.1.1. The business hearing

In November 1997 in Johannesburg, the South Africa TRC held a three-day institutional hearing to focus on the role of business during the apartheid era, with written and oral submissions by business organizations, companies, academics, civil society and political parties. The business hearing examined the relationship between apartheid and the economy, and the role of business, government and trade unions.[17] Few corporations, however, decided to come forward and take part in the process. Most businesses were deliberately uncooperative during the hearing.[18] Archbishop Desmond Tutu, Chairperson of the TRC, concluded that there were 'glaring absences' in the business submissions that the TRC received. 'No one today admits to supporting apartheid', Tutu lamented in his opening remarks to the hearings.[19] He continued, it would be 'wonderful to have someone

---

13 M Parlevliet, 'Considering Truth. Dealing with a Legacy of Gross Human Rights Violations' (1998) 16(2) *Netherlands Quarterly Human Rights*, 172–74.

14 J Barnard-Naudé, 'For Justice and Reconciliation to Come: The TRC Archive, Big Business, and the Demand for Material Reparations' in F du Bois and A du Bois-Pedain (eds), *Justice and Reconciliation in Post-Apartheid South Africa* (Cambridge Studies in Law and Society 2008), 172; Nattrass (n 8), 374–75; Darcy (n 4), 53, 54.

15 South Africa Government, Promotion of National Unity and Reconciliation Act, No. 34 of 1995, Chapter 1, section 1(ix) [South Africa TRC Act].

16 Ibid., Chapter 2, section 4(a)(i) section 4(a)(iv). See also South Africa TRC report (n 8), Vol 4.

17 South African TRC, Press Release, Statement on Business Role Submissions, 4 September 1997.

18 J Simcock, 'Unfinished Business: Reconciling the Apartheid Reparation Litigation with South Africa's Truth and Reconciliation Commission' (2011) 47 *Stan J Intl L* 239, 242, 249–53.

19 South Africa Press Association, 'Some Glaring Absences in Business Submissions to TRC: Tutu' 11 November 1997.

here saying "we did this and we did that" [...] and we want to rub some oil on the wounds'.[20]

The Commission conceded that business largely refused to participate in the hearings.[21] The broad assessment of the TRC was that 'businesses were reluctant to speak about their involvement in the former homelands'.[22] The report reserved special mention for the agriculture and mining industries, highlighting: '[I]t was particularly regrettable that representatives of commercial agriculture did not participate in the hearing, despite an invitation to do so.'[23] It was also 'regrettable that the Chamber of Mines made no mention in its submission of the active role they played in constructing and managing the migrant labour system'.[24] Arguably, given the uncertain legal consequences that the TRC posed, some corporations simply opted out of the proceedings, preferring the risk of being stigmatized for their absence to the risk of a concrete and public assessment of their direct or indirect culpability in maintaining, supporting or collaborating with the apartheid regime. Most notable among the absentees, the TRC reported, were the multinational oil corporations, such as *Shell* and *BP*, the largest foreign investors in South Africa during apartheid, which did not even respond to the invitation to take part.[25] As such, the conspicuous absence of testimony and submissions from multinational corporations doing business with the apartheid regime was a major omission from the hearings overall.[26] Although their activities were chronicled in the testimony and submission from the Anti-Apartheid Movement (AAM) Archives Committee, which focused on the role of the multinationals during the period 1960–1994, this absence permitted critical actors to be free from any scrutiny for their roles in the apartheid and related rights violations.

With few exceptions, businesses denied any active involvement with the apartheid government.[27] They rejected any notion of culpability and resisted any attempts to link their business activities with human rights violations. This also applied to the media sector, with the Afrikaans press declining to participate in the media hearing. *Nasionale Pers*, the largest Afrikaans newspaper publishing company, claimed that its affiliated papers did not commit any human rights abuses and therefore had nothing relevant to contribute to the TRC process.[28] A few representatives of the *South Africa Broadcasting Corporation* (*SABC*) were prepared to admit that *SABC* served as the propaganda arm of the government and thus contributed to abuses of human rights.[29] But justifications and excuses abounded: the government was hostile, the

---

20 Ibid.
21 South Africa TRC report (n 8), Vol 4, Ch 2, 18–19.
22 Ibid., Vol 4 'Final Recommendation on Business Hearings', 36.
23 Ibid., 28.
24 Ibid.
25 Ibid., 18.
26 Lyons (n 8), 153–54.
27 South Africa TRC report (n 8), Vol. 4, 58.
28 Ibid.
29 Ibid.

general climate was dangerous and *SABC* sought to portrait itself as valiantly seeking to do what it could in such an environment.[30] The English-language press took a similar position: in its submission *Times Media* denied that their newspaper had not done enough to oppose apartheid.[31]

Some of the business submissions accepted that apartheid benefitted certain business interests such as Afrikaner capital,[32] but all rejected the idea that apartheid was good for business. The role of businesses in supporting the government during apartheid seemed to be a case of 'selective creeping amnesia' among white businesses.[33] What was most significant in white businesses' testimony and submissions were the topics they *did not* address.[34] One of the omissions was any reference to the role of businesses' in the military-industrial complex.[35] As a representative of *Barlow Rand*, an electronic equipment manufacturer who supplied the military-industrial complex for 27 years put it: '[T]here was no direct violation of human rights that could be attributed to business.'[36] *Armaments Corporation of South Africa (Armscor)*, a state-owned armaments company that supplied weapons to the military, concluded that 'despite the covert and clandestine methods used by this organisation in the past, we have been unable to unearth what appears to be transgressions [of human rights]'.[37] One of the very few business inputs that reflected critically on business support for the ideology of apartheid was the submission from the *Afrikaner Handelsinstituut (AHI)*, the main organization of Afrikaner business:

> Without in any way detracting from the AHI's willingness to accept responsibility [...] it must be noted that support for separate development was part and parcel of the majority of the white community's thinking at the time [...] the notion that the separate development of South African population groups was seen as the best guarantee for overall justice and peace in the country. The AHI was part of that collective thinking.[38]

30 Ibid.
31 Ibid.
32 *Anglo American*, for example, complained that hostility from the National Party at times affected its ability to do business and *South African Breweries (SAB)* complained of a similar bias which forced them out of the retail liquor, wines and spirits industries. South Africa TRC report (n 8), Anglo American, Submission, 13; SAB, Submission, 15.
33 Lyons (n 8), 144.
34 Ibid., 137–41.
35 South Africa TRC report (n 8), 126: 'hundreds and probably thousands of South African private sector companies made the decision to collaborate actively with the government's war machine. This was no reluctant decision imposed on them by coercive apartheid legislation. Many businesses, including subsidiaries of leading corporations, became willing collaborators in the creation of this war machine.'
36 AM Rosholt, Business Hearings, 11 November 1997.
37 South Africa TRC report (n 8), Armscor, Submission.
38 Ibid., AHI, Submission, 4.

Some business submissions included apologies for not having done more. *Anglo American*, for example, apologized for not having provided more married accommodation for black workers.[39] This was regarded as one of the 'missed opportunities', and the corporation acknowledged 'with regret that [it] did not sufficiently progress these and many other opportunities to oppose apartheid and hasten its demise'.[40] Other than this omission, *Anglo American*'s submissions lacked any acknowledgment of its responsibility for human rights abuses perpetrated in its mines. To fill in the missing pieces, one has to turn to submissions made by trade unions that document the mining disasters, the role of the mine security during strikes, and the use of convict labour in furthering business interests and generating output, revenues and profit.[41]

Financial institutions were among the few private entities admitting that the economic sector was tied to apartheid. The submission from the *Council of South African Banks* acknowledged that apartheid was a political, social and economic system, which depended for its efficacy on all those three 'pillars', and that senior bank officials lent 'credibility' to apartheid governmental structures.[42] The submission highlighted: 'The banks were knowingly or unknowingly involved in the provision of banking services and the lending of money to the apartheid government and its agencies [...] Banks cannot exist otherwise than within the systems and structures of the country in which they operate.'[43]

With respect to its role in human rights violations, the *Development Bank of Southern Africa* admitted that it was 'an integral part of the system and part and parcel of the apartheid gross violation of human rights'.[44] In its submission, the *Land and Agricultural Bank of South Africa* acknowledged participation in policies that often, as acts of omission, supported rural and agricultural apartheid.[45] One of South Africa's former prime ministers, referring to the support financial corporations provided to the government at that time, said that 'each bank loan, each new investment [was] another brick in the wall of our continued existence'.[46]

The submissions from white businesses were contested by testimony from businesses and organizations in the black, Indian and Muslim communities, and the labour and anti-apartheid movements. Submissions critical of business argued that apartheid was a system of exploitation that benefitted capital. As the African National Congress (ANC) put it:

39 Ibid., *Anglo American*, Submission, 4.
40 Ibid., 12.
41 South Africa TRC report (n 8), Vol 4, 58, COSATU, Submission, 9, para 21. See also D Innes, 'Anglo-American and the Rise of Modern South Africa' (1984) Monthly Review Press.
42 South Africa TRC report (n 8), The Banking Industry, Submission, 6, sect 5.3.4, 6.1.
43 Ibid., 2, sect 2.3.
44 Ibid., DBSA Submission, 13.
45 South Africa TRC, Business Hearings, 11–13 November 1997, Days 1–3.
46 Quoted in JP Bohoslavsky and V Opgenhaffen, 'The Past and Present of Corporate Complicity: Financing the Argentinean Dictatorship' (2010) 23 *Harvard Human Rights J* 157, 159.

> Apartheid was associated with a highly unequal distribution of income, wealth and opportunity that largely corresponded to the racial structure of society [...] Historically privileged business as a whole must, therefore, accept a degree of co-responsibility for its role in sustaining the apartheid system of discrimination and oppression over many years.[47]

While most critical submissions recognized that apartheid affected different categories of business differently, they pointed to the association between apartheid policies, racial injustice and South Africa's racially based income distribution, and concluded that business was morally implicated in apartheid.[48] As the AAM Archives Committee concluded: '[T]he speed with which the apartheid edifice then crumbled [after the withdrawal of international business] [...] is the final proof, if any were needed, of the way in which international business sustained apartheid.'[49]

One of strongest statements came from Sampie Terreblanche, an Afrikaner academic and critic of the apartheid government. In his keynote speech at the TRC business hearings, he argued:

> The true importance of the symbiotic relationship between the white controlled state and racial capitalism was that the state was, over a period of more than 60 years, always prepared to promulgate legislation to keep black labour costs low and to suppress all kinds of black labour unrest with undue ferocity.[50]

The TRC relied on exposing the truth as a basis for accountability for crimes committed during the apartheid era.[51] For perpetrators, 'bringing the darker side of the past to the fore' was described as a chance to acknowledge their responsibility as well as fulfilling the demand for accountability.[52] The business hearing was intended as a site for contestation and the opportunity to deliver truth and accountability for alleged corporate crimes committed during apartheid. In fact, the hearing can be seen to have provided corporations 'with a subject position from which to speak and from which to represent [their] version of, and [their] position in, the past'.[53]

---

47 South Africa TRC report (n 8), ANC, Submission, 1–2.
48 See, ibid., vol. 4, 30–32 (on Afrikaner business); 33–36 (on the mining industry); 36–37 (on the armaments industry); 46–51 (on the role of business in the 1980s). See also Nattrass (n 8), 378.
49 South Africa TRC report (n 8), Anti-Apartheid Movement, Submission, 19.
50 Ibid., S Terreblanche, Testimony, 3–4, 26.
51 J Brankovic, *Responsabilidad y Reconciliación Nacional en Sudáfrica* (Ediciones InfoJus 2013), 2(4), 55–86.
52 South Africa TRC report (n 8).
53 B Harris, 'The Archive, Public History and the Essential Truth: The TRC Reading the Past' in C Hamilton (ed.), *Refiguring the Archive* (Kluwer 2002), 161, 164.

The experience of the business hearings illustrates the concern that truth commissions can be used as instruments to control collective memory.[54] The business hearings reflected the disparate versions of the past.[55] The TRC report summarized these claims collectively: 'the other position, argued mainly by business, claims that apartheid raised the costs of doing business, eroded South Africa's skill base and undermined long-term productivity and growth. In this view, the impact of apartheid was to harm the economy'.[56]

Most of the white businesses tried to refute the structural contention that they were tied to the apartheid government and that they acted in complicity with, and profited from, apartheid. They contended instead that businesses existed in a 'political vacuum.'[57] Some companies used the TRC as a forum from which they could launch complaints, claiming that they too were victims of apartheid. With no punitive incentive, 'white business tended to use the business and labour sector hearings more as public relation opportunity than as an exercise in truth telling and acknowledgment'.[58]

The TRC did not assess whether the claims of businesses were, at least partially or for some businesses, true, or whether the apartheid system could have in some way affected some types of business or not; instead, it adopted a generalized approach. The TRC did recognize that 'clearly not all businesses can be tarred with the same brush', but by condemning ordinary business activities (the 'third-order involvement' detailed in the next section) it suggested that 'all who prospered under apartheid have something to answer for, in that they took advantage of a situation which depressed the earnings of black South Africans, whilst boosting their own'.[59] It stated that:

> The current distribution of wealth (which is substantially concentrated in white hands) is a product of business activity that took place under an apartheid system that favoured whites. This acts as a counterbalance to statements by business that apartheid harmed them, a reminder that white business accumulated (sometimes vast amounts of) wealth in spite of this alleged harm.[50]

54 L Payne, *Unsettling Accounts: Neither Truth nor Reconciliation in Confessions of State Violence* (Duke University Press 2008), 36–39.
55 Lyons (n 8), 141–49.
56 South Africa TRC report (n 8), Vol 4, 19.
57 Lyons (n 8), 137; K Asmal and R Suresh Roberts (eds), *Reconciliation, Through Truth, A Reckoning of Apartheid's Criminal Governance* (David Philip Publishers 1996), 153–57.
58 A Chapman, 'Truth Recovery Through the TRC Institutional Hearings Process' in A Chapman and H van der Werwe (eds), *Truth and Reconciliation in South Africa; Did the TRC Deliver?* (University of Pennsylvania Press 2008), 169, 179.
59 South Africa TRC report (n 8), Vol 4 Ch 2, para 32.
60 Ibid., para 33.

5.1.2. The TRC's findings on business

The TRC's final report found that the business sector had been 'central to the economy that had maintained the South African state during the apartheid years'.[61] The Commission found that some sectors of business were more involved with the apartheid regime than others, but that most businesses were culpable by virtue of having benefitted from operating in a racially structured environment. The TRC concluded:

> The degree to which business maintained the status quo varied from direct involvement in shaping government policies or engaging in activities directly associated with repressive functions to simply benefiting from operating in a racially structured society in which wages were low and workers were denied basic democratic rights.[62]

The TRC thus shifted from a focus on individual perpetrators to a systematic analysis that equated profitable activity with prospering under apartheid, and drew a link between benefitting from the apartheid's system of racial privileges and having a moral culpability for it.[63] The Commission found:

> Certain businesses, especially the mining industry, were involved in helping to design and implement apartheid policies. Other businesses benefitted from co-operating with the security structures of the former State. Most businesses benefitted from operating in a racially structured context.[64]

Recognizing that businesses were not a single homogenous category, the TRC's final report identified three orders of involvement in the apartheid system.[65] The businesses that were directly involved 'with the state in the formulation of oppressive policies or practices' were considered to be those of the first order.[66] The commission concluded that business involved in this way 'must be held responsible for the suffering that resulted'.[67] The TRC focused on the mining industry, which worked with the government to shape discriminatory policies, such as the migrant labour system, to its own advantage.[68] Companies that knew 'that their products or services would be used for morally unacceptable purposes'

---

61 Ibid., Vol 6, Sect 2, Ch 5, 'Reparations and the Business Sector', 58, 140; Vol 4, Ch. 2, 58, 161.
62 Ibid., Vol 6, Sect 2, 140.
63 Nattrass (n 8), 378.
64 South Africa TRC report (n 8), Vol 4, Ch 2 'Institutional Hearings: Business and Labour', 58, paras 161–67, Vol 5, Ch 6 'Findings and Conclusions', para 161.
65 Ibid., Vol 4, Ch 2, paras 23–36.
66 Ibid., 24, para 23.
67 Ibid.
68 Ibid., 33, para 63. The TRC goes on to chastise the mining industry for not mentioning their role in the migrant labour system, or their active suppression of black

fell within those deemed to be of the second order of involvement in the apartheid system.[69] This included the armaments industry's provision of equipment used to abuse human rights, and more indirect assistance, such as banks' provision of covert credit cards for repressive security operations. For example, the TRC concluded that '[t]he banks played an instrumental role in prolonging apartheid from the time of the debt crisis in 1985 onwards'.[70]

Finally, the Commission identified a 'third-order involvement': ordinary business activities that benefitted indirectly by virtue of operating within the racially structured context of apartheid.[71] Some of the business submissions grappled with the issue of third-order involvement by asking whether, by merely doing business under apartheid, they were supporting the system.[72] The *Textile Federation*, for example, pointed out that its only link with the state was the service of clothing contracts.[73] Third-order involvement is the most problematic of the three orders because it proceeds beyond the bounds of intent and implies guilt by association. The Commission even asked, in some instances, 'whether business had done enough to end [apartheid]'.[74] A scholar argues that 'the only way in which any business could have avoided condemnation by the TRC was to have disinvested entirely from the South African economy'.[75]

The business hearings enabled the TRC to make an historical record of the complex role of businesses within apartheid. As another scholar put it: 'The efforts of white businesses to expunge their crimes from history and, in that process, revise that history, had simply failed.'[76] The findings of the TRC report on business discredited the position that white businesses did not benefit from apartheid legislation, and instead specifically affirmed the collusion and complicity of business with apartheid. Although the majority of South Africans knew this, as they had experienced it every day, the hearings helped to fill in the mechanisms crucial to the functioning of the apartheid state.[77] The South Africa TRC, which did not have any judicial power, condemned business from a moral point of view for crimes of commission and omission.[78] In the course of the South African transition from apartheid, the question of corporate accountability was approached from

    unions and their dismal health and safety record, ibid., 33–34, paras 161–67; Vol 5, Ch 6, paras 163–67.
69 Ibid., Vol 4, 25, para 26, 28.
70 Ibid., Vol 6, Sect 2, 146.
71 Ibid., Vol 4, Ch 2, para 32.
72 Ibid., para 34.
73 Ibid.
74 Nattrass (n 8), 374.
75 Ibid.
76 Lyons (n 8), 159–60.
77 Ibid.
78 South Africa TRC report (n 8). See also E Doxtrader and others, *Truth And Reconciliation In South Africa: The Fundamental Documents* (Institute for Justice and Reconciliation 2007), 427.

both moral and legal angles, allowing for a better and perhaps more balanced understanding of the truth.[79]

5.1.3. The TRC's recommendations on reparations

The transitional justice process in South Africa, through the work of the TRC, is a good example of an attempt to link corporations and reparations, despite the associated political cost of doing so.[80] The issue of reparations was a central feature of the TRC's claim to delivering justice.[81] One of the crucial tasks entrusted to the TRC was that of 'restoring the human and civil dignity of [...] victims [...] by recommending reparations measures'.[82] The TRC Act provided that reparations were to include 'any form of compensation, ex gratia payment, restitution, rehabilitation and recognition'.[83] The proposals formulated by the TRC distinguished four categories of reparations: (i) community rehabilitation programmes; (ii) symbolic reparations measures (issuing of death certificates, exhumations reburials, and other ceremonies); (iii) administrative, legal and other institutional reforms; and (iv) individual reparations in the form of financial grants.[84] The TRC adopted a constrained 'closed list' approach when it established the requirements for reparation eligibility, limited this to victims of 'killing, abduction, torture or severe ill-treatment'.[85] Approximately 17,000 of the approximately 33 million black South Africans who suffered from the injustices of apartheid were qualified for reparations.[86] One of the Commissioners explained in this way such a dilemma:

> The Act's definition of a victim immediately excluded millions of South Africans who, while they may not have suffered a gross violation of human rights in terms of the Act, nevertheless suffered the daily violation of living under apartheid. Our first painful step was thus to limit reparation recipients to

79 N Bernaz, 'Can the ICC Combat the Illegal Exploitation of Resources and "Lan Grabbing"?', 17 Aug 2017, http://rightsasusual.com/2013/10/should-multinationa l-corporations-be-held-liable-for-having-done-business-with-the-apartheid-regime.
80 C Sandoval and G Surfleet, 'Corporations and Redress in Transitional Justice Processes', in S Michalowski (ed.), *Corporate Accountability in the Context of Transitional Justice* (Routledge 2013), 93, 102.
81 South Africa TRC report (n 8), Vol 1, 126.
82 South Africa TRC Act (n 15), Sect 3(1)(c).
83 Ibid., Sect 1.
84 F du Bois, 'Reparations and the Forms of Justice' in du Bois and du Bois-Pedain (eds) *Justice and Reconciliation in Post-Apartheid South Africa* (CUP 2008), 121–22; D Ntsebeza, 'The Legacy of the Truth and Reconciliation Commission' in C Villa-Vicencio and E Doxtader (eds), *The Provocations of Amnesty: Memory, Justice and Impunity* (AfricaWorld Press 2003).
85 South Africa TRC Act (n 15), Sect 1(1)(xix)(a), 1(1)(ix). See also Simcock (n 18), 257.
86 South Africa TRC report (n 8), Vol 5, at 175–76.

those who had been found to have suffered a gross violation of human rights, as defined in the Act.[87]

Eventually, the government provided only monetary compensation (no other forms of reparations) to the 17,000 victims with a one-off payment of R30,000 (about US $4,000) each, totalling about US$70 million, which fell short of the US$360 million the TRC had requested.[88] Corporations did not provide any reparations, and victims of corporate abuses, such as labour violations, were, as a consequence, not given reparations. At the start of the business hearing, the TRC emphasized that acknowledgment and forgiveness was only part of the reconciliation process, and that this had to be followed by reparations, including from businesses. Desmond Tutu invited corporations to make donations to the President's Fund intended for the public reparations scheme designed by the TRC to rehabilitate people affected by apartheid.[89] In its final report, the Commission stated that 'business benefitted substantially during the apartheid era [...] and has, at the very least, a moral obligation to assist [...] through active reparative measures'.[90] To give effect to this, the TRC suggested to the South African government several ways for extracting reparations payments from companies. These included: a wealth tax; a one-off levy on corporate and private income; a 1% 'donation' of the market capitalization by companies listed on the Johannesburg stock exchange; and retrospective surcharges on corporate profit.[91] Yet nothing came out of these proposals.

5.1.4. Limitations of the TRC in relation to corporate accountability and reparations

There is some consensus among scholars that the South African TRC did not do all it could to obtain effective reparations for victims and properly investigate corporate human rights abuses.[92] The TRC can be seen as an embodiment of South

87 Cited in W Orr, 'Reparation Delayed in Healing Retarded' in C Villa-Vicencio and W Verwoerd, *Looking Back, Reaching Forward: Reflections on the Truth And Reconciliation Commission of South Africa* (University of Cape Town Press 2000), 243. See also M Mamdani, 'The Truth According to the Truth and Reconciliation Commission,' in I Amadiume and A An-Naim (eds), *The Politics of Memory: Truth, Healing and Social Justice* (Zed Books 2000).

88 Orr (n 87), 241; Simcock (n 18), 246–48, 250–54; F du Toit, 'Victims Challenge Business' in C Villa-Vicencio and F du Toit (eds), *Truth and Reconciliation in South Africa: 10 Years On* (New Africa Books 2006), 179; M Seekoe, 'Reparations' in Villa-Vicencio and du Toit, ibid., 36–45; *New York Times*, 'South Africa to Pay $3,900 to Each Family of Apartheid Victims' 16 April 2003.

89 Business Sector Hearings (n 45), Day 1, 11 November 1997.

90 South Africa TRC report (n 8), Vol 5, 318–19; Vol 6, 155. See also Doxtrader (n 78), 427.

91 Ibid., Vol 5, Ch 8, 318–20; Vol 6, Sect 2, Ch. 5, 143, 155. See also CJ Colvin, 'Overview of the Reparations Program in South Africa' in P de Greiff, *The Handbook of Reparations* (OUP 2006), 176.

92 Koska (n 9), 42; C Abrahams, 'Lessons from the South African Experience' in Michalowski (n 80); Barnard-Naudé (n 14); Lyons (n 8).

Africa's restorative justice approach to transition, a path that was also chosen carefully to avoid the punitive 'victors' justice' approach to corporate and other crimes.[93] Recalling the principles developed by Declan Roche, a law scholar, a restorative justice process must be guided by the need to repair and heal a relationship, and is based on the participation of offenders and their reintegration back into society.[94] In certain respects the business hearing can be seen as employing restorative justice principles described by Roche: 'personalism', reparation, reintegration and participation.[95] First, the hearing was based on personalism and focused on the experience of the workers as well as labour law violations. Second, it was clearly presented as an opportunity to remedy harm, in that the TRC directly invited businesses to seek to 'repair the wrong that accrues from whatever was done for which the person is contrite'.[96] Third, as with the entire transitional justice process in South Africa, the focus of the hearing was on the reintegration of offenders.[97] Finally, corporate involvement in human rights abuses was discussed in an open forum that included affected parties.

In key aspects, however, the process did not fulfil the essential conditions that a model of restorative justice demands.[98] First, the structure and organization of the TRC was such that equal participation was never guaranteed due to the lack of the threat of prosecution.[99] After companies failed to respond to the invitation for submission to the business hearing, the Commission acknowledged that the non-appearance of these corporations obstructed its investigation.[100] It declined, however, to use its subpoena powers to compel businesses to appear and testify, and instead simply confirmed that those companies would not be called to attend the business hearing.[101] The Commission struggled to elicit truth, compensation or redress for the crimes alleged to have been committed by corporations, notably in the mining sector. Reparations are a critical aspect of any restorative justice process and were a central feature of the TRC's claim to deliver justice.[102] But the Commission failed to secure reparations for victims of corporate abuses.

Second, the TRC lacked the power to order the payment of reparations; it was only empowered to make recommendations and remained reliant on the government to implement them subsequently.[103] Although the government accepted many of the TRC recommendations, it hesitated at imposing compulsory reparation payments, and condemned proposals for a wealth tax, believing these to be

---

93 PM Maduna, 'Declaration by Justice Minister Pennell Maduna on Apartheid Litigation in the United States', 11 July 2003 [Maduna declaration], 3.2.1.
94 D Roche, *Accountability in Restorative Justice* (OUP 2004), 26–31.
95 Ibid.; Koska (n 9), 50.
96 Business Sector Hearings (n 45).
97 Maduna declaration (n 93), 8.1
98 Koska (n 9), 52.
99 Ibid.
100 Business Sector Hearings (n 45), Day 1.
101 Ibid. See also Chapman (n 58), 182.
102 South Africa TRC report (n 8), Vol 1, 126.
103 Ibid., Vol 4, 55–58; Vol 6, 143, 727. See also Barnard-Naudé (n 14), 174.

disincentives to remain invested in the South African economy.[104] Jaco Barnard-Naudé, a South African professor, argues that 'the transitional compromise forged by the constitutional court according to which amnesty would be give on condition that comprehensive reparations would follow was disowned'.[105] He points out that the TRC 'failed to compel the legislature to enact a law that [...] would have provided some relief for the suffering that occurred in the economic sphere'.[106] No subject better encapsulates the economic and political dilemmas of transitional justice than the myriad of issues related to reparation.[107]

The political and economic context in which the TRC was established limited the Commission's capacity to exercise its authority over corporations. The TRC lacked the necessary independence from the political interests of the National Party or the African National Congress in order to be an effective arbitrator over major businesses connected to the dominant elites of the apartheid era.[108] Because the TRC was reliant on the government to implement recommendations, it had no power to compel the corporations to act and remained powerless to achieve accountability and deliver reparations when the government did not implement any of the TRC's recommendations concerning business.[109] As a non-judicial commission dealing with a business sector, on which the new South African government was disproportionately dependent, the TRC had no leverage on its own.[110]

Third, the 'new' position of business as a partner of government in the transformation controlled the process.[111] At the time that the TRC issued its final report in 2003, a post-Mandela presidency was already underway. The new administration was focused on reducing the country's high unemployment rate and on growing the nation's GDP. The new administration determined that foreign direct investment was critical to these efforts, and, as a consequence, shied away from any actions that it deemed might have the effect of deterring investors.[112] The death knell to the process came in April 2003 when South African President Thabo Mbeki announced

104 A Boraine, 'Truth and Reconciliation Commission in South Africa Amnesty: The Price of Peace' in J Elster (ed.), *Reparation and Retribution in the Transition to Democracy* (Columbia University Press 2006); Colvin (n 91).
105 Barnard-Naudé (n 14), 201–02.
106 Ibid., 174.
107 JA Carrillo, 'Justice in Context: The Relevance of Inter-American Human Rights Law and Practice to Repairing the Past' in de Greiff (n 91), 506.
108 H Van der Merwe, 'What Survivors Say About Justice: An Analysis of the TRC Victim Hearings' in H Van der Merwe and A Chapman (eds), *Truth and Reconciliation in South Africa: Did the TRC Deliver?* (University of Pennsylvania Press 2008), 23, 26; Koska (n 9), 44; K Asmal, L Asmal and R Roberts, *Reconciliation Through Truth: A Reckoning of Apartheid's Criminal Governance* (David Philip 1996), 156–57.
109 C Lekha Sriram, 'Justice as Peace? Liberal Peacebuilding and Strategies of Transitional Justice' (2017) 21(4) *Global Society* 579; Koska (n 9), 44.
110 Lyons (n 8), 159–60.
111 Ibid.; H Marais, *South Africa, Limits to Change, The Political Economy of the Transformation* (Zed Books 1998), 259.
112 T Bell and D Buhle Ntsebeza, *Unfinished Business: South Africa, Apartheid, and Truth* (Verso 2003), 348.

that the government would not implement the TRC recommendations regarding business reparations.[113]

Corporations agreed with the government. They thought that 'reparation was not the way to go [and] decided [that] the best way forward was to show that business was serious about transformation. [They] wanted to establish a project in which business could play a catalytic role to achieve agreed objectives.'[114] Finally, corporations, with the support of the government, opted for a model of financial contributions to provide development to the country. It was agreed to create a Business Trust so corporations would contribute to the country's reconstruction and provide funds to affected communities, without naming those funds as reparations.[115] The Business Trust ran from 1999 to 2011 and generated R1.2 billion of financial contributions from 140 companies, and additional government contributions.[116] Although business engagement took place on a purely voluntary basis, the process still demonstrates that corporations can play an active role in reparations.[117] The contributions, however, should not be understood as a form of compensation, given that they were not generated in response to the individual harm suffered by victims, and were not used to redress victims.[118] The Trust was not intended to provide reparations for those affected by corporate-related human rights violations, but was geared instead towards promoting economic development by attracting foreign investment.[119] Companies insisted that their contribution was referred to as 'nation-building', rather than 'community reparations'.[120]

The failure to address past abuses directly meant that the Trust did not meet a key component of a restorative justice process: that reparations target the perpetrator and repair the harm that was caused.[121] Moreover, the focus on economic growth concealed the relational aspect of economic inequality in apartheid South Africa as well as the obligation for beneficiaries, such as businesses, to repay those who were harmed.[122] As a result, this approach paved the way for corporate social responsibility in South Africa, which focused on businesses' contribution to economic development and assisting communities through social interventions, rather

---

113 Statement by President Thabo Mbeki to the National House of Parliament and the Nation, Cape Town, 15 April 2003. See also Barnard-Naudé (n 14), 194.
114 S. Makozoma, 'Winning Trust' in Business Leadership South Africa and National Business Initiative and Business Trust, *Building the Nation: A Business Contribution*, July 2007, 4.
115 Ibid. See also Colvin (n 91), 209.
116 Business Trust of South Africa, 1999–2011, www.btrust.org.za
117 Sandoval and Surfleet (n 80).
118 Ibid., 101.
119 Business Trust (n 114). See also Koska (n 9), 56.
120 B Hamber, 'Narrowing the Micro and Macro: A Psychological Perspective on Reparations in Societies in Transition' in de Greiff (n 91) 574.
121 K Clamp, *Restorative Justice in Transition* (Routledge 2014); Koska (n 9), 57.
122 P Gready, *The Era of Transitional Justice: The Aftermath of the Truth and Reconciliation Commission in South Africa and Beyond* (Routledge 2001), 220–22.

than remedying harms and addressing corporate accountability.[123] For example, *Anglo American* was also able to use the Business Trust as a vehicle to promote its own corporate social responsibility agenda and enhance its reputation in South Africa.[124] The failure of the TRC to extract acknowledgment and reparations from *Anglo American* meant that those affected were left without a remedy while the company was awarded a special status in the rebuilding of post-apartheid South Africa.[125] The term 'corporate social responsibility' was then abandoned by most South African corporations in favour of the term 'corporate social investment', in order to divert attention from calls on business to redress the results of its historical contribution to the apartheid system.[126]

Some scholars further argue that the TRC was used as a platform for businesses to transition into post-apartheid South Africa without having to deliver either truth or reparations.[127] For example, when *Anglo American*, one of South Africa's largest multinational corporations, was questioned at the business hearing, it employed 'amnesia' and other tactics to craft its own narrative and control the truth-telling process.[128] The business hearing claimed to be permeated with the spirit of reconciliation, and corporations were directly invited to take responsibility and ask for forgiveness.[129] For workers, represented by the Congress of South African Trade Unions (COSATU), reconciliation was based on the recognition that businesses were responsible for discriminatory labour practices, especially in the mines, and the exploitation of resources.[130] Members from COSATU made several references to their capacity to forgive on the condition that *Anglo American* took responsibility for labour violations in the mines.[131] Representatives from *Anglo American* accepted responsibility for their failure to support the desegregation of the industry, but they failed to respond to the specific allegations made by COSATU.[132] As a result, reconciliation was 'posited as the necessity for black South Africans to forgive, rather than Anglo American accepting blame for violations'.[133]

The fourth point is about the use of amnesties. Although the TRC had no judicial powers to penalize perpetrators for human rights violations, it could grant

---

123 D Fig, 'Manufacturing Amnesia: Corporate Social Responsibility in South Africa' (2005) 81(3) *International Affairs* 599.

124 Koska (n 9), 57.

125 Ibid., 59.

126 Fig (n 123).

127 Koska (n 9); Fig (n 123).

128 Payne (n 54), 299–339; Koska (n 9), 44, 54.

129 Business Hearing (n 45), Day 1. See also J Renner, 'A Discourse Theoretic Approach to Transitional Justice Ideals: Conceptualising "Reconciliation" as an Empty Universal in Times of Political Transition' in N Palmer, P Clark and D Granville (eds), *Critical Perspectives in Transitional Justice* (Intersentia 2012), 51, 55,

130 Business Hearing (n 45), Sam Shilowa, NARSSA, 13 November 1997, Tape 11, 13:15.

131 Ibid., Tape 11, 47:25.

132 Ibid., Bobby Godsell, NARSSA, Tape 12, 1:08:04.

133 South Africa TRC report (n 8), Vol 4, 36.

amnesties.[134] Perpetrators who came forward and admitted their guilt received amnesty against prosecution.[135] But the amnesty provisions were written for individual perpetrators, not collective entities.[136] Whereas apartheid agents were granted amnesty in return for full disclosure and encouraged to seek reconciliation with their victims, the TRC proposed that wealth taxes be considered as appropriate restitution with regard to business. As one scholar points out, 'while the TRC courageously tried to fulfil its mandate to examine systemic abuses, the statute had no built-in incentive, such as amnesty, to encourage business, or other sectors, to fully disclose the truth about their roles under apartheid'.[137] Nor was there a penal alternative, such as the prospect or threat of a criminal prosecution, for failure to tell the truth and seek amnesty.[138] Without the incentive of amnesty or the threat of criminal prosecution, there was 'nothing to hold over businesses' heads'.[139] Arguably, the TRC intended to punish businesses in a manner different from individuals. One participant in the hearings noted: '[I]n making findings about business, the TRC adopted a very different approach to culpability and restitution from that it applied to perpetrators of gross human rights abuses.'[140] Whereas apartheid agents (security policemen, members of death squads) were granted amnesty in return for full disclosure and encouraged to seek reconciliation with victims, the TRC proposed that all businesses, regardless of their different levels of involvement, were to pay a flat tax as compensation for their gains during apartheid.[141]

In doing so, and this is the fifth point, the TRC adopted a blanket approach to corporate involvement that equated any profitable activity with prospering under apartheid. In effect, all accumulated wealth was regarded by the TRC as equally deserving of punitive taxation.[142] One scholar points out that 'no attempt was made to make the proposed restitutive measures proportional to the different levels of involvement'.[143] This blanket approach meant that corporations that had participated in a relatively benign manner were to be penalized to the same extent as those that had played a more active or even collaborative role. The TRC did not demand greater accountability from the more powerful players. By opting for blanket measures, the TRC effectively 'placed small shop owners in the same group as Anglo American or Armscor', and proposed punishing them all for having operated in a racially structured environment.[144] Another scholar argues:

---

134 South Africa TRC Act (n 15), Ch 4, 'Amnesty Mechanisms and Procedures'.
135 Ibid., 3. See also S Michalowski, 'No Complicity Liability for Funding Gross Human Rights Violations?' (2012) 30 *Berkeley J Intl L* 451; Lyons (n 8), 137–41.
136 South Africa TRC Act (n 15), Ch 4, Sect 20.
137 Lyons (n 8), 137–41.
138 Ibid.
139 Ibid., 159–60.
140 Nattrass (n 8), 375, 379, 390–91.
141 Simcock (n 18), 246–48, 250–54.
142 South Africa TRC report (n 8), Vol 5, 319.
143 Nattrass (n 8), 375, 379, 390–91.
144 Ibid.

'With respect to corporations, the combination of the TRC's recommendations and the government's actions has led to a somewhat perverse form of justice.'[145] Cumulatively, the victims of corporate abuses during apartheid have yet to receive any form of reparations.

A justification of the 'blanket approach' approach of the TRC towards businesses is its focus on the systemic nature of their involvement. Terreblanche explains the importance of spelling out the systematic way in which apartheid benefittec business:

> Without a clear understanding of the systemic nature of the exploitation that has taken place, it would also not be possible for the beneficiaries (i.e. mainly whites) to make the necessary confession, to show the necessary repentance, to experience the necessary conversion and to be prepared to make the needed sacrifices.[146]

For Terreblanche, the 'necessary sacrifices' entailed the payment of a wealth tax on the grounds that it would be a 'just form of taxation, because it would be levied on wealth accumulated during the period when the structures of white political supremacy and racial capitalism were in place'.[147] This argument in favour of blanket culpability underpinned the TRC report's condemnation of business for benefitting under apartheid, and its recommendations in favour of a wealth tax. One scholar concludes: 'The South Africa TRC seems to be the only truth commission that took seriously the idea that simply by virtue of operating within the context of a repressive regime, business should bear some accountability for it.'[148]

Symptoms of the TRC's inattention are reflected in the TRC's distinction between first, second and third orders of involvement.[149] The distinction arguably masks human rights violations perpetrated in the economic sphere by representing them as mere involvements being more or less culpable than others, while the concept of responsibility is not open to evaluation of different degrees. The 'invention' of these categories on involvement ultimately worked against disclosure.[150] The TRC understood big business as beneficiaries instead of perpetrators of apartheid.[151] Business stressed that the TRC mandate was to investigate 'gross violations of human rights' during apartheid and took the view that this required investigation of active, deliberate participation by individuals.[152] As Terreblanche points out, the TRC, instead of challenging this understanding, effectively endorsed it.[153]

145 Simcock (n 18), 246–48, 250–54.
146 South Africa TRC report (n 8), S Terreblanche, Testimony, 26.
147 Ibid., S Terreblanche, Fax to Dr Fazel Randera, 8 July 1998, 1.
148 Nattrass (n 8), 246–48, 250–54.
149 Barnard-Naudé (n 14), 180.
150 Ibid.
151 Ibid., 186.
152 South Africa TRC Act (n 15), Sect. 1.
153 S Terreblanche, *A History of Inequality in South Africa: 1652–2002* (University of Natal Press 2002), 127.

Sixth, the South Africa TRC missed the opportunity to elicit significant new information on the way in which business committed abuses during apartheid.[154] The hearing did provide important insights into the manner in which apartheid reached into the business sector. But the analysis and findings are not extensive. The TRC treatment of the business sector can be understood as an exercise in forgetting 'ahead of itself'.[155] Read in isolation, the few pages that make up the TRC report account of the role of business in apartheid appear strong, he says.[156] However, a closer look at the TRC treatment of the business sector reveals that it fails to paint an adequately vivid picture of business involvement in apartheid. The TRC report, for example, did not attempt an integrated analysis to address the complex power relationship of apartheid, including the consequences of job reservation, wages, unequal access to resources, and migrant labour.[157] The report affirms that business supported and benefitted from apartheid, but it did not come to any overall conclusion as to whether the economic system was deliberately designed with the collusion of the business sector to produce white beneficiaries and black victims.

The TRC lacked the independence and authority to formally sanction businesses found to have committed human rights violations, and in particular the egregious labour violations committed in the mining industry.[158] In South Africa, the exploitation of labour provided by the majority black population became synonymous with apartheid and in 1980 the UN described the apartheid system as a modern form of slavery.[159] But international human rights instruments condemning apartheid were not invoked in the business hearings.[160] Mining companies built a compound system, which was compared to prisons and concentration camps, allegedly to restrict the free movement of the workers.[161] Health and safety standards were not observed, especially for the majority of black workers,

---

154 Chapman (n 58), 182.
155 Barnard-Naudé (n 14), 173, 176.
156 Ibid.
157 Business Hearing (n 45), 18A. See also Chapman (n 58), 184.
158 J Braithwaite, *Crime, Shame, and Reintegration* (CUP 1989).
159 UN Economic and Social Council, Commission on Human Rights, Sub-Commission on Prevention of Discrimination and Protection of Minorities, Apartheid as a Collective Form of Slavery, Report of the Secretary- General, UN Doc E/CN.4/Sub.2/449, 18 July 1980, 59.
160 The Additional Protocol I of 1977 to the Geneva Conventions of 1949 designated apartheid as a crime against humanity. The Convention on the Suppression and Punishment of the Crime of Apartheid of 1973 explicitly identified the 'exploitation of the labor of the members of a racial group or groups, in particular by submitting them to forced labor' as a crime of apartheid, International Convention on the Suppression and Punishment of the Crime of Apartheid (1973), Article III. South Africa was a signatory to the Convention to Suppress the Slave Trade and Slavery (1926) and its Protocol (1953), which prohibited slavery and its promulgation through forced labour.
161 F Johnstone, *Class, Race, and Gold: A Study of Class Relations and Racial Discrimination in South Africa* (Routledge 1976); Terreblanche (n 153), 261.

thus contributing to respiratory diseases, including tuberculosis, and a silicosis 'epidemic' within the gold mining industry.[162] While the TRC was not focused on investigating business participation in human rights violations, the TRC Act could be read as including businesses within the scope of the Commission's investigations.[163] Section 4 empowered the TRC to facilitate, initiate or coordinate inquiries into systematic human rights violations.[164] Included within the mandate, was the investigation into the 'identity of all persons, authorities, institutions and organisations involved in such violations'.[165] Some commentators argue that within the scope of its mandate, the TRC could have formally investigated allegations of labour violations.[166] The Commission, instead, chose to adopt a narrow definition of gross human rights violations and focused on isolated occurrences of physical violence. This choice had the effect of overlooking the responsibility of those who benefitted from the system of apartheid.[167] The TRC lacked independence, authority or the capacity to compel corporations to redress harms; as a result, corporations were able to evade accountability.[168]

Finally, critics also point at the short time set aside for hearing submissions on the role of business. Only three days were allocated for the accounts of decades of complicity of business with the apartheid government. Terreblanche argues:

> In the end the TRC devoted only three days of its life span of two and a half years to public hearings on the role of business in the apartheid era. Not surprisingly, the hearings were conducted in a way that obscured the systemic character of apartheid, and offered businesspeople an undeserved opportunity to clear themselves and their corporations of any guilt in respect of or responsibility for the legacy of apartheid.[169]

The TRC's approach to justice can be seen as the product of political and economic circumstances at the end of apartheid, and the transitional justice process arguably had little appetite for pursuing corporate accountability.[170] These conditions came

162 G Churchyard and others, 'Silicosis Prevalence and Exposure-Response Relations in South African Goldminers' (2004) 61(10) *Occupational Enviro* Medicine 811, 812; J McCulloch, *South Africa's Gold Mines and the Politics of Silicosis* (Woodbridge 2012).
163 C Abrahams, 'The TRC's Unfinished Business' in Villa-Vicencio and du Toit (n 88), 34.
164 South Africa TRC Act (n 15), Sect 4.
165 Ibid., Sect 4 (a)(iii).
166 Koska (n 9).
167 Gready (n 122); M Mamdani, 'The Truth According to the TRC' in I Amadiume and A Na'im (eds), *The Politics of Memory: Truth, Healing, and Social Justice* (Zed Books 2000), 176.
168 Koska (n 9), 52; Y Farah 'Toward a Multi-Dimensional Approach to Corporate Accountability' in Michalowski (n 80), 29.
169 Terreblanche (n 153), 128.
170 N Roht-Arriaza, 'Why Was the Economic Dimension Missing for so Long in Transitional Justice? An Exploratory Essay' in JP Bohoslavsky and H Verbitsky (eds), *The Economic Accomplices to the Argentine Dictatorship* (CUP 2005), 19.

to define the Commission's role in shaping the image of post-apartheid South Africa and limited its capacity to be an effective arbitrator for corporate crimes.[171] A major issue for South Africa remains the legacy of the TRC and its 'unfinished business'.[172] The legacy of the complex power relationship of apartheid continues to afflict post-apartheid society.[173]

5.2 Other truth commissions

The South Africa TRC was the first truth commission to include findings related to business involvement in abuses and to recommend reparations from companies in its report. As such, despite the limitations listed above, it assumed an innovative mandate and provided important precedents. Later truth-seeking bodies, established, for example, in Liberia, East Timor, Sierra Leone, Argentina and Brazil, adopted a similar approach, although their recommendations have been, for the most part, ignored by the government.

5.2.1. Liberia Truth and Reconciliation Commission

Liberia is a classic example of a country that suffers from the proverbial 'resource curse', as well as a case where resources perpetuated the conflict and continue to play into the risk of conflict recurrence.[174] Part of the mandate of the Liberian TRC was to look at 'economic crimes, such as the exploitation of public or natural resources to perpetuate conflict',[175] which allowed it to examine the role played by corporations. According to the TRC report:

> An economic crime is any prohibited activity committed for the purpose of generating economic gain or that in fact generates economic gain by persons and actors whose economic activities contributed to gross human rights and/

---

171 Harris (n 53), 161; Payne (n 54); Koska (n 9), 61.
172 Y Sooka, 'The TRC's Unfinished Business: Prosecutions' in Villa-Vicencio and du Toit (n 88), 17.
173 On 16 August 2012, in Marikana, the South African police killed 34 platinum miners who were striking against mining company Lonmin demanding better wages. *New Yorker*, 'A massacre and a test for South Africa', 21 August 2012; P Alexander, 'Marikana, Turning Point in South African History' (2013) 40(138) *Review of African Political Economy* 605.
174 SS Nichols, 'Reimagining Transitional Justice for an Enduring Peace: Accounting for Natural Resources in Conflict' in DN Sharp (ed.), *Justice and Economic Violence in Transition* (Springer 2014) 203, 211; SL Altman, SS Nichols, and JT Woods, 'Leveraging High Value Natural Resources to Restore the Rule of Law: The Role of the Liberia Forestry Initiative in Liberia's Transition to Stability' in P Lujala and SA Rustad (eds), *High-Value Resources and Post-Conflict Peacebuilding* (Earthscan 2012), 337.
175 Act to Establish the Truth and Reconciliation Commission (TRC) of Liberia, National Transitional Legislative Assembly on May 12, 2005, Art 4(a). See also E Schmid, 'Liberia's Truth Commission Report: Economic, Social, and Cultural Rights in Transitional Justice' (2009) 19 *Fletcher J Human Security* 5.

or humanitarian law violations in Liberia or that otherwise perpetuated armed conflict in Liberia, as well as those who benefited economically from armed conflict in Liberia. They include public and private persons, national and private corporations, and other business entities.[176]

In particular, the report analyzed crimes that occurred within the rubber, timber and mining sector.[177] Resource control and mismanagement by government and multinational corporations played a major role in the Liberian civil conflict. Throughout the period of conflict between 1979 and 2003, examined by the TRC, these resources benefitted only a small elite group of Liberians and selected companies.[178] Control of natural resources served as a motivating factor in the war, and those resources funded the armed groups perpetrating the conflict, particularly Charles Taylor's National Patriotic Front of Liberia. Successive Liberian governments were either unwilling or unable to govern and manage critical economic sectors. As a result, the TRC found, warring factions gained effective control over the timber and mining sectors and unlawfully transferred authority to exploit the resources to individual and corporate actors which conducted business in an unregulated environment and played a crucial role in contributing to the conflict in Liberia.[179] In many instances, joint corporate ventures were formed with perpetrators of grave human rights violations.[180] The Commission also found evidence that security forces associated with mining companies committed grave violations of human rights.[181] The TRC concluded that warring factions, government agencies, Liberian and foreign individuals, and corporate actors committed economic crimes in a widespread and systematic manner.[182]

The report gave particular attention to the impact of illegal timber exploitation during the conflict. Timber is one of Liberia's most significant natural resources and is a central source of government revenue. Between 1979 and 2003, timber comprised over 50% of the country's reported exports.[183] The TRC found that the timber sector contributed to the conflict in Liberia in several ways. Political elites and warring factions used logging revenue to fund the armed conflict. Logging companies shipped or facilitated the shipment of weapons and other military material to warring factions and utilized security forces that operated as militia units and that committed grave human rights abuses in Liberia.[184]

176 Liberia TRC report (n 8), Vol II, 370, para 16.1.
177 Ibid., Vol III, Title III: 'Economic Crimes and the Conflict, Exploitation and Abuse'.
178 Ibid., Vol III, Title III, paras 2, 138.
179 Ibid., paras 135–36. The TRC concluded: 'The perpetration of economic crimes in Liberia fuelled violent conflict both domestically and throughout the region.' Ibid., para 134.
180 Ibid., paras 3–4.
181 Ibid., para 81.
182 Ibid., para 137.
183 Ibid., para 18.
184 Ibid., para 19.

In its final report published in 2009, the TRC recommended that the government conduct a concession review of the mining sector to discover the extent of money laundering, bribery and other economic crimes within it, to calculate tax arrears by corporations, to determine whether mineral companies complied with Liberian law, and to document corruption, illegality and mismanagement.[185] The report included a list of 26 individuals and 19 corporations in the timber, maritime, rubber, petroleum and telecommunications sectors that allegedly committed 'economic crimes' (among them, the companies *Firestone and Oriental* and *Royal Timber*, and their president Guus Kouwenhoven, then under prosecution in the Netherlands, as discussed in Chapter 4).[186] The Commission recommended that the government 'aggressively pursue' civil and criminal actions against them.[187] Recognizing the problem of the limited *fora* for corporate accountability, the Commission recommended the inclusion of legal entities in the jurisdiction of a proposed 'Extraordinary Criminal Court for Liberia' and called upon other countries to apply universal jurisdiction to pursue corporate offenders.[188] Finally, however, the government did not initiate any judicial case against those individuals and corporations.

The commission did not explicitly link the human rights violations by corporations with an obligation to provide reparations.[189] But it called on the government to establish a Reparations Trust Fund to compensate victims.[190] The Commission suggested that the Fund could obtain sources in four ways. First, recovering tax arrears from timber, mining, petroleum and telecommunications companies that evaded tax liability under the Taylor regime. Second, obtaining funds from 'economic criminals' sentenced by Liberian courts to pay restitution or other fees.[191] To that end, the TRC recommended that the government of Liberia 'aggressively seek restitution from individuals and corporate actors that perpetrated economic crimes'.[192] Third, as an alternative to prosecution, the commission suggested that perpetrators of economic crimes could apply to the Liberia National Human Rights Commission for the purpose of making restitution 'of the full sum of all gains from their engagement in such economic crimes'.[193] Fourth, the Commission recommended that the government 'aggressively seek to trace, identify and freeze assets of those individuals and entities that committed economic crimes in Liberia' and to use both criminal confiscation laws in Liberia and civil forfeiture

---

185 Ibid., paras 166–68.
186 Ibid., Vol II, 368–70. See also Global Witness, 'Bankrolling Brutality: Why European Timber Company DLH Should Be Held to Account for Profiting From Liberian Conflict Timber' (2010).
187 Liberia TRC report (n 8), Vol II, 372.
188 Ibid., 426–59.
189 Ibid., Vol II, title IV, sect 17. See also Sandoval and Surfleet (n 80), 103.
190 Liberia TRC report (n 8), Vol. III, Title III, 43, para 158.
191 Ibid., para 160.
192 TRC report Vol. III, Title III Recommendations: 157: TRC of Liberia, Consolidated Final Report, sect 16
193 Ibid., para 157.

laws in the countries where stolen assets are located to recover funds to be repatriated to Liberia.[194]

To freeze assets the TRC also encouraged the government to utilize processes established by the UN *Convention Against Corruption* and recommended that any funds frozen under UN sanctions not be released until the new government had the opportunity to collect tax arrears.[195] The Convention codifies norms on the recovery of ill-gotten assets and against large-scale corruption.[196] These norms apply not only to individual dictators with ill-gotten assets or leaders of armed groups who may be implicated in pillage; they also explicitly cover banks and financial institutions and the profits that are the products of human rights violations or international crimes.[197] Often private companies directly or indirectly take advantage of a conflict to exploit resources and illegitimately accumulate assets.[198] Arguably, if those actors are found responsible, it is legitimate for a transitional government to attempt to trace and confiscate their assets to fund reparations programmes.[199] For example, the reparation programme in the Philippines is being funded using US$200 million out of the US$680 million recovered from the Marcos family's assets in Switzerland.[200]

In the end, the government of Liberia, as in South Africa, did not implement the TRC recommendations regarding reparations programmes. The government rejected legislation that would have given it the power to freeze assets.[201] The course of the transition in Liberia is another relevant example of the challenge in balancing the need for justice and the need to attract foreign investment in a post-conflict society. Ellen Johnson Sirleaf, Liberian president and winner of the Nobel Peace Prize, became known as a hero of Liberia's post-conflict recovery for successfully rebuilding a country destroyed by decades of conflict. 'Liberia's leading lady' succeeded in bringing high levels of aid and foreign investment into the country. Yet Johnson Sirleaf was also the target of many critical voices within Liberia. The Liberian TRC recommended that she be barred from office for her

194 Liberia TRC report (n 8), Vol III, Title III, 43–45, paras 158–61.
195 Ibid., 44–45.
196 UN Convention Against Corruption (UNCAC), UN General Assembly Resolution A/RES/58/4, entered into force 14 December 2005, Art 51.
197 J Letnar Černič, 'Sovereign Financing and Corporate Responsibility for Economic and Social Rights' in JP Bohoslavsky and J Letnar Černič, *Making Sovereign Financing and Human Rights Work* (Hart Publishing 2014).
198 NC Sánchez León, 'Corporate Accountability, Reparations and Distributive Justice in Post Conflict Societies' in Michalowski (n 80), 116–17.
199 N Roht-Arriaza, 'Reparations and Economic, Social, and Cultural Rights' in Sharp (n 174), 109, 137; Carranza (n 7), 324; A Kora, 'Dealing With a "New" Grievance: Should Anticorruption Be Part of the Transitional Justice Agenda?' (2012) 11(4) *J Human Rights* 537.
200 Decree of Urgency No. 122-2001, Art 10 (iii) and (iv). See also Carranza (n 7), 325.
201 I Al-bakri Nyei, 'Liberia after the Civil War: Victims Demand for Reparation' (2011) 1 *Conflict Trends* 43, 46–49; P James-Allen, A Weah, and L Goodfriend, *Beyond the Truth and Reconciliation Commission: Transitional Justice Options in Liberia* (ICTJ 2010), 3.

role in supporting war criminal Charles Taylor. In 2012, days after Johnson Sirleaf was elected for a second term as Liberia's president, the *New York Times* published an op-ed by two Liberian land rights campaigners, Silas Siakor and Rachel Knight.[202] They claimed: 'Mrs. Johnson Sirleaf's government may now be sowing the seeds of future conflict by handing over huge tracts of land to foreign investors and dispossessing rural Liberians.'[203] Between 2006 and 2011, Sirleaf had granted more than a third of Liberia's land to private investors for logging, mining and agro-industrial enterprises.[204] These concessions to foreign investments displaced thousands of people at a time when violent local-level land disputes were still widespread throughout Liberia.[205] Given the role that resource control played in the Liberian conflict, addressing abuses within those sectors was arguably critical to breaking down norms of impunity and achieving a sustainable transition. But policy in Liberia was geared toward attracting foreign investment rather than responding to Liberians' need for justice.[206]

5.2.2. East Timor Commission for Reception, Truth and Reconciliation

The mandate of the Commission for Reception, Truth and Reconciliation in East Timor (*Commissão de Acolhimento, Verdade e Reconciliacão* – CAVR) included looking into the 'context, causes, antecedents, motives and perspectives' that led to human rights violations that took place in the context of the political conflicts between 1974 and 1999 in East Timor.[207] As part of this mandate, CAVR examined the role in human rights violations committed by a number of actors in East Timor and Indonesia, including 'members of opposition groups, political parties, militias, corporations and other individuals'.[208] The commission found that human rights violations did not occur only as a consequence of military operations but were 'intertwined with private and corporate interests', including the Indonesian military's partnerships with business in the coffee, timber, and oil sectors.[209]

Coffee has been East Timor's single most important source of tax revenue, foreign exchange and local cash income since the late 19th century. A single company, *Sociedade Agrícola Pátria e Trabalho* (*SAPT*), dominated the production and export of plantation crops under Portuguese administration.[210] Although founded as a private venture, *SAPT* behaved as if it were a state company by virtue

202 *New York Times*, 'A Nobel's Laureate's Problem at Home', 20 January 2012.
203 Ibid.
204 Ibid.
205 Ibid.
206 Ibid.
207 CAVR East Timor, *Chega!* (n 8), part 2: 'The Mandate of the Commission', para 2, 1.
208 Ibid., paras 4, 8.
209 Ibid., Ch 7.9: 'Economic and Social Rights'.
210 J Joliffe, *East Timor: Nationalism and Colonialism* (University of Queensland Press 1978), 39–41.

of its association with the governor. Using the authority and resources of the state, *SAPT* seized the most productive land for coffee and instituted a programme of forced cultivation, overseen by the military. Later rebellions against or inability to pay the poll tax were punished by forced labour on coffee plantations.[211] State proxies had special arrangements with the Indonesian military, which gave them control of the coffee production and trade, in return for supplying 'off-budget' funds for military operations. CAVR found that revenues from the coffee industry 'financed the military campaign in East Timor as well the military's [...] repression of the local population'.[212] In addition to control of coffee, the military was also involved in the looting of East Timor's natural resources, including sandalwood, timber and oil.[213] The commission found that the private sector, including British and French arms companies who supplied arms to the regime, profited from commercial relations with Indonesia under the Suharto government.[214] By shedding light on the responsibilities of the private sector, CAVR was able to establish a more truthful account of the conflicts in East Timor.[215]

CAVR made a direct link between the violations that corporations committed or aided and abetted, and their obligations to provide reparation.[216] The Commission noted that corporations that 'profited from war and benefitted from the occupation' had a legal obligation to provide reparations to victims.[217] It referred specifically to corporations that profited from the sale of weapons, and corporations that 'supported the illegal occupation of Timor-Leste and thus indirectly allowed violations to take place'.[218] The Commission recommended that the reparation scheme be jointly funded by the state, privately owned Indonesian business and multinational corporations.[219] As in South Africa and Liberia, however, little progress was made in implementing the programme and a draft law on compensation to victims awaits enactment by the parliament.

5.2.3. Sierra Leone Truth and Reconciliation Commission

The Sierra Leone TRC also constituted an important attempt to deal with the root causes of conflict or repression and the role of different actors. In accordance with the *Truth and Reconciliation Commission Act*, the TRC was mandated 'to create an impartial historical record of violations and abuses of human rights and international humanitarian law related to the armed conflict' in Sierra Leone from

211 W Clarence-Smith, 'Planters and Smallholders in Portuguese Timor in the Nineteenth and Twentieth Centuries' (1992) 57 Indonesia Circle, 15–30.
212 CAVR East Timor, *Chega!* (n 8), Part 2, 12.
213 Ibid., Ch 7.9, paras 27–29, 45.
214 Ibid., Part 2, 95, 50. See also Darcy (n 4), 52–53.
215 Carranza (n 7), 319–21.
216 CAVR East Timor, *Chega!* (n 8), Part 11: 'Recommendations', 42.
217 Ibid.
218 Ibid., 34.
219 Ibid., 4, 42. See also Sandoval and Surfleet (n 80), 104–05.

1991 to the signing of the Lomé Peace Agreement.[220] To that end, it was to look into 'the causes, nature and extent of the violations […] [and] the context in which the violations […] occurred', as well as into the role played by different actors in the conflict.[221] At the beginning of its work, the Sierra Leone TRC considered that 'perpetrators may be both natural persons and corporate bodies, such as transnational companies or corporations' and that its mandate was not 'limited to violations committed by States or governments'.[222] In its final report *Witness to Truth*, the Commission found that the conflict happened because of the 'endemic greed, corruption and nepotism that deprived the nation of its dignity and reduced most people to a state of poverty'.[223] The TRC found that 'successive political elites plundered the nation's assets, including its mineral riches at the expense of the national good'.[224] It looked at the role of mineral resources, in particular diamonds, in fuelling the conflict.[225]

William Schabas argued that a 'useful contribution' of the commission's report was to 'debunk some of the myths of the conflict'.[226] One of these myths was related to the role of 'conflict diamonds'. The prevailing view among external observers, journalists and NGOs was that diamonds were at the root of the war in Sierra Leone.[227] The Commission concluded otherwise, noting that the rebel groups did not focus on controlling the diamondiferous regions until the final years of the conflict.[228] Because diamonds were central to the country's economy, they were inevitably a factor in conflict, but their role was largely overstated. Indeed, for much of the conflict, diamond smuggling remained under the control of the corrupt Freetown elite, where it had always been.[229] The commission found it important to emphasize, however, that this did not feature highly in the early years of the conflict, ultimately concluding that while diamonds helped to fuel and sustain the conflict, plunder was not the driving factor that precipitated the RUF's initial brutal campaign.[230]

---

220 Parliament of Sierra Leone, Truth and Reconciliation Commission Act (2000), Supplement to the Sierra Leone Gazette Vol CXXX, No. 9, Sect 6(1).
221 Ibid.
222 Sierra Leone Truth and Reconciliation Commission, *Witness to Truth* (2004) [Sierra Leone TRC, *Witness to Truth*], Vol 2, Ch 2, para 13.
223 Ibid.
224 Ibid., 27.
225 Ibid., Vol 2, Ch 2, 89; Vol 3A, Ch 3, 203; Vol 3B, Ch 1, 26–27, 68–69. See also Darcy (n 4), 53.
226 WA Schabas, 'The Special Court for Sierra Leone: Testing the Waters. Conjoined Twins of Transitional Justice? The Sierra Leone Truth and Reconciliation Commission and the Special Court' (2004) 2 *JICJ* 1082–88.
227 I Smillie, L Gberie, and R Hazelton, *The Heart of the Matter: Sierra Leone, Diamonds and Human Security* (Partnership Africa/Canada 2000).
228 Sierra Leone TRC, *Witness to Truth* (n 222), Vol. I, 12.
229 Schabas (n 226), 1082–88.
230 Sierra Leone TRC, *Witness to Truth* (n 222), Vol I, 12.

The TRC recommended specific reforms of the country's mining sector including transparency, protection against corruption, certification of diamonds, and investment of diamond revenue in rural development.[231] It recommended the establishment of a rough diamond chain-of-custody system, which eventually developed into the Kimberley Process Certification Scheme, a global regulatory framework for tracking the diamond trade to ensure that diamonds were not acquired illicitly.[232] The Commission also proposed that 'the revenue generated from mineral resources', in addition to 'seized assets from convicted persons' who 'profited from the conflict', would be used to fund reparations programmes.[233] These recommendations were not implemented.

5.2.4. Guatemala Truth Commission

The coup that took place in Guatemala in 1954 came partly as a result of pressure from a business enterprise, the *United Fruit Company* (*UFCO*), which feared the advance of agrarian reform.[234] From that time on, governments alternated with military dictatorships until the signing of the peace accords between the government and the guerrillas in 1996. Military repression peaked between 1978 and 1986, when forced disappearances and extrajudicial executions reached a massive scale and genocide was committed against the Mayan people.[235] The involvement of a considerable number of businessmen and companies in the repression of trade union activists and peasant leaders is extensively documented in the final report of the truth commission, established in 1996.[236] Some created death squads that killed a large number of lawyers, political activists, trade unionists, labour activists and environmentalists.[237] Other businessmen, while occupying important ministerial positions, also voluntarily contributed US$60 million to military campaigns

231 Sánchez León (n 198), 124; E Harwell and P Le Billon, 'Natural Connections: Linking Transitional Justice and Development Through a Focus on Natural Resources' in P de Greiff and R Duthie, *Transitional Justice and Development: Making Connections* (Social Science Research Council 2009), 282, 301; R Maconachie, 'The Diamond Area Community Development Fund: Micropolitics and Community-Led Development in Post-War Sierra Leone' in Lujala and Aas Rustad (n 174), 264.

232 JA Grant, 'Kimberley Process at Ten: Reflections on a Decade of Efforts to End the Trade in Conflict Diamonds' in Lujala and Aas Rustad (n 174); Nichols (n 174), 219.

233 Sierra Leone TRC, *Witness to Truth* (n 222), Vol 2, Ch 4, 269.

234 See P Gleijeses, *Shattered Hope: The Guatemala Revolution and the United States (1944–1954)* (Princeton University Press, 1991).

235 Comisión de Esclarecimiento Histórico (CEH), *Memoria del Silencio*, Chapter IV, Conclusion, 105.

236 For example, CEH, *Memoria del Silencio*, example case 109, Forced disappearance of members of the Pantaleón Sugar Mill Trade Union, 316; example case no. 13, Persecution and separation of the Bautista Escobar family, torture of minors and pregnant women, rape of minors, and forced disappearances, Volume VI, 297.

237 For example, CEH, *Memoria del Silencio*, example case 28, Execution of Mario López Larrave, 105; example case 100, Execution of Adolfo Mijangos López, Vol VI, 99.

that ended in genocide.[238] The Guatemalan transitional justice judicial and non-judicial mechanisms have not yet resulted in any tangible results for the victims of corporate complicity. No corporate executive or business representative has been tried in the Guatemalan justice system, nor has any company been called to face allegations of civil liability. The responsibility of businessmen and their role in the repression havw not yet been effectively addressed or even publicly discussed in Guatemala.[239] Although the Guatemala truth commission extensively documented cases of repression in which company representatives participated, these cases still have not been brought to trial.[240]

5.2.5. Brazil National Truth Commission

In 2012, Brazil's President Dilma Rousseff established a National Truth Commission (NTC) to investigate abuses during the 1964–1985 dictatorship.[241] The Brazilian Secretary of Justice urged the NTC to also 'investigate the corporations that financed the dictatorship'.[242] A few months later, the NTC announced the creation of a task force to investigate the role of companies and businesspeople during the repression.[243] The commission reported a pattern of violence and repression against workers and unions, including cases of arbitrary arrests, extra-judicial killings and forced disappearances committed by the regime, in some cases with the collusion of companies.[244] The commission reported a process of 'militarization' of the factories, based on surveillance and found documents showing that a number of companies, including *Volkswagen, Ford, Toyota* and *Mercedes-Benz*, helped the military to identify and repress suspected 'subversives' and union activists by monitoring workers, passing on information about them and handing them to the Department of Political and Social Order (DOPS), a police intelligence agency.[245] Of particular importance was the discovery in São Paulo state's archives of a document that researchers called 'the black lists' – with the names

238 This support took place during the scorched earth policy carried out between 1982 and 1986. Plaza Pública, 'Los militares y la élite, la alianza que ganó la guerra', www.plazapublica.com.gt/content/los-militares-y-la-elite-la-alianza-que-gano-la-guerra

239 Impunity Watch, 'Guatemala' in *Peace, Everyone's Business! Corporate Accountability in Transitional Justice: Lessons for Colombia*, PAX (Utrecht, May 2017), 92–97.

240 The only legal action brought so far against *Hudbay Minerals*, a Canadian mining company involved in human rights abuses in Guatemala, was initiated in Canada in response to the violent land evictions of Q'eqchí communities in El Estor, Izabal, in 2009, more than a decade after the signing of the peace accords. But the incidents referred to in this case have no relation to the armed conflict.

241 Government of Brazil, Law no. 12.528, 18 November 2011.

242 Viomundo, 'Paulo Abrão: Comissão da Verdade deve investigar empresas que financiaram a ditadura' 17 October 2011.

243 Folha de S.Paulo, 'Empresários que apoiaram tortura serão investigados' 25 September 2012.

244 Commissão Nacional de Verdade, *Relatório*, 10 December 2014, Vol 2 Texto 2: 'Violações de direitos humanos dos trabalhadores', paras 65–68.

245 Ibid., paras 67–69, 80, 81.

and home addresses of workers dismissed for political reasons – which was put together by DOPS with information provided by the companies.[246]

Further, investigations by the NTC are shedding light on how public works made or supported by the regime led to human rights violations, including the death and disappearance of farmers, and indigenous people.[247] In both cases, there is a clear connection between the economic policy of the regime, private actors (corporations, lenders and businesspeople) that exploited economic opportunities created by the regime, and human rights violations that occurred – not only deaths and disappearances, but also corruption and destruction of natural resources.[248] Arguably, in carrying out such investigations, the NTC is better fulfilling its goals of historical accountability, and may also open new possibilities for civil and criminal account-ability against perpetrators and their economic accomplices.[249] Scholars have also called for the NTC to specifically address the issue of financial complicity, some-thing within its power.[250] The NTC has the mandate to recommend changes in the institutional design of financial institutions, both in terms of regulatory measures to be enforced over private actors and the articulation of new standards and policies to be complied with by state banks and enterprises.[251]

5.2.6. A new truth commission in Argentina?

The truth and justice process in Argentina began in 1982 with the trial of the military junta and the investigations into the disappearances of persons by CON-ADEP.[252] Later innovative uses of transitional justice mechanisms have started to link corporations to the abuses committed by the dictatorship during Argentina's *Dirty War*. As detailed in Chapter 4, a number of national and multinational corporations now face criminal prosecutions and civil claims in Argentinian and US courts over their alleged involvement in human rights violations during the dictatorship. This new wave of justice calls in Argentina has also led to the estab-lishment of further truth-seeking initiatives on corporate complicity.

In December 2015, one week before leaving office, the then President of Argentina, Cristina Fernández de Kirchner signed a bill into law, mandating the

---

246 Ibid., para 66.
247 EBC, '1,2 mil camponeses mortos e desaparecidos entre 1961 e 1988', 27 September 2012.
248 JP Bohoslavsky and MD Torelly, 'Financial Complicity: The Brazilian Dictatorship Under the "Macroscope"' in Sharp (n 174), 233, 257.
249 Ibid., 262.
250 Ibid., 254–57. JS Henry, *The Blood Bankers: Tales from the Global Underground Economy* (Four Walls Eight Windows 2005), 127–77; Carranza (n 7); IV Prado Soares and L Bastos, 'A Verdade ilumina o Direito ao Desenvolvimento?: Uma análise da potencialidade dos trabalhos da Comissão Nacional da Verdade no cenário brasileiro' (2011) 6 *Revista Anistia Política e Justiça de Transição*.
251 Bohoslavsky and Torelly (n 248), 254.
252 CONADEP, *Nunca Más* (1984).

establishment of a new truth commission.[253] If established, the commission would also be tasked with investigating 'economic complicity': more specifically, the role and responsibility of businesses for violations that occurred during the dictatorship.[254] In debating and passing the bill, congress based the decision to create such a commission on evidence about the participation and collaboration of domestic and multinational companies with the dictatorship, and in response to the claim that they had benefitted directly from military action. The aim of the commission is not to 'let the events that occurred as a result of a coup to be diluted over time'.[255] As the bill creating the commission concludes, 'investigating and elaborating on the economic and financial involvement with the dictatorship will help the process of rebuilding the nation'.[256] Business leaders from the Argentine Industrial Union and the Argentine Association of Businesses, however, oppose the measure, saying the initiative was 'aimed at stigmatizing business leaders'.[257] The new government under Mauricio Macri is debating whether to move forward with the commission, arguing that it does not want to be 'used as a tool against business'.[258]

A group of UN-mandated holders of special procedures, including Pablo de Greiff and Juan Pablo Bohoslavsky, endorsed the draft law, citing the 'need to respect human rights and [that] the rule of law applies to both public and private actors'.[259] They added:

> The creation of such a commission represents a great opportunity to find out the truth and promote accountability for past violations committed with the complicity or active participation of the business sector [...] It is time to ensure accountability for corporations and transnational companies directly or indirectly responsible for violations of human rights.[260]

The Commission had been originally suggested in Bohoslavsky's book *Cuentas Pendientes*, which argued that the dictatorship could not have existed or carried out the repression without corporations' direct and indirect involvement, and advocated the establishment of a truth commission to specifically investigate corporate and financial support of the dictatorship.[261] The author argued that clarifying the role played by economic actors, and in particular investigating the financial contributions

253 Cámara de Diputados de la Nación, Ley de creación de la Comision Bicameral de la Verdad, la Memoria, la Justicia, la Reparación y el Fortalecimiento de las Instituciones de la Democracia, Law no. 27217, 3 December 2015.
254 Ibid., Arts 3, 6.
255 Ibid.
256 Ibid.
257 *Buenos Aires Herald*, 'Case of business complicity stalled in court' 24 March 2016.
258 Ibid.
259 UN OHCRH, 'Argentina dictatorship: UN experts back creation of commission on role business people played', 10 November 2015.
260 Ibid.
261 Bohoslavsky and Verbitsky (n 170).

to the *junta* was essential to understanding the dictatorship.[262] Evidence about complicity and collusion with the *junta* can also contribute to the on-going trials described in Chapter 4, and toward the overall understanding of the patterns of the 'system crimes'[263] committed, and the structural nature of the *junta*'s operations as a collective movement, similar to the way in which the South African TRC contributed to the understanding of apartheid as a 'system'.

5.3. UN investigations

In addition to TRCs, UN-mandated investigations – among others, in the Democratic Republic of the Congo (DRC), South Sudan and Myanmar – have also looked at the illegal exploitation of natural resources by different actors, including companies.

5.3.1. UN Experts Panel on the exploitation of natural resources in the Democratic Republic of the Congo

In 2012, the UN Security Council established a Panel of Experts to look into the illegal exploitation of natural resources in the DRC.[264] The Panel identified three distinct 'elite networks' – powerful groups consisting of political and military elites and businesspeople engaged in natural exploitation activities in three different areas controlled by the government of the DRC, Rwanda and Uganda.[265] The Panel compiled an extensive list of business enterprises and individuals involved in the commercial activities of the three elite networks active in the DRC.[266] It found that 157 corporations were directly or indirectly involved in illegal exploitation of natural resources, which enabled rebel groups to buy arms and commit war crimes and crimes against humanity.[267] By adding to the revenues of the elite networks, directly or indirectly, those companies and individuals contributed to the conflict and to human rights abuses.

In particular, in the area controlled by the government of the DRC, an elite network of Congolese and Zimbabwean government officials and private businesspeople exploited key mineral resources.[268] According to the Panel, this network transferred ownership of at least US$5 billion of assets from the state mining sector to private companies under its control.[269] The Panel found that the richest and

---

262 Ibid.
263 Bohoslavsky and Opgenhaffen (n 46), 197.
264 UN Security Council, Resolution 1291 (2000) of 24 February 2000.
265 Panel of Experts on the Illegal Exploitation of Natural Resources and Other Forms of Wealth of the Democratic Republic of the Congo, Final report UN Doc. S/2002/1146, 16 October 2002 [DRC Panel of Experts report], paras 5, 20, 21.
266 Ibid., 174.
267 UN Security Council, S/2003/1027, 15 October 2003.
268 DRC Panel of Experts report (n 265), para 25.
269 Ibid., para 22.

most readily exploitable of the publicly owned mineral assets of the DRC were moved into joint ventures controlled by the network's private companies.[270] 'These transactions, which are controlled through secret contracts and offshore private companies, amount to a multi-billion-dollar corporate theft of the country's mineral assets', the Panel concluded.[271] Some 30 businesspeople, politicians and military officers were the main beneficiaries of the arrangements. The Panel found that several joint-venture mining companies had strong links with the military supply companies that facilitate their operations in the DRC, and that diamond revenues were used to pay for arms purchases for the armed groups.[272] In particular, the armed conflict between members of the Hema and Lendu clans stem, in part, from attempts by powerful Hema businessmen and politicians to increase the benefits they derived from the commercial activities of the elite network through their front companies, the *Victoria Group* and *Trinity Investment*, in the Ituri area.[273]

The Panel recommended that the UN Security Council consider imposing restrictions on those business enterprises and individuals involved in illegal exploitation of natural resources, including barring them from accessing banking facilities and other financial institutions and from receiving funding or establishing a partnership or other commercial relations with international financial institutions.[274] It recommended reforms of the mining and forestry sectors, including the review of all concessions and contracts signed during the wars, and the monitoring by specialized industry organizations of commodities from conflict areas.[275]

In 2003, after the publication of the Panel's report, the Security Council released a document containing the reactions to the report.[276] According to it, the international business community

> acknowledged that companies could not avoid their responsibility in a country suffering from conflict such as the Democratic Republic of the Congo. Investors and financiers took a keen interest in the activities of corporations in the Democratic Republic of the Congo with which they were dealing. Companies themselves commented that their responsibilities extended further than they had previously acknowledged. Supply chains of raw materials, in particular came into sharp focus and prompted some of those named to reassess their activities in the Democratic Republic of the Congo.[277]

---

270 Ibid., para 35.
271 Ibid., para 36.
272 Ibid., para 54.
273 Ibid., para 118.
274 Ibid., 175–76.
275 Ibid., paras 168, 180–82. See also Final report of the Group of Experts on the Democratic Republic of the Congo, pursuant to Security Council resolution 1698 (2006) S/2007/423 18 July 2007, 173.
276 UN Security Council, S/2003/1027, 15 October 2003.
277 Ibid., para 11.

The wording of this statement is vague and generic, and companies and investors did not commit to any specific concrete action. The Security Council initiative, indeed, had a limited effect in bringing about accountability for corporate exploitation.[278] International financial institutions, such as the World Bank and the International Monetary Fund, whose focus in the DRC, as in other in post-conflict countries, is on securing foreign investments, have been unwilling to review and renegotiate contracts in the DRC, despite evidence of unaccountability, for fear of scaring off Western investors.[279] Companies involved were not investigated and the people of the DRC, who suffered the impact of the exploitation, were not provided with any form of remedy.

5.3.2. UN Commission on Human Rights in South Sudan

Despite the 2018 peace agreement in South Sudan, gross human rights violations and war crimes have continued, driven partly by fights over control of oil. Control of the country's oil resources was a 'top prize' in the struggle for political and economic power.[280] A government offensive carried out using 'extremely violent methods' in 2018 was aimed largely at securing control of areas close to oil fields.[281] South Sudan's intelligence services have increasingly taken control of the state-owned *Nile Petroleum Corporation (NILEPET)*, siphoning off money to finance the conflict. Western companies had pulled out of oil production activities in the area before South Sudan gained independence in 2011, partly because of human rights violations, opening the way for companies from Asia. Oil production is now dominated by three joint ventures between *NILEPET* and Chinese *National Petroleum Company, Petronas* of Malaysia and the Indian *Oil and Natural Gas Corporation.*

The UN Commission on Human Rights in South Sudan, with Professor Andrew Clapham as one of its members, detailed continuing war crimes and crimes against humanity, and intensifying repression by the country's security services.[282] The Commission's report, published in March 2019, emphasized the role of South Sudan's oil industry as 'a major driver for the continuing violence, the ensuing human suffering, and the violations of international humanitarian law'.[283] The Commission pointed to the strong presence of security and military forces in the oil fields: 'South Sudan's oil industry currently remains overwhelmingly militarized and even securitized, with the National Security Services increasingly expanding their

---

278 R Mani, 'Dilemmas of Expanding Transitional Justice, or Forging the Nexus between Transitional Justice and Development' (2008) 2 *Intl J Trans Just* 253, 258.

279 Ibid.

280 N Cumming-Bruce, 'Oil Companies May Be Complicit in Atrocities in South Sudan, U.N. Panel Says', *New York Times*, 20 Feb 2019.

281 Ibid.

282 UN Human Rights Council, Report of the Commission on Human Rights in South Sudan A/HRC/40/69, 18 Feb 2019.

283 Ibid., para 61.

involvement in oil production and management.'[284] There are clear elements that point to corporate complicity. The Commission stated its belief that 'international companies operating in South Sudan should be well aware of the legacy of unaddressed human rights violations associated with oil explorations in the South', referring to two previous cases of oil company complicity in South Sudan: *Talisman Energy* and *Lundin Oil*.[285] *Talisman* 'allowed the Sudanese Armed Forces to use its air strip and other facilities, despite knowing of the Sudan government's policy of forcibly displacing civilians and its commission of other human rights violations in the area'.[286] *Talisman* had faced civil litigation in the United States but the lawsuit was ultimately dismissed. *Lundin Oil* has also been accused of similar activities in South Sudan, and their former senior executives, Ian Lundin and Alex Schneiter, are awaiting trial in Sweden. The Commission noted that during the period of business activity by *Lundin Oil* in South Sudan, 'widespread and serious human rights violations were committed against the local population, as part of military operations to forcibly displace hundreds of thousands of inhabitants for the purposes of oil exploration'.[287] The Commission also proposed recommendations for the government of South Sudan including 'establishing an appropriate monitoring mechanism to monitor the transfer of an equitable share of the revenue to states and ensure public reporting', and for companies to carry out 'human rights due diligence' by assessing the risks of human rights violations posed by their activities.[288] These recommendations, however, are insufficient alone to be an effective deterrent to companies that would engage in complicit behaviour or to bring a measure of justice and accountability.[289]

While the Commission's findings underscore companies' exposure to potential criminal liability for causing or contributing to violations against civilians in their areas of operation, it is not clear from the report which if any companies have facilitated or aided and abetted the commission of these crimes. The extent to which their presence and operation in a highly militarized and securitized setting in the midst of on-going conflict contribute to the commission of crimes is not established.[290] This is, however, an argument for a full investigation into the facts rather exoneration for the companies.[291]

---

284 Ibid., para 126.
285 Ibid., para 1007.
286 bid., para 675.
287 Ibid., para 678.
288 Ibid., para 130.
289 C Lopez, 'UNCHR in South Sudan Points to Oil Companies' Complicity in Gross Human Rights Abuses', *OpinioJuris*, 15 March 2019, http://opiniojuris.org/2019/03/15/united-nations-commission-on-human-rights-in-south-sudan-points-to-oil-companies-complicity-in-gross-human-rights-abuses
290 Ibid.
291 Ibid.

5.3.3. Independent International Fact-Finding Mission in Myanmar

Since independence, Myanmar's military has been engaged in multiple internal armed conflicts with many of the country's ethnic groups, claiming an estimated hundreds of thousands of lives and displacing millions.[292] The UN and human rights organizations have documented widespread and systematic human rights violations by the junta, including war crimes and crimes against humanity.[293] The government has been accused of extrajudicial killings, beatings, rape and sexual violence, arbitrary arrests, torture, forced labour, destruction of homes, forced conscription and forced displacement.[294] Ethnic minority groups have been, and continue to be, the main target of the oppression.[295] A departure from self-imposed isolation and the adoption of market reforms in the late 1980s coincided with reports of further serious human rights violations, which led to sanctions from the United States, Canada, Australia, the United Kingdom and the European Union.[296] Business activity was under the control of the regime, and investment between 1988 and 2011 became associated with forced labour, forced displacement and torture, mostly as a result of land clearance and forced evictions, and the provision of security services by the military.[297] For example, as described in Chapter 4, in the first case brought against a corporation under the ATS, *Unocal* was accused of complicity with the Myanmar military in the commission of forced labour, murder, rape and torture during the construction of a gas pipeline.[298]

In 2011, after five decades of military rule, Myanmar accelerated its military-guided transition, culminating in partially democratic elections in 2015 and the victory of Nobel Peace Prize laureate Aung San Suu Kyi's National League for Democracy (NLD) party.[299] Ethnic and religious violence in northern Rakhine State against the Rohingya, an ethnic Muslim minority to which the government

---

292 R David and I Holliday, *Liberalism and Democracy in Myanmar* (Oxford University Press, 2018), 25–29.
293 Report of the Special Rapporteur on the situation of human rights in Myanmar, A/65/368 (15 Sept 2010); Report of the Special Rapporteur on the situation of human rights in Myanmar, A/67/383 (25 Sept 2012); UN Human Rights Council, Report of the detailed findings of the Independent International Fact-Finding Mission on Myanmar A/HRC/39/CRP.2, 17 Sept 2018 [Fact-Finding Mission report].
294 Fact-Finding Mission report (n 293).
295 AM Levin, 'Transitional Justice in Burma: A Survey of Accountability and National Reconciliation Mechanisms after Aung San Suu Kyi's Release' (2011) 18(2) *Human Rights Brief* 21.
296 David and Holliday (n 292), 21.
297 I Holliday, 'Doing Business with Rights Violating Regimes Corporate Social Responsibility and Myanmar's Military Junta' (2005) 61 *Journal of Business Ethics* 329, 332–35; JA White, 'Globalisation, Divestment and Human Rights in Burma' (2004) 14 *Journal of Corporate Citizenship* 47, 48–53.
298 *Doe v Unocal Corp.*, 963 F. Supp. 880 (C.D. Cal. 1997), 27 F. Supp. 2D 1174, 1184 (C.D. Cal. 1998), 110 F.Supp.2d 1294 (C.D. California, 2000), 248 F.3d 915 (9th Circuit, 2001), 395 F.3d 932 (9th Circuit, 2002).
299 David and Holliday (n 292).

denies citizenship rights, escalated after the transition. In August 2017, after a series of attacks by Rohingya militants on border guard police outposts, the military retaliated by launching a brutal counterinsurgency campaign that resulted in the displacement of more than 700,000 Rohingya people into Bangladesh and, according to UN investigators, constituted evidence of genocide.[300] Myanmar's transition has been managed by the military (known in Myanmar as the *Tatmadaw*), which retains legal, political and economic power over key ministries and departments within the government, and direct and indirect relationships with important state-run businesses and private businessmen.[301] Many of the same actors that dominated life under the military junta continue to do so through their economic, social and political ties to the military and government.

In March 2017, the UN Human Rights Council established a Fact-Finding Mission to establish the facts and circumstances of abuses and human rights violations by military and security forces in Myanmar.[302] The Mission established consistent patterns of serious human rights violations and abuses in Kachin, Rakhine and Shan States, in addition to serious violations of international humanitarian law, principally committed by the Myanmar security forces, particularly the military. The Mission's detailed 444-page report, published in September 2018, concluded that the actions of military, in particular in the context of 'clearance operations' in northern Rakhine, have so seriously violated international law that any engagement in any form with the military and its businesses is indefensible until and unless they are transformed.[303]

In particular, the Mission condemned *Facebook* and other social media platforms and messaging systems, and recommended an independent and thorough examination of the use of their platforms to spread messages inciting violence and discrimination.[304] This is the first time since the *Media Case* before the International Criminal Tribunal for Rwanda that the role of media in facilitating international crimes has been examined by an international body. The Mission examined *Facebook* posts and audio-visual materials that have contributed to shaping public opinion on the Rohingya and Muslims more generally. The analysis demonstrates that a carefully crafted hate campaign has developed a negative perception of Muslims among the broad population in Myanmar.[305] As elsewhere in the world, the Internet and social media platforms have enabled the spread of this kind of hateful and divisive rhetoric. The Myanmar context is distinctive, however, because of the

---

300 Fact-Finding Mission report (n 293).
301 For more details on Myanmar's experience of 'State-socialist' and then 'crony-capitalist' regimes, see David and Holliday (n 292), 20–21. On the role of the military in Myanmar's local economy and economic transition, see M Arnold, 'The Governance of Local Business in Myanamr: Confronting the Legacies of Military Rule' in M Crouch (ed.), *The Business of Transition in Myanmar* (CUP, 2017), 148–75.
302 UN Human Rights Council, Resolution A/HRC/RES/34/22, 24 March 2017.
303 Fact-Finding Mission report (n 293).
304 Ibid.
305 Ibid, para 696.

relatively new exposure of the Myanmar population to the Internet and social media.[306] The Mission concluded that the prevalence of hate speech in Myanmar significantly contributed to increased tension and a climate in which individuals and groups may become more receptive to incitement and calls for violence. This also applies to hate speech on *Facebook*:

> The extent to which the spread of messages and rumours on Facebook has increased discrimination and violence in Myanmar must be independently and thoroughly researched, so that appropriate lessons can be drawn and similar scenarios prevented. Similarly, the impact of the recent measures taken by Facebook to prevent and remedy the abuse of its platform needs to be assessed.[307]

In another report, published in September 2009 and looking specifically at the economic interests of the Myanmar military, the Fact-Finding Mission directly implicated national and international businesses in violations committed by the military and the companies it controls.[308] Through the *Union of Myanmar Economic Holdings* (*UMEHL*) and the *Myanmar Economic Corporations* (*MEC*), the key military-owned companies still 'have tentacles everywhere'.[309] The Special Rapporteur on human rights in Myanmar explained the problem in 2019:

> UMEHL and MEC are active across many sectors, including natural resource extraction. The full extent of their business operations and profits are unclear, but their main beneficiaries are most likely to be high-ranking military and ex-military officials. Military-dominated state-owned economic enterprises in natural resource extraction are regulators, revenue collectors and commercial entities, and they are permitted to retain vast profits that bypass the Government budget with no record kept on how they are spent.[310]

The Fact-Finding Mission found that *UMEHL* and *MEC* are owned and influenced by senior military leaders responsible for gross human rights violations.[311] The Mission identified 120 *UMEHL*- and *MEC*-owned businesses across diverse sectors of the economy – from construction and gem extraction to manufacturing, insurance, tourism and banking – and found that '[t]he revenue that these military

---

306 Ibid., para 1342.
307 Ibid., para 1354.
308 Independent International Fact-Finding Mission on Myanmar, 'The economic interests of the Myanmar military', A/HRC/42/CRP.3 (16 Sept2019).
309 *The Economist* Special Report, 'A Burmese Spring' (May 2013), 9.
310 Oral statement by Ms Yanghee Lee, Special Rapporteur on the situation of human rights in Myanmar at the 40th session of the Human Rights Council (11 March 2019).
311 Fact-Finding Mission on Myanmar, 'The economic interests of the Myanmar military' (n 308), para 6(a).

businesses generate strengthens the Tatmadaw's autonomy from elected civilian oversight and provides financial support for the Tatmadaw's operations with their wide array of international human rights and humanitarian law violations'.[312] The military has committed human rights and international humanitarian law violations, particularly in Kachin State, in connection with their business activities.[313] The Mission found that 15 foreign companies have joint ventures and at least 44 foreign companies have other forms of commercial ties with military businesses.[314] The Mission alerts:

> Any foreign business activity involving the Tatmadaw and its conglomerates MEHL and MEC poses a high risk of contributing to, or being linked to, violations of international human rights law and international humanitarian law. At a minimum, these foreign companies are contributing to supporting the Tatmadaw's financial capacity to wage war against ethnic minorities.[315]

The detailed findings of the Fact-Finding Mission expressly warn business about investing in Myanmar: it notes that military operations in northern Rakhine State in 2016 and 2017 have 'so seriously violated international law that any engagement in any form with the Tatmadaw, its current leadership, and its businesses, is indefensible'.[316] The Mission calls for all investors to ensure their operations and due diligence procedures are in line with international human rights standards,[317] a call echoed by the Special Rapporteur, who recommends that all businesses investing in Myanmar should 'conduct rigorous human rights due diligence in accordance with international standards, and all the more so in areas affected by violence and conflict', paying 'special attention to the potential impact of their activities on the human rights of individuals that may be at a heightened risk of vulnerability or marginalization'.[318] The Fact-Finding Mission goes one step further, calling for all investors to eschew economic relationships with the security forces or any enterprise owned or controlled by them.[319] This makes investing anywhere in Myanmar very difficult.

Conclusion

Truth-seeking initiatives established after the governance transitions in a number of countries have increasingly sought to use their mandate to scrutinize the role

312 Ibid.
313 Ibid., para 6(b).
314 Ibid., para 6(d).
315 Ibid.
316 Fact-Finding Mission report (n 293), 1675.
317 Ibid., 1716.
318 Report of the Special Rapporteur on the situation of human rights in Myanmar, A/73/332 (Aug 2018), 22.
319 Fact-Finding Mission report (n 293), 1717.

and responsibility of corporations and other economic actors in facilitating gross violations by oppressive regimes. In their final reports, each of these commissions has included recommendations for the government that specifically sought to offer redress for victims of corporate abuses. The hearings they conducted have evidenced corporate responsibility for rights violations, defined the procedural and substantive dimension of the right to reparations for victims of corporate abuses, introduced innovative recommendations that business entities should contribute to such reparations, and recommended the recovery of assets to assist in the payment of reparations.[320] Four positive aspects distinguish truth processes with such a mandate.

First, examining the role that corporations played in past abuses allows for the establishment of a more complete and holistic narrative of the violations that occurred, and facilitates a more thorough comprehension of the dynamics that contributed to the conflict or repression. The purpose of any truth-seeking initiative is to document and explain pervasive patterns of abuse, and to address the root causes of conflict in order to paint a broader portrait of culpability.[321] By examining the role of corporations in past abuses, truth commissions have been able to narrate a story about the atrocities that took place that is more representative of the multi-causal origins of the conflict or repression.[322] For example, despite the limitations of the process analyzed above, the South Africa TRC succeeded in creating an his-torical record of the complex role played by businesses during, and sometimes in conjunction with, the apartheid regime. Truth commissions in Liberia, East Timor and Sierra Leone, and UN-mandated investigations in the DRC have also helped to understand the specific role of natural resources in the maintenance of authoritarian regimes and the facilitation of armed conflicts.[323]

A second contribution of truth commissions has been the attempt and ability to counter corporate impunity. Truth-seeking initiatives often do not have judicial powers, but their findings can nonetheless serve to initiate subsequent judicial proceedings. TRCs in Liberia and East Timor, for example, have named specific companies, and this often provides the only official account of the nature and scale of corporate abuses. By reflecting on the relationship between these violations and the responsibilities of companies, they provide a more comprehensive account of corporate actions, including data on the wealth they amassed, the resources avail-able for reparations and the kind of punishments or measures of forgiveness that society should impose or can afford. Once the truth is established in this manner, other outcomes are also left open to possibility. Hayner explains that a stated intention of most truth commissions has been to contribute to justice in the courts; many have forwarded their files to the relevant authorities and have

320 Darcy (n 4), 10, 54.
321 Hayner (n 4), 1001.
322 Carranza (n 7), 319–21; I Robinson, 'Truth Commissions and Anti-Corruption: Towards a Complementary Framework?' (2015) 9 *Intl J Trans Just* 33.
323 Harwell and Le Billon (n 231), 283.

recommended prosecution.[324] For example, in its final report the South Africa's TRC submitted that there were legal grounds for instituting claims for reparations against banks and other corporations. As discussed in Chapter 4, dissatisfaction on the part of apartheid victims with the compensation awarded by the South African government, and the meagre contribution of companies, resulted in the *Apartheid Reparations* litigation filed in the United States.[325] The lawsuit was seen as a logical continuation to the incomplete work of the TRC in holding corporations accountable.[326] Also of note, as a result of the Brazil commission's findings, some of the workers named in the documents have indicated they may pursue civil lawsuits or other legal action, ask reparations for lost wages or seek an apology.[327]

A third distinct contribution of truth commissions lies in recognizing the links between the behaviour of corporations and human rights violations, which may have a potential deterrent effect on future corporate behaviour in countries that continue to suffer oppressive regimes. As a corollary, any failures to address the economic factors that contribute to a repressive government constitute a dangerous historical blindness.[328] The risk is that same factors will emerge again, resulting in the recurrence of violations. Arguably, a fuller historical record, one that includes corporate involvement, can help to ensure that a country in transition will not be left in a position where it could repeat past violations. Moreover, in line with Nelson Camilo Sánchez León, a transitional justice expert, who argues that truth commissions should pursue 'transformative reparations' that address the circumstances of affected communities, truth commissions can recommend non-monetary measures for corporations – for instance, an improving in working conditions.[329] Finally, if it is determined that corporations should be held accountable for human rights violations that occurred during an oppressive regime, this would likely provide an additional source of funding for reparations to victims and their families.

Truth commissions' recommendations for corporations to finance reparations programmes while simultaneously addressing corporate accountability have been, however, largely ignored by the governments, mostly for fear of falling foul of investors at a time of transition. Truth commissions usually only have the power to recommend reparations; they do not have the power to directly compel the

---

324 Hayner (n 4), 90.
325 M Swart, 'The Khulumani Litigation: Complementing the Work of the South African Truth And Reconciliation Commission' (2011) 16 *Tilburg L Rev* 30, 31; Barnard-Naudé (n 14), 201, 214; I Gubbay, 'Towards Making Blood Money Visible: Lessons Drawn from the Apartheid Litigation' in Bohoslavsky and Letnar Černič (n 197), 337, 344; E Daly, 'Reparations in South Africa: A Cautionary Tale' 33 (2003) *U Mem L Rev* 367, 383–87.
326 Abrahams, 'The TRC's Unfinished Business' (n 163), 34, 35.
327 Reuters, 'The "Black list": Documents suggest foreign automakers aided Brazil's dictators' 5 August 2014.
328 Bohoslavsky and Opgenhaffen (n 46), 197–201.
329 Sánchez León (n 198), 119.

payment of them, and the task of making demands for and collecting reparations usually falls to government.[330] Accordingly, governments have rarely implemented TRCs' recommendations concerning reparations, and the contributions made by businesses accused of collusion in oppression has been far less than the commissions have proposed.[331] In the end, none of the recommendations for prosecution or reparation concerning corporate involvement in abuses recommended by the TRCs in South Africa, Liberia and East Timor were followed by the respective governments. While there are no normative obstacles to expanding the focus of truth-seeking initiatives to include corporate actors, there remain economic, practical and political reasons for this struggle. As a consequence, despite their best efforts in this direction, truth commissions have struggled to secure accountability and affective remedies.[332]

Truth commissions typically face short deadlines, tight budgets and low institutional capacity, and, as a result, they may have to give priority to the most serious violations, which may not involve corporate actors.[333] Moreover, addressing questions of corporate complicity may require interdisciplinary multifaceted investigations and triangulation of information from the state, financial institutions and corporations, which demands not only specialized personnel but also a robust infrastructure that truth commissions do not usually have. Even if a truth commission was properly equipped and staffed, powerful interest groups could politically block this kind of investigation. A typical parliamentary negotiation for the establishment of a truth commission involves both victims and members of the former regime. Adding the interests of businesspeople and corporations to the mix could make it harder to approve a truth commission or to make it work after the approval.[334] This type of situation, for example, may block the path of the Argentina's commission on economic complicity. Those who may have benefitted from corporate operations and remain influential in governmental and commercial interests in contemporary Argentina may effectively obstruct commission operations if they believe this would endanger their economic interests.[335] As described above, the TRCs in South Africa, Liberia and East Timor all attributed responsibility to corporations and recommended that businesses pay reparations, but the respective governments lacked the political will to implement the commissions' proposals.[336] TRCs 'might not be functionally able to address the role and responsibility of corporations [...] TRCs are politically weak institutions, with few

330 Darcy (n 4), 43–46; Hayner (n 4), 251; T Antkowiak, 'Truth as Right and Remedy in International Human Rights Experience' (2002) 23 *Mich J Intl L* 977, 1002.
331 Darcy (n 4), 55; Sandoval and Surfleet (n 80), 100.
332 Koska (n 9), 44; Robinson (n 322).
333 Harwell and Le Billon (n 231), 299–305.
334 Bohoslavsky and Torelly (n 248), 257.
335 Sriram (n 109).
336 Sandoval and Surfleet (n 80).

economic and human resources and with expertise most often linked to violations of civil and political rights.'[337]

Remedy for corporate human rights violations in transitional justice contexts can be mandated by international and national judicial processes or recommended by truth commissions. This chapter and the previous one have discussed the limitations of such processes due to a number of normative, political and economic reasons. Remedies can, however, also be achieved through reparations programmes established at the administrative level, an issue which the next chapter discusses.

337 C Sandoval, L Filippini and R Vidal, 'Linking Transitional Justice and Corporate Accountability' in S Michalowski (ed.), *Corporate Accountability in the Context of Transitional Justice* (Routledge 2013), 18.

Chapter 6

Administrative reparation programmes

Introduction

The previous chapters have analyzed two types of remedies available to victims of corporate abuses in transitional justice contexts: judicial processes – at the international (Chapter 2), regional (Chapter 3), and domestic levels (Chapter 4) – and truth-seeking initiatives (Chapter 5). This chapter discusses another form of remedy, administrative reparations programmes – that is, reparations programmes created by legislation for whole classes of victims rather than in response to individual cases.

Reparation is one of the processes through which rights violations may be remedied, and it is a key component of transitional justice.[1] The 2005 *UN Basic Principles and Guidelines on the Right to a Remedy and Reparation for Victims of Gross Violations of International Human Rights Law and Serious Violations of International Humanitarian Law* ('the Basic Principles') define reparations as including five forms: restitution, compensation, rehabilitation, satisfaction and guarantees of non-repetition.[2] The right to reparations is primarily a right that can be claimed against the state under international human rights law, against the state and non-state actors under international humanitarian law, and against individual perpetrators under international criminal law.[3] While international law is silent in

1 M Minow, *Between Vengeance and Forgiveness: Facing History after Genocide and Mass Atrocity* (Beacon Press 1998); M Osiel, *Mass Atrocity, Collective Memory and the Law* (Transaction Publishers 1999).
2 Basic Principles and Guidelines on the Right to a Remedy and Reparation for Victims of Gross Violations of International Human Rights Law and Serious Violations of International Humanitarian Law, adopted by UN General Assembly, Resolution 60/147 of 16 December 2005 [Basic Principles], principles 19–22.
3 Most of the law applicable to state responsibility and reparations has become customary international law and codified in the Draft Articles on Responsibility of States for Internationally Wrongful Acts (International Law Commission 2001 A/56/10). The leading opinion in this regard is set out in the judgment of the Permanent Court of International Justice in the Chorzow Factory case: 'It is a principle of international law that the breach of an engagement involves an obligation to make a reparation in an adequate form' (1927, P.C.I.J. ser. A no. 9, 21). International humanitarian law contemplates the obligation of parties to armed conflict to pay compensation for violations of provisions:

relation to corporations having such an obligation, there are some non-binding principles stating that corporations have the 'responsibility' to provide redress to victims of human rights violations.[4] The UN Guiding Principles on business and human rights, for example, highlight the responsibility of corporations to address adverse human rights impacts, in addition to the state's obligation to provide redress to victims of corporate-related human rights abuses.[5] The issue of responsibility of non-state actors was also raised in the discussions and negotiations of the Basic Principles, with regard to groups that exercise effective control over a territory, but also with regard to business enterprises exercising economic power.[6] The Basic Principles provide for equal and effective access to justice, 'irrespective of who may ultimately be the bearer of responsibility for the violation'.[7] Theo Van Boven, whose work was central to the drafting of the Basic Principles, noted that these were meant to apply also 'to business enterprises exercising economic power'.[8] It was considered, from a victim-oriented perspective, that non-state actors are to be held responsible for their policies and practices, allowing victims to seek redress and reparations.[9] Under principle IX.15:

> In cases where a person, *a legal person*, or other entity is found liable for reparation to a victim, such party should provide reparation to the victim or

Hague Convention respecting the Laws and Customs of War on Land (art 3), Additional Protocol to the Geneva Conventions relating to the Protection of Victims of International Armed Conflicts (art 91). See also Study concerning the right to restitution, compensation and rehabilitation for victims of gross violations of human rights and fundamental freedoms, Theo van Boven, Special Rapporteur (E/CN.4/Sub.2/1993/8); M du Plessis, 'Reparations and International Law: How Are Reparations to Be Determined (Past Wrong or Current Effects), Against Whom, and What Form Should They Take?' (2003) 22 *Windsor YB Access Just* 61; NL Rosenblum (ed.), *Breaking the Cycles of Hatred: Memory, Law, and Repair* (Princeton University Press 2002).

4 The final version of the draft UN Norms included this paragraph: 'Transnational corporations and other business enterprises shall provide prompt, effective and adequate reparation to those persons, entities and communities that have been adversely affected by failures to comply with these Norms through, inter alia, reparations, restitution, compensation and rehabilitation for any damage done or property taken.' Draft Norms on the Responsibilities of Transnational Corporations and Other Business Enterprises with Regard to Human Rights, E/CN.4/Sub.2/2003/12 (2003), para 18. See also, D Weissbrodt and M Kruger, 'Norms on the Responsibility of Transnational Corporations and Other Business Enterprises with Regard to Human Rights' (2003) 97 *AJIL* 901.

5 Basic Principles (n 2), principle 11.

6 T van Boven, The UN Basic Principles and Guidelines on the Right to a Remedy and Reparation for Victims of Gross Violations of International Human Rights Law and Serious Violations of International Humanitarian Law, 2010. See also C Sandoval and G Surfleet, 'Corporations and Redress in Transitional Justice Processes' in S Michalowski, *Corporate Accountability in the Context of Transitional Justice* (Routledge 2014), 93, 99

7 Basic Principles (n 2), principle 3(c).

8 van Boven (n 6).

9 Ibid., 1–3.

compensate the State if the State has already provided reparation to the victim.[10]

While reparations programmes often target the most serious forms of civil and political rights violations, some reparations programmes have paid attention to a broader band of rights violations.[11] In Brazil, for example, reparations were paid to workers who had to abandon their jobs due to political persecution, especially after the 1979 Amnesty law when the labour unions joined the struggle against the dictatorship.[12] The Argentinian government passed a number of laws and decrees to provide reparations for victims of human rights abuses, including payment of compensation for lost labour time.[13] As discussed in the previous chapter, the reports of a few truth commissions followed up with recommendations regarding remedy for abuses. Of those, some focused on official policies of reparations and restitution, specifically recovery of land, jobs and other assets; the South African TRC called on businesses to voluntarily contribute to a reparation fund – an effort viewed as largely unsuccessful by most accounts; and labour and economic reforms were suggested in some cases – for example, in Honduras, Paraguay and Ecuador.

In most cases, however, the attention has centred primarily or exclusively on making only the state accountable.[14] The responsibility of corporations to provide reparations has not been given adequate consideration.[15] In theory, corporations could provide any of the five recognized forms of reparations (restitution, compensation, rehabilitation, satisfaction, guarantees of non-repetition[16]) in isolation or in combination. In practice, in the case of corporations there is a tendency to

10 Basic Principles (n 2), principle IX.15.
11 An early effort to link impunity and reparation for economic, social and cultural rights, albeit not explicitly in a transitional justice context, was UN Sub-Commission on the Promotion and Protection of Human Rights, Final Report on the Question of the Impunity of Perpetrators of Human Rights Violations (Economic, Social and Cultural rights), UN. Doc. E/CN.4/Sub.2/1997/8, 1997. See also L Magarrell, 'Reparations for Massive or Widespread Human Rights Violations: Sorting out Claims for Reparations and the Struggle for Social Justice' (2003) 22 *Windsor YB Access Just* 91–94; R Mani, *Beyond Retribution: Seeking Justice in* the Shadows of War (Polity Press 2002); Z Miller, 'Effects of Invisibility: In Search of the "Economic" in Transitional Justice' (2008) 2 *Intl J Trans Just* 266, 285.
12 JP Bohoslavsky and MD Torelly, 'Financial Complicity: The Brazilian Dictatorship Under the "Macroscope" in DN Sharp (ed.), *Justice and Economic Violence in Transition* (Springer Science Business Media 2014), 256; I Cano and P Galvão Ferreira, 'The Reparations Program in Brazil' in P de Greiff (ed.), *The Handbook of Reparations* (OUP 2006), 102; Magarrell (n 11), 91.
13 JP Bohoslavsky and V Opgenhaffen, 'The Past and Present of Corporate Complicity: Financing the Argentinean Dictatorship' (2010) 23 *Harvard Human Rights J* 157, 197–201.
14 Sandoval and Surfleet (n 6), 93, 96.
15 Ibid., 93.
16 Basic Principles, Arts 19–23.

prefer compensation to other forms of reparations.[17] In international law the preferred form of reparation both in state practice and in the theory is restitution; only when this is not possible may other forms of reparations be awarded.[18] In 1928, the Permanent Court of International Justice ruled in the *Chorzów Factory* case that restitution was the preferred remedy for correcting illegal state confiscation of property.[19]

Restitution refers to measures that restore the victim to the original situation before the violations occurred, including the return of property and land. The concept of restitution has long been accepted as an important judicial remedy in international law. The particular remedy of restitution stems from the broader right to an effective remedy for violations of human rights.[20] International law approaches restitution generally through the lens of infringements of law due to what are defined as wrongful acts or omissions attributable to states through the application of the law of state responsibility.[21] Restitution is also a key element of the remedial measures envisaged under international criminal law.[22] While corporations do not have a specific obligation to provide restitution under international law, they may be forced to provide such restitution under the national law of a country. This is because victims of human rights violations, including corporate-related abuses, have an enforceable right to have the violation remedied, repaired and reversed.[23] Restitution measures that are specifically applicable to companies include expropriation and restitution of lands.

It is on these foundations that the subsequent concepts of land restitution to those deprived of it during period of conflict or repression have been built.[24] The

17 Sandoval and Surfleet (n 6), 109.
18 Permanent Court of Justice, *Chórzow Factory (Indemnity)* case (*Germany v Poland*), 1928 PCIJ (ser. A) No. 17, Judgment of 13 September 1928, 47. See also FL Kirgis, 'Restitution as a Remedy in US Courts for Violations of International Law' (2001) 95 (2) *AJIL* 343.
19 *Chórzow Factory* (n 18), 47.
20 See Universal Declaration of Human Rights (UDHR), Art 8; International Covenant on Civil and Political Rights (CCPR), Art 2; International Convention on the Elimination of All Forms of Racial Discrimination (CERD), Art 6; Convention against Torture and Other Cruel, Inhuman or Degrading Treatment or Punishment (CAT), Art 11; Convention on the Rights of the Child (CRC), Art 39.
21 For example, a legal opinion of the Inter-American Juridical Committee has asserted that restitution is required for any violation of an international obligation: Inter-American Juridical Committee, Legal Opinion on the Decision of the Supreme Court of the United States of America, OAS Doc. CJI/RES.II-15/92, para 10 (1992).
22 For example, Rome Statute, UN Doc. A/CONF.183/9 (1998), 17 July 1998, Art 75 (1); Rules of Procedure and Evidence of the International Tribunal for the Prosecution of Persons Responsible for Serious Violations of Humanitarian Law Committed in the Territory of the Former Yugoslavia since 1991 (11 February 1994), Art 105.
23 UNHCR, Inter-Office Memorandum No. 104/2001, 28 November 2001, Field Office Memorandum No. 101/2001, 28 November 2001.
24 UN Principles on Housing and Property Restitution for Refugees and Displaced Persons, UN Doc. E/CN.4/Sub.2/2005/17 (2005) [Pinheiro principles]. The right of return can be found in Article 13(2) of the UDHR and Article 12(4) of the ICCPR.

Basic Principles state that restitution includes 'return to one's place of residence' and 'return of property', and 'should, whenever possible, restore the victim to the original situation' before the violations occurred.[25] These points were further refined in the UN *Principles on Housing and Property Restitution* (the Pinheiro Principles).[26] They constitute evidence for the preference towards restitution as an appropriate and justifiable remedy for violations of international law, in particular those violations involving the illegal confiscation of housing, property and land.[27] As such, administrative reparations programmes can in certain circumstances provide the restitution of property and land from corporations.[28] This chapter looks at administrative reparation programmes dealing with a particular type of reparation, land restitution, which can include the restitution of land taken for economic reasons during an armed conflict or time of repression.

There are a number of reasons for the focus on land restitution: land acquisition is often a key driver of conflict; land confiscation, forced evictions and population displacement are common during conflict; land disputes are a key aspect that countries in transition need to address; land is, in most cases, the most important asset that victims seek back; corporations are often involved in land confiscation either directly or in complicity with the state; land rights abuses are some of the most widespread corporate human rights abuses; and innovative reparation programmes have tried to deal with victims' grievance in this area. While contemporary conflicts – for example, in Syria, Libya, Yemen, Myanmar, Somalia and the Democratic Republic of Congo – involve massive dislocation and destruction, insufficient focus is put upon restoring housing, land and property rights.[29] This chapter focuses on efforts to return land that was taken for economic projects in transitional countries in three different regions (Colombia, Myanmar and South Africa). The analysis presented here is intended to show that innovative reparations programmes involving the responsibilities of business have been implemented and that, despite difficulties, this remains one of the most interesting avenues for remedy.

See also D Fitzpatrick and A Fishman, 'Land Policy and Transitional Justice after Armed Conflicts' in Sharp (n 12), 263, 274; RC Williams, 'Post-Conflict Property Restitution and Refugee Return in Bosnia and Herzegovina: Implications for International Standard-Setting and Practice' (2005) 37 *NYU J Intl L Policy* 448; G Paglione, 'Individual Property Restitution: From Deng to Pinheiro – and the Challenges Ahead' (2008) 20 *Intl J Refugee L* 393; E Rosand, 'The Right to Return under International Law Following Mass Dislocation: The Bosnia Precedent?' (1998) 19 *Michigan J Intl L* 1128.
25 Basic Principles (n 2), Art 18.
26 Pinheiro principles (n 24).
27 Fitzpatrick and Fishman (n 24), 276.
28 J Goebertus, 'Palma de Aceite y Desplazamiento Forzado en la Zona Bananera' (2008) 67 *Colombia Internacional* 152.
29 P Seils, 'Transitional justice – time for a re-think', OpenGlobalRights, 10 Apr 2018 www.openglobalrights.org/paul-seils/Transitional-justice-time-for-a-re-think/?lang= English

6.1 Land restitution programmes

The question of land restitution is a complex and deeply interconnected one. Its realization remains challenging and among the most sensitive topics in most transitional countries. Land access is often a key cause of conflict, and the conflict then exacerbates the problem, including as a result of population displacement and 'land grabbing' by political elites, with corporations often benefitting directly and indirectly from land seizures.[30] During the conflict in Colombia, for example, land titles and property rights were transferred directly from the population to corporations.[31] In Myanmar, the military government as well as state-owned and private companies confiscated millions of acres of land from hundreds of thousands of people.[32] Businesses were crucial to the particular development strategy that emerged in the 1960s and 1970s in Latin American.[33] Businesses allied with authoritarian systems to ensure political stability and protect 'capitalist deepening' projects during a period of labour and student revolts and challenges to the capitalist system:

> The Cold War logic prevalent at the time reinforced these policies and extended them into the countryside where the agrarian reform victories that protected peasant, indigenous, and rural workers were violently replaced with private sector land ownership, resulting in large numbers of internally and externally displaced peoples, illegal detention and torture, and massacres of leaders and communities.[34]

30 C Huggins, 'Truth, Justice, Reconciliation, and … Land Tenure Reform?' (2009) *Oxford Transitional Justice Research Working Paper Series*, 3; 'Linking Broad Constellations of Ideas: Transitional Justice, Land Tenure Reform and Development' in P de Greiff and R Duthie, *Transitional Justice and Development: Making Connections* (Social Science Research Council 2009) 332, 333; Fitzpatrick and Fishman (n 24), 263–67; R Duthie, 'Transitional Justice and Displacement' (2011) 5(2) *Intl J Trans Just* 245; B Atuahene, 'Property Rights and the Demands of Transformation' (2010) *Michigan J Intl L* 31; 'Property and Transitional Justice' (2010) *UCLA L Rev Discourse* 58.

31 T Van Ho, 'Is it Already Too Late for Colombia's Land Restitution Process? The Impact of International Investment Law on Transitional Justice Initiatives' (2016) 5 (1) *Intl Human Rights L Rev* 60.

32 I Pietropaoli, 'Corporate Accountability and Transitional Justice in Myanmar' (7 March 2016) JusticeInfo; Amnesty International, *Open for Business? Corporate Crime and Abuses at Myanmar's Copper Mine* (AI 10 February 2015); Global Witness, *Guns, Cronies and Crops* (GW 26 March 2015); FIDH, *Land of Sorrow: Human Rights Violations at Mandalay's Myotha Industrial Park* (FIDH 27 September 2107).

33 GA O'Donnell, *Modernization and Bureaucratic-Authoritarianism: Studies in South American Politics* (Institute of International Studies, University of California, 1973).

34 LA Payne, 'Corporate Complicity and Transitional Justice: Setting the Scene' in *Peace, Everyone's Business! Corporate Accountability in Transitional Justice: Lessons for Colombia*, PAX (Utrecht, May 2017) 18.

The next sections compare experiences in Colombia, Myanmar and South Africa, which suggest that the restitution of land unlawfully taken by companies during a time of conflict or repression offers an important form of corporate accountability and redress to victims, but it is met by a number of normative and practical challenges, especially in post-conflict countries where land tenure is generally insecure and customary rights are not legally recognized.

6.1.1. Colombia's victims and land restitution law

In Colombia, the issue of land has been a central part of the armed conflict since it started in the 1960s.[35] Historically a highly unequal society, the concentration of land in the hands of a few has increased dramatically in the course of the conflict.[36] During the armed conflict, warring factions forcefully displaced almost six million people from large tracts of land in mainly rural areas, which were taken over by guerrillas, paramilitaries and drug traffickers, and by companies.[37] The forced displacement of populations alongside subsequent corporate occupation was a common occurrence.[38] There are serious allegations and some compelling evidence to suggest that corporations have been complicit in the forced displacements in two ways: first, by directly paying for militants to displace people in order to gain access to land,[39] and, second, by purchasing land from armed actors after a displacement, without any attempt to compensate those who were originally displaced from it.[40] This is a part of what is often referred to as the phenomenon of the 'para-economy' in Colombia – the informal economic network that has benefitted directly in business terms from political and paramilitary violence.[41] Mining and agriculture companies, in particular, have been accused of relying on paramilitary groups to help expand and secure their operations.[42] Indeed, population

---

35 NC Sánchez León, *Tierra en transición. Justicia transicional, restitución de tierras y política agrarian en Colombia* (Centro de Estudios de Derecho, Justicia y Sociedad, Dejusticia, 2017).
36 KAO Lid and J García-Godos, 'Land Restitution in the Colombian Transitional Justice Process' (2010) 28 *Nordic J Hum Rts* 262, 263.
37 Ibid., 272, 282–83; N Summers, 'Colombia's Victims' Law: Transitional Justice in a Time of Violent Conflict?' (2012) 25(1) *Harvard Human Rights J* 219, 222; AM Ibañez and CE Velez, 'Civil Conflict and Forced Migration: Micro Determinants and Welfare Losses of Displacement in Colombia' (2008) 36 *World Development* 659, 661.
38 F Thomson, 'The Agrarian Question and Violence in Colombia: Conflict and Development' (2011) 11(3) *J Agrarian Change* 321, 347.
39 C Espinosa, 'The Constitutional Protection of IDPs in Colombia,' in RA Rivadeneira (ed.), *Judicial Protection of Internally Displaced Persons: The Colombian Experience* (Brookings Institution 2009), 3.
40 Thomson (n 38), 347.
41 VL Franco and JD Restrepo, 'Empresarios Palmeros, Poderes de Facto y Despojo de Tierras en el Bajo Atrato' in M Romero Vidal (ed.), *La Economía de los Paramilitares* (Debate 2011), 269, 317.
42 Ibid., 280.

displacement is largely concentrated in areas where mining and agro-industries activities are widespread.[43] The involvement of palm oil companies in the Colombian conflict provides a good example of the grey area between legality and illegality in which companies exploit conflict to benefit economically.[44] In the Urubá and other regions of Colombia, palm oil companies that legally bought land from which communities and individuals have been displaced by conflict continue to have direct links with the paramilitaries.[45] Several of these companies are owned by paramilitaries operating under aliases, which acts as a further economic drain in that the economic activity generated is not fed back into the formal economy, and is instead used to further undermine the security climate of the state.[46]

In November 2016, Colombia's Congress ratified the final peace agreement between the government and the *Fuerzas Armadas Revolucionarias de Colombia* (FARC). The central component of this peace agreement is its chapter on victims that envisions the creation of a comprehensive system of transitional justice. The novel feature of such a transitional justice framework is its focus, in addition to combatants in illegal armed groups and state agents, on third parties or non-combatants who 'participated directly or indirectly in the armed conflict'.[47] For some experts, this means that 'members of the country's economic and political sectors may have to clarify how they collaborated and under what circumstances, and admit their responsibility for the commission of such crimes' before the special jurisdiction.[48]

The Colombian government has embarked on an innovative restitution and reparations programme aimed at 'integral reparations', under which some corporations may be forced to turn over land and titles to land that were obtained during the conflict.[49] Transitional justice processes started in Colombia in 2005 with the

---

43 Summers (n 37), 222; Ibanez and Velez (n 37), 661; AM Ibañez and JC Muñoz, 'The Persistence of Land Concentration in Colombia: What Happened Between 2000 and 2010?' in M Bergsmo and others (eds), *Distributive Justice n Transitions* (FICHL 2010), 279, 306–07.

44 NC Sánchez León, 'Corporate Accountability, Reparations and Distributive Justice in Post Conflict Societies' in S Michalowski, *Corporate Accountability in the Context of Transitional Justice* (Routledge 2014), 114, 118.

45 Goebertus (n 28).

46 Franco and Restrepo (n 41), 286.

47 Final Agreement to End the Armed Conflict and Build a Stable and Lasting Peace, Colombian government and FARC-EP, 24 Nov 2016, Point 5. This system is due to create a truth commission, the *Comisión de Esclarecimiento de la Verdad*, and a transitional jurisdiction known as the special jurisdiction for peace (*Jurisdicción Especial para la Paz*), among other measures. For comments, see NC Sánchez León and D Marín López, 'Corporate Accountability in Transitional Justice in Colombia', in *Peace, Everyone's Business!* (n 34), 120, 121.

48 Sánchez León and Marín López (n 47), 122.

49 *Ley de Víctimas y Restitución de Tierras* (Victims and Land Restitution Law), no. 1448 (10 June 2011) [Victims' Law]. See also Van Ho (n 31), 62; Lid and García-Godos (n 36), 277, 287.

approval of the *Justice and Peace Law*.[50] The *Victims and Land Restitution Law* (Victims' Law), passed in 2011, is intended, in part, to redress the widespread forced displacements stemming from the conflict.[51] Envisaged as a component of the reparations programme, restitution of land is considered by the government to partly contribute to a sustainable solution of the land issue, and, by extension, of the Colombian armed conflict.[52] The Victims' Law aims to facilitate truth, justice and integral reparations for victims, with a 'guarantee of no repetition'.[53] The law defines as 'victims' people, or their family members, who suffered grave violations of human rights or of international humanitarian law in the context of the internal armed conflict from 1 January 1985.[54] It states that the objective of reparations is to contribute to repositioning (*recuperar*) victims as citizens in the full exercise of their rights and duties.[55] Most significantly, the Victims' Law declares a right of restitution for those who have been dispossessed of their land or who have been forced to abandon it.[56]

The heart of the law lies in the scheme for land restitution.[57] The Victims' Law establishes a clear, context-specific and extensive right to land restitution.[58] Because the problem of forced displacement is widespread, the law was specifically designed to provide an easy and accessible remedy for victims.[59] The legal and actual return of the land that was dispossessed remains a key goal in the attempt to gain transitional justice; where it is not possible to meet this goal (e.g. because of continued lack of security), then equivalent land, or compensation for the loss, is to be provided.[60] Importantly, the law shifts legal presumptions and the burden of proof regarding land ownership distinctly in favour of victims.[61] One of the most interesting aspects of the law is the way it establishes the necessary causal link to

---

50 Justice and Peace Law, no 975 (2005). See also, KAO Lid and J García-Godos, 'Transitional Justice and Victims' Rights before the End of a Conflict: The Unusual Case of Colombia (2010) 42(3) *J Latin American Studies* 487.

51 Victims' Law (n 49). See also Summers (n 37), 220; DL Attanasio and NC Sánchez, 'Return within the Bounds of the Pinheiro Principles: The Colombian Land Restitution Experience' (2012) 11 *Washington Univ Global Studies L Rev* 1, 2.

52 Lid and García-Godos (n 36), 265

53 Victims Law (n 49), Art 1. See also, Summers (n 37), 225; O Lid and García-Godos, 'Transitional Justice and Victims' Rights before the End of a Conflict' (n 50).

54 Victims Law (n 49), Art 3.

55 Ibid.

56 Ibid., Arts 71–72.

57 Ibid. It applies to land lost after 1 January 1991. See also P Martínez Cortés, 'Ley De Víctimas y Restitución de Tierras en Colombia en Contexto' (2003) FDCL and Transnational Institute.

58 Victims Law (n 49), Art 75.

59 Ibid., Art 77(3)(4). See also Summers (n 37), 223, 227–28; Van Ho (n 31), 70.

60 Victims Law (n 49), Art 72.

61 Ibid., Arts 77–78.

dispossession.[62] Rather than making the claimant prove that they fit within the definition, the law reverses the burden of proof with the use of presumptions.[63]

The law includes a presumption that land transfers were illegal if they were entered into as a business or sales contract between the victim and any individual 'convicted of membership, collaboration or financing of armed groups'.[64] It also establishes a presumption of illegality if the transfer was the result of a business transaction stipulated at less than half of its value, or where the transaction was made in areas of widespread violence, massive displacement or grave violations of human rights, in areas where land became increasingly concentrated or where crop production significantly changed, or where the leadership of the contracting community business or farming cooperatives changed after the displacement.[65] Anyone who possesses land that is ordered to be restituted through this process 'will have [his] possession declared void as if it never occurred'.[66] If a subsequent owner has purchased the land in 'good faith', he can oppose the restitution process and receive compensation for his loss.[67] As one scholar notes: 'The inversion of the burden of proof is widely considered a major achievement of the Victims' Law and one that will significantly advance the right to restitution.'[68]

The law also adopts a series of measures to address corporate involvement in displacement.[69] It attempts to regulate corporate purchases of land and also to hold businesses accountable for contributing to the displacement.[70] First, the Victims' Law stipulates that corporations may be held financially liable for their involvement in the conflict.[71] Judges in individual reparations cases can require businesses, when found responsible for 'contributing to victimization', to make payments to the Victims' Reparations Fund.[72] The *Justice and Peace Law* established the fund in 2005 as a financing mechanism for victims' reparations, including restitution and civil damages.[73] Until the Victims' Law was passed, judges were only allowed to mandate payments from paramilitary groups.[74] Under the new law, judges may declare that companies bear partial responsibility for displacement or other damages and, accordingly, may impose financial penalties on them.[75]

---

62 N Roht-Arriaza, 'Reparations and Economic, Social, and Cultural Rights' in Sharp (ed.), *Justice and Economic Violence in Transition* (Springer 2014), 109, 129.
63 Victims Law (n 49), Art 78.
64 Ibid., Art 77(1). See also Attanasio and Sánchez (n 51), 24.
65 Victims' Law (n 49), Art 77.
66 Ibid., Art 99. See also Summers (n 37), 230.
67 Attanasio and Sánchez (n 51), 24.
68 Summers (n 37), 229.
69 Victims' Law (n 49), Arts 98, 178.
70 N Summers, 'Recent Developments: Colombia's Victims' Law: Transitional Justice in a Time of Violent Conflict?' (2012) 25(1) *Harvard Human Rights Journal*, 232.
71 Summers (n 37), 232.
72 Ibid.
73 Justice and Peace Law (n 50), Art 54.
74 Ibid.
75 Victims' Law (n 49), Art 177.

Second, the law bans all sales of land that has been restituted for the two-year period post-restitution, and requires judicial authorization of all contracts for the use of this land.[76] For corporations who acquired such land or acquired licences to use the land, the law may lead to these purchases or licences being voided, even if courts previously recognized that they entailed land rights.[77] The provision applies specifically to businesses that wish to continue large agro-industrial projects on previously purchased or leased land. To be considered for authorization, companies wishing to re-contract must prove that they acted in good faith when creating the original contract.[78] If corporations fail to prove good faith, the agro-industrial project will be turned over to the government, and profits will be put towards local victims' reparations programmes.[79]

One of the most controversial provisions of the law concerns such areas where the dispossessed lands have been turned into agri-business projects. While displacements due to military considerations are relatively easily reversed (once military operations have ended, one could expect the civilian population to return to their place of origin), large-scale projects make irreparable changes to the areas where they are developed.[80] Transformation of the use of land, from subsistence farming to vast monocultures makes the reversal practically impossible. If these lands are to provide acceptable socioeconomic conditions for the displaced peoples of Colombia, a mere restitution may not be sufficient.[81] Some stakeholders support a restitution policy that focuses on correcting the illegal dispossession and clarifying land titles and individual rights to property, which would serve to boost the land market and allow for rural development policies that modernize agricultural production, fundamentally based on large, corporate ownership.[82] Arguably, a better approach is one of a restitution policy that meets the requirements of recognition and redistribution, advancing the interest of peasant, indigenous and Afro-Colombian communities.[83]

76 Ibid., Arts 99, 101.

77 Van Ho (n 31), 70.

78 Victims Law (n 49), Arts 99, 207. See also MJ Guembe and H Olea, 'No Justice, No Peace: Discussion of a Legal Framework Regarding the Demobilization of Non-State Armed Groups' in N Roht-Arriaza and J Mariezcurrena (eds), *Transitional Justice in the Twenty-First Century: Beyond Truth versus Justice* (Cambridge University Press 2006), 120.

79 Victims' Law (n 49).

80 Lid and García-Godos (n 36), 268.

81 MP Saffon and R Uprimny-Yepes, 'Reparations for Land Dispossession and Distributive Justice in Colombia', Selected Briefs from the Seminar 'Land Reform and Distributive Justice in the Settlement of Internal Armed Conflicts', Bogotá (5–6 June 2009); Roht-Arriaza (n 62), 129, 131; R Uprimny-Yepes and NC Sánchez, 'Los dilemas de la restitución de tierras en Colombia' (2010) 12(2) Revista Estudios Socio-Jurídicos 305, 325; Lid and García-Godos (n 36), 268

82 Uprimny-Yepes and Sánchez (n 81).

83 Ibid.

Some scholars propose the notion of 'transformative reparations' as a more adequate perspective from which to conceive reparations to victims of the Colombian armed conflict, and particularly to victims of land dispossession.[84] For example, Nelson Camilo Sánchez León suggests a strategy to restore illegally accumulated assets and to redistribute wealth that private actors accumulated during the conflict in Colombia.[85] This strategy is part of a theoretical elaboration of the concept of transformative reparations in an effort to combine the dominant concept of reparations backed on corrective justice with the concept of distributive justice.[86] This model differentiates the degree of responsibility of the actor that obtained the wealth into three levels: high, medium and low.[87]

The 'high responsibility' category refers to where an actor has direct responsibility for violations perpetrated: these are essentially a category that focuses on companies that directly committed illegal acts to obtain economic benefits or financed armed groups to obtain commercial advantages. For example, *Drummond* allegedly paid paramilitary groups to violently resolve labour disputes.[88] Direct responsibility cases can be dealt with through mechanisms of corrective justice, namely criminal and civil judgments – primarily using existing tort mechanisms on the basis of the principle of integral reparation, which requires that victims receive full reparations or complete restitution.[89] As discussed, the Victims' Law stipulates that money used to compensate victims should partially come from businesses that have financed paramilitaries relative to the extent to which the conflict was exacerbated by the business financial support.[90]

The category labelled as 'medium responsibility' refers to those with indirect responsibility: companies that conducted business with the knowledge that the conflict helped its commercial success, but who did not directly participate or support violations. For example, as discussed in Chapter 4, *Chiquita*, while did not directly commit violent actions, had a clear supportive link with paramilitary groups. Indirect responsibility cases are more complex to deal with since they have to address the responsibility of companies that are known to have acted illegally, but against which the available evidence is insufficient for judicial proceedings. Sánchez León argues that it is possible to design a mechanism applying both the principles of corrective and distributive justice.[91] During the conflict, cultivable

---

84 Ibid.
85 Sánchez León (n 30), 119.
86 NC Sánchez León and R Uprimny-Yepes, 'Propuestas para una restitución de tierras transformadora' in C Díaz (ed.), *Tareas Pendientes:Propuestas para la formulación de políticas públicas de reparación en Colombia* (ICTJ 2010); C Díaz Gómez, NC Sánchez León, R Uprimny-Yepes, *Reparar en Colombia: los dilemas en contextos de conflicto, pobreza y exclusión* (ICTJ and DeJusticia 2010).
87 Sánchez León (n 44), 119.
88 See Chapter 3.2.
89 Ibid., 123.
90 Victims Law (n 33), Art 117(e)(f). See also Martínez Cortés (n 57).
91 Sánchez León (n 44), 125.

land was transferred through the forced displacement of people, and companies in various sectors acquired much of that land at derisory prices.[92] A way to reverse such a large-scale dispossession could be to introduce a flexible evidence mechanism that allows land restitution without requiring victims to prove intent.[93] For example, as discussed, the Victims' Law establishes a judicial presumption that people who transferred property in an area of generalized violence did so because of the violence – they are not required to prove the nature of this violence or threat of violence.[94] This approach allows the reversing or annulling of certain legal transactions based on the idea that all land in prescribed areas affected by the violence ought to be considered abandoned land (*res derelicta*) because of the violence, and as a corollary this ferments the assumption that companies who acquired such land participated in bad faith in such displacement.

Finally, the category of 'low responsibility' refers to cases in which the company developed a successful business in Colombia, but where there was no causal nexus between the company's profits and the human rights violations that occurred.[95] The cases of many Colombian banks may exemplify low degrees of responsibility. In such cases, where there is insufficient evidence to establish any degree of responsibility, Sánchez León argues that the ethical and legal justifications for requiring those companies to contribute to the transitional justice programme is not corrective justice, but distributive justice based on the principle of solidarity with public burdens.[96] Distributive justice provides for a duty on society to assist individual members in proportion to the individual needs, contribution and responsibility, the resources available to the society and the society's responsibility to the common good.[97] For example, banks could be required to forgive loans of displaced peoples or provide debt relief.[98]

To implement the Victims' Law, however, the state would need to prevent companies from accessing, using or benefitting from the restituted land. The resulting financial impact on the corporation raises concerns under international investment law.[99] As one scholar points out, 'the potential effect [of the restitution] on multinational corporations raises the potential that international investment law's prohibition on expropriation without compensation could be used to stymie the implementation of the Victims' Law'.[100]

92 Comisión de Seguimento, Cuantificación y Valoración de las Tierra y los Bienes Abanodnados (2011).
93 Sánchez León (n 44), 126.
94 Victims' Law (n 49), Arts 77–78.
95 Sánchez León (n 44), 122.
96 Ibid., 127.
97 KT Jackson, 'Global Distributive Justice and the Corporate Duty to Aid' (1993) 12 (7) *J Business Ethics* 547.
98 Sánchez León (n 44), 129.
99 Van Ho (n 31), 71.
100 Ibid., 62.

Colombia is party to 18 investment treaties or trade agreements with investment protections.[101] Companies are protected by these treaties if they have an 'investment' – Colombia's investment treaties refer to 'any asset' in the country.[102] This means that both the property to be restituted under the Victims' Law and the licences granted to companies are considered 'investments' under Colombia's international investment law commitments.[103] As discussed, the Victims' Law requires the state to nullify transfers of property in certain cases. Despite the legitimate public purpose inherent in this law, the transfer of property may give rise to a violation of international investment law's prohibition on expropriation.[104] Most investment treaties provide foreign investors with a right to disregard domestic judicial processes and seek immediate protection before *ad hoc* arbitral panels.[105] As a result, the threat of international investment law complaints may force Colombia to either opt out of applying the law to foreign corporations, or to pay those corporations millions for violating investment law protections.[106] States like Colombia, facing potentially widespread claims, may choose to limit transitional justice initiatives that impact foreign investors, or to exempt foreign investors from the impact of those initiatives, despite the negative impact this would have on home-grown Colombian capital and investment. This can exacerbate tensions within a community as the exemption of foreign corporations from transitional justice's reach may be seen as rewarding corporations with benefits received through complicity in human rights violations, while punishing investments generated through savings and profit generation in Colombia.[107]

6.1.2. South Africa's land restitution programme

During the colonial and apartheid era in South Africa, a series of laws progressively dispossessed millions of people.[108] By 1990, only 13% of the land was reserved for occupation by black South Africans and all productive agricultural land was in the

---

101 UN Conference on Trade and Development (UNCTAD), Investment Policy Hub, Colombia.
102 See e.g. Bilateral Agreement for the Promotion and Protection of Investments between the Government of the Republic of Colombia and the Government of the People's Republic of China (2013), entered into force 2013; Agreement for the Promotion and Protection of Investments between the Government of the Republic of Colombia and the Government of the Republic of India (10 November 2009), entered into force 2013.
103 Van Ho (n 31), 72.
104 Ibid., 74. See also M Sornarajah, *The International Law on Foreign Investment* (CUP 2010), 364–66.
105 UNCTAD, Investor-State Disputes Arising from Investment Treaties: A Review (2005).
106 Van Ho (n 31), 23, 73 80.
107 Ibid., 81, 83.
108 The Natives Land Act of 1913 prohibited black South Africans from owning or leasing land outside small designated areas, later known as 'homelands' or 'Bantustans'.

hands of white farmers.[109] The South Africa TRC called for some manner of restitution to take place. It proposed that 'consideration be given to the most appropriate ways in which to provide restitution for those who have suffered'.[110] When negotiations on the Interim Constitution got underway in 1993, the protection of property became one of the most contentious issues.[111] The National Party government, the last government under the apartheid system, supported by the business lobby, insisted that such protection be provided for and initially resisted the inclusion of any provision authorizing restitution.[112] A compromise was reached at the end of the negotiation which was reflected in Section 28 of the Interim Constitution, which provided for a right 'to acquire and hold rights in property' and a concomitant duty on the state to pay compensation in the event of expropriation.[113] In this way, contrary to the case of Colombia, the beneficiaries of the right to restitution were not given a right against the current owners to demand the return of land, but rather a right against the state.[114]

In 1994, the first post-apartheid ANC government passed the *Restitution of Land Act* to restore land rights of individuals, households and communities who were dispossessed due to racial discriminatory policies that had been adopted since the *Natives' Land Act* passed in 1913.[115] Settling restitution claims, however, proved extremely complex and time-consuming.[116] Early evidence indicated that most restored farms were not producing – possibly due to the time that had passed and that people often got different land over their original land. To avoid

109 R Hall, 'Reconciling the Past, Present, and Future: The Parameters and Practices of Land Restitution in South Africa' in C Walker and others (eds), *Land, Memory, Reconstruction, and Justice: Perspectives on Land Claims in South Africa* (Ohio University Press, 2010), 18–19.

110 Truth and Reconciliation Commission of South Africa, *Final Report* (1998), Vol I, Ch 4, 48.

111 F du Bois, 'Reparations and the Forms of Justice, in F du Bois and A du Bois-Pedain (eds), *Justice and Reconciliation in Post-Apartheid South Africa* (CUP 2008), 116, 128; S Terreblanche, 'Dealing with Systemic Economic Injustice' in C Villa-Vicencio and W Verwoerd (eds), *Looking Back, Reaching Forward: Reflections on the Truth and Reconciliation Commission of South Africa* (University of Chicago Press 2000), 265, 267; J Simcock, 'Unfinished Business: Reconciling the Apartheid Reparation Litigation with South Africa's Truth and Reconciliation Commission' (2011) 47 *Stan J Intl L* 239, 259–60; Hall (n 109).

112 du Bois (n 111), 129.

113 Interim Constitution of South Africa, Sect 28; Constitution of South Africa Act, no. 200 of 1993, Sect 8.

114 du Bois (n 111), 129.

115 Restitution of Lands Act, no. 22 of 1994 as amended by Land Restitution and Reform Laws Amendment Act 63 of 1997, Sect 2(1). See also Walker and others (eds) Land, Memory, Reconstruction, and Justice: Perspectives on Land Claims in South Africa (Ohio University Press 2010), , 1; Roht-Arriaza (n 62), 123; T Roux, 'Land Restitution and Reconciliation in South Africa' in du Bois and du Bois-Pedain (n 95), 23.

116 Roht-Arriaza (n 62), 124–25; H Mostert, 'Change Through Jurisprudence: The Role of the Courts in Broadening the Scope of Restitution' in Walker and others (n 115), 64–74; Hall (n 109), 25.

the land becoming unproductive, to 'maintain food supplies and [...] to ensure that the transition is as smooth as possible',[117] the government urged people to enter into 'strategic partnerships' with the former agribusiness landholders, where the communities were encouraged to lease the land back to the former owners in exchange for a share of the profits, without being able to live on or work the land as they did prior to dispossession.[118] In the end, only about 1.5 million of the 80 million hectares of 'white agricultural land' were reallocated, while USD562 million were spent on buying alternative land, and a further USD475 million was spent on cash compensation – all with public funds.[119] The ambitious goal to redistribute 30% of white-owned agricultural land (estimated to be 67% of the country) to black South Africans was not met.[120] One of the few studies of how the money was spent in South Africa found that the amount dispensed was too small and was mostly used to pay off debts and meet immediate expenses.[121] As a consequence, despite the reconciliation process and its vaunted and celebrated goals, land ownership in South Africa today remains highly unbalanced and unequal.

6.1.3. Forced evictions and land restitution demands in Myanmar

The incomplete transition of Myanmar, described in the previous chapter, leaves the country open to continued forced evictions in the name of promoting investment and economic development. Forced evictions – the 'permanent or temporary removal against their will of individuals, families and/or communities from the homes and/or land which they occupy, without the provision of, and access to, appropriate forms of legal or other protection'[122] – is a serious human rights violation. Forced evictions in Myanmar have always been linked to business and ethnic conflict.[123] The military and other armed groups carried out most of the illegal land expropriation in the 1990s and early 2000s, during the transition to a more market-oriented model.[124] By 2010, humanitarian and human rights groups had documented the destruction and forced

---

117 ANC, Ready to Govern, 1992, Sect E.1. See also, R Hall, 'Land Restitution in South Africa: Rights, Development, and the Restrained State' (2004) 38(3) *Canadian J African Studies* 654.

118 B Derman, E Lahiff and E Sjaastad, 'Strategic Questions about Strategic Partners' in Walker and others (n 115), 306.

119 Hall (n 109), 30.

120 Roht-Arriaza (n 62), 126.

121 A Bohlin, 'A Price on the Past: Cash as Compensation in South African Land Restitution' (2004) 38(3) *Canadian J African Studies* 672.

122 UN Committee on Economic, Social and Cultural Rights, 'General Comment No. 7: The right to adequate housing (Art 11.1): forced evictions', E/1998/22 (20 May 1997).

123 Internal Displacement Monitoring Centre and Norwegian Refugee Council, 'Global Overview 2011', 88.

124 R David and I Holliday, *Liberalism and Democracy in Myanmar* (Oxford University Press, 2018), 24; W Bello, 'Paradigm Trap', Transnational Institute (2018), 15–18, 50–58.

relocation of more than 3,500 villages and sites in eastern Myanmar.[125] Land acquisition and confiscation and resultant forced displacement in Myanmar, both prior to and during the reform process, have been carried out for a number of reasons. These include military settlements and public infrastructure projects, as well as the establishment of agro-industrial plantations by private entities, large industrial development projects, special economic zones and hotel zones.[126]

Whereas before 2011 land expropriation was conducted by the ruling junta, investors have now become directly or indirectly the new driver of expropriation. The former Special Rapporteur on human rights in Myanmar, Tomás Ojea Quintana, predicted in 2012 that, 'given the expected wave of privatisations and the increase in foreign investment, along with accelerated economic development, there is likely to be an increase in land confiscations, development induced displacement'.[127] With the lifting of economic sanctions and the promulgation of business-friendly investment laws, investment has boomed.[128] But an increase in investment where land governance does not meet national or international standards and where tenure is not secure contributes to forced eviction. In August 2018, the current Special Rapporteur, Yanghee Lee, noted the legacy of land rights abuses and called upon the government to investigate on-going illegal expropriation linked to development projects and investment.[129] With the influx of investment after the lifting of economic sanctions, demand for land has increased – land that was once worthless is now expensive. Where ceasefires have been made, large areas that were previously insecure or unprofitable for investment have suddenly become amenable to private development.[130] A report by *Global Witness*, an NGO, noted that, from 2005 to 2013, 5.3 million acres of land had been leased out to investors for commercial agriculture, most without the consent of the owners.[131] Another study in 2014 found that more than 5.2 million acres of private agribusiness concessions were awarded, more than 3 million since 2010.[132]

Much of the confiscated land is given or sold on to crony businessmen and unscrupulous foreign investors with deals conducted in secrecy, enabling corruption

---

125 Report of the Special Rapporteur on the situation of human rights in Myanmar (15 Sept 2010), A/HRC/65/368, para 49.
126 Land in Our Hands Network, 'Destroying People's Lives: The Impact of Land Grabbing on Communities in Myanmar' (LOHN, Dec 2015).
127 Report of the Special Rapporteur on the situation of human rights in Myanmar, A/67/383 (25 Sept 2012).
128 J Wood, 'Special Economic Zones: Gateway or Roadblock to Reform?' in M Crouch (ed.), *The Business of Transition in Myanmar* (CUP, 2017), 182.
129 Report of the Special Rapporteur on the situation of human rights in Myanmar, A/73/332 (Aug 2018), 22.
130 Transnational Institute (TNI), 'Access Denied: Land Rights and Ethnic Conflict in Burma' (8 May 2013), www.tni.org/briefing/access-denied.
131 Global Witness, 'Guns, Cronies and Crops: How Military, Political and Business Cronies Conspired to Grab Land in Myanmar' (26 March 2015), www.globalwitness.org/en/campaigns/land-deals/guns-cronies-and-crops
132 K Woods, 'A political anatomy of land grabs', *The Myanmar Times* (3 March 2014).

to flourish.[133] Most land expropriation continues to be carried out in contravention of international standards and best practice, without consultation, informed consent, adequate compensation or a resettlement policy, and without recourse to due process, resulting in forced evictions and associated human rights abuses. Farmers and land rights activists who protest are regularly harassed and prosecuted.[134] An example of business-led land expropriation and forced evictions is the Leptadaung copper mine, operated by Chinese company *Wanbao Mining*, in partnership with military-owned *UMEHL*. Thousands of people have been forcibly evicted by the government with the knowledge, and in some cases the participation, of foreign companies.[135] In 2012, thousands of protesters were confronted by security forces that used white phosphorous to disperse the crowds, injuring between 110 and 150 people.[136] The authorities are yet to investigate either the police or the companies operating the mine.[137]

Conflict in Myanmar has been centred on minority groups' demands for autonomy but fuelled by competition over the land and natural resources, and has regularly resulted in displacement.[138] Fighting in Kachin and Shan States, for example, is based on various grievances, including land use, development projects and the exploitation of natural resources. Violence in those regions has resulted in over 100,000 internally displaced people, whose land has been now appropriated by the military and corporations.[139] The Special Rapporteur expressed concern that displaced people's land in Kachin State is increasingly being turned into banana plantations or used for mining.[140] In both Kachin and Rakhine States Special Economic Zones are planned in areas abandoned by displaced ethnic minority populations.[141]

While land grabbing is not the cause of violence against the Rohingya, it may be the result. According to the Independent International Fact-Finding Mission on Myanmar, '[t]he mass displacement and the burning of Rohingya villages were

133 Bello (n 124), 15–18, 50–58; S Leckie and J Arraiza, 'Restitution in Myanmar: Building Lasting Peace, National Reconciliation and Economic Prosperity rough a Comprehensive Housing, Land and Property Restitution Programme' (Displacement Solutions and Norwegian Refugee Council, March 2017), 7, 11.
134 FIDH, 'Land of Sorrow' (Sept 2017).
135 Amnesty International, 'Open for Business? (n 32).
136 Ibid.
137 Amnesty International, 'Myanmar: Letpadaung mine protesters still denied justice' (27 Nov 2015); D Aguirre and I Pietropaoli, 'Blame game at Letpadaung' *The Myanmar Times* (28 Jan 2015).
138 I Pietropaoli, 'Corporate Accountability and Transitional Justice in Myanmar' *Justiceinfo* (7 March 2016), www.justiceinfo.net/en/justiceinfo-comment-and-debate/opinion/26259-corporate-accountability-and-transitional-justice-in-myanmar.html
139 Report of the detailed findings of the Independent International Fact-Finding Mission on Myanmar, A/HRC/39/CRP.2 (18 Sept 2018) [hereinafter Fact-Finding Mission report], paras 289–94.
140 Report of the Special Rapporteur on the situation of human rights in Myanmar, A/73/332 (Aug 2018) 22–25.
141 Ibid., 32.

followed by the systematic appropriation of the vacated land'.[142] The expropriated land has been set aside for security outposts, housing for other ethnic groups, as well as infrastructure projects and special economic and industrial zones nearby.[143] The Fact-Finding Mission found that at least 45 companies and organizations provided the military with over USD10 million in financial donations that were solicited in September 2017 by senior military leadership in support of the 'clearance operations' that began in August 2017 against the Rohingya.[144] The Mission also found that private companies with enduring links to the military are financing development projects in northern Rakhine in furtherance of the military's objective of preventing the Rohingya's return to their homeland and communities.[145]

Since the reform process began in Myanmar, civil society organizations have increasingly called for redress for corporate human rights abuses, particularly in relation to illegal land confiscation and forced relocation.[146] Despite the formation of several non-judicial committees and commissions, however, government efforts to address land-related issues have been slow, incomplete and marred by confusion and a lack of coordination. In 2012, the parliament established the Farmland Investigation Commission (FIC), a body tasked with investigating reports of land confiscation and making recommendations for the restitution of land. From September 2013 to January 2016, the FIC submitted to the President's Office 18 reports that investigated past cases of land confiscation by various actors in a wide range of economic sectors.[147] The FIC received more than 26,000 complaints from alleged individual and community victims of land confiscation – of these, as of early 2016, it had investigated some 13,000 cases.[148] The FIC, however, did not have the power to implement its findings or to refer cases to courts or the relevant government bodies for action. When the FIC and the Land Utilization Management Central Committee –- which had been established to implement the FIC's recommendations – were dissolved in 2016, they left behind thousands of un-investigated cases.[149]

In May 2016, the President's Office formed the Central Review Committee on Confiscated Farmlands and Other Lands (CRCCF), which currently deals with

---

142 Fact-Finding Mission report (n 139), para 50.
143 Ibid., para 50.
144 Independent International Fact-Finding Mission on Myanmar, 'The economic interests of the Myanmar military', A/HRC/42/CRP.3 (16 Sept2019), para 6(c).
145 Ibid.
146 Amnesty International (n 32); Global Witness (n 131); FIDH (n 134); Land in Our Hands Network (n 126).
147 Republic of the Union of Myanmar, Farmland Investigation Commission, Report no. 1–18, Sept 2013–Jan 2016.
148 Myanmar Centre for Responsible Business, *Land* (IHRB 2015).
149 Mekong Region Land Governance, *Transparency Under Scrutiny Information Disclosure by the Parliamentary Land Investigation Commission in Myanmar* (MRLG 2017); Frontier Myanmar, 'Leftover land dispute vex government as discontent grows', 12 April 2017.

cases of land confiscation.[150] The CRCCF set the unrealistic goal of settling all land dispute cases within the first six months of its mandate (i.e. by November 2016).[151] The process of land restitution has been slow, marred by allegations of corruption, with thousands of cases still to be investigated. The CRCCF had a backlog of 10,891 cases to investigate, including 6,707 that it had inherited from the FIC.[152] Only 2,057 cases, or about 19%, had been settled and the land returned to the original land users.[153] According to one estimate, the military and local and regional governments returned about 400,000 acres of land.[154] Corporations, however, have not yet returned confiscated land, except in a few cases, which remain rare, are largely *ad hoc* in natur, and are driven more by attempts at improving company reputations than securing the rights of victims.[155]

Conclusion

This chapter has analyzed efforts in three countries (Colombia, South Africa and Myanmar) that have emerged from conflict or repression to restitute land – including land that was acquired or confiscated for economic investment. Of the three, Colombia's Victims' Law represents the best practice. Colombia, South Africa, and Myanmar experienced a different transition. Colombia is emerging from an internal armed conflict. South Africa ended the apartheid regime. And in Myanmar, despite the 2015 democratic elections, the transition to peace and democracy is far from complete – the military still holds 25% of seats in parliament and important ministerial positions, and the persecution of the Rohingya, a Muslim ethnic minority, reached peaks of crimes against humanity and genocide allegations in 2017.[156] Arguably, it is easier to return land that was confiscated by armed groups after the conflict is over (in Colombia) than land that was allocated by a repressive regime (in South Africa) or land that was confiscated by a military

150 Government of Myanmar, Union President Office, Notification 14/2006, 'Formation of the Reinspection Committee of Farmland and Other Land Acquisition', 5 May 2016.
151 *Irrawaddy*, 'Govt Committee to settle all land grabs cases in six months', 1 Jul 2016.
152 *Frontier Myanmar*, 'Leftover land dispute vex government as discontent grows', 12 April 2017.
153 Ibid.
154 Namati, *Returns of Grabbed Land in Myanmar: Progress After 2 Years* (Namati 2015). See also *The Irrawaddy*, 'Whose Land is it Anyway?' 7 July 2016.
155 Displacement Solutions, *Land Acquisition Law and Practice in Myanmar: Overview, Gap Analysis with IFC PS1 & PS5 and Scope of Due Diligence Recommendations* (Displacement Solutions 2015), 17.
156 Human Rights Watch, 'Burma: Satellite Imagery Show Mass Descruction', 19 September 2017; Amnesty International, 'Myanmar: Scorched-earth campaign fuels ethnic cleansing of Rohingya from Rakhine State', 17 September 2017; Fortify Rights, 'United Nations: Establish Independent Investigation into Genocide in Myanmar', 29 October 2015.

government that still holds power (in Myanmar). However, from the point of view of victims of land confiscation, their demands to restitution are similar.

While in Colombia the Victims' Law addressed the responsibility of companies, the transitional legal arrangements put in place in South Africa shielded individuals and businesses responsible for human rights violations and instead guaranteed the protection of existing land titles.[157] The cost of repairing injuries was placed on the shoulders of the post-apartheid state only, to be dispensed through public funds, and in that sense through a cost borne by the whole of society rather than those most responsible for the violations.[158] All transactions had to be financed with public funds, and actual land transfers were based on the 'willing buyer, willing seller' principle. A question that ought to have been addressed, but which was avoided, was whether those who benefitted from the dispossession – individuals and corporate owners who obtained land cheaply from the previous government and may have developed it with cheap labour – had any responsibility in the restitution process. In this sense, South Africa's restitution programme recognized the victims of land dispossession, but it did not address the responsibility of the beneficiaries.[159]

In Myanmar, the NLD-led government has failed to make significant progress towards the fulfilment of the party's election promises with regard to land rights. In its 'Election Manifesto', published ahead of the November 2015 general election, the NLD vowed to ensure the return to farmers of 'illegally-lost land' and the payment of compensation.[160] The document also promised the party would work towards defending farmers against 'illegal land confiscation practices' and amending the existing land laws 'that are not appropriate for the present era'.[161] Despite this stated commitment to resolve the country's land disputes, land confiscation has continued under the NLD-led administration, and military-owned and 'crony' companies still control the economy.[162]

Land restitution is a form of reparation specifically applicable to companies. This form of reparation can also help the goals of 'transformative justice' as opposed to purely corrective justice. Transformative justice is based on two tenets. First, the purpose of reparations should not be to restore victims to their previous position of vulnerability, but to transform the circumstance in which they lived. Second, it is reasonable that reparation programmes are grounded on corrective justice, as they have to address the suffering of victims. Yet this should be the source only of *prima facie* obligations – in certain circumstances, corrective actions can be outweighed by considerations of distributive justice. Given the indirect responsibilities

---

157 M Chaskalson, 'The Property Clause: Section 28 of the Constitution' (1994) 10 *South Africa J Human Rights* 131.
158 du Bois (n 111).
159 U Dhupelia-Mesthrie, 'Urban Restitution Narratives' in Walker and others (n 115), 83.
160 National League for Democracy (NLD), Election Statement, 15 September 2015.
161 Ibid.
162 FIDH (n 32); Pietropaoli (n 32).

of many corporate actors, and the regular lack of available evidence of complicity, this approach is fundamental to ensure the possibility of addressing corporate involvement in conflict and repression.[163] The next chapter discusses a further transitional justice mechanism, institution reform, which can also achieve transformative justice objectives.

---

163 D de Felice, 'Sabine Michalowski (ed.), Corporate Accountability in the Context of Transitional Justice', (2014) 14 *Human Rights Law Review* 576.

Chapter 7

Institutional reform

Introduction

While the previous chapters have dealt with judicial and non-judicial transitional justice mechanisms addressing past corporate abuses, this chapter looks at institutional reform as a mechanism to prevent future corporate human rights abuses. In a conflict or authoritarian context, public institutions – such as the police, military and judiciary – are often instruments of repression and human rights violations. When transition to democracy and peace occurs, reform of such institutions is a priority to prevent violations from happening again, disabling the structures that allowed them to occur. Institutional reform is the process of 'reviewing and restructuring state institutions so that they respect human rights and the rule of law, and are accountable to the public'.[1] Institutional reform measures do not only deal with the individual circumstances of human rights violations but aim to address the reasons why members of public institutions allowed, facilitated or promoted human rights violations – with the goal of preventing reoccurrence.[2]

Preventing reoccurrence means going beyond addressing individual human rights violations to target the laws, institutions and systems that commit or facilitate them. Institutional reform is therefore distinguished from restitution, compensation and rehabilitation; it should consist of general reform that benefits the victims, but also the potential victims in society as a whole. Justice in the aftermath of serious human rights violations cannot be limited to prosecution, truth initiatives and reparation, but should also include institutional and other permanent reforms that aim to prevent the recurrence of such violations.[3] Prevention of reoccurrence generally requires the reform of institutions and systems that allowed such violations –

---

1 International Center for Transitional Justice (ITCJ), Institutional Reform, www.ictj.org/our-work/transitional-justice-issues/institutional-reform
2 A Mayer-Rieckh, 'Guarantees of Non-Recurrence: An Approximation' (2017) 39(2) *Human Rights Quarterly* 416.
3 P Gready and S Robins (eds), *From Transitional to Transformative Justice* (CUP 2014); C Sandoval-Villalba, 'Reflections on the Transformative Potential of Transitional Justice and the Nature of Social Change in Times of Transition' in R Duthie and P Seils, *Justice Mosaics: How Context Shapes Transitional Justice in Fractured Societies* (International Center for Transitional Justice, 2017).

including corporate abuses – to occur with impunity. Institutional reform measures include security sector reform, vetting, creation of oversight bodies, disarmament, demobilization and reintegration, establishment of effective civilian complaint procedures, reforms of the judiciary and legal reforms.[4]

The Human Rights Council refers to the importance of a comprehensive approach to transitional justice

> incorporating the full range of judicial and non-judicial measures, including, among others, individual prosecutions, reparations, truth seeking, institutional reform, vetting of public employees and officials, or an appropriately conceived combination thereof, in order to, inter alia, ensure accountability, serve justice, provide remedies to victims, promote healing and reconciliation, establish independent oversight of the security system and restore confidence in the institutions of the state and promote the rule of law in accordance with international human rights law, with a view to preventing recurrence of violations and abuses.[5]

Within such a framework the scope of transitional justice is broadened to the achievement of the reform of the entire system.[6] While all processes of transitional justice complement each other and are interdependent,[7] institutional reform and guarantees of non-recurrence are lacking in almost every country undergoing a transitional justice process.[8] The UN includes institutional reform as an essential component of transitional justice, but does not develop details or prescribe obligations concerning its implementation in practice.[9] The obligation to guarantee

4 UN Secretary-General, 'Securing Peace and Development: The Role of the United Nations in Supporting Security Sector Reform', UN Doc. A/62/659-S/2008/39 (23 Jan 2008); OECD, *Handbook on Security System Reform (SSR): Supporting Security and Justice* (2007); R Duthie, 'Introduction', in A Mayer-Rieckh and P de Greif (eds), *Justice as Prevention: Vetting Public Employees in Transitional Societies* (Social Science Research Council 2007).

5 UN Human Rights Council, 'Promoting Reconciliation and Accountability in Sri Lanka', A/HRC/22/L.1/Rev.1 (18 March 2013), para 21.

6 B Fernando, 'Editorial: Institutional Reforms as an Integral Part of a Comprehensive Approach to Transitional Justice' (2014) 8 *International Journal of Transitional Justice* 187; MB Ndulo and R Duthie, 'The Role of Judicial Reform in Transitional Justice and Development', ICTJ (2009).

7 UN Human Rights Council, Report of the Special Rapporteur on the Promotion of Truth, Justice, Reparation and Guarantees of Non-Recurrence, Pablo de Greiff. UN Doc. A/HRC/21/46, 9 Aug 2012, paras 22–24.

8 C Sandoval, 'Transitional Justice and Social Change' in *SUR International Journal on Human Rights* (2004) 1(1) 'Commemorative Issue, Human Rights in Motion' 181, 185.

9 Guidance Note of the UN Secretary-General, United Nations approach to transitional justice (March 2010); Report of the Independent Expert to Update the Set of Principles to Combat Impunity, Diane Orentlicher, Updated Set of Principles for the Protection and Promotion of Human Rights through Action to Combat Impunity, UN Doc. E/CN.4/2005/102 (8 Feb 2005) [hereinafter Updated Principles to

non-recurrence is the least developed category of the four measures in response to gross human rights violations listed in the UN Principles to Combat Impunity (the other three being prosecutions, reparations and truth telling).[10] The 2005 updated version of the Principles devotes only four out of 38 principles to this obligation. Generally, little systematic attention has been paid to the topic of institutional reform, and guarantees of non-recurrence remain under-explored in academic literature – despite being crucial to achieving lasting change after conflict or repression. The origins and normative foundations of 'guarantees of non-recurrence' oblige states to prevent the recurrence of violations. International human rights law reiterates the state obligation to prevent the recurrence of violations.[11] Although preventing recurrence is a legal obligation, specific guarantees and the institutional reforms required are not necessarily defined as legal obligations. While the human rights community broadly agrees on the importance of preventing recurrence of violations, 'it has limited understanding of what it entails and how it is done'.[12]

Institutional reforms, in particular legal and judicial reforms, are also of key importance to prevent corporate human rights violations from happening again. But there has been almost no academic research in this area and few initiatives in practice. Out of the four processes that constitute the core of transitional justice (that is, justice, reparations, truth telling and institutional reform), institutional reform represents 'the most needed measure to stop business from feeling that they have immunity that protect them. Yet, it is the area of transitional justice where the least is done.'[13] Widespread impunity and lack of accountability associated with corporate abuses undermines institutional reform, which constitutes the 'missing piece of the puzzle, to pursue the full spectrum of justice'.[14] The argument of this chapter is that, as violations of human rights are increasingly intertwined with corporate abuses, a rethinking of institutional reform of violations to include a stronger element of corporate accountability is necessary. Only by reforming the institutions that have allowed or failed to address corporate human rights abuses will it be possible to guarantee the non-recurrence of such violations.

Combat Impunity]; Basic Principles and Guidelines on the Right to a Remedy and Reparation for the Victims of Gross Violations of International Human Rights Law and Serious Violations of International Humanitarian Law, UN Doc. A/RES/60/147 (21 Mar. 2006); Draft Articles on Responsibility of States for Internationally Wrongful Acts, Yearbook of the International Law Commission, Vol. II, UN Doc. A/CN.4/SER.A/2001/Add.1 (Part 2) (2001). These documents use both the term 'guarantees of non-recurrence' and the term 'guarantees of non-repetition' – these terms are interchangeable, without difference in meaning.

10 Updated Principles to Combat Impunity (n 9), Principle 1.
11 For example, ICCPR, Art 2; CAT, Art 2.
12 Mayer-Rieckh (n 2), 416.
13 Sandoval (n 8), 24.
14 Ibid. See also JP Bohoslavsky and V Opgenhaffen, 'The Past and Present of Corporate Complicity: Financing the Argentinean Dictatorship' (2010) 23 *Harvard Human Rights Journal* 157.

This chapter analyzes the reform of public institutions in transitional justice contexts that have an impact on the prevention of corporate human rights abuses. The first section (7.1) describes the importance of vetting and prosecutions in changing institutions and achieving corporate accountability. Section 7.2 analyzes how legal and judicial reforms can address corporate accountability and prevent abuses from happening again. Section 7.3 turns to land law reforms. The focus of this section is on land reforms in Myanmar. Myanmar has moved to democracy and peace without undertaking a transitional justice process. Current land law reforms, which are happening simultaneously to the dramatic rise of foreign investment in the country, risk worsening the likelihood of future corporate human rights abuses – in particular forced evictions. Myanmar provides some of the most significant recent examples of business-related human rights abuses allowed to continue with impunity by bad institutions and laws, and is thus where the need for institutional and legal reform to prevent future corporate human rights abuses is particularly clear. Finally, section 7.4 examines natural resource governance reform, as this is an area where the involvement of business in human rights violations is most significant.

7.1. Vetting and prosecutions

For transitional justice measures such as vetting and prosecutions, a significant impact on institutions is, as Pablo de Greiff, the UN Special Rapporteur on the promotion of truth, justice, reparation and guarantees of non-reoccurrence, describes it, their 'disarticulation potential' – that is, the capacity to disable the structures that allowed violations to occur in the first place.[15] Through these effects on institutions responsible for past abuses, vetting and criminal justice reforms can have a preventative impact.

In relation to prosecutions, concepts of deterrence and rehabilitation, rather than retribution, are the primary aims for sentencing corporate offenders.[16] Sanctioning the corporations with fines, criminal prosecution or prohibition of future business operations may inhibit the repetition of human rights violations.[17] If the prospect of civil or criminal suits, and the consequent adverse publicity, results in a change of corporate actions, then the legal reform process would have fulfilled its

---

15 P de Greiff, 'Transitional Justice, Security, and Development' World Development Report 2011 (29 Oct 2010), 17–18.
16 A Ramasastry, 'Corporate Complicity: From Nuremberg to Rangoon – An Examination of Forced Labor Cases and Their Impact on the Liability of Multinational Corporations' (2002) 20 *Berkeley J Intl Law* 91, 131; J Clough and C Mulhern, *The Prosecution of Corporations* (OUP 2002), 183–216.
17 E Posner and A Vermeule, 'Transitional Justice as Ordinary Justice' (2004) 117 *Harvard Law Review* 761, 792; E Harper, 'Delivering Justice in the Wake of Mass Violence: New Approaches to Transitional Justice' (2005) 10 *Journal of Conflict and Security Law* 149; Ramasastry (n 16), 96.

goal of deterrence.[18] Prosecution of corporations provide an effective impetus to improving business behaviour and deterring similar actions by other companies.[19] Judicial imposition of legal liability for certain types of human rights violations may induce companies, for example, to adopt or improve their human rights policies. A criminal conviction of a company, and the public attention and adverse publicity such a conviction may give rise to, can also provide incentives to improve business culture.[20] Prosecutions can help by 'pressuring corporations to refrain from engaging with oppressive regimes in the future'.[21] Criminal and administrative sanctions, which might include lustration of the board of directors of a company responsible for violations or even dismantling entire corporations, are fundamental to addressing corporate cultures that encourage violations and prevent abuses from recurring in the future.[22]

Vetting can also target economic violence and corporate actors.[23] Since vetting procedures are administrative rather than criminal, for example, 'they can make use of relaxed evidentiary and procedural rules that may make them more efficient than criminal trials as forms of redress for certain types of abuses', including 'typically hard-to-prove economic crimes, such as illicit enrichment, [and] money laundering'.[24] Vetting may also play a role in reforming sectors such as natural resource management. The Liberia Forest Initiative, for instance, is an initiative for assisting comprehensive institutional reform in post-conflict Liberia. As part of this process, human rights advocates collected statements about abuses committed by logging companies and their security forces during the war, which contributed to the establishment of a vetting policy for concession bidders. According to this policy, individuals providing security for forest companies are vetted using criteria that exclude those who have credible allegations of abuse against them.

Reforming state institutions can have an impact on the way corporations behave.[25] For example, reforming audit commissions, competition commissions or

18 Posner and Vermeule (n 17), 792; WA Schabas, 'Catching the Accomplices' (2001) 83 *IRRC* 842, 456; Clough and Mulhern (n 16), 6.
19 International Commission of Jurists (ICJ), 'Report of the Expert Legal Panel on Corporate Complicity in International Crime', 16 Sep 2008 Vol 2 'Criminal Law and International Crimes', 59.
20 Ibid.
21 T Van Ho, 'Transnational Civil and Criminal Litigation' in S Michalowski (ed.), *Corporate Accountability in the Context of Transitional Justice* (Routledge 2013), 52.
22 D de Felice, 'Sabine Michalowski (ed.), Corporate Accountability in the Context of Transitional Justice', (2014) 14 *Human Law Review* 576, 578.
23 R Duthie and DN Sharp, 'Transitional Justice, Development, and Economic Violence' in R Duthie and DN Sharp (eds), *Justice and Economic Rights Violence in Transition* (Springer 2014), 165–201, 189.
24 P de Greiff, 'Articulating the Links between Transitional Justice and Development: Justice and Social Integration', in P de Greiff and R Duthie (eds), *Transitional Justice and Development: Making Connections* (2009), 38.
25 C Sandoval and G Surfleet, 'Corporations and Redress in Transitional Justice Processes', in Michalowski (ed.) Corporate Accountability in the Context of Transitional Justice (Routledge 2013), 93–113, 109–111.

commissions that award licences to trade could be crucial to provide the state with the mechanisms to control and sanction corporate behaviour. In Brazil, for example, post-dictatorship institutional reforms took place in the governance field: democratic improvements in the electoral system after the 1988 Constitution, the submission of the military to civilian power, and the approval of a law of access to information.[26] But there are indications that Brazil could also work to reform its financial system. This being the case, it would be desirable for such proposed reforms to help to address financial complicity.[27] For example, specific regulations could be approved to prevent the National Bank of Economic and Social Development from supporting projects that are potentially harmful to human rights. Brazil's National Truth Commission (NTC) has the power to recommend changes in the institutional design of financial institutions, both in terms of regulatory measures to be enforced over private actors and new standards and policies for state banks and enterprises.[28] Greater attention to questions of financial complicity in the transitional justice context would likely reinforce the importance of establishing vetting programmes to bar those complicit in human rights crimes from occupying public office.[29]

VII.2. Legal and judicial reform

As seen in Chapter 4, one of the major obstacles to achieving corporate accountability is the limitation of domestic legal systems, which obstructs investigations and measures for redress.[30] Lack of legal regulation of companies' operations and ineffective and corrupt judicial systems often facilitate the commission of human rights abuses.[31] Legislative and judicial reforms are therefore particularly relevant to achieve stronger control of corporations' behaviour and, as a consequence, to prevent violations. Because of common gaps and failings in legal systems, legal reform processes are a standard aspect of transitional justice.[32] Adopting and reviewing legal frameworks, such as adopting constitutional amendments or ratifying international human rights treaties, is of particular importance in addressing corporate accountability for human rights violations.

Constitutional reform is often proposed in post-conflict situations to disable structures that may have contributed to the conflict or repression. For example, in

26 By the Complementary Law no. 97 (9 June 1999) and Law no. 12.527 (18 Nov 2011) enforced together with the Truth Commission Law, no. 12.528.
27 JP Bohoslavsky and MD Torelly, 'Financial Complicity: The Brazilian Dictatorship under the "Macroscope"' in Duthie and Sharp (eds) Justice and Economic Violence in Transition (Springer 2014), 254.
28 Ibid.
29 Mayer-Rieckh and de Greif (n 4).
30 Fernando (n 6), 187–88; N Cheesman, 'Law and Order as Asymmetrical Opposite to the Rule of Law,' (2014) 6(1) Hague Journal on the Rule of Law 96–114.
31 Sandoval (n 8); Cheesman (n 30).
32 DJ Scheffer, 'The Tool Box, Past and Present, of Justice and Reconciliation for Atrocities' (2001) 95(4) American Journal of International Law 970; Cheesman (n 30).

South Africa, a new constitution was enacted in 1996 recognizing the rights of equality and non-discrimination and establishing civil, political, economic, social and cultural rights, along with remedies for individuals and social institutions to transform the *status quo* of the apartheid regime.[33] The enactment of a new constitution, an important guarantee of non-repetition, however, does not constitute a fundamental change unless it is able to transform the ideology that supported the old system.[34] Despite the new constitution, South Africa remains a deeply unequal society, and elements of the apartheid ideology are still present today.[35] Constitutional reforms could be used to address issues where corporate human rights abuses are prevalent. A variety of principles that could help to strengthen control over corporations have been incorporated into constitutions. These include provisions that establish a right to a healthy environment,[36] ownership of resources and land,[37] procedural rights, such as the right to information, participation and accountability,[38] and governance principles, such as wealth sharing or multilevel governance.[39]

Bilateral investment agreements (BITs) negotiated with a post-conflict transition country have an immediate impact on national economic policy. Investment protection treaties are contracts between states that place a priority on protecting the property rights of foreign investors from adverse regulation.[40] They can also prevent regulation to fulfil positive human rights law obligations.[41] For example, treaty provisions may prohibit regulations protecting collective goods such as water, food or the environment.[42] The proliferation of bilateral agreements has the adverse

33 Act 108, which took effect in February 1997.
34 Clara Sandoval explains that three types of social change can happen through transitional justice measures: ordinary changes, structural changes and fundamental changes. A fundamental social change happens when transitional justice is able to put forward a new dominant ideology inspired by radically different values to those present during the repression or the conflict. Sandoval (n 8).
35 Ibid.
36 For example, Article 49 of the Constitution of Rwanda states: 'Every citizen is entitled to a healthy and satisfying environment.'
37 For example, the 2009 Constitution of Bolivia includes indigenous people's rights to natural resources, such as 'the autonomous indigenous territorial management, exclusive use and exploitation of renewable natural resources within their territories'.
38 For example, Article 2(4) of the Constitution of Peru states: 'All persons have the right [...] [t]o request, without providing a reason, information that one needs, and to receive that information from any public entity within the period specified by law, at a reasonable cost.'
39 For example, para 168(5) of the 2011 Transitional Constitution of the Republic of South Sudan states: 'The sharing and allocation of resources and national wealth shall be based on the premise that all states, localities and communities are entitled to equitable development without discrimination.'
40 D Aguirre, *The Human Right to Development in a Globalized World* (Routledge 2008), 132.
41 A Shalankany, 'Arbitration and the Third World: A Plea for Reassessing Bias under the Specter of Neoliberalism' (2002) 41 *Harvard International Law Journal* 419.
42 D Aguirre, 'Corporate Liability for ESCR Revisited: The Failure of International Cooperation' (2011) 42(1) *California Western International Law Journal* 145.

effect of rendering states more accountable to foreign investors than to the local population. Transitional, post-conflict states, often rich in natural resources and eager to attract foreign investors, may be at particular risk of undermining their institutional reforms process to abide by bilateral trade agreements. During the conflict in Colombia, for example, land titles and property rights were transferred to corporations, including foreign corporations protected by international investment law. As discussed in the previous chapter, the impact of the restitution process outlined in the Colombian Victims' Law on foreign corporations raises concerns that international investment law may inhibit the full realization of the restitution process.[43]

Under the 1965 *Convention on the Settlement of Disputes between States and Nationals of Other States*, multinational companies have standing in tribunals concerning the terms of investment treaties.[44] Investor-state dispute settlements (ISDS) improperly protect investors' interests over the rights of people. Myanmar is a case in point. The international community of states is interested in the investment opportunities in the country, but also recognizes its regulatory problem. Many, such as the European Union (EU), are negotiating BITs that guarantee investors' interests as 'rights' and give them access to ISDS mechanisms outside of Myanmar. The BITs that Myanmar has signed with major foreign investors (e.g. China, India, Japan, the Philippines and Thailand) and is negotiating with the EU all include troubling ISDS provisions that can undermine the government's 'right to regulate'. ISDS generates costly disputes – some arbitral awards run into the billions of dollars. Myanmar lacks the legal and financial capacity to defend potential challenges by multinational companies. BITs are meant to increase investment by encouraging legal certainty. But for a transitional country like Myanmar, radical legal reform is required to protect human rights during economic development. Locking in regulation by allowing investors to challenge new government policy through ISDS may discourage Myanmar from addressing poor law and undertaking necessary legal reform. Law and policy on land redistribution and the recognition of communal land rights, for example, may conflict with the interests of foreign investors and give rise to costly disputes under BITs. The threat of litigation may dissuade this type of reform.

Legal developments are currently happening in the area of mandatory corporate human rights due diligence in a number of jurisdictions across Europe.[45] Laws requiring companies to undertake human rights due diligence can have the effect

43 T van Ho, 'Is it Already Too Late for Colombia's Land Restitution Process? The Impact of International Investment Law on Transitional Justice Initiatives' (2016) 5(1) *International Human Rights Law Review* 60.

44 *Convention on the Settlement of Disputes between States and Nationals of Other States* 1965, Art 63.

45 For a comparative legal analysis of human rights due diligence and corporate liability laws in Europe, see European Coalition of Corporate Justice (ECCJ), 'Comparative Table – mHRDD with Corporate Liability Laws in Europe', Sept 2019, http://corporatejustice. org/documents/publications/eccj/eccj_hrdd_pcl-comparative-table-2019-final.pdf

of preventing corporate human rights violations. In 2017, France has been the first country to pass a law requiring large French companies to establish and implement a '*plan de vigilance*'.[46] In the UK, in April 2019, a group of civil society organizations launched a campaign for mandatory human rights and environmental due diligence legislation.[47] Also in April 2019, the UK Supreme Court handed down a judgment in *Lungowe v Vedanta*, finding that *Vedanta*, a British mining company, had a duty of care to prevent its foreign subsidiary in Zambia from causing harm to people affected by their operations.[48] Similarly, elsewhere in Europe various laws, legal proposals and legal campaigns are progressing for mandatory human rights and environmental due diligence regulation.[49] The most recent version of the draft business and human rights treaty, currently under negotiation at the UN, provides for legal liability for a failure-to-prevent mechanism:

> States Parties shall ensure that their domestic legislation provides for the liability of natural or legal persons conducting business activities, including those of transnational character, for its *failure to prevent* another natural or legal person with whom it has a contractual relationship, from *causing harm* to third parties when the former sufficiently controls or supervises the relevant activity that caused the harm, or should foresee or should have foreseen risks of human rights violations or abuses in the conduct of business activities, including those of transnational character, regardless of where the activity takes place.[50]

In addition, Article 5 on 'prevention' provides that state parties should ensure that business enterprises adopt and implement 'enhanced human rights due diligence measures to prevent human rights violations or abuses in occupied or conflict-

---

46 Loi n 2017–399 du 27 mars 2017 relative au devoir de vigilance des sociétés mères et des entreprises donneuses d'ordre (1), Art 1.

47 Civil society campaign launched in UK in April 2019, https://corporate-responsi bility.org/wp-content/uploads/2019/04/190409_UK-mHRDD-campaign-statem ent_FINAL-with-logos.pdf. Another study is looking into applying the model of the UK Bribery Act to a failure to prevent human rights abuses; see Joint Committee on Human Rights (UK), *Human Rights and Business 2017: Promoting responsibility and ensuring accountability*, Sixth Report of Session 2016–17, 5 April 2017.

48 *Lungowe v Vedanta Resources plc* [2019] UKSC 20.

49 In addition to campaigns calling for mandatory human rights due diligence at the national level in a number of European countries, there are also calls for establishing EU human rights due diligence legislation; see European Coalition for Corporate Justice, 'A call for EU human rights and environmental due diligence legislation', 3 Oct 2019, http://corporatejustice.org/final_cso_eu_due_diligence_statement_03.10. 19-compressed.pdf

50 Art 6(6) of the Revised Draft Treaty 'Legally Binding Instrument to Regulate, in International Human Rights Law, the Activities of Transnational Corporations and Other Business Enterprises', 16 July 2019.

affected areas, arising from business activities, or from contractual relationships, including with respect to their products and services'.[51]

Often parallel to legal reforms in a transitional justice context are judicial reforms. As seen in previous chapters, the lack of access to judicial remedies for victims of corporate human rights abuses is one of the main obstacles to corporate accountability. This problem is exacerbated in post-conflict situations where the judicial systems often lack capacity and resources, and are plagued with corruption. Under the Guiding Principles:

> States should take appropriate steps to ensure the effectiveness of domestic judicial mechanisms when addressing human rights-related claims against business, including considering ways to reduce legal, practical and other relevant barriers that could lead to a denial of access to remedy.[52]

Judicial reform projects include, for example, attempts to eliminate judicial corruption and to promote judicial independence.

An independent judicial system is crucial to the protection of human rights, including human rights affected by business activities. It plays a major role in ensuring that victims of corporate abuse receive effective remedy and protection, and that perpetrators, including companies, are brought to justice. The judiciary also provides an essential check and balance on other branches of government, ensuring that new laws and policies regulating corporate activities comply with the constitution as well as international human rights law standards. Improving the judicial system works both ways to protect people's rights and to promote economic development. It is actually an area of improvement sought also by international investors in post-conflict environments. This is because the primary service provided by courts is thought to be reliable and efficient dispute resolution, which is important to investors.[53] Courts enforce contract and property rights, and secure property and contract rights are important for fostering productive investment and economic transactions.[54] Moreover, judicial enforcement can make commitments more credible – particularly commitments by government, which need to convince international companies to invest in the long term.[55] Whether it is for fighting corruption, fostering good governance or attracting foreign investments, transitional countries need judges and lawyers who

---

51 Ibid., Arts 5(2) and 5(3)(e).
52 UN Guiding Principles on Business and Human Rights: Implementing the United Nations 'Protect, Respect and Remedy' Framework, annexed to Report of the Special Representative of the Secretary-General on the issue of Human Rights and Transnational Corporations and Business Enterprises, John Ruggie, A/HRC/17/31 (21 March 2011) [Guiding Principles], principle 26.
53 MC Stephenson, 'Judicial Reform in Developing Economies: Constraints and Opportunities' Annual World Bank Conference on Development Economics 2007, 3.
54 D North, *Institutions, Institutional Change, and Economic Performance* (CUP 1990).
55 A Brunetti and B Weder, 'Political Credibility and Economic Growth in Less Developed Countries' (1994) 5(1) *Constitutional Political Economy* 23; Stephenson (n 53), 3.

are able to operate independently and impartially to provide proper jurisprudence and, importantly, change the public's poor perception of the system. The next section examines land law reforms, which are also key to achieving transitional justice goals of reconciliation and guarantees of non-repetition of violations as well as preventing land rights violations by corporations.

7.3. Land reform

Land access is often a key cause of conflict, and the conflict then exacerbates the problem, including as a result of forced evictions and displacement by political elites and by corporations. Post-conflict land policy, however, has received relatively little attention in the literature on transitional justice.[56] As some scholars have argued:

> While it is clear that land policy plays a role in recovering from the effects of conflict, and ensuring that further conflict does not follow, there is an empirical lacuna on the causal relationship between post-conflict land policy and the promotion of transitional justice objectives such as redress of human rights violations.[57]

Transitional justice practice has tended to look at only one element of land rights, namely restitution of property to those deprived of it during period of conflict or repression.[58] As examined in the previous chapter, for example, one of the most recent attempts by the Colombian government to address the issue of land has been to include a restitution agenda in the transitional justice process initiated in 2005, as a component of the reparations programme designed to meet the needs of victims of internal displacement.[59] The 2011 Colombian Victims' Law is intended to provide property restitution to some of the individuals displaced as a result of human rights and humanitarian law violations.

South Africa also implemented several measures to address the legacy of apartheid in relation to land distribution.[60] By 1990 South Africa was marked by a

---

56 A notable exception is the work of Bernadette Atuahene on South Africa; see e.g. B Atuahene, 'Property Rights and the Demands of Transformation' (2010) 31 *Michigan Journal of International Law*; B Atuahene, 'Property and Transitional Justice', (2010) 58 *UCLA Law Review Discourse* 58 (2010).

57 D Fitzpatrick and A Fishman, 'Land Policy and Transitional Justice After Armed Conflicts' in Duthie and Sharp (eds) *Justice and Economic Violence in Transition* (Springer 2014), 263–88, 263.

58 D North, J Wallis, and B Weingast, 'Violence and the Rise of Open-Access Orders' (2009) 20 *Journal of Democracy* 59; D North, J Wallis and B Weingast, *Violence and Social Orders: A Conceptual Framework for Interpreting Recorded Human History* (CUP 2009); Fitzpatrick and Fishman (n 57), 265.

59 KAO Lid and J García-Godos, 'Land Restitution in the Colombian Transitional Justice Process' (2010) 28 *Nordic J Hum Rts* 262, 262.

60 S Terreblanche, *A History of Inequality in South Africa 1652–2002* (University of KwaZulu-Natal Press, 2002), 5–8, 260–64.

glaring racial divide between the 13% of land reserved for black occupation and the remaining 'white South Africa', dominated by 60,000 commercial farms, which covered 70% of the country.[61] Institutional reform measures were incorporated early on in the transition through the Interim Constitution, which covered the right to property and dealt with the restitution of land rights.[62] The new democratic parliament later approved the *Restitution of Land Rights Act*[63] and established a commission on restitution of land rights, which constituted an 'ambitious programme of redress, reconciliation, and reconstruction'.[64]

Comparative experiences in South Africa and in Colombia suggest that delays or inactivity in relation to land policy and land tenure reform may be a government strategy in terms of potential for land confiscation by political elites or corporations. Land policy delay allows uncertain chains of transactions and transfers of possession to develop from initial post-conflict conditions, and creates space for land grabbing.[65] After the conflict, 'the imperatives of state stabilization tend to favour land policy measures that allow for elite control over land rather than responses to past episodes of corruption, plunder, or systematic property violations'.[66] Reparations programmes may also have 'spill-over' effects in terms of institutional capacity.[67] For example, civil registry initiatives generated by property restitution programmes can lead to broader efforts to clarify land titles. As a result, land confiscation without proper compensation by companies may become more difficult.[68]

In addition to land restitution, comprehensive land tenure reforms are necessary to address the root causes of the conflict and ensure the non-repetition of abuses. Land tenure reform refers to a process in which the legal, institutional and regulatory framework for land ownership is altered. It is often used as the main instrument to achieve a more efficient and equitable distribution of land and resources. Land tenure reform should be part of transitional justice's reforms, especially in countries where land tenure is insecure and where there have been

---

61 R Hall, 'Reconciling the Past, Present and Future: The Parameters and Practices of Land Restitution in South Africa' in C Walker and others (eds), *Land, Memory, Reconstruction, and Justice: Perspectives on Land Claims in South Africa* (Ohio University Press, 2010), 19.
62 Section 28 and sections 121 to 123 respectively.
63 Act 22 of 1994.
64 R Hall, 'Land Restitution in South Africa: Rights, Development, and the Restrained State' (2004) 38(3) *Canadian Journal of African Studies*; A Dodson, 'Unfinished Business. The Role of Governmental Institution after Restitution of Land Rights' in C Walker and others (eds), *Land, Memory, Reconstruction, and Justice: Perspectives on Land Claims in South Africa* (Ohio University Press, 2010), 273.
65 Fitzpatrick and Fishman (n 57), 267.
66 Ibid., 265.
67 N Roht-Arriaza and K Orlovsky, 'A Complementary Relationship: Reparations and Development', July 2009, ICTJ Research Unit.
68 Duthie and Sharp (n 23), 174.

historical injustice related to land rights.[69] For example, in 2009, Kenya approved the national land policy, a practical framework for the implementation of the truth commission's recommendations regarding land. The policy was seen by many as a progressive document providing protection for those communities using land under communal tenure systems and calls for compensation and reparation for historical injustices.[70]

The Rwandan context also represents one of many examples of the interaction between conflict, resource and land distribution, transitional justice and the possibility for renewed violence.[71] In fact, the terms 'Hutu' and 'Tutsi' partially derive from unequal labour relations, land distribution and differential access to cattle.[72] Scholars have linked the genocide to tensions based not just on 'ethnic hatred', but also on economic disparity, decades-long resource inequity and unequal land distribution.[73] Some analyses link specific killings during the genocide directly to land-based grievances.[74] While post-genocide transitional justice mechanisms failed to address these issues of resource and economic inequalities, the government later passed a land law and implemented a land and development policy.[75] The Rwandan Constitution of 2003, the National Land Policy of 2004 and the Organic Land Law of 2005 set out a context in which all land shall be registered and rights gained under different means of access to land shall be considered equal.[76]

In September 2018, Liberia passed the Land Rights bill into law. Nearly 70% of Liberia's 3.3 million citizens live in rural areas and own their lands collectively according to customary laws. Despite strong customary claims, for the past six decades the Liberian government claimed all lands as owned by the state and allocated

69 C Huggins, 'Linking Broad Constellations of Ideas: Transitional Justice, Land Tenure Reform and Development in P de Greiff and R Duthie (eds), *Transitional Justice and Development: Making Connections* (2009), 332, 333.

70 C Huggins, 'Truth, Justice, Reconciliation, and…Land Tenure Reform?' (2009) *Oxford Transitional Justice Research Working Paper Series* 3.

71 Z Miller, 'Effects of Invisibility: In Search of the "Economic" in Transitional Justice' (2008) 2 *International Journal of Transitional Justice* 266, 289.

72 J Pottier, *Re-Imagining Rwanda: Conflict, Survival and Disinformation in the Late Twentieth Century* (CUP 2002).

73 Miller (n 71), 281–82; P Uvin, 'Reading the Rwandan Genocide', (2001) 3 *International Studies Review* 75.

74 H Musahara and C Huggins, 'Land Reform, Land Scarcity and Post-Conflict Reconstruction: A Case Study of Rwanda,' in C Huggins and J Clover (eds), *From the Ground Up: Land Rights, Conflict and Peace in Sub-Saharan Africa* (Johannesburg: Institute for Security Studies, 2005); S Straus, *The Order of Genocide: Race, Power, and War in Rwanda* (Cornell University Press, 2006).

75 Republic of Rwanda Ministry of Lands, Environment, Forests, Water and Mines, Organic Law No. 08/2005 Determining the Use and Management of Land in Rwanda, National Land Policy (2004). See also C Huggins and J Pottier, 'Land Tenure, Land Reform, and Conflict in Sub-Saharan Africa: Towards a Research Agenda,' in C Huggins and J Clover (n 74), 385.

76 E Daley, 'Ahead of the Game: Land Tenure Reform in Rwanda and the Process of Securing Women's Land Rights' (2010), 4(1) *Journal of Eastern African Studies* 131.

roughly 17% of the country to foreign investment without consulting community members. Liberia's *Land Rights Act* remedies this by protecting community land rights. Under the Act, communities are responsible for the management of their customary lands and tasked with drafting bylaws on how they will govern their land,[77] their members are considered to be the private owners of their customary lands,[78] they must give their free, prior and informed consent before others can use or 'interfere with' their private customary lands,[79] and all their members, including women, youth and members of minority groups, have equally strong ownership claims to customary lands, and equal rights to use and manage community land.[80] Myanmar also has a long-lasting land regulation problem.

7.3.1. Land reform in Myanmar

Despite the reforms and partial transition to democracy in Myanmar, initiated in 2011 and described in the previous chapter, the country still suffers from endemic corruption, poor governance and weak rule of law, a legacy of impunity and cronyism, unresolved conflicts and serious human rights violations – including land rights violations.[81] Nevertheless, billions of dollars of foreign and national investment are flowing into the country, further increasing the demand for land. Forced evictions and corporate abuses continue with impunity and are facilitated by weak regulation and bad institutions.[82] While transitional justice as such is not on the political agenda, Myanmar is undertaking some timid reforms to its legislative framework and its judicial system. More than 400 existing laws are at some stage of study and review, many have been revoked and amended, dozens of new laws have been adopted, and others are in draft form – including key laws in the area of business and human rights, such as the new foreign investment, labour, land, mining and environmental laws.[83]

The previous military government encouraged and expedited land law reforms introduced in the name of the rule of law and good governance to accommodate the government's reform agenda and aligned it with the development policies of international financial institutions.[84] This came at the expense of equality and substantive justice:

---

77 Land Rights Act, Arts 35.1, 36.1, 36.2 and 38.1.
78 Ibid., Arts 2 and 32.1.
79 Ibid., Art 33.
80 Ibid., Arts 2 and 34.3.
81 M Crouch (ed.), *The Business of Transition in Myanmar* (CUP 2017), 6; J Bissinger, 'Foreign Investment in Myanmar: A Resource Boom but a Development Bust?' (2012) 34(1) *Contemporary Southeast Asia*, 23–52.
82 R Egreteau, *Caretaking Democratization: The Military and Political Change in Myanmar* (OUP 2016); M Lall, *Understanding Reform in Myanmar: People and Society in the Wake of Military Rule* (Hurts and Company 2016).
83 International Bar Association (IBA), 'The Rule of Law in Myanmar' (IBA, 2012), 41; OECD, 'Myanmar: OECD Investment Policy Review' (OECD 2014).
84 S McCarthy, 'Rule of Law Expedited: Land Title Reform and Justice in Burma (Myanmar)' (2018) 42(2) *Asian Studies Review* 229, 235.

In their haste to produce these reforms while at the same time pursuing Western developmental strategies, the government created a situation where land security and titling for the majority of the population became more precarious. Small hold farmers, ethnic communities, and the most vulnerable suffered the most from these legal reforms while the government encouraged market-driven development and private (domestic and foreign) investment in agriculture.[85]

An estimated 70% of Myanmar's population lives in rural areas and depends on agricultural land as a primary means of livelihood. Few farmers in Myanmar have formal documents to prove they have any rights to the land their ancestors have used for generations. Myanmar's transition has moved the country away politically from total authoritarianism, and economically to a market-based system emphasizing foreign investment, both embedded in the 2008 Constitution and reflected in most law and policy.[86] This has opened a regulatory gap in which the legal system is deficient, and investment and economic growth happen in the absence of a fair regulatory framework. The current land framework is characterized by new and obsolete overlapping and contradicting laws that lead to confusion and loopholes exploited by the military and by companies.[87] Flaws in these laws, combined with the Constitution, which provides that the government is the 'ultimate owner of all lands and all natural resources',[88] and with the lack of legal recognition of customary land tenure, has left people vulnerable to 'legal land grabs' and forced evictions with limited access to effective remedies. Forced evictions continue where regulation and institutional reform is insufficient. Changes in land policies restricting such practice, and holding those who benefitted, including companies, accountable, are therefore key in Myanmar's political and economic transition, and for its peace process. The new government, led by Aung San Suu Kyi's National League for Democracy (NLD) party, promised to reform land laws and to deal with widespread land grabbing. But land reforms undertaken so far in Myanmar are actually more likely to facilitate those violations.

Land acquisition is generally conducted under the 1894 *Land Acquisition Act*, a legacy of the British colonial period, which allows the government to compulsorily acquire land for 'public purposes'.[89] The concept of 'public purpose' is poorly defined, granting wide discretion to the government without effective administrative or judicial review. Amendments to the *Land Acquisition Act* risk to further undermine the rights of farmers. For example, amendments provide for a broad

85 Ibid.
86 Crouch (n 81), 9.
87 Land Core Group, 'Legal Review of Recently Enacted Farmland Law and Vacant, Fallow and Virgin Lands Management Law', Nov 2012; S Leckie and E Simperingham, *Housing, Land and Property Rights in Burma: The Current Legal Code* (Displacement Solutions, 2009).
88 Constitution of the Republic of the Union of Myanmar, Section 37.
89 Land Acquisition Act 1894, Art 4, 40(b).

interpretation of public purpose that includes 'national defence and security matters of the state' as well as 'the development of the state according to national economic policy'.[90] The *Farmland Law*, passed in 2012 during the transition, also allows the government to take over farmland 'in the interests of the state' with no further procedural or substantive restrictions.[91] The *Vacant, Fallow and Virgin Lands Management Law*, also passed in 2012, gives the government the right to repossess 'vacant, virgin or fallow' lands for infrastructure projects or special projects required in the interest of the state.[92] Much of the land classified as 'vacant, virgin or fallow' is in fact occupied by people or is subject to shifting cultivation practices.[93] There is no compensation for the land because it is determined to be without ownership.[94] The adoption in 2018 of the *Law Amending the Vacant, Fallow and Virgin Lands Management Law* is also problematic. The amendment sets a deadline for land users to register where the land they occupy is considered 'vacant, fallow and virgin' land to be converted for commercial exploitation or face potential trespass charges. This amendment potentially affects millions of people who do not have land title to secure their tenure. A number of UN Special Rapporteurs have publicly stated that they are concerned that 'this law may be used to illegally dispossess land users of their land without due process or adequate notice, undermine their human rights, and have a disproportionate impact on poor, rural and minority communities, ethnic nationalities and indigenous peoples'.[95]

Myanmar began a process of reviewing law and institutions in 2016, culminating in the National Land Use Policy (NLUP).[96] The NLUP is a positive, if imperfect, step that included extensive consultation and review, a first of its kind in Myanmar. The NLUP, which sought to harmonize land use management in Myanmar, refers directly to human rights standards in chapters related to land

---

90 Land in our Hands Network, 'Destroying People's Lives: The Impacts of Land Grabbing on Communities in Myanmar', Dec 2015.
91 Farmland Law (Pyidaungsu Hluttaw Law No. 11 of 2012), Art 64.
92 Vacant, Fallow and Virgin Lands Management Law (Pyidaungsu Hluttaw Law No. 10 of 2012), Arts 3(a)(b), 55.
93 N Willis, 'Land Disputes and the Ongoing Development of the Substantive Rule of Law in Myanmar (Burma)' in S Kierkegaard (ed.), *Law and Practice: Critical Analysis and Legal Reasoning* (International Association of IT Lawyers, Denmark, 2013), 882, 888.
94 Farmland Law, Art 2(e)(f).
95 UN Rapporteurs intervened directly with the Myanmar government in opposition to the amendments: Yanghee Lee, Special Rapporteur on the situation of human rights in Myanmar; Hilal Elver, Special Rapporteur on the right to food; Victoria Lucia Tauli-Corpuz, Special Rapporteur on the rights of indigenous peoples; Leilani Farha, Special Rapporteur on adequate housing as a component of the right to an adequate standard of living, and on the right to non-discrimination in this context; Cecilia Jimenez-Damary, Special Rapporteur on the human rights of internally displaced persons; Fernand de Varennes, Special Rapporteur on minority issues; Philip Alston, Special Rapporteur on extreme poverty and human rights (21 January 2019) OL MMR 5/2018.
96 Myanmar National Land Resources Management Central Committee, National Land Use Policy (January 2016).

acquisition and recognized traditional land ownership and shifting cultivation regimes.[97] It recognizes land governance as a challenge to peace, development and human rights. The NLUP proposes a framework of institutional reform in line with international standards and affirms the need for participatory, transparent and accountable governance.[98] It recognizes customary tenure, which, if implemented in law, would bolster institutional reform and prevent repetition of forced evictions. Explicit references to responsible investment, human rights and the protection of the environment make it a 'sound basis for land law reform'.[99] The policy was envisioned as a guiding document in the drafting of a National Land Law and in reforming existing laws that facilitate 'the allocation of ethnic customary lands to investors' through forced evictions.[100] The NLD government, however, has made little progress on the land reform process envisioned by the NLUP. In 2016, a government commission in charge of the land reform process criticized the NLUP and suggested stronger land confiscation powers for the state, and a reduction of progressive rights granted to ethnic minorities and women.[101] The NLUP provides for a national law that should harmonize all laws related to land and that the process will be consultative.[102] But instead of a consultative review of all land law with a view to creating a new National Land Law, the government is currently making amendments to the existing laws.[103]

Although the *Farmland Law* and the *Vacant, Fallow and Virgin Lands Management Law* were ostensibly introduced to improve tenure security for farmers, they had the opposite effect, as the onus was placed on farmers to obtain the land titles.[104] The combined effect of these laws was to formalize the pattern of land grabbing that had developed under the previous military governments and to encourage land speculation.[105] Rather than reforming it, Myanmar has consolidated a legal system that facilitates forced evictions by ensuring impunity for government officials and businesses associated with the process. The reform process is based on laws and institutions designed to increase private ownership and investment rather

97 Ibid., esp. Art 9(b) and Part IV. For comments, see D Aguirre, 'A sound basis for land reform', *Frontier Myanmar* (19 Feb 2016), https://frontiermyanmar.net/en/a -sound-basis-for-land-reform

98 National Land Use Policy, Art 9(b), Part IV.

99 Aguirre (n 97).

100 World Rainforest Movement, 'Myanmar: New policy promoting indigenous rights under threat' (4 April 2017), https://wrm.org.uy/articles-from-the-wrm-bulletin/ section1/myanmar-new-policy-promoting-indigenous-rights-under-threat

101 The Committee is headed by Thura Shwe Mann, the former Union Solidarity and Development Party (USDP) member and powerful politician linked to land grabbing cases; 'Parliamentary commission advises overhaul of national land use policy', *Myanmar Times* (1 Dec 2016); 'Land policy a test case for new parliament's power', *The Economist* (23 Dec 2016).

102 National Land Use Policy, Art 77 'Harmonization of Laws and Enacting New Law'.

103 Land Core Group (n 87), 13–14.

104 Farmland Law, Arts 22–25.

105 McCarthy (n 84), 238.

than to secure land tenure and prevent forced evictions. The failure to regulate, or to enforce regulations protecting human rights, results in forced evictions violating Myanmar's duty to protect rights from adverse impacts of business activity.[106]

The UN Special Rapporteur on human rights in Myanmar has called for the government to fulfil its duty to protect human rights through 'robust policy and regulatory frameworks, including in relation to land, thereby ensuring that businesses accept their responsibility to respect human rights'.[107] The responsibility to protect human rights is part of Myanmar's general duties under international human rights law, particularly its recent commitment to the *International Covenant on Economic, Social and Cultural Rights* (ICESCR), and it is outlined in the Guiding Principles in the business context. As a party to the ICESCR, Myanmar is in violation of the Covenant if it fails to prevent forced evictions.[108] Essential elements of the right to adequate housing in the ICESCR are security of tenure and protection against forced eviction.[109] In order to protect those rights, the state must take measures to ensure that third parties, such as business enterprises, do not interfere with them.[110] In her March 2019 report to the UN, the Special Rapporteur stated that by denying people access to lands essential for their livelihood and culture, the *Law Amending the Vacant, Fallow and Virgin Lands Management Law* 'likely contravenes Myanmar's obligations under ICESCR'.[111] Institutional reform should ensure that laws, policy and institutions governing land acquisition guarantee a process of meaningful consultation in which the public is provided with access to relevant information in a timely manner and has an opportunity to present comments, objections and alternatives.[112] By conforming to these obligations, Myanmar can prevent or mitigate land-related human rights violations.

106 Crouch (n 81), 17.
107 Report of the Special Rapporteur on the situation of human rights in Myanmar, A/73/332 (Aug 2018), 22.
108 CESCR, General Comment No.7 The Right to Adequate Housing (Art 11.1): Forced Evictions (20 May 1997) E/1998/22; CESCR, General Comment No.12 The Right to Adequate Food (Art 11) (12 May 1999) E/C/12/1999/5; CESCR, General Comment No.15 The Right to Water (Arts 11 and 12) (23 Jan 2003) E/C/12/2002/11; CESCR General Comment No.4 The Right to Adequate Housing (Art 11) (13 Dec 1991) E/1992/23.
109 General Comment 7 (n 108).
110 General Comment 12 (n 108), para 15. General Comment 7 (n 108), paras 2, 9. General Comment 4 (n 108), para 8a.
111 Report of the Special Rapporteur on the situation of human rights in Myanmar, A/HRC/40/68 (5 March 2019), para 21.
112 Every citizen is entitled to participate in the decisions of their government; see UDHR, Art 21 (right to participate in government) and Arts 19, 20 (rights to information, association, assembly, and freedom of expression, which includes right to receive and impart information); CEDAW, Art 7 (right to participate in formulation of government policy); CRC, Art 13 (right to information); ICCPR, Art 19 (right to freedom of expression includes right to receive and impart information); ICESCR, Art 13 (component of right to education is the right to participate effectively in a free society).

7.4. Natural resource governance reform

While rarely the single, driving cause of conflict, links between conflict and natural resources are present in every conflict.[113] The final reports of the South Africa and Sierra Leone truth commissions, for example, directly addressed the question of structural inequality as a direct result of crimes committed in association with natural resource extraction.[114] In Liberia, the root of the conflict was disparate access to land and revenues from natural resources. In Myanmar, armed conflict between ethnic armed groups and the military government is fuelled by competition over natural resources. Weak governance institutions are frequently associated with an abundance of natural resources and commonly relate to violence and human rights abuses, including by companies, in several ways.

First, high-value resources can sustain repressive regimes by providing revenues to the ruling elite and allowing them to avoid accountability. Second, resource exploitation can result in rights abuses against communities. In resource-rich and weak governance countries, companies operating in the natural resource extractive sector have often been involved in human rights abuses. Third, resources can motivate and sustain abuses committed by armed groups by financing and rewarding their activities and prolonging conflicts. Finally, in economies dependent on natural resources, much of the performance of the state is related to how it manages natural resources and their revenues. If natural resources revenues are being misdirected to meet the needs of one small group rather than the whole population, the government is failing to equitably distribute the resources and to provide education, health care and other socioeconomic rights. Some of the countries rich in natural resources are among the least developed in the world.[115] Not only has natural resource wealth failed to bring prosperity, but it is instead associated with violent conflict.[116] This is part of the phenomenon known as the 'resource curse' – the paradox that many resource-rich countries tend to be more impoverished, more unequal, more authoritarian and more conflict-prone than otherwise similarly situated countries.[117] But the abundance of resources is not really the problem.[118] Rather, the problems stem from governance structures that

---

113 SS Nichols, 'Reimagining Transitional Justice for an Enduring Peace: Accounting for Natural Resources in Conflict' in Duthie and Sharp (eds) *Justice and Economic Violence in Transition* (Springer 2014), 203–36, 203.

114 Sierra Leone TRC report, vol 2, ch 4, 269; South Africa TRC report, vol 6, sec 2, ch 5, 155. See Chapter 5.

115 P Lujala and S Aas Rustad, 'High-Value Natural Resources: A Blessing or a Curse for Peace?' in P Lujala and S Aas Rustad (eds), *High-Value Resources and Post-Conflict Peacebuilding* (Earthscan 2012), 3–18, 4.

116 L Patey, 'Lurking Beneath the Surface: Oil, Environmental Degradation, and Armed Conflict in Sudan' in P Lujala and S Aas Rustad (eds) *High-Value Resources and Post-Conflict Peacebuilding* (Earthscan 2012), 563–70; V Boege and D Franks, 'Reopening and Developing Mines in Post-Conflict Situations: The Challenge of Company-Community Relations' in Lujala and Aas Rustad (ibid.), 87–120.

117 M Ross, *Extractive Sectors and the Poor* (Oxfam America 2001).

118 Nichols (n 113), 209.

determine how the resources or their revenues are managed, who is able to access them and for what purpose.[119]

Natural resources are increasingly being recognized as a priority in post-conflict and transitional justice processes.[120] They often serve to motivate support and prolong conflict, but they may also present opportunities for reconciliation and stability. Understanding the specific role of natural resources in the maintenance of authoritarian regimes and the facilitation of armed conflicts is central to such transitional justice aims.[121] Examining the role of natural resources in conflict through a transitional justice lens can also help to bring attention to the role that corporations play in conflicts and make long-term structural changes.[122] A resource focus may support the vetting of positions of authority in resource ministries, banning of companies from future concession licences, and the reform of structures that enabled the corrupt control of resource revenues.[123] Well-managed natural resources can also make significant contributions to post-conflict processes by encouraging responsible investment and sustainable economic growth.

For example, the report by the UN Panel of Experts on the Illegal Exploitation of Natural Resources of the DRC recommended that reforms of the mining and the forestry sectors should include the review of all concessions and contracts signed during both wars.[124] The Panel recommended that specialized industry organizations could be requested to monitor trade in commodities from conflict areas. The data produced could be the basis of industry policing of individuals, companies and financial institutions that trade in commodities from conflict areas.[125] Liberia is another classic example of the 'resource curse' as well as a case where resources perpetuated the conflict and play into the risk of conflict recurrence.[126] Society in pre-war Liberia was extremely inequitable, with almost all benefits of the country's mineral wealth going to the urban elites. When war erupted, hostilities were funded by revenues first from illegally extracted diamonds and then from harvesting of timber.[127] The Liberia truth commission recommended that the government

119 Ibid.; P Collier and I Bannon (eds), *Natural Resources and Violent Conflict: Options and Actions* (World Bank 2003); M Ross, 'What Do We Know About Natural Resources and Civil War?' (2004) 41(3) *Journal of Peace Research* 337.
120 Nichols (n 113), 211.
121 E Harwell and P Le Billon, 'Natural Connections: Linking Transitional Justice and Development Through a Focus on Natural Resources' in P de Greiff and R Duthie (eds), *Transitional Justice and Development: Making Connections* (2009), 283.
122 Nichols (n 113), 205.
123 Harwell and Le Billon (n 121), 286.
124 Final report of the Panel of Experts on the Illegal Exploitation of Natural Resources and Other Forms of Wealth of the Democratic Republic of the Congo, S/2002/1146, 16 Oct 2002, para 168.
125 Ibid., paras 180–82.
126 Nichols (n 113), 211.
127 SL Altman, SS Nichols, and JT Woods, 'Leveraging High Value Natural Resources to Restore the Rule of Law: The Role of the Liberia Forestry Initiative in Liberia's Transition to Stability' in Lujala and Aas Rustad (n 116), 337–66.

conduct a concession review of the mining sector to discover the extent of economic crimes within that sector.[128] Such a concession review could be used to clarify mining rights within the mining sector, calculate tax arrears by corporations, determine whether mineral companies complied with Liberian law, document corruption, illegality and mismanagement, and provide a platform to advocate for institutional controls to prevent future abuse.[129]

The Sierra Leone Truth and Reconciliation Commission (TRC) was also mandated to consider the political economy of resource extraction. Its report revealed the role that diamonds had played in supporting the chiefdoms and aligning them with the central government rather than with the population.[130] The TRC recommended specific reforms of the country's mining sector including transparency, protection against corruption, certification of diamonds and investment of diamond revenue in rural development.[131] The TRC recommendations for reforms included the establishment of a rough diamond chain-of-custody system, which eventually developed into the Kimberley Process Certification Scheme, a global regulatory framework for tracking the diamond trade to ensure that diamonds were not acquired illicitly.

Another aspect of natural resources that the transitional justice's reform process may help to address is revenue management and allocation.[132] Many of the inequalities associated with natural resources stem from how government uses the revenues that it collects from extractive and other natural resources industries. When such inequitable use of revenues was a factor in a conflict, changing the system is necessary to reduce the potential for renewed conflict.[133] In cases of inequitable distribution of benefits from natural resources, changing the ownership of the resources or their proceeds can be an important component of post-conflict development. This is known as revenue sharing, which involves the transfer of resources from extractive industries or their government regulators to communities that are affected by the resource extraction. Revenue sharing can take different forms, including agreements negotiated between the community and the company conducting the extraction, procurement opportunities and financing of development projects through trust funds. Through these benefit-sharing trust funds, governance of revenues is devolved, at least in part, to regional or local bodies, which have access to funds held in a trust.

One example of this approach is Sierra Leone's Diamond Area Community Development Fund (DACDF). In order to redistribute the power that comes

---

128 Liberia TRC report, Vol 3, Title III, paras 166–68. See Chapter 5.
129 Ibid., para 168.
130 R Maconachie, 'The Diamond Area Community Development Fund: Micropolitics and Community-Led Development in Post-War Sierra Leone' in Lujala and Aas Rustad (n 116), 264.
131 Harwell and Le Billon (n 121), 301.
132 A Wennemann, 'Sharing Natural Resource Wealth in War-to-Peace Transitions' in Lujala and Aas Rustad (n 116), 228.
133 Nichols (n 113), 221.

from diamond revenues, in 2001 the government established DACDF to channel 0.75% of the export value of diamonds to communities. In the first five years of the programme, US$3.5 million were distributed to communities in amounts based on the number of licences issued and diamonds recovered there. Similar mechanisms have been developed for a number of industries. For example, each of the countries in the Congo Basin has legal requirements for sharing forestry revenues with communities affected by logging. In its 2005 Mineral Development Agreement (MDA) with the government of Liberia, *ArcelorMittal* made a social agreement to establish a public–private partnership called the County Social Development Fund. This arrangement provided the model for the social agreements and the revenue sharing trust, which were later developed in the forest sector. As agreed in the MDA, the fund receives US$3 million each year to be shared between the three affected counties.[134]

Some international initiatives have been developed explicitly to improve transparency in natural resources sectors. The Extractive Industries Transparency Initiative (EITI) is perhaps the best known and most extensive initiative attempting to increase transparency in the management of revenues from high-value natural resources. The EITI promotes improved governance and revenue transparency in resource-rich countries through the disclosures of company payments and government revenues from oil, gas and mining.[135] It is a voluntary initiative, but only in the sense that it is voluntary for countries to sign up. Once a country is a member, it is mandatory for extractive companies operating in such country to declare what they pay to the government, and, conversely, for the government to declare what it receives from companies. In addition, many EITI member countries convert their international EITI commitments into binding national laws by enacting legislation that implements the EITI requirements.

Conclusion

The foundational principle of the Guiding Principles' Pillar I is that 'States must protect against human rights abuse within their territory and/or jurisdiction by third parties, including business enterprises. This requires taking appropriate steps to prevent, investigate, punish and redress such abuse through effective regulations and adjudication.'[136] Pillar I is a standard of conduct according to which the state must take appropriate steps to prevent abuses.[137] Where conflict exacerbates the

---

134 Distribution of these funds, however, has been plagued with abuses. See Friends of the Earth, 'Government of Liberia and ArcelorMittal Complicit in the Misuse of Social Development Funds', Press Release, 7 June 2010, www.foeeurope.org/press/2010/Jun07_Government%20of%20Liberia%20and%20AM_complicit_in_misuse_of_county_development_funds.html

135 E Rich and N Warner, 'Addressing the Roots of Liberia's Conflict through the Extractive Industries Transparency Initiative' in Lujala and Aas Rustad (n 116), 201–10.

136 Guiding Principles, Principle 1.A.1.

137 Ibid.

risk of business and human rights abuses, institutional reform should, as outlined in the Guiding Principles, ensure that their 'current policies, legislation, regulations and enforcement measures are effective in addressing the risk of business involvement in gross human rights abuses'.[138] The state duty to protect requires regulating the conduct of business – whether private or state-owned – through procedural legislation as well as by providing access to an effective remedy.[139] The Guiding Principles explain that in meeting the duty to protect human rights, states must ensure that other laws and policies governing the operations of business prevent violations.[140] The Commentary to Principle 3 also calls for greater human rights clarity in, for example, laws and policy governing 'access to land, including entitlements in relation to ownership or use of land'.[141] It is only through institutional reform and appropriate regulation that the Guiding Principles' Pillar II on corporate 'responsibility to respect' and Pillar III on 'access to remedy' can help prevention.

This Guiding Principles framework alone could form the basis of an institutional reform process designed to prevent the repetition of corporate human rights abuses. States, however, are often unwilling and unable to implement their obligations, particularly in regulating business in the transitional context. Preventing corporate human rights abuses requires identifying opportunities and confronting vested business interests. Preventative institutional reform measures should change the state structures and institutions that facilitated or failed to prevent abuses and that allowed business to participate in or benefit from human rights violations.[142] To do so, institutional reform should address institutions normally considered part of the economic development paradigm, such as those regulating investment and land governance, ensuring they go beyond simply enabling market activity[143] by including procedural safeguards and accountability mechanisms. Yet the neoliberal temptation to deregulate, privatize and rely on investment-led economic growth has proven strong.

The UN Working Group on Business and Human Rights has sought to encourage states to act on these obligations by preparing National Action Plans (NAPs) to implement the Guiding Principles.[144] NAPs should develop the Guiding Principles in policy terms, starting with the state's legal institutions. States should examine their ability to transpose binding international law into binding

138 Ibid., Principle 2.B.7.
139 Ibid., Principles 1, 2, 4.
140 Ibid., Principle 1.B.3.
141 Ibid.
142 C Sandoval, L Filippini and R Vidal, 'Linking Transitional Justice and Corporate Accountability' in S Michalowski (ed.), *Corporate Accountability in the Context of Transitional Justice* (Routledge 2013), 23.
143 D Desai, D Isser, and M Woolcock, 'Rethinking Justice Reform in Fragile and Conflict-Affected States: Lessons for Enhancing the Capacity of Development Agencies' (2012) 4 *Hague Journal on the Rule of Law*, 54, 60–61.
144 OHCHR, State National Action Plans (June 2014).

national law and policy that guides administrative institutions. The NAP process has instead focused on private-sector duties to respect human rights and on the regulation of their activities, rather than developing state policy and institutions that improve the scope to protect rights.[145] This betrays an understanding of the state duty to protect simply as one to legislate the business duty to respect its laws.[146] This approach creates a duty to respect the national legal system even if it does not adequately protect human rights. The result is that the baseline for implementing the Guiding Principles is the domestic legal order as it stands, omitting a review of whether or not it sufficiently protects human rights in the context of business operations.[147]

The classical distinction between corrective and distributive justice can help the understanding of guarantees of non-recurrence. Corrective justice refers to redressing past harms while distributive justice deals with equitably distributing goods and opportunities.[148] Corrective justice aims to 'bring people back to where they were before the harm suffered'.[149] Distributive justice 'creates not agent-relative but general reasons for action, central among which is that of upholding and supporting just social institutions'.[150] Prosecution, truth telling and reparation generally fall in the sphere of corrective justice in that they represent efforts of redressing past human rights violations and repairing the harms suffered.[151] Guarantees of non-recurrence mostly fall in the sphere of distributive justice as they primarily aim at equitable outcomes.[152] In particular, institutional reforms that address structural discrimination and redistribute opportunities belong in this category. In addition, policies to redress socioeconomic inequalities also fall in the sphere of distributive justice. Such policies aim to address root causes of violations

---

145 For example, the United Kingdom's National Action Plan focuses on the state's regulation of its corporations to conform to human rights norms already part of the domestic legal order of the United Kingdom. UK Secretary of State for Foreign and Commonwealth Affairs *Good Business: Implementing the Guiding Principles on Business and Human Rights* (Sep 2013).

146 LC Backer, 'Moving Forward the UN Guiding Principles for Business and Human Rights: Between Enterprise Social Norm, State Domestic Legal Orders, and the Treaty Law that Might Bind Them All' (2015) 38 *Fordham International Law Journal* 457, 473.

147 Ibid., 472.

148 R Duthie, 'Transitional Justice, Development, and Economic Violence' in Duthie and Sharp (eds) *Justice and Economic Violence in Transition* (Springer 2014), 171.

149 P Kalmanovitz, 'Corrective Justice versus Social Justice in the Aftermath of War' in M Bergsmo, C Rodríguez-Garavito, P Kalmanovitz, and M Paula Saffon (eds), *Distributive Justice in Transitions* (FICHL, 2010), 75.

150 Ibid., 77.

151 P de Greiff, 'Articulating the Links Between Transitional Justice and Development: Justice and Social Integration' in P de Greiff and R Duthie (eds), *Transitional Justice and Development: Making Connections* (2009), 63.

152 To the extent that guarantees of non-recurrence are conceived as direct efforts to address past human rights violations, they also constitute forms of corrective justice. Mayer-Rieckh (n 2), 440.

and to establish conditions of equality that render conflict over resources and opportunities less likely. The preventative measures listed in the Principles to Combat Impunity, the Basic Principles and the Draft Articles on State Responsibility aim either to disable abusive capacities or to strengthen integrity capacities – and therefore fall in the domain of corrective justice. Those documents do not discuss distributive measures that address socioeconomic inequalities. Such measures focus on the more immediate structural causes of human rights violations such as inadequate civilian oversight of the security sector or the existence of parastatal armed groups. Usually, such immediate structural causes are not the root causes of a situation that resulted in serious violations.[153] Often, the immediate structural causes of human rights violations are symptoms of underlying root causes that are related to economic or social inequalities such as controversies over access to land and resources.

> Correcting past wrongs and establishing conditions to correct future wrongs may not be enough to prevent future violations if it leads to restoring an original status of socio-economic inequality that triggered the commission of the violations in the first place.[154]

Next to corrective measures, some form of socioeconomic transformation of society that entails a redistribution of goods and opportunities may be needed to construct a more just order and so effectively prevent recurrence.[155] In his 2011 report on rule of law and transitional justice, the Secretary-General states that the UN 'must promote dialogue on the realization of economic and social rights and provide concrete results through transitional justice mechanisms, legal reform, capacity-building, and land and identity registration efforts, among other initiatives'.[156]

Effectively preventing the recurrence of corporate abuses requires a comprehensive effort to address their immediate and root causes. What specific measures need to be adopted depends on a 'thorough analysis of the human rights violations, the agents, structures and resources used to perpetrate them, the reasons for perpetrating them, as well as the effects of these violations on the victims and society as a whole'.[157] Institutional reform offers the best route to implement human rights law in transitional states. As such, it also presents an opportunity to break from the past and regulate business enterprises to ensure that they contribute to sustainable

---

153 Ibid., 441–42.
154 Ibid., 442.
155 I Muvingi, 'Sitting on Powder Kegs: Socioeconomic Rights in Transitional Societies', (2009) 3 *International Journal of Transitional Justice* 178: 'The transition phase creates space for redistribution during which the main objective is not the protection of privilege but the correction of injustice as groundwork for the construction of a more just order.'
156 UN Secretary-General, The Rule of Law and Transitional Justice in Conflict and Post-Conflict Societies, UN Doc. S/2011/634, para 52 (12 Oct 2011).
157 Mayer-Rieckh (n 2), 434.

development and human rights in the future. Institutional reform also contributes to the emerging field of transformative justice, which addresses inequality and marginalization.[158] It can confront powerful economic interests and unjust business activity, allowing people to question the development model adopted, the hierarchies of power[159] and the role of business in fulfilling economic, social and cultural rights in the future.[160]

While institutional reform is an overlooked area of transitional justice, and commonly associated only with the reform of public institutions, it is an important aspect of corporate accountability. Institutional reforms, especially legal and judicial reform, land reform and natural resource governance reform are key to prevent the reoccurrence of corporate human rights violations. New laws, such as new land rights law, can provide elements of corporate accountability and provide access to justice avenues for victims of corporate abuses. More equitable management of natural resources and revenue sharing can help to achieve a more sustainable peace process. Unregulated business activities have adverse impact on people in repressive and conflict-affected settings. Yet institutional reform has not normally addressed the business sector, despite the opportunity that transition presents for combating business impunity and creating lasting changes.[161] Institutional reform can prevent reoccurrence of business and human rights violations while improving accountability.[162] To do so, reform should change the relationship between the state, the community and business to prevent human rights violations. Land confiscation without procedural participation, due process and proper compensation should become illegal and the businesses and individuals involved held accountable. This type of comprehensive institutional reform of land tenure to prevent forced evictions can help prevent a return to conflict and repression. Holding perpetrators of human rights violations accountable and providing reparations that return victims to the conditions that prevailed before or during conflict and repression is not enough. Preventing reoccurrence is not about dealing with an abstract threat, but specifically targeting widespread abuses that underpinned or characterized conflict and repression. This transitional context of institutional reform connects the past with the future, taking the state beyond its duty to protect in human rights law to preventing reoccurrence and contributing to transitional justice.

---

158 P Gready and S Robins, 'From Transitional to Transformative Justice: A New Agenda for Practice' (2014) 8(3) *International Journal of Transitional Justice* 339.
159 Ibid., 351.
160 Z Miller, 'Effects of Invisibility: In search of the Economic in Transitional Justice' (2008) 2 *International Journal of Transitional Justice* 266, 267.
161 Sandoval, Filippini and Vidal (n 142), 24.
162 Sandoval and Surfleet (n 25), 93, 109–111; P de Greiff and R Duthie (eds), *Transitional Justice and Development: Making Connections* (2009).

Conclusion

Innovative use of litigation, truth-seeking and reparations programmes in transitional justice countries across the world have addressed, even if still only in a marginal way, corporate accountability for human rights abuses and crimes under international law, and have attempted to provide redress for victims. The limitations of the traditional mechanisms of corporate accountability have triggered the exploration of innovative approaches. Sporadic victories for victims of business-related human rights abuses have occurred. For the most part, however, victims face major obstacles to achieve corporate accountability, and corporations involved in violations often enjoy impunity. Put simply, if corporations have committed human rights violations or crimes under international laws during a time of conflict or repression, either directly or in complicity with states or with individuals, then they should be held accountable and reparations should be made to the victims.[1] Addressing corporations' responsibility and providing reparations to the victims are not a voluntary pursuit by the state, which has the obligation to bring those alleged to have committed human rights abuses and crimes to justice within their domestic criminal justice systems and to repair the harm suffered by victims. There are, however, complex legal, political and practical obstacles to this seemly fair concept. Some of these problems, common to all victims of corporate abuses, are accentuated in transitional justice contexts due to the prevalence of weak rule of law, dysfunctional judicial systems, corruption and logistical difficulties.

This book has sought to show how accountability and remedies for corporate human rights abuses and crimes under international law can be achieved in transitional justice contexts. It has done so by analyzing how different mechanisms available to victims of corporate abuses in transitional justice contexts across history and across countries have, or have not, achieved corporate accountability and provided appropriate reparations to victims of corporate abuses. The analysis has

---

1 A Clapham, 'Extending International Criminal Law beyond the Individual to Corporations and Armed Opposition Groups' (2008) 6 *JICJ* 899; E Duruigbo, 'Corporate Accountability and Liability for International Human Rights Abuses: Recent Changes and Recurring Challenges' (2008) 6 *Northwestern JIHR* 222; SS Beale, 'A Response to the Critics of Corporate Criminal Liability' (2009) 46 *American Crim LR* 1481.

focused on the four processes that constitute the core of transitional justice: (i) judicial mechanisms at the international, regional and national level; (ii) truth-seeking initiatives; (iii) administrative reparations programmes; and (iv) institutional reform.

Corporate accountability for human rights violations during conflict or repression is not a new transitional justice phenomenon. Rough justice for such violations was sought at Nuremberg when, for example, Bruno Tesch was tried, found guilty and executed for the sale of the Zyklon B gas used in extermination camps in Nazi Germany. While corporations were not prosecuted as legal entities *per se*, the post–World War II trials, analyzed in Chapter 2, have helped to understand the role that business enterprises play in times of conflict or repression and to develop criteria of responsibility, and there is evidence that criminal charges against corporations were considered entirely permissible.[2] Just as the notion of transitional justice is said to have begun with the Nuremberg trials, so too 'corporate complicity was included in that process from its very origins'.[3] Continuity from Nuremberg, however, has not happened. Transitional justice has ignored corporate responsibility for human rights violations. More than five decades later, a proposal for a restricted form of corporate criminal liability in the *Rome Statute of the International Criminal Court* failed.[4] At present, the only business actors capable of being prosecuted before the ICC are individual businesspeople, although so far the court has not done so. An expansion of the ICC jurisdiction to include corporations may in theory happen in the future, but this is currently unlikely. The new Office of the Prosecutor (OTP) focus on thematic prosecutions of crimes committed by means of natural resources exploitation and land confiscation may expand the remit of the ICC to address crimes where corporations are often involved, but how this may result in corporate accountability remains to be seen. Even if corporations were in the future accepted as subjects of the ICC, and even considering the focus of the OTP on the destruction of the environment, the illegal exploitation of natural resources or the illegal dispossession of land, corporations remain unlikely to become the primary focus of an ICC prosecutor. The contextual element of war crimes and crimes against humanity and the specific intent required for genocide limit the scope of application of international

2 JA Bush, 'The Prehistory of Corporations and Conspiracy in International Criminal Law: What Nuremberg Really Said' (2009) 109 *Colom LR* 1094, 1239; A Ramasastry, 'Corporate Complicity: From Nuremberg to Rangoon – An Examination of Forced Labor Cases and their Impact on the Liability of Multinational Corporations' (2002) 20 *Berkeley J Intl L* 105.

3 LA. Payne, 'Corporate Complicity and Transitional Justice: Setting the Scene' in *Peace, Everyone's Business! Corporate Accountability In Transitional Justice: Lessons For Colombia*, PAX (Utrecht, May 2017) 18.

4 See also K Haigh, 'Extending the International Criminal Court's Jurisdiction to Corporations: Overcoming Complementarity Concerns' (2008) 14 *Australian J Human Rights* 199; L Van den Herik, 'Subjecting Corporations to the ICC Regime: Analysing the Legal Counterarguments' in C Burchard, O Triffterer and J Vogel (eds), *The Review Conference and the Future of the International Criminal Court* (Kluwer 2010), 155.

crimes, at least in practical terms. Thus, while international criminal law could address crimes attributable to corporations, it would intervene only in extra-ordinary circumstances.[5] Businesspeople and corporations would rarely meet the criteria for ICC prosecution as in most cases they are not among those mas-terminding international crimes; instead, for the most part, they benefit from a given situation and exploit the financial opportunities. Therefore, the responsibility of corporations for their involvement in international crimes has been of marginal interest in international prosecution efforts.[6] This is arguably a necessary limitation of international criminal law that remains unlikely to be overcome. For these rea-sons, international criminal law does not currently offer an effective avenue for seeking remedy for corporate human rights abuses in transitional justice contexts.

The regional systems are rarely mentioned in the scholarship on business and human rights or on transitional justice. But Chapter 3 demonstrates that regional systems have indirectly provided, and could further do so, remedies for victims of corporate abuses and shaped national reparation programmes in transitional justice contexts by examining complaints against states for failing to prevent, investigate or redress human rights violations related to corporate activities.[7] The Inter-American Court of Human Rights, in particular, has provided important contributions to the analysis of evidence of corporate abuses and the provision of remedy and reparations for victims, including in transitional justice contexts.[8] A decision of the African Commission of August 2017 ordering the Democratic Republic of the Congo to investigate the role of *Anvil Mining* in a village massacre during the 1998 civil war also provides innovative precedents in this area, which could grow into more meaningful and effective quests.[9] As such, the regional systems can offer a com-plementary avenue for victims that have failed to obtain justice and reparations at the national level. This is particularly important in transitional justice contexts where national litigation is rarely an effective option. But their effectiveness is undermined by a number of limitations. Proceedings are extremely lengthy, as the case against *Anvil Mining* demonstrates. And, ultimately, the national governments have to

---

5 N Farrell, 'Attributing Criminal Liability to Corporate Actors: Some Lessons from the International Tribunals' (2010) 8(3) *JICJ* 872.

6 F Jessberger, 'On the Origins of Individual Criminal Responsibility under Interna-tional Law for Business Activity: IG Farben on Trial' (2010) 8(3) *JICJ* 783, 801; W Kaleck and M Saage-Maab, 'Corporate Accountability for Human Rights Violations Amounting to International Crimes The Status Quo and its Challenges' (2010) 8(3) *JICJ* 700, 710.

7 A Huneeus, 'International Criminal Law by Other Means: The Quasi-Criminal Jur-isdiction of the Human Rights Courts' (2013) 107 *AJIL* 1.

8 For example, Inter-American Court of Human Rights (IACtHR), *Santo Domingo Massacre v Colombia* (2012), 135; *Afro-Descendant Communities Displaced from the Cacarica River Basin (Operation Genesis) v Colombia* (2013).

9 African Commission on Human and Peoples' Rights (ACHPR), *Institute for Human Rights and Development in Africa and Others v Democratic Republic of Congo*, Com-munication 393/10, 9 June 2016.

implement the recommendations of the regional systems. To date they have done so only to a limited extend.

Civil claims and prosecutions against companies for violations committed in times of conflict or repression have been attempted in a number of countries, as detailed in Chapter 4, but they are still the exception and have rarely been successful in establishing corporate accountability and providing redress for victims.[10] There are obstacles both in the host and the home state. Systematic flaws in domestic regulation and the judicial system due to lack of institutional capacity and resources are likely to occur in the host states in a transitional context, and as a result victims are often not in a position to bring claims against companies in the countries where the abuses have occurred. The political instability in post-conflict and transitional contexts adds to the challenge. Home states remain equally reluctant to hold multinational companies accountable. Attempts to achieve legal accountability of corporations through extraterritorial jurisdiction face serious obstacles as the complicated history of the *South Africa Apartheid Litigation* and the narrowing of the exercise of extraterritorial jurisdiction in *Kiobel* and then *Jasner* demonstrate.[11] Most human rights lawsuits against corporations are dismissed on procedural grounds in the early stages of litigation.[12] Many have dragged on for years or even decades after the violations allegedly occurred, questioning whether even a decision on the merits could ever provide real accountability and redress.[13] To date, the few cases that have survived legal procedural challenges, and have not been dismissed, have been settled before trial.[14] No case against a corporation alleging violation of human rights or crimes under international law has yet been decided on the merits. Few businessmen have been convicted for crimes under international law, but to date no criminal case alleging criminal responsibility of corporations for human rights violations or crimes under international law has resulted in a conviction (although this is currently being attempted in France and a few other countries).[15]

As part of their mandate, some truth and reconciliation commissions (TRCs), detailed in Chapter 5, have investigated the different actors involved in the past

---

10 B Stephens, 'Conceptualizing Violence Under International Law: Do Tort Remedies Fit the Crime?' (1997) 60 *Alb L Rev* 579, 604.

11 C Abrahams, 'Lessons from the South African Experience' in S Michalowski (ed.), *Corporate Accountability in the Context of Transitional Justice* (Routledge 2013), 153.

12 For example, *Sarei v Rio Tinto*, 221 F. Supp. 2d 1116 (C.D. Cal. 2002), *In re Union Carbide Corp Gas Plant Disaster at Bhopal*, 634 F. Supp 842, 850–51 (S.D.N.Y. 1986). See also S Joseph, *Corporations and Transnational Human Rights Litigation* (Hart 2004); K Gallagher, 'Civil Litigation and Transnational Business: An Alien Tort Statute Primer' (2010) 8 *JICJ* 745, 751–53; R Meeran, 'Tort Litigation Against Multinational Corporations for Violation of Human Rights: An Overview of the Position Outside the United States' (2011) 3(1) *City Univ Hong Kong L Rev* 1

13 For example, *ExxonMobil*.

14 For example, *Talisman*, *Shell* (in *Kiobel*), *Chiquita*, *Drummond*, *Total*.

15 French courts are currently investigating *Amesys*, *Qosmos* and *LafargeHolcim* for complicity with the regimes in Libya and Syria.

conflict or repression, including corporations. As such, they have played a unique role in establishing an official record of corporations' involvement in past abuses. TRCs have named specific companies, published data on the wealth they amassed, and recommended prosecutions. For example, the South Africa TRC recognized the role of business in maintaining the *status quo* of apartheid society.[16] It submitted that there were legal grounds for instituting claims for reparations against corporations (which finally resulted in the *Apartheid Litigation* filed in the United States)[17] and recommended that business provide reparations. The Liberian TRC concluded that corporate actors across different sectors were involved in human rights violations.[18] Truth commissions' recommendations to finance reparations programmes and simultaneously address corporate responsibility have, however, largely been ignored by the governments. Truth commissions usually only have the power to recommend reparations; they do not have the power to pay them directly, and the task of making reparations usually falls to government.[19] In the end, none of the commissions' recommendations for prosecution or reparation concerning corporate involvement in abuses was followed by the respective governments.

As discussed in Chapter 6, administrative reparation programmes can provide a variety of measures for violations related to business activities, for whole classes of victims rather than in response to individualized justice sought through the courts. New administrative programmes in relation to redress for victims of corporate abuses have been attempted in the area of restitution, in particular land restitution. Colombia, for example, is attempting an innovative land restitution programme, under which some companies may be forced to return land obtained during the conflict.[20] Finally, in relation to institutional reform, Chapter 7 has argued that preventing corporate human rights abuses requires changing the state structures and institutions that facilitated or failed to prevent abuses and that allowed business to participate in or benefit from human rights violations. To do so, institutional reform should address institutions normally considered part of the economic development paradigm, such as those regulating investment and land governance, ensuring they go beyond simply enabling market activity by including procedural safeguards and accountability mechanisms. Yet the neoliberal temptation to deregulate, privatize and rely on investment-led economic growth has inhibited governments from doing so. Transitional justice has not yet advanced sufficiently to address the rights of

16 Truth and Reconciliation Commission of South Africa, *Final Report* (1998), Vol 4, Ch 2.
17 *In re South African Apartheid Litigation*, 617 F. Supp. 2d 228 (S.D.N.Y. 2009). See also M Swart, 'The Khulumani Litigation: Complementing the Work of the South African Truth and Reconciliation Commission' (2011) 16 *Tilburg Law Review* 30.
18 Truth and Reconciliation Commission of Liberia, *Consolidated Final* Report, 30 June 2009, Vol 3.
19 T Antkowiak, 'Truth as Right and Remedy in International Human Rights Experience' (2002) 23 *Mich J Intl L* 977, 1002.
20 Government of Colombia, *Ley de Víctimas y Restitución de Tierras* (Victims and Land Restitution Law), no. 1448 (10 June 2011).

victims of corporate abuses: the right to justice, the right to know, the right to reparations, and the aim to prevent future victimization.

The analysis of the way transitional justice mechanisms have dealt with corporate accountability leads to a number of conclusive points: (i) transitional justice and corporate accountability – and their goals – are linked and overlapping; (ii) transitional justice cannot be 'holistic' if it overlooks the responsibility of companies; (iii) transitional justice's 'toolbox' can offer unique remedies for corporate human rights violations committed during times of conflict or violence; (iv) different transitional justice mechanisms achieve corporate accountability and remedy in a different but complementary way; (v) corporations can contribute to the financing of reparations based on a 'polluter pays' type principle; (vi) the 'power versus justice' dilemmas of societies in transition are one of the main obstacles to corporate accountability; (vii) reparations programmes and institutional reform – and their potential to align with 'transformative justice' goals – are the transitional justice mechanisms with the most important part to play in the field of business and human rights.

First, as both fields of transitional justice and corporate accountability are expanding, they may, arguably, converge. In the words of Ruben Carranza:

> There is now more pluralism and transitional justice has evolved from being narrowly focused on physical integrity violations to recognizing that armed conflict, political violence and repression cannot be de-linked from their economic and social causes and consequences. The way taken by transitional justice to get to where it is now might be a helpful map for those working on corporate accountability.[21]

Both transitional justice and corporate accountability approaches are continually developing. Transitional justice has moved away from a narrow focus on the most serious civil and political rights violations committed by state actors, to include also economic, social and cultural rights, to then explore 'economic violence' such as corruption and the unlawful exploitation of natural resources, to finally consider also the role of economic actors.[22] The case of Argentina is emblematic: in 1983, CONADEP was mandated to investigate only cases of enforced disappearances during the dictatorship; in 2015, the government passed a bill establishing another

---

21 R Carranza, 'Transitional Justice, Corporate Responsibility and Learning from the Global South', 28 April 2015, http://jamesgstewart.com/transitional-justice-corporate-responsibility-and-learning-from-the-global-south/?subscribe=success#blog_subscription-2

22 J Cavallaro and S Albuja, 'The Lost Agenda: Economic Crimes and Truth Commissions in Latin America and Beyond' in K McEvoy and L McGregor (eds), *Transitional Justice from Below, Grassroots Activism and the Struggle for Change* (Hart 2008), 122; E Andreevska, 'Transitional Justice and Democratic Change: Key Concepts' (2013) 20 *Lex et Scientia Intl J* 54, 55; M Mutua, 'What Is the Future of Transitional Justice?' (2015) 9 *Intl J Trans Just* 1; R Duthie, 'Transitional Justice, Development, and Economic Violence' in R Duthie and ND Sharp (eds), *Justice and Economic Violence in Transition* (Springer 2014), 165, 168.

truth commission, mandated to investigate the complicity of corporations and financial institutions in the repression.[23] When Latin American countries emerging from military dictatorships began their pursuit of transitional justice, they were not concerned with holding corporations accountable; they were concerned with finding a balance between prosecuting individual perpetrators and responding to demands for truth and reparations.[24] Later, however, Argentina, Brazil and Colombia, among other countries, have started to seek the truth about economic crimes and the links between businesses and perpetrators of human rights violations during the conflict and dictatorships.

Simultaneously to the expansion of transitional justice, the business and human rights field is also developing. While international human rights treaties impose obligations only on states, it is now accepted that corporations do have responsibilities. The international legal framework has evolved accordingly with the adoption, for example, of the UN Guiding Principles on business and human rights in 2011. An international treaty on business and human rights is currently under negotiation at the UN. The proposed treaty may provide what is still lacking: a proper enforcement mechanism to address the current accountability gap.

Although the path has not been a linear and smooth one, criminal and civil litigation alleging corporate involvement in past abuses in both the home and host countries is being incessantly pursued. Currently, impunity is still the norm and cases resulting in corporate accountability are few and far between, but progress is in the direction of more accountability, not less. Business enterprises involved in human rights abuses or international crimes are, and will continue to be, pursued in domestic jurisdictions. In April 2019, the UK Supreme Court found that *Vedanta* had a duty of care to prevent its foreign subsidiary in Zambia from causing harm to people. In June 2018, French investigative judges indicted *Lafarge* on charges of complicity in crimes against humanity in Syria – the first time a parent company has been indicted for such crime. Victims and their representatives across jurisdictions are challenging normative and practical obstacles and fighting to develop standards for imposing liability upon corporations for their human rights abuses.[25]

Second, bringing the economic perpetrators or accomplices that made many of the violations possible into the orbit of transitional justice would provide for a more complete and holistic justice. Transitional justice aims to achieve justice, to establish an account of the truth about the past, to provide reparations for victims and their families. Corporate accountability mechanisms share some of the same aims – to provide justice for victims of corporate abuses, to provide them with access to justice and remedy. Transitional justice is intended to address past abuses, and corporations

---

23 Government of Argentina, Ley de creación de la Comision Bicameral de la Verdad, la Memoria, la Justicia, la Reparación y el Fortalecimiento de las Instituciones de la Democracia, Law no. 27217, 3 December 2015.

24 Carranza (n 21).

25 MB Taylor, RC Thompson and A Ramasastry, *Overcoming Obstacles to Justice: Improving Access to Judicial Remedies for Business Involvement in Grave Human Rights Abuses* (Fafo 2010).

are often tied up with these abuses. As the field of transitional justice and corporate accountability are continually evolving, and converging, future approaches should give greater attention to the accountability of companies responsible for past violations.

Corporate accountability is part of a broader debate within transitional justice and international criminal law about how economic crimes should be addressed.[26] It has become impossible to overlook the reality that in an increasing number of conflicts, alongside atrocities perpetrated by state actors on civilians, a pattern of war economies has emerged, particularly around the exploitation of natural and mineral resources. The way in which war is fought, supplied and financed is more complicated than ever, and there is a concomitant need for transitional justice to adapt to these modern realities. Arguably, transitional justice's focus on business enterprises operating in regions affected by armed conflict and instability, and their potential involvement in, or contribution to, human rights abuses and crimes under international law is going to increase. Corruption and other economic crimes, illegal land confiscation and natural resources exploitation, as well as corporate accountability, are all part of a broader set of grievances that many in the field of transitional justice simply regarded as background, but did not consider inherent to the work of prosecutors, truth commissions or reparations programmes. That is changing.

Third, the most serious corporate abuses happen in times of conflict, and it is precisely transitional justice with its 'toolbox' that offers the most interesting avenues for corporate accountability. In a 'non-conflict' situation, corporate accountability is generally limited by the legal obstacles at the national level and the lack of personality under international human rights law. In transitional justice contexts, there are other processes available to establish corporate accountability and redress for victims, namely truth commissions and reparations measures. Disputes related to access to land provide the clearest example of the convergence of the two fields.

Illegal land confiscation and forced evictions often occur outside the context of armed conflict – millions of people have been displaced, often without compensation, by dams, extractive projects, palm oil plantations, large infrastructure and other 'development' projects. In this sense, the line between conflict- and repression-related violations and the 'normal' development process is blurry. One such case is Kenya. Successive waves of land dispossession and transfer lie at the heart of Kenya's ethnic and political tensions. Disputed access to land is often cited as one of the key structural causes of violence in the country.[27] The question is whether the forced

---

26 ND Sharp, 'Addressing Economic Violence in Times of Transition: Toward a Positive-Peace Paradigm for Transitional Justice' (2012) 35 *Fordham Intl L J* 780; R Duthie, 'Toward a Development-Sensitive Approach to Transitional Justice' (2008) 2 *Intl J Trans Just* 292; P Gready, *The Era of Transitional Justice: The Aftermath of the Truth and Reconciliation Commission in South Africa and Beyond* (Routledge 2007); K Andrieu, 'Dealing With A "New" Grievance: Should Anticorruption Be Part of the Transitional Justice Agenda?' (2012) 11(4) *J Human Rights* 537.

27 N Roht-Arriaza, 'Reparations and Economic, Social, and Cultural Rights' in Duthie and Sharp (n 22), 109, 131.

dispossession of the traditional lands in Kenya is part of a transitional justice narrative connected to forced dispossession for political gain, or part of a resource privatization narrative connected to economic investment[28] – in other words, whether or not this is a 'transitional' violation that can be redressed using the mechanisms of transitional justice. Unlike the South African or Colombian cases, here the dispossession was not in the service of a violent political or military campaign, but simply a result of greed and misplaced development objectives. From a victim's point of view, however, the effect on the dispossessed is similar, as is the denial of remedy and corporate accountability.

In a case of land confiscation by a company, directly or in complicity with the government, in a 'non-conflict' situation (i.e. for natural resources extraction, large infrastructure projects or agribusiness activities), corporate accountability and remedies can only be attempted through litigation in the host country, and possibly in the host country the company is multinational. For 'ordinary' land expropriations or dispossessions, justice and remedy are supposed to happen as a matter of due process. If the same land confiscation happened in a conflict situation, transitional justice would offer other options: truth commissions can recommend the restitution of land and the prosecution of companies; reparations measures, as in Colombia, can force companies to return land; institutional reform could address weak laws and institutions that have allowed forced evictions to happen with impunity, as it is recommended for Myanmar; and there could even be the possibility of the ICC Prosecutor's Office examining the case to verify if an international crime has been committed by means of such illegal land dispossession. What makes transitional justice processes programmes feasible is precisely that they are 'transitional' – that is, exceptional.

Fourth, transitional justice offers tools for human rights advocates that have adopted a 'hybrid' approach to promoting corporate accountability and use both transnational litigation and non-judicial mechanisms. Courts are clearly critical for setting standards of legal obligation, and through litigation it is possible to secure financial damages for victims of corporate abuses.[29] But pursuing individual cases through the courts tends to be an incomplete way of addressing the scale of the challenge represented by victims in post-conflict settings. Courts only have the capacity to attend to a limited number of cases and rely heavily on victims being able to come forward and articulate their claims before the legal system. The scale of the challenge and the difficulties associated with access to justice for all make this a piecemeal effort. In addition, compensation achieved through tort litigation is limited to a narrow number of victims, who qualify as plaintiffs under procedural rules. Decisions, as outcome of a legal process, may be of considerable importance

---

28 Ibid.
29 E Harper, 'Delivering Justice in the Wake of Mass Violence: New Approaches in Transitional Justice' (2005) 10 *J Conflict Security Law* 149; SR Ratner, 'Corporations and Human Rights: A Theory of Legal Responsibility' (2001) 111 *Yale L J* 443, 446–48, 461–75; B Stephens, 'The Amorality of Profit' (2002) 20 *Berkeley J Intl L* 45, 46–48.

for those applicant victims, but would not have an effect on other victims, who may have also suffered similar violations. Judicial reparations can work well in contexts where human rights violations are the exception rather than the rule, and as a consequence the number of victims is limited, the specific human rights violations are easy to establish, and the evidence to prove is not too problematic. The existing judicial routes by which multinational corporations can be held accountable for their human rights abuses are not sufficient if taken in isolation. Rather, it is vital to acknowledge the 'multi-directional relationship' between different transitional justice mechanisms.[30]

In transitional justice contexts where governments seek to repair massive violations of human rights to a large number of victims, administrative reparations programmes may be a better-suited mechanism for redressing harm.[31] They offer reparation to broader categories of victims, instead of just the plaintiffs in a legal case, thus preventing unequal treatment of victims for reparations, and can be implemented through faster procedures with more flexible evidentiary standards.[32] While not usually able to respond to the variables of each individual case, a reparations programme can create generally descriptive classes of victims or their surviving family members who, given similar circumstances, can be treated alike. When implemented well, such programmes can have a much broader reach than court-ordered redress, both in terms of the number of people who obtain some reparation and also in terms of the holistic nature of the measures undertaken.[33] While the state is responsible for implementing them, administrative reparation programmes may result from recommendations made by TRCs and even by the regional systems. Such recommendations might include the responsibility of business to contribute to reparations programmes, an avenue that would need to be pursued with greater vigour if societies are to achieve the full benefits of a transitional justice journey. Administrative programmes and civil litigations are, anyway, not always mutually exclusive options. The Peruvian TRC formulated an interesting position in this respect: receiving benefits from the reparations plan does not leave civil lawsuits against the state without effect, and should not interrupt or impede penal cases against perpetrators.[34] This approach preserves victims' access to judicial avenues, while protecting the stability of the reparations programme.[35]

Fifth, corporations found responsible for past abuses can finance reparations programmes. Different countries have adopted different models for the financing

---

30 Y Farah, 'Toward a Multi-Directional Approach to Corporate Accountability' in S Michalowski (n 11), 29.
31 UN OHCHR, Rule of Law Tools for Post-conflict States: Reparations Programmes (2008).
32 Ibid.
33 International Center for Transitional Justice, *Reparations in Theory and Practice* (ICTJ 2007), 3–4.
34 Comisión de la Verdad y Reconciliación de Perú, *Final Report*, 28 August 2003.
35 L Magarrell and G Guillerot, *Memorias de un Proceso Inacabado: las Reparaciones en Perú* (ICTJ 2006).

of reparations.[36] For the most part, however, states have paid for reparations even when non-state actors committed violations, on the basis that the state failed to protect and ensure rights. For example, transitional justice developments in Brazil initially focused on an 'abstract model' of accountability whereby the state as a whole assumed responsibility for the violations carried out by government officials, but avoided investigation or prosecution of the individual or corporate perpetrators and accomplices.[37] Corporate responsibility to achieve reparation is difficult to address within the binding legal framework because many situations of corporate abuses lack an adequate legal-factual link that establishes responsibility. Consequently, the state assumed the responsibility of providing reparations through a programme of moral and economic redress to the victims, without looking for specific individual or corporate accountability.[38] While this may be legally correct, normally a much wider range of actors would be expected to bear responsibility for endemic and long-lasting systems of oppression.[39]

All reparations programmes face two fundamental and related questions: first, clearly articulating the parameters of who ought to be considered a 'victim'; and, second, how to select the human rights violations, from among the many that occurred, that would and ought to trigger reparations. For a reparations programme to ensure that every victim is a beneficiary, it would have to extend benefits to *all* the victims of *all* the violations that may have taken place during the conflict or repression. No programme has achieved such comprehensiveness and it is hard to foresee how this could be reasonably achieved. Generally, reparations, both through courts and through administrative programmes, have been limited to monetary compensation for violations of what are perceived as core rights to physical integrity – killings, forced disappearances, torture, and arbitrary detention – to the survivors or to the families of the victims of those violations.[40] This is the case of early reparations – for example, in Chile and Argentina.[41] South Africa's TRC also adopted a constrained 'closed list' approach when it established the requirements for reparation eligibility.[42]

---

36 S Darcy, 'Truth Commissions, the European Union and Reparations from Business' in F Medjouba (ed.), *Building Peace in Post-Conflict Situations* (BIICL 2011), 47.
37 JP Bohoslavsky and MD Torelly, 'Financial Complicity: The Brazilian Dictatorship Under the "Macroscope"' in Duthie and Sharp (n 22), 249.
38 Ibid., 252.
39 E Schmid, 'War Crimes Related to Violations of Economic, Social and Cultural Rights' (2011) 71(3) *Heidelberg J Intl L* 540.
40 P Gready, *The Era of Transitional Justice: The Aftermath of the Truth and Reconciliation Commission in South Africa and Beyond* (Routledge 2011).
41 Government of Argentina, Presidential decree number 70 of 1991; Law 24.043 of 1991; Law 24.411 of 1994. Government of Chile, Law 19.123 of 1992. See also CH Acuña, 'Transitional Justice in Argentina and Chile. A Never-Ending Story' in J Elster (ed.), *Reparation and Retribution in the Transition to Democracy* (Columbia University Press 2006), 206, 215–16.
42 Government of South Africa, Promotion of National Unity and Reconciliation Act (1995), Sect 1(1)(xix)(a), 1(1)(ix).

That reparation programmes have concentrated on these types of violations is not unjustified. The states where reparations are needed are generally poor, with many competing challenges and few resources. The number of victims and survivors may run to the tens or hundreds of thousands, with varied needs. When the resources available for reparations are scarce, choices have to be made and, arguably, it makes sense to concentrate on what are perceived to be the most serious crimes. Conversely, attempting to provide reparations for too broad a category of violations would be prohibitively expensive, and would also risk turning reparations into a 'theory of everything'.[43] As Naomi Roht-Arriaza puts it: 'Reparations are...a limited category of responses to harm.'[44] No programme has, however, explained why the victims of some violations were eligible for reparations and others not. As a consequence of this omission, most programmes have ignored types of violations that perhaps ought to have been included. In particular, only a few reparation programmes have addressed rights violations mostly associated with business activities, such as land expropriation without compensation and forced displacement. In this sense, only certain victims became fully part of the process of reconciliation, and wider accountability for the economic structure that supported past violations may be lost.[45] Overall, administrative programmes in transitional justice contexts have often overlooked the role of corporations in reparations programmes both from the point of view of the victims (the harms suffered by victims of corporate abuses have rarely been fully repaired) and the perpetrators (corporate actors responsible for violations have rarely paid reparations). The responsibility of companies to provide reparations has, as a consequence, not been given adequate consideration. There may even be a 'business case' for effective reparations: after all, some scholars have argued, it is 'in the economic interest [of corporations] to make sure that the country, and its people, move toward recovery and that the path is paved for the reconciliation of victims and perpetrators, as this is believed to have a positive impact on economic recovery'.[46]

Sixth, the investment and economic activity that a corporation (especially a multinational corporation) could bring may be more appealing to a post-conflict state than the need to provide redress to its citizens for violations committed by the company. Transitional governments, often reliant on revenues generated by corporate entities, have a vested interest in not investigating or prosecuting corporations. In addition, as a rule, it is the political or the military elites that change first. As a result, situations of transition after conflicts and repression have often led to the prosecution of political elites. By contrast, industry and business constitute a

---

43 N Roht-Arriaza, 'Reparations and Economic, Social, and Cultural Rights' in Duthie and Sharp (n 22), 110.

44 Ibid., 114.

45 R Meister, 'Human Rights and the Politics of Victimhood' (2002) 16(2) *Ethics Intl Affairs* 91, 95; M Humphrey, *The Politics of Atrocity and Reconciliation: From Terror to Trauma* (Routledge 2002), 121.

46 C Sandoval, L Filippini and R Vidal, 'Linking Transitional Justice and Corporate Accountability' in Michalowski (n 11), 21.

continuum in most societies, which may explain why there is often no drive for a determined legal remedy in these cases. For example, conscious of the need to harness the economic power of well-connected businessmen and attract foreign investment, the new Myanmar government accepts leaving the past unaddressed. Investors are key actors for the country's economic development, and the government fears that holding businesses accountable may escalate existing tensions, cause instability and jeopardize investment, development and even democracy.[47] Instead of reforming land governance to prevent abuses, the government is adopting neoliberal strategies, rewarding those who benefit from repression, conflict and systemic human rights abuses.[48]

Countries in transition are often in state of economic collapse, and corporations are seen as critical for economic progress. As a result, even if economic actors have substantially contributed to the systemic injustice, they may not be held accountable, in a tacit promise to contribute to the economic recovery. This tendency can be observed in the post–World War II cases, as well as later in the South African truth and reconciliation process and the initial position of the South African government towards claims of the *Apartheid Litigation*. It can also explain the lack of political will by the part of governments in implementing TRCs' recommendations regarding business. Those who may have benefitted from corporate operations and remain influential in government may obstruct commissions' operations if they believe they endanger their economic interests. For instance, the South Africa, Liberia and East Timor TRCs all attributed responsibility to corporations and recommended that businesses pay reparations, but the respective governments lacked the political will to implement the commissions' proposals.

Transitional societies have both weak governments and fragile legal systems. The attraction of foreign investment seems an easy short-term solution to meet pressing economic needs. Yet it is often corporations, and not the host state, that ultimately benefit from lax standards. Even if corporations may play a critical role in fostering the economic progress needed to bring societies out of the risk of falling back into conflict and repression, this is not a sufficient reason to trade a contribution to economic recovery with immunity from accountability. In order to address the root causes of conflict and repression, it is fundamental to consider the role of all actors, including corporations. In addition, at least for cases of gross human rights violations, justice should take precedence over economic development.[49] For example, as far as the South African experience is concerned, 'claims of victims of certain violations of civil and political rights, such as torture or the killing of a close family member, should not be conflated with general claims

---

47 See R David and I Holliday, *Liberalism and Democracy in Myanmar* (OUP 2018), 158; P Pierce and C Reiger, 'Navigating paths to justice in Myanmar's transition', International Center for Transitional Justice (June 2014).
48 See W Bello, 'Paradigm Trap', Transnational Institute (2018).
49 D de Felice, 'Sabine Michalowski (ed.), Corporate Accountability in the Context of Transitional Justice' (2014) 14 *Human Rights Law Review* 576, 577.

of all victims of apartheid to be lifted out of apartheid-related poverty and social exclusion'.[50]

Finally, including business and human rights concepts in the development of reparations programmes and institutional reform is arguably the most important way to prevent the reoccurrence of corporate human rights abuses. It is also important to achieve distributive and 'transformative' justice. As explained by Nelson Camilo Sánchez León, the 'transformative justice' concept is

> an effort to combine the dominant concept of reparations, which in current legal theory is backward looking and founded in corrective justice, with the concept of distributive justice, which is forward looking and takes into consideration current needs of the population.[51]

The perspective adopted by Sánchez León leads to the conclusion that

> a model that seeks a lasting democratic transition should avoid the temptation to pursue quick economic recovery at the expense of long-term democratic governance... [E]ven though some measure[s] that address corporations... may be undesirable, allowing the perpetuation of undemocratic practice that benefit the wealthy at the expense of the general welfare of the population does not facilitate the non-repetition of events and might even endanger the already-settled elements of transition in a democratic transformation.[52]

Dependence on business for global or domestic economic stability and wellbeing results in an unwillingness to sanction abusive behaviour. States are unlikely to sanction businesses for abusive behaviour where those companies or sectors are integral to the national economy or national security.[53] The absence of settled law leaves states free to do so without constraint. Direct action by businesses to block accountability is also evident. The history of the Guiding Principles and the current negotiations on a business and human rights treaty reveal powerful pressure from businesses in favour of voluntary mechanisms and against binding obligations. Transitional states face pressure to deregulate and privatize in an attempt to attract investment rather than regulate corporate behaviour and enact policy to protect, respect and fulfil human rights.[54] Even in countries where transitional justice has successfully challenged antidemocratic military power, the individuals

---

50 Abrahams (n 11), 161.
51 NC Sánchez León, 'Corporate Accountability, Reparations, and Distributive Justice in Post Conflict Societies' in Michalowski (n 11), 119.
52 Ibid., 130.
53 Payne (n 3), 26, 27.
54 T van Ho, 'Due Diligence in Transitional Justice States: An Obligation for Greater Transparency?' J Letner Černič and T van Ho (eds.), *Human Rights and Business: Direct Corporate Accountability for Human Rights* (Wolf Legal Publishers 2015), 229, 236.

and companies that sustained or benefitted from the regime often remain in place. 'The redistribution of power is perhaps the primary demand of any transitional process that has as a goal the democratic transformation of society. Confronting power is, at the same time, one of the greatest challenges of a transition.'[55] Both transitional justice and business and human rights mechanisms must confront unequal power relations and deal with the redistribution of legal, political and natural resources – land, for example. Liberal state building is inadequate if it reinforces power imbalances and inequality; worse yet, if it rewards companies who profited during a repressive, rights-abusing regime, it is counterproductive to human rights.[56] To address the inequalities of economic and social power, transitional justice must be 'transformative'.

This book has explored the legal, practical and political challenges in achieving accountability and obtaining reparations from complexly structured multinational companies that sit outside both the state-centred framework of international human rights law and the individual-centred approach of international criminal law. It has highlighted the potential dilemma between ensuring effective remedies for victims of past human rights abuses by companies and partnering with the same actors to build peaceful and prosperous societies. It has illustrated the numerous difficulties that weak governments and divided societies face when addressing adverse corporate impacts – from under-resourced TRCs to limited evidence in support of criminal and civil proceedings. Transitional justice potentially advances the same moral and practical arguments for corporate violations as for perpetrators of state violations. The moral argument is the duty to victims, to provide them with justice and compensation for the atrocities committed against them. The practical argument is about deterrence and non-repetition: without attaching a tangible cost – such as the credible threat of prosecution – to corporate human rights violations, they are likely to continue in future dictatorships and armed conflicts.[57] Transitional justice offers a way to overcome a governance gap in which victims' rights exist in international human rights law, but no international legal institutions exist to allow them to secure those rights.[58] Transition requires economic, social and cultural development by securing human rights and sustainable development in the future.[59] Transitional justice offers legal and non-legal tools to address the inequalities that constitute

55 Sánchez León (n 51), 114.
56 R Paris, *At War's End: Building Peace after Civil Conflict* (Cambridge University Press, 2004).
57 Payne (n 3), 23.
58 Ibid., 22, 23.
59 L Arbour, 'Economic and Social Justice for Societies in Transition' (2007) 40(1) *Intl Law and Politics* 1 (based on her speech at Second Annual Transitional Justice Lecture, New York University School of Law, New York, 25 Oct 2006), 2; A Orford, 'Globalization and the Right to Development' in Philip Alston (ed.), *Peoples' Rights* (OUP 2002), 139; J Bohman, 'Beyond Distributive Justice and Struggles for Recognition: Freedom, Democracy, and Critical Theory' (2007) 6(3) *European Journal of Political Theory* 271.

conflict and repression.[60] Transitional justice processes need to take corporations into account if they want to address the root causes of conflict and repression, and, in parallel, corporate accountability mechanisms need to recognize the specific needs of transitional societies if they want to achieve long-lasting changes in corporate culture and behaviour.

---

60 RG Teitel, 'Transitional Justice Globalized' (2008) 2(1) *International Journal of Transitional Justice*, 1–4; DN Sharp, 'Interrogating the Peripheries: The Preoccupations of Fourth Generation Transitional Justice' (2013) 26 *Harvard Human Rights Journal* 149; R Mani, 'Rebuilding an Inclusive Political Community after War' (2005) 36(4) *Security Dialogue* 511.

Bibliography

Abrahams, C, 'Lessons from the South African Experience' in Michalowski (ed.), *Corporate Accountability in the Context of Transitional Justice* (Routledge 2013), 153

Abrahams, C, 'The TRC's Unfinished Business: Reparations' in Villa-Vicencio and du Toit (eds), *Truth and Reconciliation in South Africa: 10 Years On* (New Africa Books 2006), 34

Acuña, C, 'Transitional Justice in Argentina and Chile: A Never-Ending Story?' in Elster (ed.), *Retribution and Reparation in the Transition to Democracy* (Columbia University Press 2006), 223

Addo, M, *Human Rights Standards and the Responsibility of Transnational Corporations* (Kluwer 1999)

Aguirre, D, 'Corporate Liability for ESCR Revisited: The Failure of International Cooperation' (2011) 42(1) *California Western International Law Journal* 145

Aguirre, D, 'Corporate Social Responsibility and Human Rights Law in Africa' (2005) 5(2) *African Human Rights LJ* 239

Alford, R, 'The Future of Human Rights Litigation After Kiobel' (2014) 89 *Notre Dame L Rev* 1749

Alston, P (ed.), *Non-State Actors and Human Rights* (OUP 2005)

Altschuller, AW, 'Two Ways to Think about the Punishment of Corporations' (2009) 46 *American Criminal L Rev* 1359

Alvarez, JA, 'Are Corporations "Subjects" of International Law?' (2011) 9(1) *Santa Clara JIL* 1

Amerson, JM, '"The End of the Beginning?": A Comprehensive Look at the Business and Human Rights Agenda from a Bystander Perspective' (2012) 17 *Fordham J Corporate Finance L* 871

Amnesty International, *Open for Business? Corporate Crime and Abuses at Myanmar's Copper Mine* (AI 10 February 2015)

Anderson, M, 'Transnational Corporations and Environmental Damage: Is Tort Law an Answer?' (2002) 41 *Washburn L J* 405

Andreevska, E, 'Transitional Justice and Democratic Change: Key Concepts' (2013) 20 *Lex et Scientia Intl J* 54

Andrieu, K, 'Dealing with a "New" Grievance: Should Anticorruption Be Part of the Transitional Justice Agenda?' (2012) 11(4) *J Human Rights* 537

Antkowiak, T, 'Truth as Right and Remedy in International Human Rights Experience' (2002) 23 *Mich J Intl L* 977

Antkowiak, TM, 'An Emerging Mandate for International Courts: Victim-Centered Remedies and Restorative Justice' (2001) 4(7) *Stan J Intl L* 279

Arbour, L, 'Economic and Social Justice for Societies in Transition' (2007–2008) 40 *Intl JL and Politics* 1

Arnold, DG, 'Corporations and Human Rights Obligations' (2016) 1(2) *BHRJ* 255

Arnold, M, 'The Governance of Local Business in Myanamr: Confronting the Legacies of Military Rule' in Crouch (ed.), *The Business of Transition in Myanmar* (CUP 2017)

Arthur, P, 'How "Transitions" Reshaped Human Rights: A Conceptual History of Transitional Justice' (2009) 31 *HRQ* 321

Attanasio, DL and Sánchez, NC, 'Return within the Bounds of the Pinheiro Principles: The Colombian Land Restitution Experience' (2012) 11 *Washington Univ Global Studies L Rev* 1

Backer, LC, 'Multinational Corporations, Transnational Law: The United Nation's Norms on the Responsibilities of Transnational Corporations as a Harbinger of Corporate Social Responsibility as International Law' (2006) 37 *Columbia HRLR* 287

Backer, LC, 'On the Evolution of the United Nations' "Protect-Respect-Remedy" Project: The State, the Corporation and Human Rights in a Global Governance Context' (2011) 9 *Santa Clara J Intl L* 37

Backer, LC, 'Rights and Accountability in Development ("RAID") v Das Air and Global Witness v Afrimex: Small Steps Toward an Autonomous Transnational Legal System for the Regulation of Multinational Corporations' (2009) 10 *Melbourne JIL* 258

Baleza, M, 'Corporate Complicity in Human Rights Violations. When is it Time to Leave a Country?' (2011) 8 *Información Filosófica*, 55

Barkan, E, *The Guilt of Nations: Restitution and Negotiating Historical Injustices* (WW Norton 2001)

Barnard-Naudé, J, 'For Justice and Reconciliation to Come: The TRC Archive, Big Business, and the Demand for Material Reparations' in du Bois and du Bois-Pedain (eds), *Justice and Reconciliation in Post-Apartheid South Africa* (CUP 2008), 172

Bass, G, *Stay the Hand of Vengeance: The Politics of War Crimes Tribunals* (Princeton University Press 2000)

Bassiouni, MC, *The Statute of The International Criminal Court: A Documentary History* (Transnational Publisher 1998)

Batesmith, A, 'Corporate Criminal Responsibility for War Crimes and Other Violations of International Humanitarian Law: The Impact of the Business and Human Rights Movement' in Harvey, Summers, and White (eds), *Contemporary Challenges to the Laws of War: Essay in Honour of Professor Peter Rowe* (CUP 2014), 292

Bazyler, MJ and Alford, R (eds), *Holocaust Restitution: Perspectives on the Litigation and Its Legacy* (NYU Press 2006)

Bazyler, MJ, 'Nuremberg in America: Litigating the Holocaust in United States Courts' (2000) 34 *U Rich L Rev* 1

Beale, SS, 'A Response to the Critics of Corporate Criminal Liability' (2009) 46 *American Crim LR* (2009) 1481

Beale, SS and Safwat, A, 'What Developments in Western Europe Tell Us about American Critique of Corporate Criminal Liability' (2005) 8 *Buffalo Criminal L Rev* 89

Bell, T and Buhle Ntsebeza, D, *Unfinished Business: South Africa, Apartheid, and Truth* (Verso 2003)

Berdal, M and Malone, D, *Greed and Grievance: Economic Agendas in Civil Wars* (International Development Research Centre 2000)

Bernaz, N, 'An Analysis of the ICC Office of the Prosecutor's Policy Paper on Case Selection and Prioritization from the Perspective of Business and Human Rights' (2017) *JICJ* 527

Bernaz, N, 'Book Reviews: Leora Bilsky, *The Holocaust, Corporations, and the Law. Unfinished Business*' (2019) 21 *Journal of the History of International Law* 1

Bernaz, N, 'Corporate Criminal Liability under International Law. The New TV S.A.L. and Akhbar Beirut S.A.L. Cases at the Special Tribunal for Lebanon' (2015) 13 *JICJ* 313

Bernaz, N, 'Enhancing Corporate Accountability for Human Rights Violations: Is Extra-territoriality the Magic Potion?' (2013) 117 *J Business Ethics* 494

Bernaz, N, 'Establishing Liability for Financial Complicity in International Crimes' in Bohoslavsky and Letnar Cernic (eds), *Making Sovereign Financing & Human Rights Work* (Hart 2014), 61

Bernaz, N and Pietropaoli, I, 'The Role of NGOs in the Business and Human Rights Treaty Negotiations' (2017) *Oxford J Human Rights Practice* 1

Bhashyam, S, 'Knowledge or Purpose? The Khulumani Litigation and the Standard for Aiding and Abetting Liability Under Alien Tort Claims Act' (2008) 30 *Cardozo L Rev* 245

Bilchitz, D, 'A Chasm Between "Is" and "Ought"? A Critique of the Normative Foundations of the SRSG's Framework and Guiding Principles' in Bilchitz and Deva (eds), *Human Rights Obligations of Business: Beyond the Corporate Responsibility to Respect* (CUP 2013), 107

Bilchitz, D, 'The Necessity for a Business and Human Rights Treaty' 1(2) *Business and Human Rights Journal* (2016) 203

Bilchitz, D, 'The Ruggie Framework: An Adequate Rubric for Corporate Human Rights Obligations?' (2010) 12 *IJHR* 199

Bilchitz, D and Deva, S (eds), *Human Rights Obligations of Business: Beyond the Corporate Responsibility to Respect* (CUP 2013)

Bilsky, L, *The Holocaust, Corporations, and the Law: Unfinished Business* (University of Michigan Press 2017)

Bilsky, L 'Transnational Holocaust Litigation' (2012) 23(2) *Eur J Int Law* 349

Bishop, JD, 'The Limits of Corporate Human Rights Obligations and the Rights of For-profit Corporations' (2012) 22(1) *Business Ethics Quarterly* 119

Bismuth, R, 'Mapping a Responsibility of Corporations for Violations of International Humanitarian Law Sailing Between International and Domestic Legal Orders' (2009) 38 *Denver J Intl L Policy* 203

Black, E, *IBM and The Holocaust: The Strategic Alliance Between Nazi Germany and America's Most Powerful Corporation* (Crown Books 2001)

Blitt, RC, 'Beyond Ruggie's Guiding Principles on Business and Human Rights: Charting an Embracive Approach to Corporate Human Rights Compliance' (2012) 48 *Texas Intl L J* 33

Bloxham, D, '"The Trial that Never Was": Why There Was No Second International Trial of Major War Criminals at Nuremberg' (2002) 87 *J Hist Assn* 41

Blumberg, PI, 'Asserting Human Rights against Multinational Corporations under United States Law: Conceptual and Procedural Problems' (2002) 50 *American J Comp L* 493

Bohlin, A, 'A Price on the Past: Cash as Compensation in South African Land Restitution' (2004) 38(3) *Canadian J African Studies* 672

Bohoslavsky, JP and Letnar Černič, J (eds), *Making Sovereign Financing & Human Rights Work* (Hart 2014)

Bohoslavsky, JP and Michalowski, S, 'Jus Cogens, Transitional Justice and Other Trends of the Debate on Odious Debts − A Response to the World Bank Discussion Paper on Odious Debts' (2010) 48 *Colum J Transnatl L* 61

Bohoslavsky, JP and Opgenhaffen, V, 'The Past and Present of Bank Responsibility for Financing the Argentinean Dictatorship' (2009) 23 *Harvard Human Rights J* 157

Bohoslavsky, JP and Rulli, M, 'Corporate Complicity and Finance as a "Killing Agent": The Relevance of the Chilean Case' (2010) 8 *JICJ* 829

Bohoslavsky, JP and Torelly, MD, 'Financial Complicity: The Brazilian Dictatorship Under the "Macroscope"' in Duthie and Sharp (eds) *Justice and Economic Violence in Transition* (Springer 2014), 233

Bohoslavsky, JP and Verbitsky, H, *Cuentas Pendientes* (Siglo Ventiuno Editores 2015)

Bohoslavsky, JP and Verbitsky, H, *Cuentas Pendientes: Los cómplices ecónomicos de la dictadura* (Siglo Ventiuno Editores 2015).

Bohoslavsky, JP and Verbitsky, H (eds), *The Economic Accomplices to the Argentine Dictatorship* (CUP 2015)

Boraine, A, 'Transitional Justice: A Holistic Interpretation' (2006) 60 *J Intl Affairs* 18

Boraine, A, 'Truth and Reconciliation Commission in South Africa Amnesty: The Price of Peace' in Elster (ed.) *Retribution and Reparation in the Transition to Democracy* (Columbia University Press 2006), 299

Borer, TA (ed.), *Telling the Truths: Truth Telling and Peacebuilding in Post-Conflict Societies* (University of Notre Dame Press 2006)

Borkin, J, *The Crime and the Punishment of I.G. Farben* (The Free Press 1978)

Braithwaite, J, *Crime, Shame, and Reintegration* (CUP 1989)

Braithwaite, J, *Restorative Justice and Responsive Regulation* (OUP 2002)

Braithwaite, J and Fisse, B, *The Impact of Publicity on Corporate Offenders* (State University of New York Press 1983)

Braithwaite, J and Fisse, B, *Corporations, Crime, and Accountability* (CUP 1993)

Bratspies, RM, '"Organs of Society": A Plea for Human Rights Accountability for Transnational Enterprises and Other Business Entities' (2005) 13 *Michigan State J Intl L* 9

Brickey, KF, 'Corporate Criminal Accountability: A Brief History and an Observation' (1982) 60 *Wash Univ LQ* 393

Buchheit, LC, Mitu Gulati, G and Thompson, RB, 'The Dilemma of Odious Debts' (2007) 56 *Duke LJ* 1201

Buhmann, K, Roseberry, L and Morsing, M (eds) *Corporate Social and Human Rights Responsibilities: Global Legal and Management Perspectives* (Palgrave 2011)

Burchard, C, Triffterer, O and Vogel, J (eds), *The Review Conference and the Future of the International Criminal Court* (Kluwer 2010)

Bush, JA, 'The Prehistory of Corporations and Conspiracy in International Criminal Law: What Nuremberg Really Said' (2009) 109 *Colom LR* 1094

Cambou, D, 'The Dutch Shell Case: Foreign Direct Liability Claims as an Avenue for Holding Multinational Corporations Accountable for Human Rights Violations' in Letnar Černič and van Ho (eds), *Human Rights and Business: Direct Corporate Accountability for Human Rights* (Wolf Legal 2015), 347

Cano, I and Galvão Ferreira, P, 'The Reparations Program in Brazil' in de Greiff (ed.), *The Handbook of Reparations* (OUP 2006), 102

Carranza, R, 'Plunder and Pain: Should Transitional Justice Engage with Corruption and Economic Crimes?' (2008) *Intl J Trans Just* 310

Carrillo, JA, 'Justice in Context: The Relevance of Inter-American Human Rights Law and Practice to Repairing the Past' in de Greiff (ed.), *The Handbook of Reparations* (OUP 2006), 506

Cassel, D, 'Corporate Aiding and Abetting of Human Rights Violations: Confusion in the Courts' (2008) 6 *Northwestern Univ J Intl Human Rights* 304

Cassese, A, 'Foreign Economic Assistance and Respect for Civil and Political Rights: Chile – A Case Study' (1979) 14 *Texas Intl LJ* 251

Cavallaro, J and Albuja, S, 'The Lost Agenda: Economic Crimes and Truth Commissions in Latin America and Beyond' in McEvoy and McGregor (eds), *Transitional Justice from Below, Grassroots Activism and the Struggle for Change* (Hart 2008), 121

Chambers, R, 'The Unocal Settlement: Implications for the Developing Law on Corporate Complicity in Human Rights Abuses' (2005) 1 *Human Rights Brief* 13

Chandler, G, 'The Curse of "Corporate Social Responsibility"' (2003) 2 *New Academy Review* 1

Chapman, AR, 'Truth Recovery Through the TRC Institutional Hearings Process' in Chapman and Van der Werwe (eds), *Truth and Reconciliation in South Africa: Did the TRC Deliver?* (University of Pennsylvania Press 2008), 169

Chapman, AR and van der Werwe, H, 'Reflections on the South African Experience' in Chapman and Van der Werwe (eds), *Truth and Reconciliation in South Africa: Did the TRC Deliver?* (University of Pennsylvania Press 2008), 286

Chapman, AR and Van der Werwe, H (eds), *Truth and Reconciliation in South Africa: Did the TRC Deliver?* (University of Pennsylvania Press 2008)

Chaskalson, M, 'The Property Clause: Section 28 of the Constitution' (1994) 10 *South Africa J Human Rights* 131

Chiomenti, C, 'Corporations and the International Court', in de Schutter (ed.), *Transnational Corporations and Human Rights* (Hart 2006), 287

Chirwa, DM, 'The Doctrine of State Responsibility as a Potential Means of Holding Private Actors Accountable for Human Rights' (2004) 5 *Melb JIL* 1

Chirwa, DM, 'The Long March to Binding Obligations of Transnational Corporations in International Human Rights Law' (2006) *South African J Human Rights* 76

Clamp, K, *Restorative Justice in Transition* (Routledge 2014)

Clapham, A, 'Extending International Criminal Law beyond the Individual to Corporations and Armed Opposition Groups' (2008) 6 *JICJ* 899

Clapham, A, *Human Rights Obligations of Non-State Actors* (OUP 2006)

Clapham, A, 'The Question of Jurisdiction under International Criminal Law over Legal Persons: Lessons from the Rome Conference' in Kamminga and Zia-Zarifi (eds), *Liability of Multinational Corporations under International Law* (Kluwer 2000), 139

Clapham, A and Jerbi, S, 'Categories of Corporate Complicity in Human Rights Abuses' (2011) 24(3) *Hastings Intl Comp L Rev* 339

Clark, P, and others, 'Justice for Apartheid Crimes: Corporations, States, and Human Rights' (2009) *Oxford Transitional Justice Research*

Cleveland, SH, 'The Alien Tort Statute, Civil Society, and Corporate Responsibility' (2004) 56 *Rutgers L Rev* 971

Clough J and Mulhern, C, *The Prosecution of Corporations* (OUP 2002)

Coliver, S and others, 'Holding Human Rights Violators Accountable by Using International Law in U.S. Courts: Advocacy Efforts and Complementary Strategies' (2005) 19 *Emory Intl L Rev* 169

Colvin, CJ, 'Overview of the Reparations Program in South Africa' in de Greiff (ed.), *The Handbook of Reparations* (OUP 2006), 176

Comisión Interamericana de Derechos Humanos, Relatoría Especial sobre Derechos Económicos SocialesCulturales y Ambientales, *Informe Empresas y Derechos Humanos:*

Estándares Interamericanos OEA/Ser.L/V/II CIDH/REDESCA/INF.1/19, 1 November 2019

Crawford, J, 'Corporate Responsibility in War Crimes, A New Legal Battlefield' *JusticeInfo*, 15 November 2019, www.justiceinfo.net/en/tribunals/national-tribunals/42906-corporate-responsibility-war-crimes-new-legal-battlefield.html

Crouch, M (ed.), *The Business of Transition in Myanmar* (CUP 2017)

Daly, E, 'Reparations in South Africa: A Cautionary Tale' (2003) 33 *U Mem L Rev* 367

Darcy, S, 'Truth Commissions, the European Union and Reparations from Business' in Medjouba (ed.), *Building Peace in Post-Conflict Situations: British Institute of International and Comparative Law* (BIICL 2011), 43

Davitti, D, *Investment and Human Rights in Armed Conflict: Charting an Elusive Intersection* (Hart Publishing, 2019)

de Doelder, H and Tiedemann, K (eds), *Criminal Liability of Corporations* (Brill 1996)

de Felice, D, 'Sabine Michalowski (ed.), Corporate Accountability in the Context of Transitional Justice' (2014) 14 *Human Rights Law Review* 576

de Greiff, P, 'Articulating the Links between Transitional Justice and Development: Justice and Social Integration' in de Greiff and Duthie (eds), *Transitional Justice and Development: Making Connections* (Social Science Research Council 2009), 38

de Greiff, P, 'Repairing the Past: Compensation for Victims of Human Rights Violations' in de Greiff (ed.), *The Handbook of Reparations* (OUP 2006), 1

de Greiff, P, *Report of the Special Rapporteur on the Promotion of Truth, Justice, Reparation and Guarantees of Non-Recurrence*, A/HRC/21/46 (9 August 2012)

de Greiff, P (ed.), *The Handbook of Reparations* (OUP 2006)

de Greiff, P, 'Theorizing Transitional Justice' in Elster, Nagy and Williams (eds) *Transitional Justice* (NYU Press 2012), 31

de Greiff, P, 'Truth Telling and the Rule of Law' in Borer (ed.) *Telling the Truths: Truth Telling and Peacebuilding in Post-Conflict Societies* (University of Notre Dame Press 2006), 181

de Greiff, P and Duthie, R, *Transitional Justice and Development: Making Connections* (Social Science Research Council 2009)

de Schutter, O, 'The Accountability of Multinationals for Human Rights Violations in European Law' in Alston (ed.), *Non-State Actors and Human Rights* (OUP 2005), 227

Deva, S, 'Human Rights Violations by Multinational Corporations and International Law: Where from Here?' (2003) 19 *Connecticut JIL* 1

Deva, S, 'Protect, Respect and Remedy? A Critique of the SRSG's Framework for Business and Human Rights' in Buhmann, Roseberry and Morsing (eds), *Corporate Social and Human Rights Responsibilities: Global Legal and Management Perspectives* (Palgrave 2011), 108

Deva, S, 'Treating Human Rights Lightly: A Critique of the Consensus Rhetoric and Language Employed by the Guiding Principles' in Bilchitz and Deva (eds), *Human Rights Obligations of Business: Beyond the Corporate Responsibility to Respect* (CUP 2013), 78

Dhooge, LJ, 'A Modest Proposal to Amend the Alien Tort Stat Jägers ute to Provide Guidance to Transnational Corporations' (2007) 13 *U.C. Davis J Intl L Policy* 119

Dhooge, LJ, 'Accessorial Liability of Transnational Corporations Pursuant to the Alien Tort Statute: The South African Apartheid Litigation and the Lessons of Central Bank' (2009) 18 *Transnatl L Contemp Probs* 247

Doxtrader, E and others, *Truth And Reconciliation In South Africa: The Fundamental Documents* (Institute for Justice and Reconciliation 2007)

du Bois, F, 'Reparations and the Forms of Justice' in du Bois and du Bois-Pedain (eds), *Justice and Reconciliation in Post-Apartheid South Africa* (CUP 2008), 116

du Bois, F and du Bois-Pedain, A (eds), *Justice and Reconciliation in Post-Apartheid South Africa* (CUP 2008)

du Plessis, M, 'Reparations and International Law: How Are Reparations to Be Determined (Past Wrong or Current Effects), Against Whom, and What Form Should They Take?' (2003) 22 *Windsor YB Access Just* 44

du Toit, F, 'Victims Challenge Business' in Villa-Vicencio and du Toit (eds), *Truth and Reconciliation in South Africa: 10 Years On* (New Africa Books 2006), 179

Duruigbo, E, 'Corporate Accountability and Liability for International Human Rights Abuses: Recent Changes and Recurring Challenges' (2008) 6 *Northwestern JIHR* 222

Duthie, R, 'Toward a Development-Sensitive Approach to Transitional Justice' (2008) 2 *Intl J Trans Just* 292

Duthie, R, 'Transitional Justice and Displacement' (2011) 5(2) *Intl J Trans Just* 245

Duthie, R, 'Transitional Justice, Development, and Economic Violence' in Duthie and Sharp (eds), *Justice and Economic Violence in Transition* (Springer 2014), 165

Elster, J, *Closing the Books: Transitional Justice in Historical Perspective* (CUP 2004)

Elster, J, (ed.), *Retribution and Reparation in the Transition to Democracy* (Columbia University Press 2006)

Elster, J, Nagy, R and Williams, M (eds), *Transitional Justice* (NYU Press 2012)

Embree, J, 'Criminalizing Land-Grabbing: Arguing for ICC Involvement in the Cambodian Land Concession Crisis' (2015) 27 *Florida JIL* 399

Engle, E, 'Extraterritorial Corporate Criminal Liability: A Remedy for Human Rights Violations?' (2006) 20 *St John's J Legal Commentary* 291

Engle, E, 'Kiobel v. Royal Dutch Petroleum Co.: Corporate Liability Under The Alien Tort Statute' (2012) 34 *Hous J Intl L* 499

Enneking, L, *Foreign Direct Liability and Beyond* (Eleven International 2009)

Enneking, LF, 'The Future of Foreign Direct Liability? Exploring the International Relevance of the Dutch Shell Nigeria Case' (2014) 10(1) *Utrecht L Rev* 44

Ezeudu, M, 'Revisiting Corporate Violations of Human Rights in Nigeria's Niger Delta Region: Canvassing the Potential Role of the International Criminal Court' (2011) 11 *African Human Rights LJ* 23

Fafo, *Business and International Crimes. Assessing the Liability of Business Entities for Grave Violations of International Law* (Fafo 2005)

Fernando, B, 'Editorial: Institutional Reforms as an Integral Part of a Comprehensive Approach to Transitional Justice' (2014) 8 *International Journal of Transitional Justice* 187

Fairlie, MA, 'The Hidden Costs of Strategic Communications for the International Criminal Court' (2016) 51 *Texas ILJ* 281

Farah, Y, 'Toward a Multi-Directional Approach to Corporate Accountability' in Michalowski (ed.), *Corporate Accountability in the Context of Transitional Justice* (Routledge 2013), 29

Farrell, N, 'Attributing Criminal Liability to Corporate Actors: Some Lessons from the International Tribunals' (2010) 8(3) *JICJ* 872

Fasterling, B and Demuijnck, G, 'Human Rights in the Void? Due Diligence in the UN Guiding Principles on Business and Human Rights' (2013) 116 *J Business Ethics* 799

Fauchald, OK and Stigen, J, 'Corporate Responsibility Before International Institutions' (2005) 40 *Geo Wash Intl L Rev* 1025

Feldman, G, 'The Historian and Holocaust Restitution: Personal Experiences and Reflections' (2005) 23 *Berkeley J Intl L* 347

Fig, D, 'Manufacturing Amnesia: Corporate Social Responsibility in South Africa' (2005) 81(3) *International Affairs* 599

Fitzpatrick, D and Fishman, A, 'Land Policy and Transitional Justice after Armed Conflicts' in Sharp (ed.), *Justice and Economic Violence in Transition* (Springer 2014), 263

Gallagher, K, 'Civil Litigation and Transnational Business: An Alien Tort Statute Primer' (2010) 8 *JICJ* 745

Giannini, T and Farbstein, S, 'Corporate Accountability in Conflict Zones: How Kiobel Undermines the Nuremberg Legacy and Modern Human Rights' (2010) 52 *HILJ* 119

Goldhaber, MD, 'Corporate Human Rights Litigation in Non-US Courts – A Comparative Scorecard' (2013) 3 *Univ California Irvine L Rev* 127

Gonza, A, 'Integrating Business and Human Rights in the Inter-American Human Rights System' (2016) 1 *Business Human Rights J* 357

Goodstein, J and Butterfield, K, 'Extending the Horizon of Business Ethics: Restorative Justice and the Aftermath of Unethical Behaviour' (2010), 20(3) *Business Ethics Quarterly* 453

Gray, D, 'Devilry, Complicity and Greed: Transitional Justice and Odious Debt' (2007) 70 *L Contemporary Problems* 137

Gray, D, 'An Excuse-Centered Approach to Transitional Justice' (2006) 74 *Ford L Rev* 2621

Gready, P, *The Era of Transitional Justice: The Aftermath of the Truth and Reconciliation Commission in South Africa and Beyond* (Routledge 2001)

Gready, P, and Robins, S, 'From Transitional to Transformative Justice: A New Agenda for Practice' (2014) 8(3) *International Journal of Transitional Justice* 339

Gross, AM, 'The Constitution, Reconciliation and Transitional Justice: Lessons from South Africa and Israel' (2004) 40(1) *Stanford J Intl L* 47

Gubbay, I, 'Towards Making Blood Money Visible: Lessons Drawn from the Apartheid Litigation' in Bohoslavsky and Letnar Černič (eds) *Making Sovereign Financing & Human Rights Work* (Hart 2014), 337

Guembe, MJ, 'Economic Reparations for Grave Human Rights Violations: the Argentine Experience', in de Greiff (ed.) *The Handbook of Reparations* (OUP 2006), 21

Haigh, K, 'Extending the International Criminal Court's Jurisdiction to Corporations' (2008) 14(1) *Australian J Human Rights* 199

Hall, R, 'Land Restitution in South Africa: Rights, Development, and the Restrained State' (2004) 38(3) *Canadian J African Studies* 654

Hall, R, 'Reconciling the Past, Present, and Future: The Parameters and Practices of Land Restitution in South Africa' in Walker and others (eds), *Land, Memory, Reconstruction, and Justice: Perspectives on Land Claims in South Africa* (Ohio University Press 2010), 18

Hamber, B, 'Narrowing the Micro and Macro: A Psychological Perspective on Reparations in Societies in Transition' in de Greiff (ed.), *The Handbook of Reparations* (OUP 2006), 574

Harper, E, 'Delivering Justice in the Wake of Mass Violence: New Approaches to Transitional Justice' (2005) 10 *J Conflict Security L* 149

Harvey, C, Summers, J and White, ND (eds), *Contemporary Challenges to the Laws of War: Essay in Honour of Professor Peter Rowe* (CUP 2014)

Harwell, E and Le Billon, P, *Natural Connections: Linking Transitional Justice and Development Through a Focus on Natural Resources* (International Center of Transitional Justice 2009).

Hasnas, J, 'The Centenary of a Mistake: One Hundred Years of Corporate Criminal Liability' (2009) 46 *American Criminal LR* 1329

Hayner, P, *Unspeakable Truths: Confronting State Terror and Atrocities* (Routledge 2000)

Hayner, P, *Unspeakable Truths: Facing the Challenge of Truth Commissions* (Routledge 2001)

Hazan, P, *Judging War, Judging History: Behind Truth and Reconciliation* (Stanford University Press 2010)

Hecht, L and Michalowski, S, 'The Economic and Social Dimensions of Transitional Justice' (2012) *ETJN Concept Paper* 2

Heller, KJ, *The Nuremberg Military Tribunals and the Origins of International Criminal Law* (OUP 2011)

Henry, JS, *The Blood Bankers: Tales from the Global Underground Economy* (Four Walls Eight Windows 2005)

Herz, RL, 'The Liberalizing Effects of Tort: How Corporate Complicity Liability under the Alien Tort Statute Advances Constructive Engagement' (2008) 21 *Harvard Human Rights J* 207

Holliday, I, 'Doing Business with Rights Violating Regimes Corporate Social Responsibility and Myanmar's Military Junta' (2005) 61 *Journal of Business Ethics* 329

Hongju Koh, H, 'Separating Myth from Reality About Corporate Responsibility Litigation' (2004) 7 *J Intl Econ L* 263

Hristova, MV, 'The Alien Tort Statute: A Vehicle for Implementing the United Nations Guiding Principles for Business and Human Rights and Promoting Corporate Social Responsibility' (2012) 47 *Univ San Francisco L Rev* 89

Huggins, C, 'Linking Broad Constellations of Ideas: Transitional Justice, Land Tenure Reform and Development' in de Greiff and Duthie (eds), *Transitional Justice and Development: Making Connections* (Social Science Research Council 2009), 332

Huggins, C, 'Truth, Justice, Reconciliation, and … Land Tenure Reform?' (2009) *Oxford Transitional Justice Research Working Paper Series*, 3

Huisman, W and van Sliedregt, E, 'Rogue Traders: Dutch Businessmen, International Crimes and Corporate Complicity' (2010) 8 *JICJ* 803

Huneeus, A, 'International Criminal Law by Other Means: The Quasi-Criminal Jurisdiction of the Human Rights Courts' (2013) 107 *AJIL* 1

International Commission of Jurists, *Access to Justice: Human Rights Abuses Involving Corporations. The Netherlands* (ICJ 2010)

International Council on Human Rights Policy (ICHRP), *Beyond Voluntarism: Human Rights and the Developing International Legal Obligations of Companies* (ICHRP 2002)

Jackson, KT, 'Global Distributive Justice and the Corporate Duty to Aid' (1993) 12(7) *J Business Ethics* 547

Jägers, N, *Corporate Human Rights Obligations: In Search of Accountability* (Intersentia 2002)

Jägers, N, 'UN Guiding Principles on Business And Human Rights: Making Headway Towards Real Corporate Accountability?' (2011) 29 *Netherlands QHR* 159

Jakobsen, CR, 'Doing Business with the Devil: The Challenges of Prosecuting Corporate Officials Whose Business Transactions Facilitate War Crimes and Crimes Against Humanity' (2005) 56 *Air Force LR* 176

James-Allen, P, Weah, A and Goodfriend, L, *Beyond the Truth and Reconciliation Commission: Transitional Justice Options in Liberia* (ICTJ 2010)

Jessberger, F, 'On the Origins of Individual Criminal Responsibility under International Law for Business Activity: IG Farben on Trial' (2010) 8(3) *JICJ* 783

Joseph, S, *Corporations and Transnational Human Rights Litigation* (Hart 2004)

Kaeb, C, 'The Shifting Sands of Corporate Liability under International Criminal Law' (2016) 49 *George Washington International Law Review* 351

Kaleck, W, 'International Criminal Law and Transnational Businesses: Cases from Argentina and Colombia' in Michalowski (ed.), *Corporate Accountability in the Context of Transitional Justice* (Routledge 2013), 174

Kaleck, W and Kroker, P, 'Syrian Torture Investigations in Germany and Beyond: Breathing New Life into Universal Jurisdiction in Europe?' (2018) 16(1) *Journal of International Criminal Justice* 165

Kaleck, W and Saage-Maab, M, 'Corporate Accountability for Human Rights Violations Amounting to International Crimes The Status Quo and its Challenges' (2010) 8(3) *JICJ* 700

Kalmanovitz, P, 'Corrective Justice versus Social Justice in the Aftermath of War' in Bergsmo, Rodríguez-Garavito, Kalmanovitz and Paula Saffon (eds), *Distributive Justice in Transitions* (FICHL 2010), 75

Kamminga, MT and Zia-Zarifi, S (eds), *Liability of Multinational Corporations under International Law* (Kluwer 2000)

Karp, DJ, *Responsibility for Human Rights, Transnational Corporations in Imperfect States* (CUP 2014)

Keenan, PJ, 'Conflict Minerals and the Law of Pillage' (2013–2014) 14 *Chicago JIL* 524

Keitner, CI, 'Conceptualizing Complicity in Alien Tort Cases' (2008) 60 *Hastings LJ* 61

Kelly, MJ, 'Grafting the Command Responsibility Doctrine onto Corporate Criminal Liability for Atrocities' (2010) 24 *Emory Intl L Rev* 671

Khanna, VS, 'Corporate Criminal Liability: What Purpose Does It Serve?' (1996) 109 *Harv L Rev* 1477

Kinley, D and Chambers, R, 'The UN Human Rights Norms for Corporations: The Private Implications of Public International Law' (2006) *HRLR* 1

Kinley, D and Tadaki, J, 'From Talk to Walk: The Emergence of Human Rights Responsibilities for Corporations at International Law' (2004) 44 *Va J Intl L* 931

Kinley, D, Murray, O and Pitts, C, 'Exaggerated Rumors of the Death of an Alien Tort? Corporations, Human Rights and the Remarkable Case of Kiobel' (2011) 12 *Melb J Intl L* 57

Kohl, U, 'Corporate Human Rights Accountability: The Objections of Western Governments to the Alien Tort Statute' (2014) 63 *Intl Comp L Quarterly* 665

Kora, A, 'Dealing with a "New" Grievance: Should Anticorruption Be Part of the Transitional Justice Agenda?' (2012) 11(4) *J Human Rights* 537

Korman, EG, 'Rewriting the Holocaust History of the Swiss Banks: A Growing Scandal' in Bazyler and Alford (eds), *Holocasut Restitution: Perspectives on the Litigation and Its Legacy* (NYU Press 2006), 115

Koska, G, 'Corporate Accountability in Times of Transition: The Role of Restorative Justice in the South African Truth and Reconciliation Commission' (2016) 4(1) *Restorative Justice* 41

Kremnitzer, M, 'A Possible Case for Imposing Criminal Liability on Corporations in International Criminal Law' (2010) 8(3) *JICJ* 913

Kritz, N (ed.), *Transitional Justice: How Emerging Democracies Reckon with Former Regimes* (US Institute of Peace 1995)

Krsticevic, V, 'Reparations in the Inter-American System: A Comparative Approach' (2007) 56 *Am Univ L Rev* 1375

Ku, J, 'The Curious Case of Corporate Liability under the Alien Tort Statute: A Flawed System of Judicial Lawmaking' (2011) 51 *Va J Intl L* 353

Kyriakakis, J, 'Corporate Criminal Liability and the ICC Statute: The Comparative Law Challenge' (2006) 56(3) *Netherlands Intl LR* 333

Kyriakakis, J, 'Corporations and the International Criminal Court: The Complementary Objection Stripped Bare' (2008) 19 *Criminal L Forum* 115

Kyriakakis, J, 'Corporations Before International Criminal Courts: Implications for the International Criminal Justice Project' (2017) 30(1) *Leiden J Intl L* 221

Kyriakakis, J, 'Prosecuting Corporations for International Crimes: The Role for Domestic Criminal Law' in May and Hoskins (eds), *International Criminal Law and Philosophy* (CUP 2010)

Laplante, LJ, 'On the Indivisibility of Rights: Truth Commissions, Reparations, and the Right to Development' (2007) 10 *Yale Human Rights Development LJ* 141

Laplante, LJ, 'Outlawing Amnesty: The Return of Criminal Justice in Transitional Justice Schemes' (2009) 49 *Va J Intl L* 915

Laplante, LJ, 'Transitional Justice and Peace Building: Diagnosing and Addressing the Socioeconomic Roots of Violence through a Human Rights Framework' (2008) 2 *Intl J Transitional Just* 331

Le Billon, P, *Wars of Plunder* (Columbia University Press 2012)

Leader, D, 'Business and Human Rights: Time to Hold Companies to Account' (2008) 8 *ICLR* 447

Leigh, LH, 'The Criminal Liability of Corporations and Other Groups: A Comparative View' (1982) 80 *Mich L Rev* 1508

Lekha Sriram, C, 'Transitional Justice Comes of Age: Enduring Lessons and Challenges' (2005) 23(2) *Berkeley J Intl L* 506

Letnar Černič, J, 'Corporate Human Rights Obligations at the International Level' (2008) 16 *Willamette J Intl L* 130

Letnar Černič, J, *Human Rights Law and Business* (Europa Law 2010)

Letnar Černič, J, 'Sovereign Financing and Corporate Responsibility for Economic and Social Rights' in Bohoslavsky and Letnar Černič (eds) *Making Sovereign Financing & Human Rights Work* (Hart 2014), 139

Letnar Černič, J and Van Ho, T (eds), *Human Rights and Business: Direct Corporate Accountability for Human Rights* (Wolf Legal 2015)

Levin, AM, 'Transitional Justice in Burma: A Survey of Accountability and National Reconciliation Mechanisms after Aung San Suu Kyi's Release' (2011) 18(2) *Human Rights Brief* 21

Lid, KAO and García-Godos, J, 'Land Restitution in the Colombian Transitional Justice Process' (2010) 28 *Nordic J Hum Rts* 262

Lid, KAO and García-Godos, J, 'Transitional Justice and Victims' Rights before the End of a Conflict: The Unusual Case of Colombia' (2010) 42(3) *J Latin American Studies* 487

Lippman, M, 'War Crimes Trials of German Industrialists: The "Other Schindlers"' (1995) 9 *Temple Intl Comp LJ* 173

Lopez, C, 'The Revised Draft of a Treaty on Business and Human Rights: A Big Leap Forward', *Opinio Juris*, 15 August 2019

Lopez, C, 'The "Ruggie Process": From Legal Obligations to Corporate Social Responsibility' in Bilchitz and Deva (eds), *Human Rights Obligations of Business: Beyond the Corporate Responsibility to Respect* (CUP 2013), 58

Lucke, K, 'States' and Private Actors' Obligations Under International Human Rights Law and the Draft UN Norms', in Cottier, Pauwelyn and Burgi (eds), *Human Rights and International Trade* (OUP 2005), 148

Lujala, P and Aas Rustad, S (eds) *High-Value Resources and Post-Conflict Peacebuilding* (Earthscan 2012)

Lundberg, MA, 'The Plunder of Natural Resources During War: A War Crime' (2007) 39 *Georgetown JIL* 495

Lyons, BS, 'Getting to Accountability: Business, Apartheid and Human Rights' (1999) 17 *Neth Q Hum Rts* 135

McCarthy, S, 'Rule of Law Expedited: Land Title Reform and Justice in Burma (Myanmar)' (2018) 42(2) *Asian Studies Review* 229

McConnell, L, 'Assessing the Feasibility of a Business and Human Rights Treaty' (2017) 66 *International and Comparative Law Quarterly* 143

McCorquodale, R and Simons, P, 'Responsibility Beyond Borders: State Responsibility for Extraterritorial Violations by Corporations of International Human Rights Law' (2007) 70 *Modern L Rev* 618

McCorquodale, R, 'Debate: The Alien Tort Statute and Corporate Liability' (2011) 160 *Univ Pennsylvania L Rev* 99

McCorquodale, R, 'Waving Not Drowning: Kiobel Outside the United States' (2013) 107 *AJIL* 846

McCulloch, J, *South Africa's Gold Mines and the Politics of Silicosis* (Woodbridge 2012)

McEvoy, K and McGregor, L (eds), *Transitional Justice from Below, Grassroots Activism and the Struggle for Change* (Hart 2008)

McEvoy, K, 'Beyond Legalism: Towards a Thicker Understanding of Transitional Justice' (2007) 34(4) *J Law Society* 412

Magarrell, L, 'Reparations for Massive or Widespread Human Rights Violations: Sorting out Claims for Reparations and the Struggle for Social Justice' (2003) 22 *Windsor YB Access Just* 91

Malamud-Goti, J and Grosman, L, 'Reparations and Civil Litigation: Compensation for Human Rights Violations in Transitional Democracies' in de Greiff (ed.), *The Handbook of Reparations* (OUP 2006), 539

Mamolea, A, 'The Future of Corporate Aiding and Abetting Liability Under the Alien Tort Statute: A Roadmap' (2011) 51 *Santa Clara L Rev* 79

Mani, R, *Beyond Retribution: Seeking Justice in the Shadows of War* (Polity Press 2002)

Mani, R, 'Dilemmas of Expanding Transitional Justice, or Forging the Nexus between Transitional Justice and Development' (2008) 2 *Intl J Trans Just* 253

Marais, H, *South Africa, Limits to Change, The Political Economy of the Transformation* (Zed Books 1998)

Marrus, MR, *Some Measure of Justice: The Holocaust Era Restitution Campaign of the 1990s* (University of Wisconsin Press 2009)

Marston Danner, A and Martinez, JS, 'Guilty Associations: Joint Criminal Enterprise, Command Responsibility and the Development of International Criminal Law' (2005) 93 *California L Rev* 75

Martin-Ortega, O, 'Business and Human Rights in Conflict' (2008) *Carnegie Council for Ethics in International Affairs*, 280

Mayer-Rieckh, A, 'Guarantees of Non-Recurrence: An Approximation' (2017) 39(2) *Human Rights Quarterly* 416

Medjouba, F (ed.), *Building Peace in Post-Conflict Situations: British Institute of International and Comparative Law* (BIICL 2011)

Meeran, R, 'Access to Remedy: The UK Experience of MNC Tort Litigation for Human Rights Violations' in Bilchitz and Deva (eds), *Human Rights Obligations of Business: Beyond the Corporate Responsibility to Respect* (CUP 2013), 378

Meeran, R, 'Tort Litigation Against Multinational Corporations for Violation of Human Rights: A View of the Position Outside the United States' (2001) 3(1) *City Univ Hong Kong L Rev* 1

Michalowski, S (ed.), *Corporate Accountability in the Context of Transitional Justice* (Routledge 2013)

Michalowski, S, 'Due Diligence and Complicity – a Relationship in Need of Clarification' in Bilchitz and Deva (eds), *Human Rights Obligations of Business: Beyond the Corporate Responsibility to Respect* (CUP 2013), 218

Michalowski, S, 'No Complicity Liability for Funding Gross Human Rights Violations?' (2012) 30 *Berkeley J Intl L* 451

Michalowski, S, *Unconstitutional Regimes and the Validity of Sovereign Debt: A Legal Perspective* (Routledge 2007)

Michalowski, S and Bohoslavsky, JP, 'Ius Cogens, Transitional Justice and other Trends of the Debate on Odious Debts. A Response to the World Bank Discussion Paper on Odious Debts' (2010) 48 *Columbia J Transnatl L* 61

Miller, Z, 'Effects of Invisibility: In Search of the "Economic" in Transitional Justice' (2008) 2 *Intl J Trans Just* 266

Muchlinski, P, 'Human Rights and Multinationals: Is there a Problem?' (2001) 77(1) *Intl Affairs* 31

Muchlinski, P, 'Implementing the New UN Corporate Human Rights Framework: Implications for Corporate Law, Governance, and Regulation' (2012) 22(1) *Business Ethics Quarterly* 145

Muchlinski, P, 'Limited Liability and Multinational Enterprises: A Case for Reform?' (2010) 34(5) *Cambridge J Economics* 915

Muchlinski, PT, *Multinational Enterprises and the Law* (OUP 2007)

Musahara, H and Huggins, C, 'Land Reform, Land Scarcity and Post-Conflict Reconstruction: A Case Study of Rwanda' in Huggins and Clover (eds), *From the Ground Up: Land Rights, Conflict and Peace in Sub-Saharan Africa* (Institute for Security Studies 2005)

Mutua, M, 'What Is the Future of Transitional Justice?' (2015) 9 *Intl J Trans Just* 1

Muvingi, I, 'Sitting on Powder Kegs: Socioeconomic Rights in Transitional Societies' (2009) 3 *Intl J Trans Just* 163

Naffine, N, 'Who are Law's Persons? From Cheshire Cats to Responsible Subjects' (2003) 66 *Modern L Rev* 346

Nattrass, N, 'The Truth and Reconciliation Commission on Business and Apartheid: A Critical Evaluation' (1999) 98 *African Affairs* 373

Ndulo, MB and Duthie, R, 'The Role of Judicial Reform in Transitional Justice and Development' in ICTJ Research Unit, *Transitional Justice and Development*

Nerlich, V, 'Core Crimes and International Business Corporations' (2010) 8 *JICJ* 895

Neuborne, B, 'Holocaust Reparations Litigation: Lessons for the Slavery Reparations Movement' (2003) 58 *New York Univ Annual Survey American L* 615

Neuborne, B, 'Preliminary Reflections on Aspects of Holocaust-Era Litigation in American Courts' (2002) *Washington U LQ* 795

Neumann Vu, S, 'Corporate Criminal Liability: Patchwork Verdicts and the Problem of Locating a Guilty Agent' (2004) 104 *Columbia LR* 459

Nichols, SS, 'Reimagining Transitional Justice for an Enduring Peace: Accounting for Natural Resources in Conflict'in Sharp (ed.), *Justice and Economic Violence in Transition* (Springer 2014), 203

Ohlin, JD, 'Joint Intentions to Commit International Crimes' (2011) 11 *Chicago J Intl L* 721

Olsen, T, Payne, L and Reiter, A, *Transitional Justice in Balance* (US Institute for Peace Press 2010)

Pasqualucci, J, 'The Whole Truth and Nothing but the Truth: Truth Commissions, Impunity and the Inter-American Human Rights System' (1994) 12 *BU Intl LJ* 333

Paul, G and Schönsteiner, J, 'Transitional Justice and the UN Guiding Principles on Business and Human Rights' in Michalowski (ed.), *Corporate Accountability in the Context of Transitional Justice* (Routledge 2013), 77

Payne, LA, 'Corporate Complicity and Transitional Justice: Setting the Scene' in Peace, Everyone's Business! Corporate Accountability in Transitional Justice: Lessons for Colombia (PAX, Utrecht, May 2017) 18

Payne, LA and Pereira, G, 'Accountability for Corporate Complicity in Human Rights Violations: Argentina's Transitional Justice Innovation?' in Bohoslavsky and Verbitsky (eds), *The Economic Accomplices to the Argentine Dictatorship* (CUP 2015), 29

Payne, LA and Pereira, G, 'Corporate Complicity in Dictatorships' (Saïd Business School and University of Oxford)

Payne, LA and Pereira, G, 'Corporate Complicity in International Human Rights Violations' (2016) 12 *Annual Rev L Social Science* 63

Pietropaoli, I, 'Corporate Accountability and Transitional Justice in Myanmar', JusticeInfo (7 March 2016)

Posner, EA and Vermeule, A, 'Transitional Justice as Ordinary Justice' (2004) 117 *Harvard L Rev* 761

Priemel, KC, 'Tales of Totalitarianism: Conflicting Narratives in the Industrialist Cases at Nuremberg' in Priemel and Stiller (eds), *Reassessing the Nuremberg Military Tribunals Transitional Justice, Trial Narratives, and Historiography* (Berghahn 2012), 170

Priemel, KC and Stiller, A (eds), *Reassessing the Nuremberg Military Tribunals Transitional Justice, Trial Narratives, and Historiography* (Berghahn 2012)

Ramasastry, A, 'Closing The Governance Gap in the Business and Human Rights Arena: Lessons from the Anti-Corruption Movement', in Bilchitz and Deva (eds), *Human Rights Obligations of Business: Beyond the Corporate Responsibility to Respect* (CUP 2013), 162

Ramasastry, A, 'Corporate Complicity: From Nuremberg to Rangoon – An Examination of Forced Labor Cases and Their Impact on the Liability of Multinational Corporations' (2002) 20 *Berkeley J Intl L* 91

Ramasastry, A, 'Odious Debt or Odious Payments? Using Anti-Corruption Measures to Prevent Odious Debt' (2007) 32 *NC J Intl L Com Reg* 819

Ramasastry, A, 'Secrets and Lies? Swiss Banks and International Human Rights' (1998) 31 *V and J Transnatl L* 325

Ramasastry, A and Thompson, RC, *Commerce, Crime and Conflict: Legal Remedies for Private Sector Liability for Grave Breaches of International Law* (Fafo 2006)

Ratner, SR, 'Corporations and Human Rights: A Theory of Legal Responsibility' (2001) 111 *Yale LJ* 443

Reguart-Segarra, N, 'Business, Indigenous Peoples' Rights and Security in the Case Law of the Inter-American Court of Human Rights' (2019) 4 *Business and Human Rights Journal* 109

Robinson, I, 'Truth Commissions and Anti-Corruption: Towards a Complementary Framework?' (2015) 9 *Intl J Trans Just* 33

Roche, D, *Accountability in Restorative Justice* (OUP 2004)

Roche, D, 'Dimensions of Restorative Justice' (2006) 62(2) *J Social Issues* 217

Rodriguez-Garavito, C (ed.), *Business and Human Rights: Beyond the End of the Beginning* (CUP 2018)

Roht-Arriaza, N, 'Reparations and Economic, Social, and Cultural Rights' in Sharp (ed.), *Justice and Economic Violence in Transition* (Springer 2014), 109

Roht-Arriaza, N, 'State Responsibility to Investigate and Prosecute Grave Human Rights Violations in International Law' (1990) 78 *Calif L Rev* 451.

Roht-Arriaza, N, 'The New Landscape of Transitional Justice' in Roht-Arriaza and Mariezcurrena (eds), *Transitional Justice in the Twenty-First Century: Beyond Truth Versus Justice* (CUP 2006), 2

Roht-Arriaza, N, 'Why Was the Economic Dimension Missing for So Long in Transitional Justice? An Exploratory Essay' in Bohoslavsky and Verbitsky (eds), *The Economic Accomplices to the Argentine Dictatorship* (CUP 2015), 19

Roht-Arriaza, N and Mariezcurrena, J (eds), *Transitional Justice in the Twenty-First Century: Beyond Truth Versus Justice* (CUP 2006)

Ross, M, 'What Do We Know About Natural Resources and Civil War?' (2004) 41(3) *J Peace Research* 337

Ross, ML, 'Does Oil Hinder Democracy?' (2001) 53(3) *World Politics* 325

Roux, T, 'Land Restitution and Reconciliation in South Africa' in du Bois and du Bois-Pedain (eds), *Justice and Reconciliation in Post-Apartheid South Africa* (CUP 2008), 23

Ruggie, JG, 'Business and Human Rights: The Evolving International Agenda' (2007) *AJIL* 101

Ruggie, JG, 'Global Governance and "New Governance Theory": Lessons from Business and Human Rights' (2014) 20 *Global Governance* 5

Ruggie, RG, 'Hierarchy or Ecosystem? Regulating Human Rights Risks of Multinational Enterprises' in Rodriguez-Garavito (ed.), *Business and Human Rights: Beyond the End of the Beginning* (CUP 2018), 46

Ruggie, JG, *Just Business: Multinational Corporations and Human Rights* (WW Norton 2013)

Ruggie, JG, 'Regulating Multinationals: The UN Guiding Principles, Civil Society, and International Legalization' in Rodriguez-Garavito (ed.), *Business and Human Rights: Beyond the End of the Beginning* (CUP 2013)

Ryngaert, C, 'Dealing with Organisations and Corporations' in Malcontent (ed.) *Facing the Past: Amending Historical Injustices through Instruments of Transitional Justice* (Intersentia 2016)

Sánchez León, NC and Marín López, D, 'Corporate Accountability in Transitional Justice in Colombia' in *Peace, Everyone's Business! Corporate Accountability in Transitional Justice: Lessons for Colombia* (PAX, Utrecht, May 2017)

Sánchez León, NC, *Tierra en transición. Justicia transicional, restitución de tierras y política agrarian en Colombia* (Centro de Estudios de Derecho, Justicia y Sociedad, Dejusticia 2017)

Sánchez León, NC, 'Corporate Accountability, Reparations and Distributive Justice in Post Conflict Societies' in Michalowski (ed.), *Corporate Accountability in the Context of Transitional Justice* (Routledge 2013), 114

Sandoval, C, 'Transitional Justice and Social Change' (2004) 1(1) *SUR International Journal on Human Rights* 'Commemorative Issue, Human Rights in Motion' 181

Sandoval, C and Surfleet, G, 'Corporations and Redress in Transitional Justice Processes' in Michalowski (ed.), *Corporate Accountability in the Context of Transitional Justice* (Routledge 2013), 93

Sandoval, C, Filippini, L and Vidal, R, 'Linking Transitional Justice and Corporate Accountability' in Michalowski (ed.) *Corporate Accountability in the Context of Transitional Justice* (Routledge 2013), 9

Sandoval-Villalba, C, 'Reflections on the Transformative Potential of Transitional Justice and the Nature of Social Change in Times of Transition' in Duthie and Seils (eds), *Justice Mosaics: How Context Shapes Transitional Justice in Fractured Societies* (International Center for Transitional Justice 2017)

Schabas, W, *The UN International Criminal Tribunals* (CUP 2006)

Schabas, W and Darcy, S (eds), *Truth Commissions and Courts: The Tension between Criminal Justice and the Search for Truth* (Kluwer 2005)

Schabas, WA, *An Introduction to the International Criminal Court* (CUP 2007)

Schabas, WA, 'Catching the Accomplices' (2001) 83 *IRRC* 842

Schabas, WA, 'Enforcing International Humanitarian Law: Catching the Accomplices' (2001) 83 *IRRC* 842

Schabas, WA, 'The Special Court for Sierra Leone: Testing the Waters. Conjoined Twins of Transitional Justice? The Sierra Leone Truth and Reconciliation Commission and the Special Court' (2004) 2 *JICJ* 1082

Scheffer, DJ, 'The Tool Box, Past and Present, of Justice and Reconciliation for Atrocities' (2001) 95(4) *AJIL* 970.

Schmid, E, 'Liberia's Truth Commission Report: Economic, Social, and Cultural Rights in Transitional Justice' (2009) 19 *Fletcher J Human Security* 5

Schmid, E, *Taking Economic, Social and Cultural Rights Seriously in International Criminal Law* (CUP 2005)

Schmid, E, 'War Crimes Related to Violations of Economic, Social and Cultural Rights' (2011) 71(3) *Heidelberg J Intl L* 540.

Schrempf-Stirling, J and Wettstein, F, 'Beyond Guilty Verdicts: Human Rights Litigation and Its Impacts on Corporations' Human Rights Policies' (2017) 145 *J Bus Ethics* 545

Scott, SW, 'Taking Riggs Seriously: The ATCA Case Against a Corporate Abettor of Pinochet Atrocities' (2005) 89 *Minn L Rev* 1497

Seekoe, M, 'Reparations' in Villa-Vicencio and du Toit (eds), *Truth and Reconciliation in South Africa: 10 Years On* (New Africa Books 2006), 36

Segovia, A, 'Financing Reparations Programs: Reflections from International Experience'in de Greiff (ed.), *The Handbook of Reparations* (OUP 2006), 651

Sharp, DN, 'Addressing Economic Violence in Times of Transition: Toward a Positive-Peace Paradigm for Transitional Justice' (2012) 35 *Fordham Intl L J* 780

Sharp, DN (ed.), *Justice and Economic Violence in Transition* (Springer 2014)

Shelton, D, 'The United Nations Principles and Guidelines on Reparations: Context and Contents' in De Feyter and others (eds), *Out of the Ashes: Reparation for Victims of Gross and Systematic Human Rights Violations* (Intersentia 2006)

Simcock, J, 'Unfinished Business: Reconciling The Apartheid Reparation Litigation With South Africa's Truth and Reconciliation Commission' (2011) 47 *Stan J Intl L* 239

Simpson, C (ed.), *War Crimes of the Deutsche Bank and the Dresdner Bank* (Holmes & Meyer 2002)

Skinner, G, 'Nuremberg's Legacy Continues: The Nuremberg Trials' Influence on Human Rights Litigation in U.S. Courts Under the Alien Tort Statute' (2008) 71 *Alb L Rev* 321

Slye, RC, 'Corporations, Veils and International Criminal Liability' (2008) 33 *Brooklyn J Intl L* 955

Spar, D and Yoffie, D, 'Multinational Enterprises and the Prospects for Justice' (1999) 52(2) *J Intl Affairs* 557

Stahn, C and Van den Herik, L (eds), *Future Perspectives on International Criminal Justice* (Asser Press 2010)

Steinhardt, RG, 'Fulfilling the Promise of Filartiga: Litigating Human Rights Claims Against the Estate of Ferdinand Marcos' 20(195) *Yale J Intl L* 65

Stephens, B, 'Conceptualizing Violence Under International Law: Do Tort Remedies Fit the Crime?' (1997) 60 *Alb L Rev* 579

Stephens, B, *Corporate Accountability: International Human Rights Litigation against Corporations in US Courts* (Martinus Nijhoff 2008)

Stephens, B, 'The Amorality of Profit: Transnational Corporations and Human Rights' (2002) 20 *Berkeley J Intl L* 45

Stephens, B, 'The Curious History of the Alien Tort Statute' (2014) 89 *Notre Dame L Rev* 1467

Stephens, B and others, *International Human Rights Litigation In U.S. Courts* (Brill 2008)

Stessens, G, 'Corporate Criminal Liability: A Comparative Perspective' (1994) 43 *Intl Comp LQ* 493

Stoitchkova, D, 'Towards Corporate Liability in International Criminal Law' (2010) 38 *Intersentia*

Summers, N, 'Colombia's Victims' Law: Transitional Justice in a Time of Violent Conflict?' (2012) 25(1) *Harvard Human Rights J* 219

Summers, N, 'Recent Developments: Colombia's Victims' Law: Transitional Justice in a Time of Violent Conflict?' (2012) 25(1) *Harvard Human Rights Journal* 232

Sundell, J, 'Ill-Gotten Gains: The Case for International Corporate Criminal Liability' (2011) 20 *Minnesota JIL* 648

Swart, M, 'The Khulumani Litigation: Complementing The Work of the South African Truth and Reconciliation Commission' (2011) 16 *Tilburg L Rev* 30

Tamo, A, 'Corporate Complicity for Human Rights Violations in Africa Post-Kiobel Case' in Letnar Černič and Van Ho (eds) *Human Rights and Business: Direct Corporate Accountability for Human Rights* (Wolf Legal 2015), 447

Taylor, MB, Thompson, RC and Ramasastry, A, *Overcoming Obstacles to Justice: Improving Access to Judicial Remedies for Business Involvement in Grave Human Rights Abuses* (Fafo 2010)

Taylor, T, *The Anatomy of the Nuremberg Trials: A Personal Memoir* (Knopf Doubleday 1992)

Teitel, R, *Globalizing Transitional Justice* (OUP 2014)

Teitel, RG, 'Globalizing Transitional Justice: Contemporary Essays' (2014) *Oxford Scholarship Online*

Teitel, RG, *Transitional Justice* (OUP 2000)

Teitel, RG, 'Transitional Justice Genealogy' (2003) 16 *Harvard Human Rights J* 69

Terreblanche, S, *A History of Inequality in South Africa. 1652–2002* (University of Natal Press 2002)

Terreblanche, S, 'Dealing with Systemic Economic Injustice' in Villa-Vicencio and Verwoerd (eds), *Looking Back, Reaching Forward: Reflections on the Truth and Reconciliation Commission of South Africa* (University of Chicago Press 2000), 265

Thompson, B, 'Was Kiobel Detrimental to Corporate Social Responsibility: Applying Lessons Learnt from American Exceptionalism' (2014) 30 *Utrecht J Intl Europ L* 82

Thomson, F, 'The Agrarian Question and Violence in Colombia: Conflict and Development' (2011) 11(3) *J Agrarian Change* 321

Tripathi, S, 'Business in Armed Conflict Zones: How to Avoid Complicity and Comply with International Standards' (2010) 50 *Politorbis* 131

Van den Herik, L, 'Corporations as Future Subjects of the International Criminal Court: An Exploration of the Counterarguments and Consequences' in Stahn and Van den Herik (eds), *Future Perspectives on International Criminal Justice* (Asser Press 2010), 350

Van den Herik, L, 'Subjecting Corporations to the ICC Regime: Analysing the Legal Counterarguments' in Burchard, Triffterer, and Vogel (eds), *The Review Conference and the Future of the International Criminal Court* (Kluwer 2010), 155

Van den Herik, L and Dam-de Jong, D, 'Revitalizing the Antique War Crime of Pillage: The Potential and Pitfalls of Using International Criminal Law to Address Illegal Resource Exploitation During Armed Conflict' (2011) 15 *Criminal L Forum* 250

Van den Herik, L and Letnar, J, 'Regulating Corporations under International Law: From Human Rights to International Criminal Law and Back Again' (2010) 8 *JICJ* 725

Van der Merwe, H, 'What Survivors Say About Justice: An Analysis of the TRC Victim Hearings' in Chapman and Van der Merwe (eds), *Truth and Reconciliation in South Africa: Did the TRC Deliver?* (University of Pennsylvania Press 2008), 23

Van der Wilt, H, 'Genocide v. War Crimes in the Van Anraat Appeal' (2008) 6 *JICJ* 557

Van Ho, T, 'Due Diligence in Transitional Justice States: An Obligation For Greater Transparency?' in Letnar Černič and Van Ho (eds), *Human Rights and Business: Direct Corporate Accountability for Human Rights* (Wolf Legal 2015), 229

Van Ho, T, 'Is it Already Too Late for Colombia's Land Restitution Process? The Impact of International Investment Law on Transitional Justice Initiatives' (2016) 5 *Intl Human Rights LR* 60

Van Ho, T, 'Transnational Civil and Criminal Litigation' in Michalowski (ed.), *Corporate Accountability in the Context of Transitional Justice* (Routledge 2013), 55

van Rossum, R, 'Adjudication of International Crime in the Netherlands' (2011) 39 *Intl J Legal Information* 202

Vasquez, CM, 'Direct vs. Indirect Obligations of Corporations under International Law' (2005) 43 *Columbia J Transnatl L* 927

Vest, H, 'Business Leaders and the Modes of Individual Criminal Responsibility under International Law' (2010) 8(3) *JICJ* 852

Villa-Vicencio, C and du Toit, F (eds), *Truth and Reconciliation in South Africa: 10 Years On* (New Africa Books 2006)

Villa-Vicencio, C and Verwoerd, W (eds), *Looking Back, Reaching Forward: Reflections on the Truth and Reconciliation Commission of South Africa* (University of Chicago Press 2000)

Walker, C, and others (eds), *Land, Memory, Reconstruction, and Justice: Perspectives on Land Claims in South Africa* (Ohio University Press 2010)

Wanless, WC, 'Corporate Liability for International Crimes under Canada's Crimes Against Humanity and War Crimes Act' (2009) 7(1) *JICJ* 201

Weigend, T, 'Societas delinquere non potest? A German Perspective' (2008) 6 *J Intl Criminal Justice* 927.

Weissbrodt, D, 'International Standard-Setting on the Human Rights Responsibilities of Businesses' (2008) 26 *Berkeley J Intl. L* 373

Weissbrodt, D, 'U.N. Perspectives on "Business and Humanitarian and Human Rights Obligations"' (2006) 100 *American Society Intl L Proceedings* 135

Weissbrodt, D and Kruger, M, 'Norms on the Responsibility of Transnational Corporations and Other Business Enterprises with Regard to Human Rights' (2003) 97 *AJIL* 901

Wells, C, *Corporations and Criminal Responsibility* (OUP 1993)

White, JA, 'Globalisation, Divestment and Human Rights in Burma' (2004) 14 *Journal of Corporate Citizenship* 47

Wiebelhaus-Brahm, E, 'Truth Commissions and Other Investigative Bodies' in Bassiouni (ed.), *The Pursuit of International Criminal Justice: A World Study on Conflicts, Victimization, and Post-Conflict Justice* (Intersentia 2010)

Woods, JM 'A Human Rights Framework for Corporate Accountability' (2010) 17 *ILSA J Intl Comp L* 321

Wouters, J and Ryngaert, C, 'Litigation for Overseas Corporate Human Rights Abuses in the European Union: The Challenge of Jurisdiction' (2009) 40 *George Washington Intl L Rev* 939

Wuerth, I, 'The Supreme Court and the Alien Tort Statute: Kiobel v. Royal Dutch Petroleum Co.' (2013) 107 *AJIL* 601

Zerk, J, 'Corporate Liability for Gross Human Rights Abuses: Towards a Fairer and More Effective System of Domestic Law Remedies', February 2014, www.ohchr.org/Documents/Issues/Business/DomesticLawRemedies/StudyDomesticLawRemedies.pdf

Zwanenburg, M and den Dekker, G, 'Prosecutor v. Frans van Anraat, case No. 07/10742' (2011) 104 *AJIL* 86

Index

Ad Hoc Tribunals 40–43
African Charter On Human and Peoples' Rights 74–77
African Commission On Human and Peoples' Rights 72–77
Alien Tort Statute 105–107, 110–117
Allied Control Council 35
Almog V. Arab Bank 125–28
American Convention On Human Rights 65–71
Amesys 86–88
Anglo American 126, 133–34, 149, 159
Anglogold Ashanti 126, 133–34
Anvil Mining 58–61, 65, 73, 237
Apartheid: Apartheid Convention 4; Apartheid Litigation 103–110
Argentina 84–88, 115–18, 240–41; Truth Commission 173–75

Barclays Bank 104, 108
Basic Principles On the Right to a Remedy and Reparation 187–91
Binding Treaty *See* Business and Human Rights Treaty
Bnp Paribas 77, 88, 116, 124–25
Brazil: National Truth Commission of 172–73
business and human rights: Guiding Principles on xii, 6–10, 66, 188, 218, 230–32; Special Representative on vii, 5–7, 45; treaty 9–10, 64, 217, 248; Working Group on ix, 7–10, 231
Businesspeople: Prosecution of 80–89

Canada 132
Cape 126
Cassese Report 112
Chevron 34

Chile 112
Chiquita 35, 99, 134, 198
Colombia 99–100 192–93; Victims and Land Restitution Law of 193–200
ComisióN Nacional Sobre La DesaparicióN de Personas (Conadep) 85, 240
Corporate Complicity Ix, 11–12, 109, 111–14, 118
Concentration Camps 21–26
Control Council Law No. 10 21–25
Convention On the Settlement of Disputes 216
Corporate Veil 128
Corruption 170–73, 218, 240–42
Crimes Against Humanity 21–29, 31, 34–41, 47, 75–79, 86–88, 124–25, 132, 175–79

Dalhoff, Larsen and Horneman (Dlh) 73
Democratic Republic of Congo (DRC) 33, 38–39, 51, 58–61, 82; UN Experts Panel on the Exploitation of Natural Resources in the 175–77
Diamond 170–71, 228–30
Drummond 99–100

East Timor: Commission for Reception, Truth and Reconciliation of 168–69
Economic Crimes 16–17, 164–66, 240–42
Economic, Social, and Cultural Rights 14–17; Committee On 3, 71
Enforced Disappearances 86, 92
European Court of Human Rights 63–64
Extrajudicial Killing 94, 99, 105, 172, 179
Extraterritorial Jurisdiction 71–74, 139–40, 238
Exxelia Technologies 74–75
Exxonmobil 95–96

Facebook 180–81
Farben 22–23, 29–31, 97, 120–21
Financial Complicity 110–119
Financial Institution 114–18, 176–77
Flick 24–25, 29
Forced Eviction 202–04, 222–26
Forced Labour *See* Slavery
Ford Motor 86–87, 123–24
Forum Non Conveniens 102, 128–29
France 74–75

General Motors 108–09
Genocide 77, 79–81, 94, 97–98, 124–25, 180, 221
Germany 26, 30–31, 83, 88, 120–21
Guarantee of Non-Repetition *See* Guarantee of Non-Reoccurrence
guarantee of non-reoccurrence 187, 189, 211, 215, 219–20, 248–49; Special Rapporteur on truth, justice, reparation and x, 212
Guatemala 56–57; Truth Commission of 171–72

Holocaust: Reparations Lawsuits 120–24
Human Rights Due Diligence 10, 131, 216–17

Ibm 108–10
Impunity Xii–Xiv, 183; Un Principle to Combat 211–12, 233–35
Indigenous Peoples' Rights 52–54, 224–25
Indonesia 95–96, 168–69
Industrial Cases 21–25
Inter-American Court of Human Rights 51–58
International Criminal Court 26–31; Thematic Prosecutions 36–40
International Criminal Tribunal for Rwanda 41
International Criminal Tribunal for the Former Yugoslavia 40
International Military Tribunal 19–21
Investment Law 199–200, 203, 216
Iraq 80–81
Israel 78
Ius Cogens 111, 117–18

Jesner V. Arab Bank 101–03, 125–27
Judicial Reform 218

Kouwenhoven, G. 82
Khulumani V. Barclays See Apartheid Litigation
Kiobel 96–101
Krupp 20–23

Lafargeholcim 75–77
land: restitution of 190–95 199–202, 220, 239; unlawful confiscation of xiii, 37, 39, 191, 205–07, 220, 225, 234–36, 242–43; reform of 219–226
Lebanon: Special Tribunal for 42
Ledesma 86–87
Legal Reform 214–16
Liberia 228–30, 73, 81–82; Truth and Reconciliation Commission of 164–68
Lundin Oil 83–84, 178
Libya 12, 73

MadariéN 55
Marcos Litigation 119–20
Media Case 41
Mens Reas 68, 94, 118–19
Mercedes-Benz 85–88
Ministries Trial 25–28
Myanmar Economic Corporations (Mec) 181
Myanmar 35–36, 79–80, 93–94, 133–34, 216: Independent International Fact-Finding Mission in 179–82; land restitution in 202–206; land reform in 222–26; Special Rapporteur on the situation of human rights in 179–82, 203–04, 226

natural resources: corporate exploitation of viii-ix, 36–39,47, 164–65, 169, 175–76, 204, 236, 240, 242–43; governance of 227–30, 234
Nazi Regime 19–22, 26, 121–22
Nestlé 63–64
Nigeria 61–62, 127
Nuremburg 28–31; Trial 19–21

Odious Debt 116–18
Ogoni People 61–63
Out-of-Court Settlement 133–37

Palestine 77, 99
Paramilitary Groups 55–57, 99–100, 135–37, 193, 196–98
Philippines 119

Pillaging 37–38
Pinheiro Principles 191, 195
Pinochet 112
Propaganda 41, 147

Qosmos 74
Radio TéLéVision Libre Des Mille
    Collines 41
Rasche 26–29, 41
Responsibility to Respect 10
Restorative Justice 156–58
Riggs 112
Riwal 77–78
Rohingya People 35–36, 179–80,
    204–06
Rome Statute of the International Criminal
    Court 31–39, 42, 46–48, 69–70
Ruggie, J. 5–7, 9, 11

Serac V Nigeria 61–62
Shell 127–29, 133, 137
Siemens 123
Sierra Leone 38, 77, 81; Special Court for
    40–41; Truth and Reconciliation
    Commission of 169–71
Slavery 105, 122–24, 132, 162
South Africa 126; Truth and Reconciliation
    Commission of 146–64; land restitution
    programme of 200–02, 206–07, 219–20
South Sudan 83, 94: Un Commission On
    Human Rights in 177–79
Sudan 73, 77, 83
Syria 73–78

Talisman Energy 94–95, 178
Terrorism 76–77, 99
Tesch & Stabenow 24
The Netherlands 90, 127–30
Timber 73, 81–83, 165–68
Tort Law 124–27

Torture 54, 58–60, 63, 73–79, 86–88,
    91–95, 98–100, 105–06, 112, 119,
    124–26, 130–32, 179
Total 79–80, 93
Toyota 172
Trade Unions 63, 86–87, 146, 149, 171
Transformative: Reparations 184, 198;
    Justice 207–09, 234, 248–49
Trial of the Major War Criminal 19–22
Truth: Right to Xi–Xiii
Norms on the Responsibility of Transna-
    tional Corporations and other Business
    Enterprises with regards to Human
    Rights 5

Union of Myanmar Economic Holdings
    (Umehl) 181, 204
United Kingdom 77, 79, 131
United States 21–25, 90–93, 97–107,
    119–24, 127–29, 178–79: United States
    Military Tribunal 22
Universal Declaration of Human Rights 4
Universal Jurisdiction 46, 68, 78–80, 84,
    131, 166
Unocal 93–94, 133–34, 179

Van Anraat, F. 80–81
Vedanta 130–31, 217
Vetting 210–14
Volkswagen 123–172

War Crimes 14, 18, 21–31, 37, 45, 47, 54,
    58–60, 75, 77–82, 84, 93, 116, 120,
    175, 177, 179
War World II: 14, 19, 25, 28, 30, 43,
    120–22, 133–34

Yemen 84

Zyklon B 24, 31, 111